17.95

ASPECTS OF EDUCATIONAL TECHNOLOGY

Aspects
of Educational Technology
Volume XVIII

New Directions in
Education
and Training Technology

*Edited for the Association for Educational
and Training Technology by*
B S Alloway and G M Mills

General Editor
A J Trott *Bulmershe College*

**Kogan Page, London/Nichols Publishing
Company, New York**

First published in Great Britain in 1985
by Kogan Page Limited
120 Pentonville Road, London N1 9JN

British Library Cataloguing in Publication Data
  Aspects of educational technology.
  Vol. 18: New directions in education and
  training technology.
  1. Educational technology
  I. Association for Educational and Training
  Technology II. Alloway, B.S. III. Mills, G.M.
  371.3'07'8   LB1028.3

  ISBN 0-85038-944-5(UK)
  ISBN 0-89397-211-8(USA)
  ISSN 0141-5956

Printed in Great Britain by The Anchor Press Ltd and
bound by Wm Brendon and Son Ltd, both of Tiptree, Essex

Published in the USA by Nichols Publishing Company
PO Box 96, New York, NY 10024

Contents

Author Index

Editorial

Although the organizers of ETIC84 suggested that there should two main themes – the impact of microcomputers on education, and industrial training – it was made clear to potential authors that other topic areas would be included. In the event, papers for the first of these themes (microcomputers) could be classified into three sections. Industrial training is sub-divided into training design and professional training. Each of the editors has provided a separate overview for one of these main themes. The final four sections are devoted to miscellaneous educational technology topics.

Professor Tom Stonier's opening address sets the scene by plotting future developments in computer-based learning in both hardware and software. His provocative paper is admirably complemented by a full range of general and theoretical issues covered in Section 1 beginning with John Anderson's outline of the philosophy behind some of the latest developments in the UK government-sponsored Microelectronics in Education Programme.

The practical integration of computer based learning approaches within the curriculum of education and training is the focus of the contributions in Section 2. Some of the specific techniques which are becoming significant for the development of such systems are outlined in Section 3. The growing use of microcomputers in educational and training technology is recognized in several papers in other sections.

The UK Manpower Services Commission's training programmes (New Training Initiative) are now beginning to make a large impact. Two contributions outline some of their philosophy in Sections 4 and 5. Other papers give accounts of practice in a wide variety of training situations in both public and private sectors of the economy.

For the more general educational technology presentations, the editors take full responsibility for sometimes making an arbitrary choice about which paper should fit into which section. For example, those on teleconferencing and on the analysis of media impact could just as well have fitted into Section 6 which concentrates on both the content and the methodology of communication and diffusion in the educational process.

Most of the contributions under the 'Technology Developments' are workshop reports. The final section includes some significant papers of which those from overseas participants are of particular interest. The last paper includes the closing address of John Sinclair, the outgoing AETT president.

With over 200 participants, of whom over 50 were from overseas, the conference proved to be one of the most lively of recent years. This amount of enthusiasm bodes well for future conferences. The social programme included a civic reception, visits to the Bradford Industrial Museum, to the National Museum of Film, Photography and Television (for an unforgettable) 'flying' experience at the IMAX cinema, and to the Bronte Museum at Haworth. We are grateful to the Vice-Chancellor of Bradford University, Professor John West, for his encouragement and the excellent accommodation arrangements. His after-dinner speech at the conference dinner was particularly enjoyed. We must also pay tribute to everybody who assisted, particularly to the band of technicians and other helpers who ensured that very few technical hitches occurred despite an unusually large amount of computer hardware.

B S Alloway and G M Mills
Science and Society
University of Bradford

In memoriam: we regret to announce the death of Mr G A Shearer who co-authored paper 6.3.

Overview of Microcomputers at ETIC84

G M Mills
University of Bradford

That microcomputers have now really arrived is amply demonstrated by the very large number of contributions to ETIC84 which not only indicate the impact which microcomputers are having on educational and training technology but also discuss the implications for future developments. The impression one gets when one reads these papers is of an enormous outpouring of fresh ideas. This is particularly so in the papers from Tom Stonier, Anderson, Sewell Ward & Rotheray, Boyd, MacDonald & Windsor, but many other authors have very interesting ideas about the organization and development of educational microcomputer systems.

One of the main changes in thinking about computer based learning in recent years is the switch from a concentration almost entirely on computer-assisted instruction (CAI), which was caused largely by the limitations of the old teletype interfaces to mainframe computers of the 1970s, to the much more flexible arrangements which the latest microcomputers can provide through their graphics, colour and sound facilities. When these are combined with packages of educational materials in other formats (text, pictures etc), they can provide a complete range of learning styles such as discovery learning, use of simulations, and the re-organization of collected data. The key word here is flexibility.

Nevertheless, as several authors have indicated, we are still very much in a transitional stage. Some of the technical developments mentioned in some papers may well be outmoded in a relatively short period of time. But most of the ideas behind their work will continue to stimulate further developments – many of which we will look forward to hearing about in future ETICs.

The problems of devising systems for the efficient use of microcomputers in education and training are recurrent themes. Several authors contend that the motivational effect (due to the greater control which learners have over their own learning) may be the most significant factor in increasing learning efficiency. This is merely one of the human/computer interactions which will increasingly become the concern of the educational technologist. More than ever, the latter must extend his/her interdisciplinary base into such fields as psychology, information technology, and the expert systems area of 'artificial intelligence' if he/she is to keep abreast of the current microelectronics revolution as it affects education and training.

While the main education sector is responsible for the majority of new ideas and innovations in techniques, the industrial sector has been slowly but surely making use of the more tried and tested computer based learning methods. Rightly, they adopt the position that their systems must work and place the emphasis on evaluation (eg papers by Kochar & McLean, Roebuck). In a few years time, the integration of microcomputers/microelectronics into all aspects of educational and training technology will be so complete that the separation of papers on microcomputers from those on training,used in this year's conference proceedings, will make no sense. Until then, we are in for an interesting time!

Gordon Mills

Overview of Training at ETIC84

B S Alloway
University of Bradford

It was with a real concern for the commercial and industrial training areas that the conference committee decided to devote a major part of the conference time to new developments in training. With hindsight, it does seem to have been a worthwhile exercise, allowing many of the conference delegates with a commitment to vocational education and training an opportunity to explore many new approaches.

This sector of the conference started with a keynote address on 'New Perspectives for Training' by Paul Keen, Principal Officer for Training at the Headquarters of the Manpower Services Commission (MSC) in Sheffield. Stressing the ways in which MSC was seeking to meet the major change factors in British industry and commerce, he outlined some of the schemes which the Commission was actively promoting in training development. While revised forms of training were now required for traditional industries, ie steel making, shipbuilding, motor vehicles, construction, and agriculture etc, completely new types of training were evolving for areas in which large numbers of jobs were being created. This was particularly so in the high technology and service industries within society.

Extensive details were given of the schemes which the MSC now organized, and conference members were advised to contact the Commission for further information about new developments. This information on schemes, although very wide ranging, obviously had considerable relevance to delegates as a large number of the audience were quickly drawn into a lively discussion. This continued throughout all of the 'Training' centred sessions. Some of the sessions sampled in which delegate participation was observed included:

* Hotel and Catering Open Tech Resources Network
* Team Approach to Patient Education
* Towards Industrial Understanding
* Training Teachers in Eduucational Technology
* A Youth Trainer's Course
* Teleconferencing for Education and Training
* NUMINE for Nurses
* Computer Based Training in the Provident Financial Group
* Computer Based Training as a Management Tool.

Also, on a random sampling basis, within these sessions, the follow-up to papers, seminars, and workshops included contributions from the following organizations:

Provident Financial Group PLC
The Agricultural Training Board
The Ministry of Defence
The Engineering Training Board
Civil Service College, Sunningdale
The Royal Engineers
The National Health Service
Royal Society for the Prevention of Cruelty to Animals (RSPCA)
East Midlands Gas Board
The Home Office
Ford Motor Company
Royal Air Force (RAF) Training Support
Royal Army Engineering Corps (RAEC)
Trustee Savings Bank (TSB)
BBC Engineering Training
The Co-operative Bank

Central Electricity Generating Board (CEGB)
John Lewis Management Training
The Metropolitan Police
The Construction Industry Training Board
Control Data Ltd
Royal Naval School of Educational and Training Technology

It should also be noted that many interesting comparisons with recent British experience were made possible by the valuable contributions presented by the delegates from a wide range of overseas countries who were directly involved with their own patterns of training development.

Over the complete period of the conference it was interesting to observe how the two main themes, 'Microcomputers in Education' and 'Training Development', overlapped in many sessions. This hopefully indicates that there is a close relationship between educational and training issues, and that both sectors have a part to play in each other's development. The microelectronics aspect is the latest, and perhaps the most important, 'technology' commitment to education and training in a long history of applications. Certainly there are many purely educational technology contributions as papers and workshops, indicating the continuing need to provide a platform for the raison d'être for the ETIC conferences.

Within the workshop organized by the Association for Educational and Training Technology on 'Membership' it was disclosed that the Association has a longstanding commitment to new applications of educational technology and recently re-started a programme of one-day conferences to this effect. The first day conference at Imperial College this year was on 'Authoring Languages' for education and training. Having been oversubscribed by three times the possible number that could be accommodated, a further day on the same theme was arranged for Sheffield University. The significance of 'Interactive Video' for training, as demonstrated at ETIC84 also suggests that AETT will be providing more training opportunities in this area.

The Chairman of the AETT's Conferences Standing Committee, Margaret Proctor, conducted an 'opinion survey' during ETIC84. From her analysis, it is clear that the industrial and training sectors are still highly committed to the new technologies. With this in mind, it is encouraging to note that Nick Rushby (Conference Chairman for ETIC85) has put forward a conference theme that will continue the exploration started with the Educational Technology International Conference in 1984 at the University of Bradford.

Bernard Alloway

Keynote Address: The Computer: Most Powerful Technology Ever?

T T Stonier

School of Science and Society, University of Bradford

INTRODUCTION

The first genuine revolution in over a century is beginning. It is based on the emergence of the home computer, and will result in a significant shift from school-based to home-based education.

This forecast is not derived from the assessment of educational needs or education technology, but simply from the economic dynamics of the situation. In December 1983, under the impetus of the Christmas rush, during that single month alone, about half a million personal computers were sold in the United Kingdom. In January 1984, there were an estimated 2,100,000 homes in the UK owning microcomputers (Gowling Marketing Services, 1984). It is apparent that the next consumer boom will be in home information technology. Some estimates have forecast that ten years from now, in the early 1990s, the average middle-class family will spend as much on information technology as on the family car.

In addition to the personal computer itself, householders of the future will own (or lease) many peripherals. The computer will have its own visual display unit (VDU) rather than sharing the family TV set. The usefulness of the family TV set will be extended in three ways:

* It will have a built-in videorecorder.
* It will be connected to a vastly extended network by cable television.
* A dish on the roof will link it to satellites.

The lucky areas will be wired up with optical fibres. Optical fibres facilitate two-way television transmission which, using the family video camera, opens up new possibilities for artistic endeavours and personal communications systems.

To achieve a proper link between the computer and the telephone system requires a modem to allow home users to network with other people, and to enter massive databases such as Prestel (VIEWDATA). These systems have been proliferating around the world. The householder of the future will tap into a wide range of general and specialist databases. Those used by doctors, lawyers, and other professionals will be the so-called expert systems which provide user-friendly organized data. Others, such as those used by travel agents, theatre ticket agents and estate agents, will also be available. Finally, it will become a matter of course to interrogate, from the home, the more general databases, such as those provided by the Library of Congress, other libraries, museums, government archives, etc. In addition, there already exist the databases provided by the Financial Times in London, the New York Times, the Wall Street Journal, and the Washington Post.

These systems will set the stage for electronic newspapers which will induce the householder to purchase a high-speed printer to obtain hard copy of his or her personally designed newspaper, containing information entered into the system by some reporter half-way across the world, perhaps only minutes earlier. The householder may be very upset by the latest news, in which case he or she sits down at the word processor and telexes a strongly worded letter in reply. Actually, by the mid-1990s, voice-to-print devices may be good enough and cheap enough so that our householder talks to the computer, rather than types in the message. In fact the householder, under the stress of the moment, may wish to yell at it, being careful not to distort the vocalization too much, lest the computer, unable to follow the message, misprints it.

Alternatively, a few people may get together to create a short television drama as an editorial comment to be transmitted over the neighbourhood cable television network. If of sufficient quality or interest, it might be picked up nationally - even internationally. The home computer, coupled to the rest of the home information technology (IT) system, will become not only a vastly expanded family entertainment centre; for many it will also become the home work station. In addition, it will permit electronic shopping for the sick, the infirm, or the just plain lazy, and it will become the home environment control system, automatically adjusting ventilation, heating, lighting, and sound systems to the user's specifications. Home security systems to alert the householder to faulty equipment, fires, or intruders will also become prevalent, including devices to monitor, in the crib, the baby's breathing and heart-beat, particularly during bouts of illness. We shall return to this feature later.

COMPUTERS AND HOME EDUCATION

In many ways, the main impact that computers will have on the home relates to the computer as an instrument of education.

1. As already indicated, the computer-based system will allow access to incredible amounts of information:- newspaper databases, the major libraries of the world, museums, special collections, government offices, and a host of other professional information providers. In 20 years, owning a first-rate encyclopedia will be as quaint as owning a Victorian slate to scratch on.
2. The system will allow tele-conferencing.
3. The widespread use of video recording equipment will allow education programs, eg via the Open University, to broadcast at off-peak hours, such as late at night. Local education groups will be able to broadcast via cable TV. In some cases, an hour's programme may be down-loaded on to the user's video cassette in a matter of seconds. Whole collections of local computer software will become available, some to be stored in the home, others in the local school, some in the city library. The ability to use laser-based video disks interactively with computers is an important aspect of the technology leading to computer-based education.

It is seldom that a revolution begins within a well established institution. The education system is no exception. That is not to say that there are not large numbers of teachers and educators who would like to see the system change. However, the pressure will come from outside, from the millions of homes with computers.

At the moment, it is the lack of good educational software which is the limiting factor in the spread of home computers. However, this will change during the mid-1980s as we move into the fourth generation of microcomputer education software packages.

The first stage occurred in the mid-1970s as relatively cheap micros first appeared on the scene. Some hardware manufacturers considered the education market as a serious possibility and produced software for it. The result was drill and practice of the dreariest sort. Modelled after the worst features of Skinner's system, it was largely an educational disaster. Only the interactive nature of the computer saved the micros from educational oblivion.

The second stage began in the late 1970s. Teachers working with computers began to convert crude drill and practice into games, and then moved on to bypass drill and practice altogether as they developed games with specific educational objectives. The problem with much of this material was that it was badly programmed. Often there was no escape mechanism or even worse, the programs would frequently crash.

We are now in the third stage. The age of the amateur is rapidly being left behind as education software publishers combine educational expertise with professional design and programming teams. By creating idiot-proof packages, properly backed up by instructions for parents or teachers, educationally sound games are entering the market at an accelerating pace.

The trouble is that the programs available at present, although excellent in themselves, are still ad hoc. Neither curriculum nor systematic body of knowledge can be built on them. Nevertheless, even with all these limitations, the computer is beginning to invade the education system at an accelerating pace.

Table 1 illustrates the responses of a child who wrote 'Why I liked the computer' as part of a class exercise. It was, in fact, part of a class report which, under the aegis of the teacher, was to become part of a successful effort to raise funds for buying a computer. The original computer had been on loan from our department. It is hard to tell how much of what was written was Emma's idea, how much those of her peers, how much reflected parental attitudes and, in particular, how much represented her teacher's influence. Nevertheless, at least in part, it is not atypical of the responses computers elicit from children.

> Why I liked the computer.
>
> I liked the computer because it played games with us.
> I think the best game was hang man. ·
> It helped do my times tables.
> The first thing it says is hello then it said
> What is your name?
> So I typed my name.
> It was very polite.
> It never got cross.
> It was like a typewriter with a telly on top.
> I liked it because it did all the writing.
> All we did was the thinking.
> It was like a friend and it's very helpful.
> There are very exciting pictures.

Table 1 <u>Report from an eight-year-old school girl Emma (Leeds, May 1982)</u>

There are several interesting features in Emma's 13-line treatise. Most profound, and therefore perhaps somewhat suspect, is the statement: 'I liked it because it did all the writing. All we did was the thinking.' Was Emma having difficulty writing and found typing superior? Did someone else do the typing? What does Emma conceive thinking to be?

More typical is the opening statement: 'I liked the computer because it played games with us.' She picks 'Hangman' as best. This fits in with a report of Malone (1981b) in his study of what makes computer games fun. In his case, boys and girls from Palo Alto, California, also liked 'Hangman', although it came only twentieth out of the top 25 games. The range of software available to Emma's class in 1982 was extremely limited, so that her comparisons with other games would have been severely restricted.

The liking for computer games is virtually universal. The motivation for play is complex. It must be, at least to a large extent, biologically based. Biologically useful activities activate the pleasure centres. A kitten, chasing a ball, enjoys chasing as an activity in its own right. Considering the fact that the kitten will have to make its living as a hunter, chasing is a highly desirable activity. One of the questions computer psychologists need to answer is whether the almost compulsive preoccupation of boys with computer arcade games reflects their need to develop the hand-eye co-ordination required of human hunters, who were not blessed with large claws or fangs, but did evolve hunting techniques using weapons.

It is interesting to observe the marked sex differences apparent in the enjoyment of certain games. This is borne out in Malone's studies where the game 'Darts' was modified to provide eight different variants. In the original version, a dart aimed accurately at the correct answer exploded a balloon as a reward. This proved to be of greatest interest to boys. It was of much less interest to girls. They liked the version in which the balloons were popped in another part of the screen and which also introduced music. Malone (1981b) quotes one girl as saying: 'Darts is more like a boy's game.'

Shaylor tested five educational programs on 9- to 13-year-olds in schools in the Bradford area (Shaylor and Stonier,1983). Her results showed that, as one might expect, age was an important factor in determining the acceptability or desirability of programs. What was surprising was that in this age range, children of only slightly different ages reacted quite differently to the same program. Those younger than optimum found certain programs too complicated; those older than optimum found the programs not challenging enough, and therefore boring. One could also interpret the limited data as implying that games had a broader age appeal than drill and practice related programs.

All this is of relevance to educators trying to utilise a computer for instructional purposes. As an author of several educational programs (eg,Mills and Stonier,1982; Stonier cited in Futcher,1984), it becomes apparent that practice precedes theory. One such program, 'Letters Learn', was developed further by one of our students (H Swain). In her field testing, she found that the delight was not in looking at good pictures, but in pressing the right key and being the person responsible for allowing the picture to be displayed. This phenomenon extends to older people as well. She also tested out the program on an elderly lady, who was thrilled at being able to work a computer and make things happen on screen. Unfortunately, most adults still view the computer as a complicated piece of technology, well beyond their competence.

Children do not have such inhibitions. To them the computer is a toy. It is associated with playing games. A four-year-old boy who had never used capital letters, when offered the 'Letters Learn' program '... was thrilled to bits by the game, yet had no interest in alphabet books at home'.

An important and typical response of children is illustrated in Emma's perception of the computer: Not only was it 'like a typewriter with a telly on top' but also, 'It was very polite. It never got cross.' This type of anthropomorphic projection on to the machine is even stronger in younger children. For example, Conlin (personal communication) reports the response of a four-year-old in her infant school: 'at the end of the program he read from the screen "GOODBYE MARTIN". Martin said "Goodbye"; then kissed the PET.' A reasonable hypothesis for explaining this phenomenon is that the computer is interactive, and therefore gives the illusion that it is a being, rather than a thing.

CLINICAL IMPRESSIONS OF THE ADVANTAGES OF COMPUTERS FOR CAL/CBE

The above, plus other lines of evidence, suggest at least nine reasons why the computer constitutes such a powerful pedagogic tool:

1. The most important reason is that the computer is interactive. Unlike books, tapes, films, radio and television, the user's response determines what happens next. This gives children a sense of control. It also elicits active, motor involvement.
2. Computers are fun. Human beings love to respond to challenges, love to make things happen. The computer games industry has grown rich on that basic axiom. By coupling education to games of challenge, computer-assisted learning becomes fun.
3. Computers have infinite patience. A computer does not care how slowly the user responds or how often a user makes mistakes. Among the earliest uses of computer-assisted learning on a wide scale was the use of computers in Ontario in the late 1960s designed to help innumerate teenagers to fulfil the maths requirement for college courses. The programme was successful from a number of points of view, not the least of them the attitude expressed by one girl who stated that the computer was the first maths teacher who had never yelled at her.
4. Good education programs never put a child down. Instead they provide effective positive reinforcement.
5. Computers can provide privacy. Children, or for that matter teachers, can make embarrassing mistakes without anyone seeing them. Ignorance, lack of skill, slowness to comprehend, poor co-ordination, can all be overcome in the privacy of one's home. The computer will not tell!
6. Conversely, the computer can be used in a variety of social situations. These include classroom activities involving groups, or a teacher and single pupil only, or two neighbourhood children, or party games, or a grandparent and grandchild, etc. Many education programs are designed to allow for either individual practice, or for two or more children to play games.
7. A computer can explain concepts in a more interesting and understandable manner by means of animated material. No amount of talking, writing, or providing diagrams, can compare with making things come alive on the screen.
8. Whereas it is very difficult to hide things in a book, it becomes possible to hide things in a program which become apparent only occasionally. A book, on re-reading, holds few surprises (although the reader may have missed points the first time). In contrast, a computer program can be full of surprises. Good programs contain an element of mystery and uncertainty which keep the user interested. It means that the learning experience provides new situations not only for the students, but also for the teacher or parent as well.
9. The ability to simulate complex situations such as chemical reactions, ecosystems, demographic or economic changes is a particularly powerful reason for using computers in education. Training pilots, managers, doctors, chemical engineers, ie, any profession or activity where a mistake in the real world could be very costly, is best served by learning on a computer which simulates real-life situations. In addition, simulating real events often makes it possible to train students to think 'laterally' across traditional subject boundaries.

TEACHING ABOUT LIFE SKILLS

In the popular mind, and among many educators, computers are associated with mathematics, or at least with science and the computational aspects of other disciplines such as statistics associated with geography or economics. For this reason, this section will focus entirely on the area of communications and life skills, and outline some of the features of a cradle-to-grave, computer-based education system.

There is an increasing body of evidence that brain development in infants is enhanced by a stimulating environment. We have already alluded to the baby-minding computer which could monitor the infant's vital functions. The computer could be programmed to rock the crib slightly, provide pleasant sounds (including tapes of mama singing a lullaby), throw patterns of light above the crib, etc. This will never substitute for the actual continuous 24 hour, physical contact that human babies are entitled to. It will, however, be a great improvement over what babies in Western cultures have been getting since the Industrial Revolution.

The serious education programme begins as follows:

1. <u>Babbling</u> is periodically reinforced by means of a microphone coupled to a computer which provides optical feedback by flashing colours and shapes on to the ceiling. As voice analysers (used in voice-to-print devices) become cheap, such a system could be refined so that appropriate visual shapes appear. These shapes should correspond roughly to the shape of the mouth making the sound, eg, circular shapes for 'oh', vertical ellipses for 'ah', vertical rectangles for 'i', horizontal ellipses for 'ell', jagged lines for hissing sounds, etc.

   The purpose of this exercise is to convey to the child that, just as with a rattle clutched in its fist, its actions can affect aspects of the environment. In other words, the computer becomes an 'electronic rattle'. However, unlike the rattle which encourages control over the arm muscles, a computer encourages vocalization. In due course the child will recognize that there is a correlation between the kind of sounds made and the visual effects produced.

   To teach the older infant this most important of all lessons - that its actions can effect the environment - one introduces computer-controlled robot toys such as a remote-controlled LOGO turtle, the BBC Buggy, or the sort of toy described by R G Dyke (1984) at Manchester SEMERC. Dyke has also described the MICROMIKE system to encourage babbling and vocal play in handicapped children. Much of what will be in use for the education of all infants and young children in the future, is already under development in special education for the disabled (see review by Hogg,1984).

2. <u>Pre-Reading:</u> before a child is able to recognize words and letters it is necessary to teach it other skills such as recognizing shapes, recognizing objects, and recognizing relationships. Calloway's program 'Hide and Seek' is designed to do just this sort of thing. It uses a pelmanism to encourage the child to remember to look for simple shapes such as a tree, a flower, or a house. At the more advanced level 'Hide and Seek' substitutes words for these objects to allow the child to begin associating the idea of words with objects (Calloway,1983b). Similarly, Hull University's 'Square and Cross', although perhaps too complex for this young age group, in principle provides the sort of program to help a child become conscious of terms such as 'right' and 'left', 'over' and 'under' (Sewell and Ward,1985).

3. <u>Reading:</u> in order to recognize words and letters, a whole series of programs is emerging. The author has been involved with simple programs to teach alphabet skills, the program 'Letters Learn', and a second program which has been widely distributed commercially by ASK entitled 'Words, Words, Words' (Stonier,1983). In this latter program, the bottom of the screen asks the question 'I see a ...' followed by a picture of an object such as a house, a tree, a girl, and so on. If the child types in the appropriate word correctly ('house', 'tree', 'girl', etc) the picture moves up to the main part of the screen. The child can thus build up an entire scene consisting of about eight objects. The reward for the child is not only that the scene becomes a completed picture but also, upon completion of the task, which is possible only if all the words have been spelled correctly, the scene will show animation. This has proved to be a very strong motivator for children and, in our field testing, we have found children, with very little interest in books of words, playing intensely at this game. It has also proved useful in the classroom as a centre of discussion and further activity.

4. Writing and Spelling: writing words by copying them is one way to learn. Calloway's (1983a) program 'Facemaker' is designed to encourage the use of adjectives as well as to help the child become more observant while creating a face on the screen. Recognizing statements brings us to the next kind of skill.

Lally and MacLeod (1983) have described computer-based handwriting exercises in which students use a digitizer pen to track various letter shapes on a graphic display. A more rapid feedback and much greater degree of control over the handwriting learning process is possible than with conventional techniques. The procedure emphasizes the process of handwriting as well as the appearance of the final product.

Of great educational interest is the 'Writing to Read' program originated by J H Martin in 1981 and currently under development by IBM. It uses the IBM Personal Computer equipped with voice output and colour graphics. The structure of the program is based on 30 key words and 42 phonemes which compose them. It teaches students to write words the way they sound. Basically, the children are learning to write almost before they are learning to read. According to one teacher working with the system: 'Students' progress is phenomenal'.

5. Syntax and Grammar: here, the University of Hull Psychology Department's 'Square and Cross' game cited above is very useful, as is the idea of Conlin's 'Children from Space' (Conlin,1983). Don Walton's 'Blob' (Walton,1984) allows the child to look for up to 300 verbs which make 'Blob' do things. The process of finding the activating verbs, as well as the ones which do not have an effect on 'Blob', is an excellent technique for building vocabulary. In a social situation such as a classroom many of the programs listed above are ideal for engendering talking and verbal skills.

6. Talking and Developing Verbal Skills: using the computer as a centre for social activity applies not only to children but to adults as well. Ives (1984) has reported on work done at the Islington Adult Education Unit, where it was found that the use of a computer in English as a second language course greatly facilitated intra-group communication. It was the opinion of the course organizer, when comparing the group with computers and the one without, that 'it was the computer group whose English improved the most'.

An increasing number of programs are available which utilize an old technique: 'Pictures and Questions' or 'Stories and Questions'. These are particularly useful for increasing comprehension. Young children like to hear and see things over and over again, driving their mothers or teachers mad with repetition. This is an area where the computer, with infinite patience, makes an ideal supplement to the child's education.

7. Creative Writing: writing a simple story, in part, is already implied in the 'Words, Words, Words' game described above, where the child can choose to move from one scene to any of the other six scenes. This will become particularly exciting as interactive video systems become cheap enough for home computers. At the written level, the use of word-processing reminds us of Emma's comment, 'I liked it because it did all the writing. All we did was the thinking.'

In some of the more advanced spelling programs which are in the commercial pipe-line, there will be ones in which the writing of words is to be coupled with actually writing them down on a postcard (and drawing a picture on the other side). These home-produced postcards will, it is hoped, engender a proclivity for correspondence, lacking in many people. Such proclivity will be fostered even more by the use of 'Econet' and similar systems which should allow electronic pen pals to emerge across the country and finally across the world. What is so important about using the electronic media is that it is possible to have almost instant feedback. Instead of waiting for a letter or a card to take two weeks, or more, to get into another part of the world and then come back, by using electronic mail facilities it is possible to receive a reply within a matter of minutes or certainly later that same day.

Computers will be used for building vocabularies, utilizing programs (already in existence) of antonyms and synonyms, and of alphabetizing and dictionary skills. Grammar, syntax and punctuation can all be illustrated in a game context - one which makes sense.

8. Linguistics: one can go much deeper into language. On mainframe computers, there already exist algorithms for mis-spelling (Yannakoudakis and Fawthrop,1983). These are what are used to correct typing mistakes in word-processors (those which possess sufficient memory to do so). These programs also set the stage for creating your own language by starting off with the random appearance of letters, spaces and punctuation, and slowly introducing rules and algorithms into the system so that the pattern of

letters begins to sound more and more like English, or like Hawaiian, or whatever. Similarly, one can create patterns of words such as the 'Poetry from Logo' program discussed by Sharples (1984).

9. Library and Research Skills: the availability of large databases and increasingly complex information resources will require higher and higher levels of library and research skills. To help train students, there will be a need for software to help interrogate these databases and other information resources. Furthermore, computer programs will be created (if they do not already exist), to help develop skills in abstracting, speed reading, and comprehension.

10. Literature: the introduction of cheap interactive video systems, which could run a film on a computer for 50 minutes or so with virtually instant access to any portion of that film, allows great plays and dramatization of great literature to be placed on such discs and should greatly facilitate the study and comprehension of such literature. Interactive video systems, with their spacial data management systems should allow geographical trips, historical trips, logical trips, etc.

11. Adventure Games: these are emerging by leaps and bounds and reflect not just an attempt at mere entertainment, but increasingly an effort at education. Some of these are historically based. A different type is Spinnaker's 'Snooper Trooper' which is, to my mind, one of the best examples of training children in the rudiments of logic and systematic thinking and as good an introduction to scientific investigations under the guise of being a detective, as I have ever seen.

12. Simulations: one form would involve simulation interviewing or bargaining situations. These would include job interviews with employers, interviews for universities, polytechnics, etc, interviews with doctors, dealing with car salesmen, bank managers, social workers, bureaucrats, travel agents, and so on. Another form of simulation involves fostering sensitivity in human relationships. One of our postgraduate students has done an interesting boy-meets-girl simulation designed to stimulate classroom discussion and personal thought (Price, 1984). For, although the computer will never substitute for a girl, or for a boy, it does allow an awkward teenager to start thinking out what might be the responses given different types of personalities and different types of situation. One can see this principle extended to nurse-meets-patient, how parents might handle children, how children might handle parents, etc. Several authors at this conference are presenting papers on the use of computer-based training for a wide range of managerial posts and related activities. As our experience with such CBT systems grows, so will our application to wider and wider areas of human interactions.

13. Artificial Intelligence and Expert Systems: some very sophisticated expert systems already exist to interview prospective employees. These are based on using standard aptitude tests which have been converted from a written form into an interactive computer form. They are extremely helpful in providing personnel officers with clues to the potential candidate. They can also be very helpful to a candidate in assessing his or her own strengths and weaknesses. They constitute a sort of personality mirror which could be used for a number of other situations such as retirement choices, choices of life decisions, and in the last analysis, how to face death.

CONCLUDING OBSERVATIONS AND REMARKS

The computer will invade the home and the education system in a way unparalleled in previous education history. This leads to a number of questions, both practical and social. Among the practical questions, we need to know what are the most appropriate reward systems for motivating children to learn with the help of computers. Do all audio or visual rewards reinforce the learning experience, or do they distract? Are such rewards merely frivolous? Might computer-based learning systems hinder certain kinds of learning? Might they inhibit genuine curiosity? Might they undermine long-term interests in a topic?

At the social level we should ask many questions. What will be the impact on society? What will be the impact on children? Will the violence observed on computer screens reinforce violent behaviour? Will the anthropomophization of computers and, in due course, robot toys, cause children to behave like robots themselves? Alternatively, if the computer or robot is the perfect slave to be turned on and off at will, will children confuse accepted behaviour of robot toys with how they ought to behave with real people? Considering the incredible amount of information which will comprise the environment of children of the future, will it cause information overload? What are the symptoms and pathologies of information overload? The hypnotic effect of computers is well-known. In the United States there is a phenomenon called computer divorces where one spouse, so intrigued with working with a computer, begins to overlook the responsibilities and affections due other members of the household. Lastly, a very real problem is shaping up in the technologically advanced countries where middle-class families will avail themselves of this new technology to give their children maximum educational advantages. Will this lead to a new polarization in Western societies between the information 'haves' and the information 'have-nots'? To what extent will this process exacerbate a global society structured along potentially divisive lines?

On the positive side, boys playing football, girls jumping rope (or vice versa), games, parties and discos are all fun. We have overlooked the enormous educational value of these activities in teaching both physical and social skills. In contrast, our Victorian puritanism has made learning intellectual skills, most of the time, into an onerous task. The computer will reintroduce fun into that process of learning.

Children having an early experience with computers will develop a technical expertise as second nature. One of the sources of amazement to teachers and parents watching young children working computers, is the rapidity with which they learn how to load a program, run a tape recorder, and carry out all the procedures necessary for making a computer work. In part, this astonishment reflects our own cultural experience. We overlook the fact that early in the nineteenth century, five-year-old children used to work machinery in the industrial mills of northern England and that, in Third World countries, five-year-olds will have significant responsibilities: the girls in bringing up younger siblings, the boys in taking care of the family cattle, or helping out in other ways. A helpless childhood is a Western construct.

Perhaps this will be the most important impact the computers will have: teaching children how to think more effectively. Seymour Papert (1980) complains that our tendency is to categorize children into smart and dumb people when, in fact, it is often a question of context and experience. Working out flow charts, developing habits of precision and discipline, building in checks, carrying out sub-routines in order to build larger structures. All of these foster intellectual qualities which are not produced in the same way in the present system. We know that handicapped children have shown substantial improvements in IQ tests when given the proper tools. This principle will be found applicable to virtually all children. The human mind is an exquisite information processing device reflecting the evolution of intelligence over a period of a few hundred million years. The late Chris Evans (1979) believed that the scale of intelligence should begin with a rock or some other inert matter which has zero intelligence, then work up from an amoeba which clearly has enough intelligence to move away from an undesirable environment and towards a more desirable one, through a variety of invertebrates to fish, amphibians, etc, to mammals. Finally, our closest relative, the chimpanzee, can be taught the rudiments of logic with no difficulty whatsoever.

The high motivational state induced in children working with good education software, coupled to the emergence of a global network of databases, which allow the child access to information with unprecedented ease, must have an impact on the understanding that children develop of the world they live in and, for that matter, in understanding themselves. Furthermore, as indicated above, children encouraged to write their own programs, will develop intellectual skills of precision, logic, a systematic and orderly method for producing work, and a much more sophisticated approach to the methods of solving problems. The cumulative improvements in intellectual skills coupled to their markedly expanded understanding of the world, will differentiate such children almost to the extent of being a new sub-species: <u>Homo sapiens cerebrus</u>, perhaps.

The matter is analogous to a situation some time probably between five and ten million years ago, when our pre-human hominid ancestors began to use weapons, both to ward off predators and to subdue prey. That earliest of all technological revolutions differentiated the hominid stock from the rest of the primates. The hominids were able to extend their econiche to hunting large game. In due course, as they mastered fire, they were able to extend their geographic range more successfully than any other primate. In human history it was always those who were able to develop and use new technologies adroitly who, in the long run, not only survived better but came to dominate the others. <u>Homo sapiens cerebrus</u> will survive, prosper, and in due course dominate all those who do not partake of the new intellectual technology. Among higher organisms new behaviour patterns rather than new anatomical features, set the stage for new patterns of evolution. The computer is setting the stage for a revolution as profound as the hominid revolution of a half a dozen, or so, million years ago. Will we be able to cope with it?

REFERENCES

Calloway, G (1983a) Facemaker (Computer Program). Applied Systems Knowledge (ASK), London.

Calloway, G (1983b) Hide and Seek (Computer Program). Applied Systems Knowledge (ASK), London.

Conlin, C (1983) Children in Space (Computer Program). Applied Systems Knowledge (ASK), London.

Dyke, R G (1984) Manchester SEMERC Newsletter Jan 1984, Manchester Polytechnic, pp24-27.

Evans, C (1979) The Mighty Micro. Victor Gollancz, London.

Futcher, D (1984) All-action software: ASK style. Educational Computing Feb 1984, p 25.

Gowling Marketing Services (1984) as cited by Glogg, J. In Micro Business April 1984, p 35.

Hogg, B (1984) Microcomputers and Special Educational Needs: A Guide to Good Practice. National Council for Special Education, Stratford-upon-Avon.

Ives, R (1984) Trying out new ideas in ESL work. Educational Computing Mar 1984, p 41.

Lally, M and MacLeod (1983) The promise of microcomputers in developing basic skills. In Megarry, J et al (eds) World-Yearbook of Education 1982/83: Computers and Education. Kogan Page, London.

Malone, T W (1981a) Toward a theory of intrinsically motivating instruction. Cognitive Science 4, pp 333-369.

Malone, T W (1981b) What makes computer games fun?. Byte Dec 1981, pp 258-277.

Mills, G M and Stonier, T T (1982) Trends and prospects for microcomputer-based education. International Journal of Man-Machine Studies 17, pp 143-148.

Papert, S (1980) Mindstorms: Children, Computers, and Powerful Ideas. The Harvester Press, Brighton, Sussex.

Price, C (1984) Boy Meets Girl (Computer Program). Micro-computers in Religious Education (MIRE), Keighley, West Yorkshire.

Sewell, D F, Ward, R D and Rotheray, D (1985) Theoretical influences on the design and implementation of computer-mediated learning. In Alloway, B S and Mills, G M (eds) Aspects of Educational Technology XVIII Kogan Page, London.

Sharples, M (1984) Patterns of words. Personal Computer World (In press).

Shaylor, J and Stonier, T T (1983) Evaluating educational software. Educational Computing May 1983, p 9.

Stonier, T T (1979) Changes in western society: educational implications. In Schuller, T and Megarry, J (eds) World Year Book of Education 1979. Kogan Page, London.

Stonier, T T (1983) Words Words Words (Computer Program). Applied Systems Knowledge (ASK), London.

Walton, D (1984) Blob (Computer Program). Applied Systems Knowledge (ASK), London.

Yannakoudakis, E J and Fawthrop, D (1983) An intelligent spelling error corrector. Information Processing and-Management 19, 2, pp 101-108.

Section 1: Computer-Based Learning— General and Theoretical Issues

1.1 Can Information Technology Change the Curriculum?

J S A Anderson

Deputy Director, Microelectronics Education Programme, Newcastle

Abstract: The Microelectronics Education Programme set up by the UK government initially concentrated on information for teachers and in-service training. Latterly, curriculum development has become more prominent. This paper identifies a number of aspects of the programme which have created change.

INTRODUCTION

There has been an undeniably large growth in the development of educational applications of computers and in teaching about information technology in the past three years. Building upon a small base of developments in a few authorities and schools, MEP (the government Microelectronics Education Programme) has directly brought about innovation and indirectly stimulated much more. Two major aims of the programme are:

a) to help children understand the technology, its uses and its effects on society, and
b) to encourage teachers to use the technology in improving the effectiveness of their teaching.

However, while new technology can be used as a classroom resource, it is not always the case that substantial curriculum change will follow. There are plenty of examples of how the curriculum can remain the same.

The past two years have seen the emergence and identification of some educational concepts which are needed as a basis for curriculum change. The first is concerned with identifying the basic 'literacy' in microelectronics which, it is believed, should be understood by all children of all abilities and preparing the ground for its introduction into the curriculum. The second of these is concerned with developing in children the information handling skills which they will require as more information comes to them electronically rather than in traditional ways. Helping children to acquire these skills is a concern for teachers of every subject. The first could go some way to help to create a new area of the curriculum. The second has the potential to introduce learning skills through the classroom use of information technology which will have life-long currency for those who acquire them, both within the existing curriculum divisions and across those boundaries.

I will first summarize the way in which the programme has operated in pursuit of its aims and what has so far been achieved. I will also consider the omens for UK government funding intervention in this field for the remainder of the decade. Then, I will examine in detail two of the most significant developments which may prove to be successful in the long term in changing the nature of the curriculum on the one hand, and of the nature of learning in school on the other.

OBJECTIVES OF THE PROGRAMME

In 1980, the British government announced a project for education to meet the challenge of the new technology. Richard Fothergill was appointed to lead what has become known as MEP. While initiated by the government through the Departments of Education and Science (DES), and Industry, and receiving its funds from them, the programme has been given a relatively free hand to approach the problems in its own way. This sense of independence continues to be very important in encouraging teachers to work closely with us. After a preparatory period, the main part of the programme got under way in April 1981.

All curriculum subjects are affected by our aims, not just science and mathematics, but also history, geography, music, English, and many others. Likewise, the programme is providing for children of all ages, from five- to eighteen-year-olds. Indeed the five- to eleven-year-olds are some of the most responsive of all.

In addition, it must be emphasized that it is also concerned with children of all abilities. As we are not concerned solely with turning children into bright computer scientists, we are not focusing our work on the clever children alone. Rather, this is for all children because all are are going to live in a world influenced by this new technology and they all need to adjust to it. It is also true to say that computer technology can bring out abilities, interests and enthusiasms which have been ignored by other areas of study, particularly in work with technology itself.

There are over 400,000 teachers in Britain, and the question we faced was how to reach them all and enable them to participate in the work of the programme. The 109 local authorities, each with an independent viewpoint, were, with their co-operation, organized into 14 regions for the purposes of the programme. This has given us the opportunity to get closer to the teachers in every part of the country for there are MEP activities scattered around in every one of these regions. Thus the innovative strategy that we have adopted is based on encouraging teachers all over the country to join in a campaign of action. Many are working directly for the programme, while others are using its materials or taking part in training courses. All have a national direction, amended locally to meet the particular needs of the area in which the teachers live. To make this succeed, it requires a coherent plan and a co-operative approach. The programme operates in three areas:

* information for the teachers
* in-service training
* curriculum development

INFORMATION

First there is the information service based in 14 regional centres with staff to issue newsletters, show equipment and a wide variety of teaching materials to visiting teachers, help them over their problems and give them advice and instruction but, above all, keep them well-informed about curriculum developments, new software and devices in their subject areas.

We provide central information in newsletters and on electronic systems like our word-processor disks which go out for our word-processor network. We use an interactive mail service also - British Telecom Gold. This standardization means that all the centres can share information, exchange disks of databases and make use of regionally produced information sheets which they can personalize and print without major re-typing. In addition, MEP has many pages on Prestel which schools are increasingly able to acess through their computers. National discussions are under way regarding a national information service for education in these fields.

TEACHER EDUCATION

Second, there is an in-service training programme for teachers in all subjects and at all levels. This programme is divided into four domains, electronics and control technology, computer education, computer-based learning, and communications and information systems. These cover the breadth of the programme's remit. In a typical year of operation, over 30,000 teachers have been on the courses offered. The course length ranges from one to ten days. Each is run in the region by regional staff so that local needs and interests are covered but the main elements of the courses are planned and developed by national co-ordinators. The aim is to concentrate on teachers in the regions who will become trainers themselves and then go on to train their colleagues so that the whole approach cascades down from the national initiative into the classroom itself. It is difficult to account accurately with this method of training but a rough estimate suggests that over 100,000 teachers will now have met some training from this approach. Much will have been done at the familiarization level, and the programme is now concentrating on providing training at a deeper level. One of the useful results of this work has been the growth of the number of courses that the local authorities running the schools themselves provide. These courses plus those provided directly through the programme ensure a fairly thorough coverage of the necessary in-service provision. Support for those responsible for the initial training of teachers is now beginning, based on the in-service work, and thus based on real applications in the classroom. The regional staff also go on regular updating courses to keep them abreast of the latest developments and new materials.

The four domains also relate to the primary curriculum but, in addition, a primary team provide specialist training for primary teaching educators and teachers. Special education is specially treated by four national centres which provide information and training services.

Nationally, we have a considerable project being prepared by the Open University. This will generally reflect much of the in-service training programme and will be particularly valuable for those who find it difficult to attend courses or who are not very happy about attending them.

CURRICULUM DEVELOPMENT

The third feature of the work is curriculum development. Generally this means the development of materials that enhance the current curriculum. I will now consider those which have created change.

Initially, we were concerned to broaden the base of those who were developing those materials, to identify talent, and to encourage new writers. We were not concerned to seek out teachers who could program a computer, although many were spending many hours of their own time learning how to do this. Rather, we were looking for teachers who could specify the structure of a program that professional programmers could then realize for them. The topics chosen were varied and spread right throughout the curriculum. We sponsored many of these. At the same time, we were using the three national units that currently existed and were seeking to develop other units based on the expertize that was emerging from these early regional activities. This strategy has proved successful as we now have some eight units with more to come. The topics now to be developed are much more centrally guided as certain curriculum areas have been identified as needing particular treatment and support. However, we are not going to neglect the leading edge of development as this is where we will find the imaginative responses to the new technical developments that are coming.

This is an active programme, producing considerable quantities of tried and tested materials in a wide range of subjects and media – over 1800 items of software by summer of 1984, some published commercially, with many more made freely available to teachers. In addition, some 20 books, 70 internal publications, 35 videos, 19 hardware devices and nine tape/slide sequences have been produced. Our catalogue, issued to every school in the summer of 1984, listed 333 separate packages of materials – videos, OHP sets, wallets of software, books, kits, etc. One of the strengths of the programme has been the manner in which it has worked closely with the education publishers and manufacturers – some 30 in all so far. The majority of our products are published and distributed by them, and I believe that the programme has influenced their own approach to the technology as well. We have aimed at high quality publications because we believe strongly that our children deserve to learn from such materials. Collaboration with industry has also been a major feature of our work · so that the materials we developed were relevant and presented modern practice. However the driving force of the programme has been the close collaboration with the teachers.

Our work is firmly based on the curriculum and teachers needs in meeting the learning requirements of the children. If we are to have any success, it is important to ensure that teachers can adjust and interpret our materials and training to a style that fits them and the particular group of children with whom we are working.

LOOKING FORWARD

For the local authorities, who have recently been asked by the DES to say how they plan to arrange the continuation of these activities when central government pump-priming ends in March 1986, the majority have replied that they value their MEP information services. They say that they see that new technological developments will continue to be important in education and that there will be advantages for them in consortium arrangements of the kind which MEP regionalization introduced. The majority intend, without advance commitment, to continue the funding of their regional centres. On the teacher education side, most regions have improved in their ability to manage the careers of teachers who will be their future teacher trainers and are happy that they will be able to cater for the continued demand for teacher education at the lower levels.

Without exception all agree that there are certain kinds of help which they will continue to need from central government funds. UK ministers have left open these questions for MEP to consider with DES during the coming year. All see a need for a national information service and particularly stress the need for a database comprising curriculum and teaching materials and other information. All see the need for national initiatives which provide training, briefing, and updating support for teacher educators. This training needs to be set at a high level, designed to keep teachers and educators abreast of the continuing developments in technology and its implications for schools, the curriculum, and for future members of the information generation.

CURRICULUM AND PEDAGOGIC CHANGE

I will not assess further in this paper the broad range of activity and development within MEP. A recent issue of the Computer Education Group journal (Computer Education Nov 1984) is wholly devoted to such a review. Now I will consider two developments which are perhaps the most significant so far. The first is concerned with the 'technology' of information technology; the second with the 'information'.

MICROELECTRONICS FOR ALL

The MEP Microelectronics For All (MFA) is one of the most important developments to emerge from the work of the programme. Its aim is to give schools the means by which all pupils between the ages of 11 and 13 can achieve some insight into microelectronics and information technology. Given the social impact of microelectronics, MFA represents the minimum preparation for the future which our pupils should be offered now.

The case for a 'curriculum niche' for MFA is simple to state and to accept. The learning activities involved in the course, however, must have the highest educational validity. Little could be more sterile than wiring up transistors and integrated circuits using, for example, recipe sheets. Deliberately MFA sets out to avoid any hint of circuit construction, so that the 'electronics' element of the course has a very slight emphasis. For the majority of pupils, it could well remain unrecognized. MFA is about ideas, and about understanding the ways in which ideas may be handled. Activities in the course are arranged under the headings of decision, counting, memory, music, movement; all areas of human activity. Throughout, pupils' abilities are stretched and their curiosity engaged by problems to solve and new situations to tackle. It has been designed as a low-cost practical course which introduces the principles underlying information technology and demonstrates the action of basic simple IT systems illustrated by Figure 1.

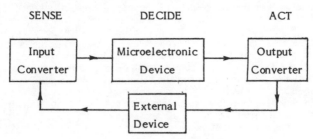

Figure 1   A basic IT system

The aims are:

1. To enhance pupils' awareness of the potential impact of microelectronics on industry, work, education and leisure.
2. To form an understanding of the basic principles of microelectronics and information technology.

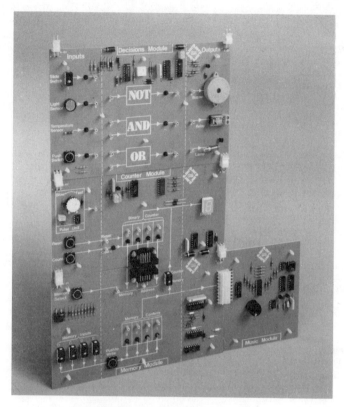

Figure 2   The demonstration unit

3. To encourage the development of communication skills and the processes of design.
4. To develop understanding of specific areas such as systems thinking, binary arithmetic, logical operations, instruction sequences etc.

THE GENERAL INFORMATION SYSTEM

The course utilizes the hardware system shown in Figure 2.

Figure 2 shows the three basic MFA modules connected together to form the demonstration system. Pupils begin work with the 'decision' module and then progessively add the 'counter' and 'memory' modules. The 'decision' module is arranged so that information enters the system on the left-hand side. Here there are four two–state input devices. The light sensor indicates whether it is dark or light. The temperature sensor detects a rise in temperature above room temperature. A slide switch and push switch provide the other two information inputs. If the light sensor output is connected to the buzzer, it sounds until the sensor detects darkness and causes it to be turned off.

Pupils first explore the interaction of input sensors and output devices before discovering ways of using more than one piece of information to control output devices. They are then in a position to be able to use their new-found knowledge to solve problems given to them or conceived by themselves.

The pupils then add the 'counter' module to the system to count how many times an event occurs, eg, how many times the bellpush has been operated. Clearly, a microelectronic system which can detect events is much more useful if it can count their occurrence as well. After exploring the principles of these boards, many problems can be posed and solved. Some typical pupil problems are:

1. Design a circuit which will sound a buzzer when a 'doorbell' (the push button) is pressed and it is light. (Who wants to be woken up at night?)
2. A cutting machine is usually fitted with a safety guard to protect the operator from injury. Design a system which will allow the machine to be started (by switching on the relay) only when the safety guard is in position and the start button is pressed. Which sensor would you use for the safety guard? Can you arrange for the buzzer to sound if the safety guard is not in place?
3. a) Design a door alarm for the deaf. A lamp must flash when someone pushes the 'doorbell' (the push button).
   b) Add to your circuit so that, even after the push switch has been released, the lamp carries on flashing.

So with the 'decisions' and 'counter' modules together, the MFA microelectronics system can sense, decide, act, and count. The next stage is to add a memory capability. The 'memory' module can output a sequence of binary patterns, for example data which controls a simple traffic light sequence. The binary counter may be incremented by a pulse unit and the binary counter inputs used address data for the memory unit. As the counter increases by one, the next memory cell contents appear at the memory outputs.

Note the format of the boards. Information comes in at the left-hand side, is processed in the centre, and actions or a display are provided on the right-hand side. This powerful but uncomplicated system is able to output through the edge connector a sequence of four-bit binary patterns from the memory. This provides examples of a very simple stored programmed control sequence.

Two other distintive elements of the course are the 'control extension boards' for the 'memory' module ,and work which links microelectronics to the capabilities of a microcomputer. Having learned how to store and read sequences of instruction with the 'memory' module, pupils put this knowledge to good use in the control of a small vehicle (with the 'movement' module), and in writing simple tunes (with the 'music' module). The 'computer' module allows a microcomputer to mimic the action of the MFA system. In this way, the electronic hardware and computer system are integrated in a natural fashion.

The course was devised to meet an evident demand and the development was carried out as an MEP Regional Curriculum Development Project of the Greater Manchester and Lancashire region. The work was co-ordinated by Dr John Martin of the Department of Electrical and Electronic Engineering of Salford University, who was the region's ECT co-ordinator. The work utilized the existing experience and expertise of practising teachers in the region and was supported both locally and nationally by industrial companies and higher education. The course has been extensively trialled in local schools. To enable an extension of this work into wider areas, in both examined and non-examined courses, MEP has established a development unit at Salford University. This unit will continue to work closely with schools and industry and with examination boards.

A QUESTION OF INFORMATION

The development of understanding of information skills by teachers of all subjects is an in-service aim. It is necessary to provide classroom materials which teachers can use to teach about IT applications, and to provide learning materials which can be used to promote a 'process learning' approach to information-handling and skills-acquisition in all subjects.

The process of information-handling, which is the fundamental activity in all subject applications of IT, is the priority for this domain. While it would be easy to suggest that primary schools are already half-way there, when employing project topic approaches to learning, it is also obvious that poor topic work fails to have information-handling as its primary activity.

In the secondary curriculum, even in most IT subjects, the potential for pupils to practise and acquire these skills exists but it is not always cultivated. The core activities and skills which we aim to promote in every subject are:

* The need to be adept at handling information.
* Identifying a need for information through an ability to identify sources to obtain information.
* The ability to make information work by applying it to everyday tasks.

One part of this involves acquisition from various sources (including electronic), and using electronic devices to communicate and apply knowledge. There may also be the use of electronic media for self-appraisal.

There has been a notable growth in the past year of 'information technology' awareness courses, mainly for lower secondary and middle school 11- to 14-year-old pupils. There are at least six published sets of course materials already, some from MEP-funded projects. A TVEI inspired O level is under consideration by at least one examining board.

Many of these courses exemplify what I would describe as a 'content' education approach to the subject which seems wholly inappropriate to the aim of giving children practical experience of activities in which they are handling information themselves rather than simply being told or shown how technology handles information. This is not to claim that such courses are wholly 'content' based but rather that, in comparison with an alternative 'process' education approach, they can be caricatured as such. Courses which tend to be more 'content' based provide the teacher with words and pictures which allow the teacher to teach about contemporaneous applications of information technology such as teleshopping or telebanking. The methodology usually involves the teacher in explaining or telling the story of the application while the pupils may be involved in some minor revision activity. This contrasts strongly with the 'process' approach taken by developments with which the Communications and Informations Systems (CAIS) domain of MEP has been involved.

The CAIS domain is producing a series of modules entitled 'A Question of Information' exploring many aspects of information – especially to develop the wide range of skills for handling information. An initial volume will set the scene; this will be followed by short modules for use in classrooms. A unique feature of the modules will be their attempt to include relevant teacher education among the ideas and activities outlined for learners. 'Handling Information in the Classroom' introduces the series and addresses some of the fundamental pedagogical issues. For example, how is the teacher to prepare for the experience of working with students who have direct personal and independent access to the wider range of information made possible by the availability of information technology? The volume explores this and other issues by drawing upon original work by Norman Longworth, work commisioned by MEP at the Universities of East Anglia and Southampton, and from others associated with the development of information skills over the past decade.

Coverage includes developing information skills in middle schools, information, thinking and action, school information systems, and missing ingredients in the teaching of informatics. The modules will cover many mainstream curriculum areas and several will take a cross-curriculum approach.

One such module is 'Writing the CEEFAX News' – a multi-purpose activity which develops thinking, writing, interpreting, abbreviating, interrogating, and structuring information in order to write electronic news. It uses word-processing, information retrieval and teletext software, and is applicable to most curricular areas. The module is based on the work of the BBC Ceefax unit but the materials do not provide a description of the operation or work of the unit. Instead, they provide raw text from the press association's teleprinter gathered on a particular day in the unit.

The pupils' task is to act as Ceefax news editors in exactly the same way as the editors had to act on that day, editing and preparing a story for Ceefax, applying all their skills and making similar kinds of decisions and judgements. They work with Edfax, a teletext emulator, available for the BBC microcomputer, to actually create teletext format pages which are identical to those which appear on Ceefax. A news update then appears (is handed out) and the pages have to be changed. This happens twice.

They certainly acquire the mechanical skills of using the Edfax editor – but the other skills of precising and editing, and editorial judgement are much more important. Both the operation of an IT system and the issue of news bias, distortion and propaganda are all experienced -rather than presented didactically.

Another approach is to take children into the neighbourhood of the school to provide 'insights into the richness and diversity of types of information and allow them to experience information, to grapple with the problems of observation, perception and classification!' The flavour of the impact that this can have on pedagogy in an information technology context can best be described by the following extracts from a teacher's diary.

First she holds a classroom discussion.

"'Any other information source?" I enquired, introducing a new term.

"What's that?" a boy exclaimed, grinning.

"Like tomato ketchup," said his friend. The grins spread, plus a few giggles.
Smiling because my over-familiarization with words had prevented my anticipating the
obvious, I said "You tell me what it is!"
He thought for a minute - "Lots of bits of information mixed together," he replied.
I thought this was a compelling image and told him so, but went on to explain how source
was spelt, and that it was associated with the beginning rather than the end of the enquiry.
I reflected later that "information sauce" was a very apt descriptive term for the end
products of the project work.'
Then she took them outdoors to gather information about the neighbourhood. They returned
to class and began trying to sort out their copious notes for entry into a microcomputer
database.
'To help them get started, I asked for some possible headings, and they volunteered
buildings, traffic signs, notices, advertisements, sports, etc. Taking traffic signs as an
example, I asked each person to tell me an item that could go in that column. Once I felt
that they were clear as to the nature of the task, I gave out some large blank sheets of
paper saying they could work in their original pairs or form into fours. For about ten
minutes everyone worked quietly and confidently; then they began encountering problems
and turned to each other and to me for help.
"You can't put telegraph pole under buildings."
"I don't know what to do with electric post."
"I've put memorial and garden windmill under buildings - is that right?"
"Can I put brass knocker on a column on its own - it doesn't fit anywhere."
A girl reprimanded her friend for putting duck's feathers under animals saying she needed
a column for birds, animals, plants and insects. Overhearing this, another girl said that
she had put those sorts of items together under nature as there were only a few of them.
Some of the children then re-examined their groups to see if any could be combined under
under broader headings.
The realization that there were alternative placings for a number of items came to
everyone. Some selected a preferred group to put them in, others chose to write them
down several times in different columns. "Honey for Sale" was both an advertisement and a
notice. "No Cycling in the Churchyard" was a traffic sign and a notice. In fact, as
someone pointed out, nearly half the items collected could be put under notices but that
did not sort them out enough so should they divide that group into smaller groups of types
of notices?
Confusion and frustration began to set in.'

And that, I suspect, is when real learning began to occur! The activities described in that
teacher's diary would benefit many teachers and pupils. Whether the tremendous interest
shown by the teaching profession in microcomputer technology is sufficient at the moment to
help bring about the new curriculum (and pedagogic changes which that technology has
inspired and could enable) remains to be seen.

ACKNOWLEDGEMENTS

I wish to acknowledge the work of Graham Bevis, MEP national co-ordinator for Electronics
and Control Technology (ECT), Ann Irving, MEP national co-ordinator for CAIS, Dr John
Martin, Director of MEP Salford Centre, Beverley Labbett and Rosemary Webb of the
University of East Anglia, and Richard Fothergill and Maureen Brown of MEP for their
assistance in preparing this address.

REFERENCE

Computer Education 48. Computer Education Group, British Computer Society.

1.2 The Nature of Computer-Assisted Learning

J Whiting

School of Life Sciences, Ulster Polytechnic

Abstract: Computer-assisted learning (CAL) has been a feature of tertiary education for 20 years. Cheap microcomputers and government aid have introduced it to the rest of education. No one yet knows the effect of this. Previous to CAL, limitations on educational media and methods have been financial and operational. CAL makes these less obtrusive since microcomputers are easy to program and use. The major limitation to the use of CAL is a human one. Teachers can either ignore or take part in the development of CAL. There is no middle ground. The latter alternative is preferable for a variety of reasons. There is a need for good software; most of what is currently available is based upon 'drill and practice' behaviourism and lacks integration with the curriculum. Practising teachers, with or without professional help, are the ones who must produce the software.

CAL can be seen as a <u>medium</u>, as a teaching <u>method</u>, and as a means towards current objectives in education and society. These are to meet the challenge of producing innovative, creative and adaptable human beings in order that they may best cope with the complex and increasingly fragmented post-industrial society which is developing all around us. CAL is one way towards these objectives; others exist and ought not to be ignored.

INTRODUCTION

Computer-assisted learning (CAL) is not a new idea; it has been with us for 30 years. However, through a combination of cheap and versatile equipment, popular imagination and government funding in the United Kingdom, a great deal of new interest has been generated in the primary and secondary sectors of education. What most forget is that CAL is an educational technology which should take its place alongside all the others.

EDUCATIONAL LIFE CYCLES

What happens when a new educational technology arises, or an older one (like CAL) develops a new lease of life? Much the same sort of thing in all cases; there is a common life cycle. A prototype idea is devised and is publicized through the journals of conference circuits. If the idea possesses any merit at all, and especially if it looks as though funds may be available for its development, then a bandwagon starts to roll. Transitory reputations are made, groups of zealots arise and missionaries spread the word to the heathen.

At about the same time, the defects inherent in the prototype start to show themselves; no prototype is perfect. Knowledge or experience of these spreads disillusion, and prejudices the uncommitted. Many of the converted recant of their heresies, and often become condemnatory on the slightest of evidence. Those who see their transitory reputations being tarnished rapidly sidestep on to the next bandwagon. Work on the prototype is abandoned except for a few devotees working away in obscurity. These latter eventually produce a working system. When they attempt to publicize this they are disregarded since 'everyone knows' that the idea has been discredited long ago.

This has happened once already with CAL, but now the general-purpose microcomputer has started the bandwagon rolling again. Whether CAL will be disregarded again is problematic, but the pervasive nature of the cheap microcomputer and its ever expanding capabilities make it unlikely. Facile truisms about the so-called 'microchip revolution' do have a basis in the real world, and it is from the real world that the stimulus for use of computers in education comes, unlike most other educational innovations.

PURPOSES AND LIMITATIONS

It is worth reminding ourselves what computers can do, both in general and in education. Simply stated, there are four things:

1. Reduce data to a directly comprehensible form.
2. Reduce administration, or rather to be more realistic, allow one to cope with most of its increase.
3. Communicate worldwide; exchange, store and retrieve data.
4. Last but not least, teach.

None of these tasks is beyond comprehension, none is difficult and none can be efficiently or completely done without sophisticated computer assistance - except, of course, the last. As far as CAL is concerned, the limitation upon its use is where it ought to be for any educational technology, ie, the wit, ability and perceptive nature of its user. Financial limitations still exist of course, but cheap computers are now much the same price as overhead projectors, slide projectors or a fortnight's pay for a vice-principal. Operational considerations are minor, compared to what they used to be when a large mainframe computer was the only resource for CAL. Anyone can use a microcomputer within a few hours of acquiring it.

ALTERNATIVES FOR TEACHERS

There are only two alternatives: ignore CAL and computing in the hope that it will go away, or get involved with it. From my viewpoint, as a writer and user of CAL for only a few years, the choice between the two is now obvious. Get involved! The nature of the involvement, however, is unlike involvement with any other educational technology. Ask anyone who has bought a computer for the children, or for themselves. The message is simple; involvement very often means total involvement for varying periods of time, perhaps months. Computers are very absorbing and can easily become an end in themselves. Raw fingertips at three in the morning are not unknown. Nor is a regrettably common lack of discernment about software. Most educational software currently available seems to be based upon behaviourist principles of 'drill and practice', though the position in the United Kingdom has been improving over the last year or so. There is one golden rule to remember when either assessing or writing software (or anything else for that matter), devised by the science fiction author Theodore Sturgeon, which states: 90 per cent of everything is rubbish.

While it would be foolish to condemn unseen software, much of it advertised as 'educational' seems to be based on 'drill and practice' methods beloved of the operant conditioners. Teaching something by behaviourist methods undoubtedly results in learning when multiple choice is used for assessment. Learning is less apparent when tested by methods which emphasize understanding or evaluation of what has been 'learnt'. This implies that the teacher's role becomes one of encouraging understanding and cognitive development, rather than rote learning of facts. Behaviourist CAL is, unfortunately, very easy to program. It is much more difficult to write programs which encourage the higher cognitive abilities. In turn, this implies that CAL should only be used in circumstances which are appropriate for it.

APPROPRIATE CIRCUMSTANCES FOR THE USE OF CAL

The first set of circumstances ought to be self-evident; ie when it is difficult or impossible to teach the topic in any other way. There are some circumstances which have successfully been used to my knowledge. You can no doubt imagine similar circumstances within your own disciplines. Most of the available programs are simulations of one sort or another, in which the user is encouraged to input parameters to an algorithm and view the results. A process of gradual optimization follows, via inductive reasoning, and the user comes to understand the model. Most models of this kind do not give any tutorial assistance and are thus wasteful of time, though once learnt, the knowledge remains for a long period. Remedial tuition is the second set of circumstances. This can be very boring and repetitive for both teacher and pupil. Motivation to learn is discouraged precisely when it ought to be stimulated. If a flexible tutorial program is written instead, the pupils can use it whenever they wish, as often as they wish and without much contact with the teacher. This sort of CAL is best written in an author language with good text recognition facilities such as 'STAF2' for mainframe and CP/M machines, Acornsoft's 'Microtext' for the BBC machine or Super PILOT on Apple or other computers. It results in easier programming plus much more flexible and interesting tutorial or adventure type programs.

Practical experiments can be replaced by computer simulations. Provided that the object of the experiment is not to inculcate practical skills, then this is appropriate. Often, experiments require a lot of tedious and repetitious calculations of doubtful educational relevance. Also, computer mediated control of laboratory equipment can be used both:

* to log data, analyse them and present the results.
* to reproduce data from computer memory to run machinery or robots.

There are one or two other reasons where the use of computers to assist learning would not be regarded as CAL by purists. I agree with them in respect of their nature, but not in respect of their purpose, since any use of computers which either frees a teacher's time or makes the teaching more efficient or both is, to my mind, CAL.

The first of these is what information technology is all about, viz. finding the information. It is now possible to access information stores and databases almost anywhere in the world from the keyboard of most computers. Prestel in the UK and equivalent systems elsewhere are one example. Another is a system like Dialog or ERIC, which many teachers and lecturers use to scan research literature. Why spend three weeks looking through a cubic metre of abstracting journals when half an hour on line to a computer in California at three dollars a minute will search them for you? This is simpler and much more cost effective. Children can learn from constructing simple versions of these, mostly using declarative language such as Prolog, as can anyone trying to learn how to use a commercially available database software system.

A second impure circumstance is computer-managed learning, usually found under the acronyms CML or CAMOL. These systems are meant to make the administration of learning easier. However, what usually happens is that the software system has been written for the benefit of the administrator rather than the teacher. Anyone familiar with BEC/TEC courses will know what I mean. But the concept is right even if its execution in practice is corrupted. There is no reason why more sensible programs cannot be written by the teachers themselves, and it is heartening to know that this is beginning to happen.

A third circumstance, derived from both of the above, is the use of electronic mail and networking, both currently very fashionable. It is conceivable to run distance learning through database networks like Prestel or in LAN within a smaller area. The Council for Educational Technology has been investigating this sort of approach for some time, as has the Open University in Britain, among others. Given a sufficiently dense network to which the majority of any population has access for little if any cash, this part of the educational information explosion will soon grow exponentially.

CHARACTERISTICS OF CAL

If the foregoing were the appropriate circumstances for the use of CAL, what sort of characteristics ought the CAL itself to possess? This may be approached from two points of view: that of the teacher and that of the users of the CAL programs.

I was critical earlier about currently available educational software because of its 'programmed learning' nature. Most often this type of programming arises for two reasons; first, it is the easiest to program and second, because much educational software has been written by professional programmers - thus, these differences. A professional progammer will write efficient programs which run quickly and produce the expected results with the minimum expenditure of processing power or other computer resources. That is what professional programmers are trained to do. The resulting progams are inhuman in outward aspect. On the other hand, if a teacher writes a CAL program, it is likely to be relatively inefficient, slow running, but have some human characteristics, because the teacher knows about education from experience and formal learning. This difference is often seen most clearly in the input routines of menu-driven modelling programs, where informality coupled to explicit advice should be the rule instead of inhuman instructions, that one can identify immediately as machine generated.

Thus, to summarize, a CAL program ought to be as close as possible in its nature to the manner, characteristics and attributes of the human being who wrote it. In other words, a replica of the teacher inside the computer. But what precise characteristics ought a 'good' CAL program to have?

* First, it ought to make maximum use of colour, sound and movement. The lesson was learnt long ago by educational technologists that a performance is better than its description on paper. With cheap microcomputers like the BBC machine there is now no excuse for monochrome displays without motion or sound. The software to design such routines is available very cheaply and is easy to use. A program that actually says 'Rubbish! Try another input!' instead of printing it on a screen is a lot better.
* Second, the whole program should be visually and intellectually stimulating – the difference between the script of a TV programme and its actuality on the screen.
* Third, get the user of the program involved in responding with lots of opportunity to respond in as many ways as possible. Arcade game routines can be programmed into parts of the program, as can adventure sequences like 'Dungeons and Dragons', where relevant. Additionally, programs must <u>never</u> be at a loss for an answer, and must <u>never</u> crash, leaving the poor user in a situation that he or she cannot understand or remedy.
* Fourth, there must be plenty of criticism, help and advice throughout the program. There should also be some form of assessment. I shall have more to say about this later.

This brings up the problem of getting a quart into a pint pot. To produce a CAL program of the kind that I have indicated above can seem almost impossible because of the severe memory limitations of microcomputers. This is a fallacy which derives from thinking of a CAL program (or any other program) as a single entity, complete in itself. However, if one has off-line storage in the form of a disc system, there is absolutely no limit to the total size of the program at all. Where the limit applies is to a segment of the program. This accords well with the current doctrines of 'structured programming', which is a sensible doctrine since it means that programs have a logical sequence, flow and design, without a spaghetti tangle of GOTOs. Thus, one file in RAM loads the next one from disk, and so on and so on. The only limitation is the available RAM for one segment of the program at a time or, in other words, total freedom within the limitations of the machine in use. Such a concept is regrettably uncommon largely, I suspect, because of the classical attitudes to professional programming.

EVALUATION AND RESEARCH

One great lack at present is information about how well good CAL induces learning in its users. From the point of view of a scientist, a new test or procedure has to be evaluated in order to show that it works, otherwise it will not be used for the innovation it is, and new knowledge will not be acquired. This procedure has not been followed very much for CAL as yet. This will be absolutely essential information if CAL is to realize its full promise as another powerful educational technology. The problems in evaluating educational models are well known, and are in part responsible for the lack of effort or result in the field of educational research into the topic.

What needs to be done is to assess the results of the learning via CAL in cognitive terms and, not only this, but also to assess <u>formatively</u>, ie, to make the assessment part of the learning and teaching process. I have already indicated that good CAL should be designed to encourage reasoning, understanding and not just inculcate facts. Unless these abilities are assessed, how are we to discover whether they are being encouraged in the first place? Such data, when acquired and analysed, can be used in two ways which are familiar to any educational technologist. First, to improve the quality and teaching potential of a CAL program, and second, to influence the students formatively. The benefits of both these processes are well known. What is less well realized by most academics and teachers (who are subject specialists first and educational technologists second, only because they are concerned about learning and teaching as well as their own subject) is that the results of such assessments ought to be made known through publication in the educational journals and at educational conferences. There is not enough of this research being published. The best attitude towards this is enshrined in an axiom used by science fiction: 'What would happen if...' One does not know until one tries to find out.

CC.ICLUSION

We are in a strange and changing society as Alvin Toffler (1980) has said. The rate of change is accelerating and nobody can predict what will happen in the next few years, though I suspect that the 'Third Wave' is all around us and we do not know it. We are in the middle of the third human revolution. The first was agricultural when humans started to cultivate the grasses around the campsites instead of banging animals on the head with antelope thighbones. The second followed the Reformation when we began to control our environment instead of submitting to it, largely through the Industrial Revolution. Now, we are into the third revolution – perhaps one could call it 'informational'? I do not know any more than you do. As teachers and educational technologists, we are at the forefront of this explosive change, if we wish to be. CAL is part of the answer but it is certainly not all of it. Computers are part of it too. But in the last analysis, all of the young and not so young minds which contribute to the third revolution have to be educated, taught to think, reason and cope with it all. Go to it!

REFERENCE

Toffler, A (1980) The Third Wave. Collins, London.

1.3 CAL: Motivating Students for Lifelong Learning

J A Chambers and J W Sprecher
Co-ordination Center for Computer-Assisted Instruction, The California State University

Abstract: The goal of this presentation is to acquaint educators with motivation theory and how it is being applied in the development of computer-assisted (CAL) learning modules in the 'Personal Adventures in Learning' project of the California State University. The purpose of this project is to stimulate the 20,000 faculty and 320,000 students on the 19 California State University (CSU) campuses to design original computer-assisted learning modules for microcomputers which will be both exciting and pleasurable to students. The ultimate goal of the project is to help students to enjoy learning and to accept it as a life-long activity. The completed computer-assisted instruction (CAI) modules will be disseminated for use at no charge throughout the California State system, and will be marketed commercially world-wide. Approximately 20 programs are expected to be released each year, beginning in late spring 1984. The presentation will discuss and illustrate the team approach to design, and the application of learning and motivation theory to CAL courseware development, by using slides plus demonstrations of recently completed projects.

INTRODUCTION

Early CAL projects, such as Plato, TICCIT, and the NDPCAL, were costly both in development of courseware and in regard to the equipment on which the programs functioned. In addition, content and learning theory were the predominant concerns of the early developers, with little time devoted to the motivational aspects of the materials. For these and other reasons, early CAL programs failed to have a significant effect in the educational field prior to 1980.

With the advent of microcomputers providing a low-cost medium with significant motivational enhancements (color, graphics, and sound), a new era arrived, and with it came the California State University's Personal Adventures in Learning (PAL) project. Commissioned in 1981, the PAL project is concerned with the design and development of educational courseware for use with microcomputers. Directed by Jack A Chambers and Jerry W Sprecher, the project is centralized at the CAI Co-ordination Centre on the CSU, Fresno campus and encompasses all 19 campuses in the CSU system. Funding for the project, anticipated to be continued through fiscal year 1984/85, is shared by the Chancellor's Office of The California State University and CSU, Fresno. The project is expected to be self-supporting through the sales of its completed PAL courseware by July 1985.

PURPOSE OF THE PROJECT

The most immediate purpose of the project is to stimulate the 20,000 faculty and 320,000 students in the CSU system to design high-quality instructional and motivational computer courseware for eventual systemwide use. This important first step in the process, ie motivating faculty and students to prepare designs, is being achieved through campus awareness techniques using various forms of media. Once the designs have been submitted, peer reviewed, evaluated, and winners chosen, the Co-ordination Centre on the Fresno campus develops and distributes the materials throughout the 19 campuses for use in CSU courses. A secondary purpose or goal of the project is to make completed courseware materials available commercially on an international basis, and through this commercial distribution, to become completely self-sufficient.

METHODS

As a means of organizing and localizing the project throughout the CSU system, each campus appoints a campus co-ordinator. The campus co-ordinators are trained in methods of design in CAL materials and in the peer review process. The primary responsibilities of these co-ordinators are to assist faculty and students to design CAL modules and to train faculty to evaluate proposed courseware in the peer review process.

Conceptual designs are prepared by the designers and evaluated by faculty from other campuses in the peer review process in two specific areas. The first area of review involves faculty who are currently teaching in the field in which the courseware is intended and concentrates on content-related issues. The second area of review focuses on faculty in psychology, education and related fields who have a working knowledge of learning theory and/or motivational aspects of instruction.

In the next step of the process, each campus designates the top choice design from among the designs which were generated from its own faculty/student design teams and which passed peer review. A panel of experts then reviews the remaining designs from all campuses which passed peer review and selects additional winning designs to be programmed at the Co-ordination Centre on the Fresno campus. The winning design teams must then prepare detailed design specifications for programming. Once the detailed designs have gone through the initial phase of programming and instructor/student guides have been prepared, the programs are field tested in CSU classes. After this period of field testing, the programs and guides are revised and disseminated for use throughout the system and, finally, are made available commercially with designers receiving royalties from sales.

PAL PROJECT 1982-83 YEAR

In the 1982-83 year, an encouraging amount of support and involvement surfaced within the CSU. Sixty seven designs were submitted from the 18 campuses that participated in the project and a total of 30 designs were chosen as winners. The completed programs (the culmination of this concerted effort) are now being programmed and are anticipated to be completed for distribution this autumn.

PAL PROJECT 1983-84 YEAR

The 1983-84 year already looks even better than the project's first year. All 19 campuses are participating and over 300 faculty have agreed to serve as peer reviewers. The project directors anticipate that at least another 20 completed programs will result from this year's activities.

For 1983-84, the PAL project has solicited designs to be submitted in three areas or 'tracks'. The first track is general and includes designs in any field in which courses are offered in the CSU system. Track 2 covers only those designs that deal with topics relating to the CSU Entry Level Mathematics examination, with a special emphasis on designs dealing with elementary algebra skills. The third track is limited to faculty only (ie, no student lead designers) and involves identification of an entire general education lower division course for CAL development along with the design of the beginning module of the courseware.

GOAL OF THE PROJECT

The Personal Adventures in Learning project's first priority is to provide an important and indispensable educational tool for university students. As a student-oriented venture, the project's primary goal is to help motivate students to enjoy learning and to want to continue to explore life and to enjoy learning as a life-long experience.

Faculty designs are, obviously, the starting point for the PAL project's CAL. A common concern among educators relating to CAL designs is that a knowledge of the microcomputer or computer programming is necessary to even attempt program designing. The project emphasizes the contrary, in that the only essentials of designing are a pencil, paper, an idea, and the knowledge of the topic. The technical aspects of final development and 'computerizing' a design are carried out at the Co-ordination Centre.

TEAM APPROACH

The lack of designer expertise in one or more areas of the design process is overcome by a design team approach. A design team consists of, ideally,one or two faculty experts in the specific field of design, a team member with experience in learning theory and learner-motivation, and an individual with a background in microcomputer concepts and capabilities (but not necessarily in programming skills) (Chambers and Sprecher 1983). This combination of expertise forms a broader range of design skills than can normally be obtained by a single author.

To effectively communicate design concepts in a 19-campus system,to permit them to be evaluated, and to allow computer programs to be developed, a forms-oriented approach was adopted by the project. The designers serve as subject area experts and prepare the conceptual designs relatively independently using the printed guidelines. However, when the conceptual designs pass peer review, they require an in-depth, somewhat technically oriented detailed design to be developed. Preparation of these designs (again forms-oriented) usually requires the assistance of an educational technologist who can assist the design team with consultation in the area of motivation, learning theory and microcomputer technology. The educational technologist also serves as the intermediary person who helps the programmer and graphics artist interpret the design.

In summary, the team approach involves the design team (at a specific campus), the educational technologist, a large pool of peer reviewers, and the development staff (programmers, graphic artists and quality control specialists). The reality of quality CAL development today is that it has surpassed the cottage industry stage and now requires the expertise of a diverse and highly skilled team.

HUMANIZING THE COMPUTER

Humanizing the computer in the PAL project has taken the form of applying the principles of Bandura's social learning theory (Chambers and Sprecher 1983). Briefly social learning theory combines cognitive psychology and the principles of behavior modification with strong emphasis on the person in the social setting. Its major concern is with vicarious learning, ie, learning through observation with subsequent modelling of the observed behavior.

Social learning theory's main contributions to CAL are in relation to attention and motivation, both largely ignored in CAL developments of the past. Attention, for example, can be focused through on-line instructions to programs. These instructions can develop expectations to reinforce learning, can motivate the student to want to use the program (ie, show it to be an interesting, exciting and relevant task), can provide goals (and thus focus learning), and can further elicit student interest by advising of the benefits of adopting the behavior observed in the program.

Modelling, the central thrust of this theory, is postulated as most likely to occur when the task is relevant, when positive results are anticipated if the model is adopted, when the model is as human as possible, and especially when high status models are used. (Thus, if you want to be successful like the Prime Minister, you should smile like the Prime Minister!)

MOTIVATION

Motivation, in terms of PAL project activities, relates to the learner's attitude about the lesson. In this regard, learners are motivated when they want to complete a lesson more than they want not to complete it (Moore,1983). An important concept in this definition is the 'balance' between competing desires and not simply a single dimension of increased or decreased motivation levels.

The motivational balance can be shifted by: 1) the learner's desire for the information; or 2) by increasing the pleasantness of the lesson. The first factor, relating to a desire for knowledge for its own sake, simplifies the teaching process regardless of the medium used. In these cases, even an unpleasant activity will be continued if the end result is desired badly enough. (A reasonable analogy is dieting to achieve a slimmer figure). However, many learners are not motivated, by at least some of the required subjects, and therefore do not continue the learning experience for an adequate period of time. A solution then, at least for CAL, is to increase the pleasantness of the lesson since a sufficiently pleasant activity may be continued even if the end result is not desired. An added benefit of the pleasant activity approach is that if learners enjoy the learning experience, it can improve their attitude toward the subject area or learning in general and lead them to learn more on their own.

From a more applied viewpoint, there remains the practical problem of how to make a CAL lesson pleasant. In addition to the effective use of color, sound and graphics, there are other less frequently used techniques. Generalizing from the area of computer games (Malone, 1981), there are several factors which appear to influence broad numbers of individuals. Six of these factors have been adapted by the PAL Project and are included in a scenario or story-line approach that offers an interesting, sometimes even entertaining, method of motivation. These factors are:

1. Set a clear goal for the learner.
2. Make the final goal depend upon intermediate goals.
3. Make attainment of the goals uncertain.
4. Make the standards for success clear.
5. Provide prompt feedback of performance.
6. Provide variable difficulty levels.

A scenario is best described by comparing a lecture to a play. Assuming that both a lecture and a play dealt with the same topic, the playwright would embed the content in a scenario or story-line and attempt to leave the audience with a deeper understanding of the topic while at the same time motivating them to return to future performances. Since a play is not usually an interactive exchange, the computer may prove to be an even more effective motivator.

COURSEWARE EXAMPLE

An example of a design produced by the project is Ten Common Inferences. Designed by Dr Brooke N Moore, a Professor of Philosophy at CSU, Chico, Ten Common Inferences (TCI) implements the user-friendly and student appeal concepts encouraged by the project. The purpose of TCI is to develop a student's ability to differentiate between five common, valid reasoning patterns and five invalid reasoning patterns. In order to help motivate the student, the tutorial occurs within the framework of a colourful scenario that depicts the adventures of a hero - Oscar the Pig - as he tries to elude a villain, Farmer McDonald. On his way out of Bacon County, Oscar must pass through ten traffic lights. It is at these traffic lights that the instructional content is presented. At each signal there is a policeman who will allow the hero and by implication, of course, the student to pass only if he or she answers a question correctly.

The learning process in this courseware is firmly integrated within the adventure scenario. The correct answer to each question can be reached only through logical thinking. If the student fails to answer a question correctly, the concept behind that question is presented in a scenario-based remediation unit and then the student is presented other questions related to that reasoning pattern. The scenario, then, continues. Once the student has successfully completed the program (and Oscar has escaped safely across the county line), a humorous gift or reward that has been promised throughout the lesson is presented to the successful learner.

CONCLUSION

The PAL project supports the position that motivation is an essential and often missing component in current microcomputer-based development of CAL. PAL encourages the use of scenarios, colour, graphics and sound. Educating CAL designers in basic motivational techniques can result in enriched CAL production in the future; and perhaps most importantly, such enriched courseware may result in what most educators desire - students who enjoy learning as a life-long activity.

REFERENCES

Chambers, J A and Sprecher, J W (1983) Computer assisted instruction: its use in the classroom. Prentice-Hall, Englewood Cliffs, NJ.

Malone, T W (1981) Toward a theory of intrinsically motivating instruction. Cognitive Science 4, pp 333-369.

Moore, B N (1983) Motivation in CAI. PAL Project presentation, Co-ordination Centre for CAI. Fresno, CA.

1.4 The Electronic Notebook: Integrating Learning Strategies in Courseware to Raise the Levels of Processing

D H Jonassen
School of Education, University of North Carolina at Greensboro, USA

Abstract: Seventy per cent of commercial microcomputer courseware is 'drill and practice'. The typical design of such courseware is similar to linear programmed instruction, where information is presented and the learner is immediately asked to recall (or recognize) some of the material. The learner's input is then immediately followed by feedback, which varies considerably in modality and elaborateness. Many provide games showing high resolution scenarios as reinforcers for mundane behaviour. The problem is that the level of mental processing required of learners is too shallow. No attempt is made to relate the information to prior knowledge, ie, to make it meaningful and therefore retrievable (except from short-term memory) by the learner.

In order to increase the level of processing required by the courseware, generative processing of the material presented in it must be stimulated. This entails the integration of learning strategies in the learner response structure of the program. A particular comprehension/strategy with the aim of increasing conceptual connectivity requires learners to recognize, integrate, and elaborate on information presented in the program. Principles for designing learner responses in courseware, illustrated by BASIC subroutines for implementing them, are examined for the following comprehension/retention strategies:
* Paraphrasing and elaboration of various types
* Imagery
* Analysis of key ideas
* Networking

In studying from traditional media, it is more difficult to control the level of processing, but in courseware, it is easier to 'force' deeper processing of material by making further presentation contingent on response of a certain type, length, or modality.

THE PROBLEM

Background: Computer Uses

At present, a majority (as much as 70 per cent) of commercially available instructional microcomputer software, otherwise known as courseware, is in the 'drill and practice' mode (Cohen,1983). The paradigmatic design of drill and practice courseware (often referred to as educational computer games) is similar to that of linear programmed learning. Information or problems usually, though not always, in prose form, are presented on the screen followed immediately by recall or recognition question about the information. Often, no new information is provided at all. The courseware merely presents a set (inexhaustible if randomly generated) of practice items followed by knowledge of results. The nature of the feedback that learners receive provides the greatest variety among such programs – from a simple yes/no confirmation of results to elaborate graphic scenarios.

Based largely on connectionism, the use of drill and practice courseware assumes that enough practice ultimately produces correct performance. What is of concern to me is the level of processing produced by such practice.

The next most common mode of instructional courseware is tutorial, in which the courseware represents a dialogue between the coursewriter and the learners. Tutorial courseware normally is designed to adapt the presentation of information and practice in some way, accommodating to individual differences in such characteristics as the learners' abilities to comprehend the material, prior knowledge, or information needs. Such adaptations to learners' abilities resemble branching programmed learning. While microcomputers possess the capability of more rapidly presenting many more options to learners than print programs, tutorial courseware normally follows print-oriented rules about the level of adaptations to the learners.

The dominance of drill and practice and tutorial programs, hereafter tutorial (because of the similarity in intent, presentation, an adaptation), is being supplanted gradually by other more sophisticated simulation and problem-solving modes of instruction. Also, increased learning involvement with programming languages such as LOGO is replacing the tutorial functions of microcomputers with practices aimed at using the microcomputer as a tool or even a tutee (Taylor,1980). For the immediate future, however, the micro as a tutor will remain a popular if not dominate mode of microcomputer use.

Conceptual Problems with the Model

At a conceptual level of analysis, it seems that tutorial uses of powerful machines like microcomputers are basically overgeneralizations of the programmed learning model of instruction. This model of instruction traditionally has dominated educational technology. Since the programmed learning model is easily confused with the procedure or technique of programmed instruction, it is better conceptually subsumed by the mathemagenic hypothesis.

Mathemagenic behaviours are 'those student activities that are relevant to the achievement of specified instructional objectives in specified situations or places', that is, those which 'give birth to learning' (Rothkopf,1970). These behaviours, according to the hypothesis, can be controlled or manipulated by specific design attributes of instruction. The form of structure of instruction or the activities stimulated by it induce the necessary cognitive operations to produce desired learning. So, the instructor merely needs to specify the appropriate orienting, acquisition, and translation processes that most efficiently result in the acquisition of a specified skill or body of knowledge and incorporate learning activities in instruction which presumably require learners to perform them. The purpose of mathemagenic activities, such as inserted questions (which are the basis of programmed learning), is to control the way in which information is transformed and encoded into memory. It is therefore a reductive approach to learning (Jonassen,1984a). That is, educational technologies, such as programmed learning, regard learners as active performers but mentally passive receptors and encoders of information presented by the medium. So, at least three problems with computer applications of the mathemagenic model exist: the model is no longer valid with regard to cognitive principles of psychology; the levels of processing normally produced by mathemagenic behaviours (especially in programmed learning materials) is too low or shallow, and the microcomputer technology has simply outgrown the mathemagenic/programmed learning model of learning. I shall consider each of these in turn.

Cognitive Principles of Psychology

Based upon almost universally accepted principles of cognitive psychology, we now make an entirely different set of assumptions about how learners process information. Rather than passively responding to instructional controls imposed by the author/designer/teacher while integrating stimuli of any sort, learners actually need to attend to stimuli, access existing knowledge to relate to it, realign the structure of that knowledge in order to accommodate the new information, and finally encode the restructured knowledge into memory, which then becomes accessible in order to explain and interpret new bits of information. The meaning generated by each learner for presented material cannot be largely controlled by the author. Rather it is constructed by the learner, using existing knowledge as the foundation for interpreting information and building new knowledge. Learning is not 'a passive reception of someone else's organisations and abstractions' (Wittrock,1974a). Rather it is an active, constructive process. It is my argument that these cognitive principles of learning are not extensively represented in the design or nature of learning activities embedded in tutorial microcomputer courseware. Rather the instructional designs of such software normally represent the application of mathemagenic principles of instruction, ie, the programmed learning model, which are not consistent with constructive principles of learning.

Level of Processing

Craik and Lockhart(1972) proposed that what gets encoded into memory depends upon the level or depth of processing of the presented information as it is encoded into memory. Processing deepens on a continuum as one progresses from sensory to semantic processing. Assigning meaning to materials naturally entails semantic processing. Only deeper, semantic processing of information requires the learning to access prior knowledge in order to interpret new material. As the level of processing deepens, more information will be recalled because more meaning will be assigned to it. The activities embedded in courseware should begin to reflect this deeper level of processing. Why? Because it is exactly this level of meaningful learning that is most frequently missing from tutorial types of courseware. The emphasis is too frequently on rote practice of existing connections or of information recently presented in the courseware, again similar to the programmed learning model of instruction.

Powerful Technologies

A third problem with applying the mathemagenic/programmed learning model to instructional software design, is that virtually all computer technologies, including microcomputers, have outgrown it. These technologies and those now evolving are clearly more powerful than the model can accommodate. As with our understanding of human learning, the capability of microcomputers to manipulate information have already stretched the model to the limit. Artificial intelligence work of all types have shown us that the computer can simulate the thinking process in ways that are inconceivable by the mathemagenic/programmed learning model. The use of these technologies simply for iterative presentation-feedback cycles is analogous to using a Formula One racing car to drive to the supermarket. The application model needs to fit the technology.

I am not contending in my argument that tutorial modes of microcomputer courseware are subject to a rapid and ignominous demise; nor should they be necessarily. They are too ensconced in educational practice. I am assuming that drill-and-practice and tutorial programs will continue to be published for at least the immediate future. The argument I am making is that designers of tutorial modes of software should expand their conceptions of learning in order to accommodate more constructive conceptions of instruction, that is, to include tutorial responses that are more varied and more generative – that necessarily require deeper levels of processing.

A SOLUTION

Conceptual Solution: Generative Learning Activities

According to the accepted principles of learning (stated above), learning is an active, constructive process whereby learners generate meaning for information by accessing and applying existing knowledge. An instructional model which is based on these principles is the generative hypothesis. The generative hypothesis (Wittrock,1974b,1978) asserts that meaning for presented material is generated by activating and altering existing knowledge structures in order to interpret it and then encoding the amended structures as distinctive features of memory that may later be accessed to explain new information. Essentially, comprehension requires the proactive transfer of existing knowledge. While this may sound simple enough, it actually depends upon a complex set of cognitive transformatons and elaborations. These processes are integral to such tasks as generating mental images, making inferences about information from existing knowledge, or selecting the appropriate references from memory. Generative learning activities are those which require learners consciously and intentionally to relate new information to existing knowledge. Instructional activities that may involve generative processing include producing mnemonics, note-taking, underlining, paraphrasing, summarizing, generating questions, creating images, outlining, and cognitive mapping. In these activities, information is transformed into an encodable form and elaborated to make it more memorable. This is the type of cognitive activity which is not represented in most tutorial modes of software, which rely on short-term recall of presented information – information which is not properly integrated with prior knowledge. These are the kind of activities that should be included in courseware, so that the levels of processing of material becomes deeper. The emphasis of instructional activities embedded in courseware should be on facilitating knowledge acquisition, not controlling it. While this is a noble and conceptually sound idea, how can it be implemented?

Practical Solution: Include Learning Strategies

The generative model of learning is most clearly manifested in <u>learning strategies</u> - activities designed to foster not only learning but also <u>learning to learn</u> (Brown et al,1981). Learning strategies, sometimes referred to as cognitive strategies, are mental 'operations or procedures that the student may use to acquire, retain, and retrieve different kinds of knowledge and performance' (Rigney,1978,p165). They represent information processing skills (eg, organization), study strategies (eg, notetaking), support strategies (eg, relaxation techniques), and metacognitive strategies (eg, monitoring learning behaviour) (Weinstein and Underwood,1983). Learning strategies are intended to increase the number of links between stores concepts in order to enhance retention. They include three types of activities:

* <u>reorganization</u> - asking questions that require a shift in perspective
* <u>integration</u> - linking incoming material with previously stores material
* <u>elaboration</u> - making links interesting and unusual through imagery, analogies, humour

The rationale is simple - learning is an individual, constructive activity, so learning activities need to allow for individual encoding of instructional materials rather than constraining the encoding process.

Types of Learning Strategies

The types of learning strategies most effectively embedded in learning materials are the information processing or study skills. The two most common types of those skills are recall and transformation strategies and elaboration strategies.

* Recall and transformation strategies focus on the recall stage of learning, where learners integrate, organize, and encode material for retention. Such strategies include paraphrasing, analysis of key ideas (eg, identifying and defining key concepts, interrelating them, and networking, or constructing a map of the structure of ideas in a presentation) (Dansereau et al,1979).
* Elaboration strategies require the learner to elaborate on, expand, or add to presented information in order to make it more meaningful and therefore more memorable. Such strategies include drawing inferences, analogies, implications or creating images (mental or physical). The important point is that including learning activities in instructional materials which require learners to systematically relate presented information to existing knowledge, encourages generative processing of that material.

Learning Strategies in Courseware

Learning strategies may be explicitly taught study skills or they may be embedded in instructional materials. Incorporating learning strategies, and hence generative processing, in microcomputer courseware would exemplify embedded strategies. The simplest method for embedding strategies is to replace adjunct, mathemagenic activities with specific comprehension or elaboration strategies - depending of course upon the nature of the material, the state's objectives, and the type of learners involved. For example, rather than inserting multiple-choice questions to test immediate recall or comprehension of information in a program, you might periodically insert any of the following directions: 'summarize in your own words' the ideas presented; recall and record key ideas and use them to create analogies, outlines, or cognitive maps; draw a picture or generate a mental image of the subject matter; or list the implications of the material. How or where this information is recorded and how it is later used for review or integration are researchable design issues as well.

Here is the connection. It is my contention that microcomputer courseware is particularly amenable to the inclusion of such strategies, because of the ability of microcomputers to store, manipulate, and retrieve information. Simply presenting recall questions and recording the percentage of correct learner responses doesn't begin to tap the potential of the machine, let alone predictably contribute much to learning. The literature does not strongly support the effectiveness of adjunct questions intext (Lindner and Rickards, 1984). There is no reason to suspect or any empirical support for the belief that they work any better in courseware. The processing capabilities of microcomputers can become an electronic notebook for storing, manipulating, and retrieving individual learner constrictions as well as facilitating comparisons among learners. As an electronic notebook, the microcomputer can foster not only learning but also learning to learn. In the remainder of this paper, I will suggest selected applications of the electronic notebook, that is, ways in which selected learning strategies can be incorporated into courseware. The suggested strategy applications are not intended to represent an exhaustive list of potential applications, merely to substantiate the electronic notebook concept.

INTEGRATING LEARNING STRATEGIES INTO COURSEWARE: THE ELECTRONIC NOTEBOOK

The simplest conceptualization of the electronic notebook is to think of it in terms of paper notebooks. While there is 'good evidence to suggest that notetaking can aid the learning process in certain situations and that reviewing one's notes can be a useful procedure' (Hartley,1983,p36), note-taking strategies most often employed by learners tend toward note recording of ideas with little reference to prior knowledge. Therefore, embedding generative learning strategies that require learners to integrate material with prior knowledge should improve comprehension even more - in both paper and electronic notebooks.

The strategies I will discuss could certainly be implemented with paper notebooks. I am not implying that their usefulness is limited to electronic recording. However, there are three reasons why they should be implemented in the electronic notebook.

* First, because they are not currently implemented. Since tutorial-type courseware relies so heavily on rote recall, efforts to raise the levels of processing should produce greater comprehension of material.
* Second, the reason it may be more successful in courseware in that the software can 'force' deeper processing by making further presentation of material contingent upon responses of a certain type, length, or modality. With print notebooks, few if any constraints on their content or use can be exercised, so learners most frequently employ the strategies that require the least mental effort, ie, rote recording.
* Third, it should become obvious from this discussion that computer procesing can make the use of these strategies easier for the student by performing many of the mechanical/numerical tasks for them, allowing them to concentrate on meaning.

Integrating Comprehension/Retention Strategies

I shall now describe the implementation of some proven comprehension strategies with the electronic notebook. These are intended to encourage integration of presented material with prior knowledge and organization of what it committed to memory.

Paraphrasing Strategy

Paraphrasing is a straightforward comprehension/retention strategy that requires learners to recall all parts of the presented information and then to describe it in their own words. In doing so, leaners presumably are required to access appropriate existing knowledge in order to interpret the presented material and then generate a description of what it means based upon their amended knowledge structures.

This strategy can be implemented in courseware in a variety of ways. The simplest means would be to include it in the courseware program as a subroutine. At the end of each block or unit of an instructional presentation (graphics, text, or combination), the program would call a paraphrasing subroutine. A very simple BASIC language example, written for the Apple II computer, is presented in Figure 1. Essentially the subroutine consists of a simple text file handling sequence and a keyboard routine for constructing text. The program creates a file, enables the learner to type in their text, paraphrasing the meaning of some previously presented information, and then, somewhere near the end of the program, prints out their paraphrasing on a printer. The learners' paraphrasing is retained on the disc and may be presented for on-line review by the learner or the teacher. Parenthetically, these presentation options present some interesting research variables. The directions could be elaborated to include virtually any contingency the courseware author would want to impose. It could be written in any language normally used for producing courseware (ie, it is not limited to BASIC), including authoring systems. The primary advantage of the electronic

```
100  REM ESTABLISH FILE
110  D$ = CHR$(4): R$ = CHR$(13)
120  HOME: INPUT "WHAT IS YOUR SURNAME? ";NAME$
130  PRINT D$; "OPEN "NAME$
140  PRINT D$; "CLOSE "NAME$
1000 REM DATA ENTRY
1010 HOME* I = 0
1020 PRINT TAB(11) "RELATING KEY TERMS": PRINT
1030 PRINT "YOU JUST COMPLETED A UNIT OF MATERIAL. ": PRINT "IN THE
     INFORMATION YOU SAW, SOME IDEAS": PRINT "WERE KEY TO THE OVERALL
     MEANING OF THE"
1040 PRINT "UNIT. TRY TO REMEMBER EACH OF THOSE": PRINT "IDEAS. WHEN
     YOU ARE READY, A NUMBER": PRINT "WILL APPEAR ON THE SCREEN. TYPE
     IN A"
1050 PRINT "TERM YOU REMEMBER AND PRESS RETURN.": PRINT "CONTINUE UNTIL
     YOU CAN'T REMEMBER ANY": PRINT "MORE TERMS. WHEN FINISHED, PRESS
     RETURN": PRINT "ON AN EMPTY LINE.": PRINT
1060 PRINT "    PRESS ";:INVERSE: PRINT "RETURN";: NORMAL: PRINT "WHEN
     YOU ARE READY.": PRINT
1065 PRINT: PRINT
1070 POKE 34,18
1080 I = I + 1: PRINT I;": ";
1090 INPUT A$
1100 IF A$ = "" AND I<4 THEN PRINT "THERE ARE MORE KEY TERMS." I = I - 1:
     GOTO 1080
1110 IF A$ = "" THEN 1200
1120 L$(I) = A$: GOTO 1080
1200 TEXT: HOME: PRINT "NOW THAT YOU HAVE RECALLED ALL OF THE": PRINT
     "KEY CONCEPTS, WE NEED TO ANALYSE THE"
1210 PRINT "RELATIONSHIPS BETWEEN THEM. AT THE TOP": PRINT "OF THE SCREEN,
     YOU WILL SEE 12 NUMBERED": PRINT "STATEMENTS DESCRIBING THE
     RELATIONSHIP"
1220 PRINT "BETWEEN TWO CONCEPTS - 'A' AND 'B'.": PRINT "UNDERNEATH THOSE,
     YOU WILL SEE TWO": PRINT "TERMS WHICH YOU RECALLED, ONE 'A' AND":
     PRINT "THE OTHER 'B'. DECIDE WHICH OF THE 12"
1230 PRINT "STATEMENTS BEST DESCRIBES THE": PRINT "RELATIONSHIP OF 'A' TO
     'B'.  ENTER THAT": PRINT " NUMBER AND PRESS RETURN. YOU WILL THEN":
     PRINT "SEE A STATEMENT WHICH REPEATS YOUR"
1240 PRINT "CHOICE FOR YOU TO CONFIRM."
1250 PRINT: PRINT "   PRESS ";: INVERSE: PRINT "RETURN";: NORMAL: PRINT
     "WHEN YOU ARE READY."
1260 GET Y$
1300 HOME: PRINT "*********************************"
1310 PRINT "1. 'A' IS (ARE) THE SAME AS 'B'."
1320 PRINT "2. 'A' IS (ARE) SIMILAR TO 'B'."
1330 PRINT "3. 'A' IS (ARE) THE OPPOSITE OF 'B'."
1340 PRINT "4. 'A' DESCRIBE(S) OR IDENTIFIES 'B'."
1350 PRINT "5. 'A' IS AN EXAMPLE OF 'B'."
1360 PRINT "6. 'A' IS A PART OF THE LARGER 'B'."
1370 PRINT "7. 'A' & 'B' ARE EXAMPLES OF THE SAME CLASS"
1380 PRINT "8. 'A' PRECEDES 'B' IN A SEQUENCE."
1390 PRINT "9. 'A' FOLLOWS 'B' IN A SEQUENCE."
1400 PRINT "10. 'A' CAUSES 'B'."
1410 PRINT "11. 'A' RESULTS FROM 'B'."
1420 PRINT "12. 'A' SUPPORTS OR DOCUMENTS 'B'."
1430 PRINT "*********************************"
1440 PRINT: PRINT


100  REM ESTABLISH FILES
110  D$ = CHR$(4): R$ = CHR$(13)
120  HOME: INPUT "WHAT IS YOUR SURNAME?";NAME$
130  PRINT D$; "OPEN "NAME$
140  PRINT D$; "CLOSE "NAME$
1000 REM PARAPHRASING SUBROUTINE
1005 HOME: I = 0
1010 PRINT TAB(11)"PARAPHRASING MEANING": PRINT
1020 PRINT "YOU JUST SAW SOME INFORMATION ON THE ": PRINT "SCREEN. TRY TO
     REMEMBER ALL OF IT AND": PRINT "THINK ABOUT WHAT IT MEANT. THEN "
1025 PRINT "DESCRIBE WHAT IT MEANT";: INVERSE :PRINT "IN YOUR OWN WORDS";:
     NORMAL: PRINT ".": PRINT: PRINT "PRESS RETURN AFTER EACH THOUGHT."
1030 PRINT: PRINT "WHEN FINISHED, PRESS RETURN ON AN EMPTY": PRINT "LINE."
1100 POKE 34,12: REM SET TOP OF SCREEN TO LINE 12
1110 I = I + 1: PRINT I;": ";
1120 GOSUB 2000
1130 IF L$(I) = "" THEN VTAB(18): PRINT "YOU MUST REMEMBER SOMETHING.
     PLEASE TRY": I = 0: GOTO 1110
1140 IF L$(I) <> "" THEN GOTO 1110
1145 REM WRITE PARAPHRASE TO FILE
1150 PRINT D$; "APPEND "NAME$
1160 PRINT D$; "WRITE "NAME$
1170 FOR X = 1 TO I -1: PRINT L$(X): NEXT X
1180 PRINT D$; "CLOSE "NAME$
1190 TEXT: GOTO 5000
2000 REM KEYBOARD ENTRY SUBROUTINE
2005 GET A$: PRINT A$;: REM GET EACH CHR AND PRINT TO SCREEN
2010 IF A$ = R$ THEN GOTO 2040
2020 L$(I) = L$(I) + A$
2030 GOTO 2005
2040 RETURN
5000 PRINT D$; "OPEN "NAME$
5010 PRINT D$; "READ "NAME$
5020 L = 0
5025 INPUT L$: L = L + 1
5030 ONERR GOTO 5050
5040 GOTO 5025
5050 PRINT D$; "CLOSE "NAME$
5060 PRINT D$; "PR#1"
5070 FOR X = 1 TO L: PRINT L$(X): NEXT X
5080 END
```

Figure 1 Program Listing for Paraphrasing Strategy Routine

notebook for presenting a paraphrasing strategy is that the material is removed from the screen, which precludes referral to the presented material with its resultant rote recording of ideas. The program could easily allow this if it is in the interests of the learner. Also, learners cannot continue the lesson until they have responded. You could easily add program statements which evaluate the length of the paraphrasing or which look for certain key concepts to be included. So, learners are obligated to process the information in a way that presumably entails generative processing of the material rather than rote recall.

Other Comprehension/Retention Strategies

Using a subroutine similar to that in Figure 1, you could easily alter the nature of the strategy employed. Simply by changing the directions (lines 1000-1060), you could direct learners to write a summary as opposed to paraphrasing. The latter more specifically requires the learner to relate the information to prior knowledge, however the former has been shown to be an effective study strategy. Another effective strategy is to have learners generate questions about the material rather than answering them (Frase and Schwartz, 1975). Some researchers classify generated questions as an elaboration strategy, but the classification matters less than the process. So, after presentation of a unit of material, you could direct learners to write questions about the material as if they were writing a test for their peers. These questions could be written off to file and later be presented to the learner for review either prior to re-reading the material (as an organizer) or presented without the material as a retrieval aid. These are a few of the optional comprehension/retention strategies that could be integrated in the electronic notebook. In this paper, I am only trying to present a model not a comprehensive review.

Analysis of Key Ideas

Another important set of comprehension/retention or recall strategies involves the analysis of key concepts or ideas presented in the material. In such strategies, the learners identify the key ideas, systematically define and elaborate on them, and interrelate them in some way. Text processing strategies involving analysis of key ideas sometimes use worksheets that specify the types of definitions and comparisons required (eg, Diekhoff et al,1982). The worksheet format is easily adaptable to courseware, with the users' responses and interrelationships stored by the computer.

The analysis of key ideas is supported by the teaching strategy of direct, systematic vocabulary instruction. Theoretical support derives from schema theory and advance organizers as well as empirical research. Understanding important concepts and their interrelationships is the basis of comprehension. So, rather than including learning activities in courseware which exercise recall of isolated concepts out of context, integrating analysis of key ideas into your electronic notebook should assist learners in understanding and interrelating the important concepts which have been presented.

Identifying Key Concepts

The first and perhaps most critical step in the anlysis of key concepts is to identify them. Any network representation of information must include nodes representing key concepts (Diekhoff et al,1982). A primary decision here is whether learners should be required to select the key concepts from presented information or whether they should be identified by the courseware writer. After working through a unit of information, learners could be directed to recall all of the key ideas presented. Since this is such a critical stage in the process, some program assistance may ensure the inclusion of all important ideas. The courseware, for instance, could cue important concepts by presenting them in inverse or flashing (for very important concepts) type. Terms could be set out in headings or included in a special glossary of key terms. The courseware could also allow the learners to mark important terms while working through the presentation, perhaps by moving the cursor over a word which would be marked by the program and presented later (electronic underlining, as it were). Whatever method you choose, it should ensure the identification of the most important concepts. Without some help, learners may identify too few or perhaps too many concepts, which would lead to content structures that are too lean or too tedious and time-consuming.

Relationship-Guided Definition

The next critical stage in building a semantic network of concepts, having identified its constituents, is to describe the links between those concepts. The method for doing this suggested by the Node Acquisition and Integration Technique (NAIT) (Diekhoff et al,1982) is the completion of a definition worksheet, which requires learners to identify six types of relationships for each key concept; characteristics and descriptors, antecedents, consequences, evidence, subsets, and supersets. As information is encountered during reading which relates in any of these ways to key concepts, learners fill it in on the worksheets. This could be easily implemented in courseware by using a type of key, an interrupt which breaks out of a program sequence and presents a subroutine. This subroutine would first call up the worksheet for the appropriate concept and allow learners to input information related to any of the six (or other) relationships. The learners could then return to the main program to continue processing the information. The result of this activity would be a series of structured summaries of concepts providing links to each other. Research has shown that following training using this technique, learners producing more varied and complete concept definitions, integrate information better, and more consistently identify what is important in a passage (Diekhoff et al,1982).

Comparing Relationships

The method for comparing and contrasting concepts suggested by NAIT is to use a comparison worksheet, which is simply a sheet that presents two concepts side-by-side and requires learners to identify simultaneously the six relationships listed above for both concepts. This is intended to lead learners through a relationship-by-relationship comparison of the definitions of selected pairs of concepts. It could be integrated into the electronic notebook in the same way as the relationship-guided definition procedure presented above.

An optional method for storing and comparing different dimensions of the interrelationships between concepts is to use a database management system. Each record in the database would represent a key concept. Each field would represent one of the six (or other) relationships stated above. The resulting database would represent the semantic network of concepts related to an instructional unit. Learners could search or sort on each field to group like or similar concepts. These groupings or any combinations could be printed out using the report function available in most systems.

Another related strategy for systematically analysing relationships among key concepts is to classify each relationship. Based upon a technique for semantically analysing pattern notes (Jonassen,1984b), key concepts are identified in a pattern note. A quasi-algorithm is used to help learners classify each link between the concepts included in the patterned note. While pattern note representation in the electronic notebook would be difficult, a simplified version of the technique could be easily implemented in the electronic notebook. The Apple BASIC routine shown in Figure 2, included in courseware as a subroutine, first asked learners to identify the key concepts presented (see above for alternative methods). These are then presented in pairs along with the algorithm. Learners select the best description of the relationship between each pair. A statement expressing the pair and the relationship is then presented for confirmation. If confirmed, it is written off to disk for printing or later review. This is a simple but systematic way to make learners think about the interrelationship of ideas, a necessary intellectual component in developing an adequate network of concepts for interpreting information. This strategy could be expanded or altered to include other functions, such as selecting pairs and creating analogies using a third term. The possibilities are numerous.

Cognitive Mapping

With a large microcomputer and a high level of programming and statistical skills, you would be able to integrate into your electronic notebook a very powerful learning strategy - cognitive mapping (Diekhoff and Diekhoff, 1982). Having identified the key concepts in your material, the procedure forms all possible pairs of concepts and requires learners to rate the strength of each relationship on a scale from one to nine, forming a correlation-type matrix of values (simple so far). These values are then scaled using a multi-dimensional scaling procedure (very complex statistical procedure). When plotted in two dimensions, it produces a map which spatially depicts the conceptual distance between all concepts included (see

```
100  REM ESTABLISH FILE
110  D$ = CHR$(4): R$ = CHR$(13)
120  HOME: INPUT "WHAT IS YOUR SURNAME? ";NAME$
130  PRINT D$; "OPEN "NAME$
140  PRINT D$; "CLOSE "NAME$
1000 REM DATA ENTRY
1010 HOME* I = 0
1020 PRINT TAB(11) "RELATING KEY TERMS": PRINT
1030 PRINT "YOU JUST COMPLETED A UNIT OF MATERIAL. ": PRINT "IN THE
     INFORMATION YOU SAW, SOME IDEAS": PRINT "WERE KEY TO THE OVERALL
     MEANING OF THE"
1040 PRINT "UNIT. TRY TO REMEMBER EACH OF THOSE": PRINT "IDEAS. WHEN
     YOU ARE READY, A NUMBER": PRINT "WILL APPEAR ON THE SCREEN. TYPE
     IN A"
1050 PRINT "TERM YOU REMEMBER AND PRESS RETURN.": PRINT "CONTINUE UNTIL
     YOU CAN'T REMEMBER ANY": PRINT "MORE TERMS. WHEN FINISHED, PRESS
     RETURN": PRINT "ON AN EMPTY LINE.": PRINT
1060 PRINT "    PRESS ";:INVERSE: PRINT "RETURN";: NORMAL: PRINT "WHEN
     YOU ARE READY.": PRINT
1065 PRINT: PRINT
1070 POKE 34,18
1080 I = I + 1: PRINT I;": ";
1090 INPUT A$
1100 IF A$ = "" AND I<4 THEN PRINT "THERE ARE MORE KEY TERMS." I = I - 1:
     GOTO 1080
1110 IF A$ = "" THEN 1200
1120 L$(I) = A$: GOTO 1080
1200 TEXT: HOME: PRINT "NOW THAT YOU HAVE RECALLED ALL OF THE": PRINT
     "KEY CONCEPTS, WE NEED TO ANALYSE THE"
1210 PRINT "RELATIONSHIPS BETWEEN THEM. AT THE TOP": PRINT "OF THE SCREEN,
     YOU WILL SEE 12 NUMBERED": PRINT "STATEMENTS DESCRIBING THE
     RELATIONSHIP"
1220 PRINT "BETWEEN TWO CONCEPTS - 'A' AND 'B'.": PRINT "UNDERNEATH THOSE,
     YOU WILL SEE TWO": PRINT "TERMS WHICH YOU RECALLED, ONE 'A' AND":
     PRINT "THE OTHER 'B'. DECIDE WHICH OF THE 12"
1230 PRINT "STATEMENTS BEST DESCRIBES THE": PRINT "RELATIONSHIP OF 'A' TO
     'B'. ENTER THAT": PRINT " NUMBER AND PRESS RETURN. YOU WILL THEN":
     PRINT "SEE A STATEMENT WHICH REPEATS YOUR"
1240 PRINT "CHOICE FOR YOU TO CONFIRM."
1250 PRINT: PRINT "    PRESS ";: INVERSE: PRINT "RETURN";: NORMAL: PRINT
     "WHEN YOU ARE READY."
1260 GET Y$
1300 HOME: PRINT "*************************************"
1310 PRINT "1. 'A' IS (ARE) THE SAME AS 'B'."
1320 PRINT "2. 'A' IS (ARE) SIMILAR TO 'B'."
1330 PRINT "3. 'A' IS (ARE) THE OPPOSITE OF 'B'."
1340 PRINT "4. 'A' DESCRIBE(S) OR IDENTIFIES 'B'."
1350 PRINT "5. 'A' IS AN EXAMPLE OF 'B'."
1360 PRINT "6. 'A' IS A PART OF THE LARGER 'B'."
1370 PRINT "7. 'A' & 'B' ARE EXAMPLES OF THE SAME CLASS"
1380 PRINT "8. 'A' PRECEDES 'B' IN A SEQUENCE."
1390 PRINT "9. 'A' FOLLOWS 'B' IN A SEQUENCE."
1400 PRINT "10. 'A' CAUSES 'B'."
1410 PRINT "11. 'A' RESULTS FROM 'B'."
1420 PRINT "12. 'A' SUPPORTS OR DOCUMENTS 'B'."
1430 PRINT "*************************************"
1440 PRINT: PRINT
```

Figure 2   Program Listing for Semantic Analysis of Key Words Routine

```
1500 POKE 34,18: C = 0
1510 FOR X = 1 TO I - 2
1512 FOR Y = 1 TO I - X - 1
1513 C = C + 1
1515 PRINT " 'A'"," 'B'": PRINT
1520 PRINT L$(X),L$(X + Y)
1530 PRINT: PRINT "WHICH NUMBER BEST DESCRIBES THE": PRINT
     RELATIONSHIP BETWEEN THESE";: INPUT R
1540 IF R = 1 THEN S$(C) = L$(X) + " IS THE SAME AS " + L$(X + Y)
1550 IF R = 2 THEN S$(C) = L$(X) + " IS SIMILAR TO " + L$(X + Y)
1560 IF R = 3 THEN S$(C) = L$(X) + " IS THE OPPOSITE OF " + L$(X + Y)
1570 IF R = 4 THEN S$(C) = L$(X) + " DESCRIBES OR IDENTIFIES " + L$(X + Y)
1580 IF R = 5 THEN S$(C) = L$(X) + " IS AN EXAMPLE OF " + L$(X + Y)
1590 IF R = 6 THEN S$(C) = L$(X) + " IS A PART OF THE LARGER " + L$(X + Y)
1600 IF R = 7 THEN S$(C) = L$(X) + " AND " + L$(X + Y) + " ARE BOTH EXAMPLES
     OF THE SAME CLASS."
1610 IF R = 8 THEN S$(C) = L$(X) + " PRECEDES " + L$(X + Y) + " IN A SEQUENCE."
1620 IF R = 9 THEN S$(C) = L$(X) + " FOLLOWS " + L$(X + Y) + " IN A SEQUENCE."
1630 IF R = 10 THEN S$(C) = L$(X) + " CAUSES " + L$(X + Y)
1640 IF R = 11 THEN S$(C) = L$(X) + " RESULTS FROM " + L$(X + Y)
1650 IF R = 12 THEN S$(C) = L$(X) + " SUPPORTS OR DOCUMENTS " + L$(X + Y)
1660 PRINT: PRINT S$(X)
1670 PRINT: PRINT "DO YOU AGREE? ";R$
1680 IF LEFT$(R$,1) = "N" THEN HOME: GOTO 1520
1685 NEXT Y,X
3000 PRINT D$; "APPEND "NAME$
3010 PRINT D$; "WRITE "NAME$
3020 FOR X = 1 TO C: PRINT S$(X): NEXT X
3030 PRINT D$; "CLOSE "NAME$
3040 TEXT
```

(lines 5000 to 5080 exactly as in the program of Figure 1)

Figure 2 Continued

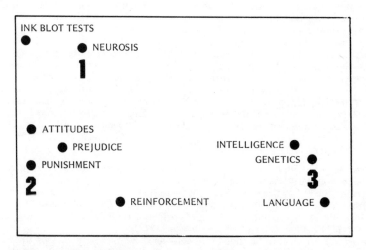

Figure 3   Example of a cognitive map (Diekhoff & Diekhoff,1982)
Reprinted with permission of Educational Technology Publications.

Figure 3 for an example of output). The programming and statistics are too complex to be considered here but, if implemented, the strategy is useful for showing the structure of relationships (ie, structural knowledge).

Elaboration Strategies

Elaboration strategies are those which require learners to add to the material presented, that is, elaborate or expand it. In so doing, learners are adding personal meaning to the material, presumably because such elaborations necessitate accessing prior knowledge in order to interpret and expand on the information. These strategies assume a variety of forms which have implications for the electronic notebook.

Imagery

One of the most popular elaboration strategies is mental imagery. Many learners voluntarily generate mental images of ideas, objects, or events about which they are reading. They naturally see the event in their 'mind's-eye' or 'get a picture of it'. Those who naturally use imagery command a powerful retention technique. When they form an image of an event or object, they are encoding the information in a separate store. Learners can also be trained to generate mental images by periodically directing them to stop reading, close their eyes, and try to create a mental picture of what they are reading. The more elaborate the image they generate or the more they are able to manipulate or expand that image, the more retrieval cues they will have at their disposal. Recall and retention have been shown to improve substantially (Kulhavy and Swenson,1975) as a result of generating images.

An optional strategy is to actually draw a simple image representing events or objects, a map etc. The creation of a physical image has been shown to have benefits similar to generating mental images. Most people, even the young, are able to draw simple cartoon figures. In fact, drawing in paper notebooks is a commonly employed strategy. The images need not be accomplished, because they will have personal relevance to the learner. The simplest application of this strategy is to provide sheets of paper for the drawing. However, the imagery strategy can also be integrated into the electronic notebook – a sort of electronic sketchpad. The easiest method for learners would be to use a graphics tablet in conjunction with your courseware. At intervals, the program would shift into draw mode, enabling its use to produce freehand drawings on the tablet, and digitize and store them. However, the cost of the tablet (£250 or more) would prohibit a great deal of use. Also, the command structure for each tablet is different, so standardization of software would present problems.

Another option is to incorporate a graphics editing program in your courseware. Such programs are often written in machine language. You might be able to adapt a BASIC language graphics program. Like other forms of the electronic notebook, it could be included in programs as a subroutine or as a separate program accessed by the main program.

The advantages of the electronic sketchpad are similar to those for the notebook. You can make further presentation of information contingent upon some form of learning activity. You can store the images and make them available for review or as retrieval cues. In addition, the graphics capabilities of most microcomputers allow you to manipulate the images easily. One simple program allows you to create and store shapes, expand and reduce them, rotate them 360 degrees, and move them anywhere on the screen. The ability to play around with various spatial relationships, simply by making a simple command, enables the learner a degree of control not available on paper.

CAVEATS AND LIMITATIONS

While I believe the electronic notebook concept for integrating learning strategies into courseware is conceptually sound, there are constraints and limitations.

The strategies that I have recommended in this paper by no means represent an exhaustive list of the strategies that might be implemented in the electronic notebook. The learning strategies literature is burgeoning. For a brief review of the kind of work being done, you are referred to O'Neil(1978) and O'Neil and Spielberger(1979).

These recommendations are intended primarily as short-term approaches to improving the quality of courseware rather than a revolution in the design of courseware. As we develop richer conceptual models of learning based upon artificial intelligence work and implement those in computer software, traditional conceptions of the computer as an information presentation device, including the electronic notebook, will become obsolete.

The particular learning strategies that are implemented through the electronic notebook need to be carefully matched to the processing requirements of the objectives stated for the program. Learning strategies are not implicitly good or effective. They represent technologies that, like any other technology, can facilitate the completion of specified objectives. If inappropriately applied, like any other technology, they can be counter-productive. The point I want to emphasize is that the electronic notebook is not universally applicable to all types of courseware or all types of content. A proper task analysis of the objectives and the strategies employed by the notebook should produce a match before the notebook is utilized.

Learning strategies, regardless of the instructional conditions of their presentation, are more effective if they are practised. In fact, the more comprehensive learning strategy systems (Dansereau et al,1979; Rood and Weinstein,1983; Weinstein,1978) entail many hours of training time. The amount of time required for practising any strategy implemented through the electronic notebook will vary with the complexity of the strategy, the ability and background of the learners, and the difficulty of the material with which they are being used. However, some practice with feedback will promote more effective integration and utilization of learning strategies in courseware.

Without practice, and even with practice, simply giving directions to learners to engage in certain forms of generative processing will not ensure that generative processing of material, in fact, occurs (Jonnassen,1984c). Learners usually habituate a preferred set of study strategies that are not generative in nature. Breaking such habits can be difficult.

By requiring learners, through the electronic notebook, to process information in a particular way, you may be contradicting their preferred, productive mode of studying, thereby decrementing learning. This is especially probable with higher ability learners, who have been frequently shown to be deterred by compensatory instructional treatments in the aptitude-treatment interaction research (Cronbach and Snow,1977). Not enough is yet known about individual differences in normal processing strategies to make firm predictions about who will be most positively affected by such strategies.

ACKNOWLEDGEMENT

This paper was written while the author was a Visiting Research Fellow in the Department of Psychology, University of Keele. I gratefully acknowledge the support of the department and its Head, James Hartley.

REFERENCES

Brown, A, Campione, J C, and Day, J D (1981) Learning to learn: on training students to learn from text. Educational Researcher, 10, 2, pp14-21.

Cohen, V B (1983) A learner-based evaluation of microcomputer software. Paper presented at the annual meeting of the American Educational Research Association, Montreal,Canada, April, 1983. (ED 233 534)

Craik, F I M and Lockhart, R S(1972) Levels of processing: a framework for memory research. Journal of Verbal Learning and Verbal Behaviour, 12, pp599-607

Cronbach, L J and Snow, R E (1977) Aptitudes and Instructional Methods. Irvington Press, New York.

Dansereau, D F (1978) The development of a learning strategies curriculum. In O'Neil, H F (ed) Learning Strategies. Academic Press. New York.

Dansereau, D F, McDonald, B A, Collins, K W, Garland, J, Holley, C D, Diekhoff, G M and Evans, S H (1979) Evaluation of a learning strategy system. In O'Neil, H F and Spielberger, C D (eds) Cognitive and Effective Learning Strategies. Academic Press, New York.

Diekhoff, G M, Brown, P, and Dansereau, D F (1982) A prose learning strategy training program based on network and depth of processing models. Journal of Experimental Education, 50, 4, pp180-184.

Diekhoff, G M and Diekhoff, K K (1982) Cognitive maps as a tool for communicating structural knowledge. Educational Technology. 26, 4, pp28-30.

Frase, L T and Schwartz, B J (1975) Effect of question production and answering on prose recall. Journal of Educational Psychology, 67, pp628-635.

Hartley, J (1983) Note-taking research resetting the scoreboard. Bulletin of the British Psychological Society, 36, pp13-14.

Jonassen, D H (1984a) Developing a learning strategy using pattern notes: a new technology. Programmed Learning and Educational Technology, 21, 3, pp163-175.

Jonassen, D H (1984b) Generative learning vs. mathemagenic control of text processing. In Jonassen, D H (ed) The Technology of Text: Principles for Structuring, Designing, and Displaying Text, Vol 2. Educational Technology Publications. Englewood Cliffe, NJ

Jonassen, D H (1984c) Effects of levels of generative processing of text. Paper presented at the annual meeting of the British Psychological Society, Warwick, 31 March, 1984.

Jones, B F and Friedman, L (1983) Content-Driven Comprehension Instruction and Assessment: A Model for Army Training Literature. Chicago Public School. Chicago.

Kulhavy, R W and Swenson, I (1975) Imagery instructions and the comprehension of text. British Journal of Educational Psychology, 45, 2, pp47-51.

Lindner, R W and Rickards, J P (1984) Questions inserted in text: issues and implications. In Jonassen, D H (ed) The Technology of Text: Principles for Structuring, Designing, and Displaying Text, Vol 2. Educational Technology Publications. Englewood Cliffe, NJ.

O'Neil, H F (1978) Learning Strategies. Academic Press, New York.

O'Neil, H F and Spielberger, C D (1979) Cognitive and Affective Learning Strategies. Academic Press, New York.

Rigney, J (1978) Learning strategies: a theoretical perspective. In O'Neil, H F (Ed.) Learning Strategies. Academic Press, New York.

Rood, M M and Weinstein, C E (1983) Improving higher order learning skills: elaborative cognitive learning strategies training. Paper presented at the annual meeting of the American Educational Research Association, Montreal, Canada, April 1983.

Rothkopf, E Z(1970) The concept of mathemagenic activities. Review of Educational Research, 40, pp325-336.

Taylor, R (1980) The Computer in the School: Tutor, Tutee, and Tool. Teachers College Press. New York.

Weinstein, C E (1978) Elaboration skills as a learning strategy. In O'Neil, H F (ed) Learning Strategies. Academic Press, New York.

Weinstein, C E and Underwood, V L (1983) Learning strategies: the how of learning. In Segal, J, Shipman,S and Glaser,R (Eds) Relating Instruction to Basic Research. Lawrence Erlbaum Associates, Hillsdale NJ.

Wittrock, M C (1974a) A generative model of mathematics learning. Journal of Research in Mathematics Education, 5, pp181-197.

Wittrock, M C (1974b) Learninng as a generative activity. Educational Psychologist, 11, pp87-95.

Wittrock, M C (1978) The cognitive movement in instruction. Educational Psychologist, 13, pp15-28.

1.5 Categories of Educational Microcomputer Programs: Theories of Learning and Implications for Future Research

G M Mills
University of Bradford

Abstract: A number of models of learning have been proposed of which I have selected four which seem to have particular relevance to microcomputer-based learning. These can be categorized as (a) skills, (b) hierarchical, (c) frameworks, and (d) feedback models. The relationships between these models, theories put forward by educational theorists such as Skinner, Piaget, Gagné, Papert, Schank, and various types of educational microcomputer programs are examined. In order to make the most efficient use of microcomputer-based educational technology, it is suggested that investigations are urgently required into the following.
(a) At what ages do children develop different intellectual skills?
(b) What are the optimum models and strategies for developing educational microcomputer programs?
(c) What criteria for assessment should be used for such programs?
(d) How will attitudes be changed by the use of microcomputers (both passively and actively)?

GROUPING OF PROGRAMS BY PREDOMINANT ACTIVITY

Various writers (Kemmis et al,1977; Howe and Du Boulay,1979) have suggested classifying teaching strategies according to type of activity or by the amount of teacher control. Typical classifications of microcomputer-based strategies placed roughly in the order of increasing control exercised by the learner in their choice of activity are shown in Table 1. Note that games may be placed in either of the instructional or revelatory categories.

1. Demonstration/textbook mode	
2. Drill and practice	
3. Programmed learning – linear mode	INSTRUCTIONAL
4. Programmed learning – branching mode	
5. Educational games	
6. Case studies and simulations	REVELATORY
7. Problem solving	
8. Creative activities, eg LOGO	EXPLORATORY (conjectural)
9. Maths packages (statistics/spreadsheets)	
10. Word-processing	UTILITY (emancipatory)
11. Database packages	

Table 1 <u>Classification of educational microcomputer programs</u>

Instructional programs are available for many topics and for a wide age range. Such sound and useful programs can readily be designed by using the following presentation principles:

1. aim for the minimum material on the screen at one time which will satisfy the educational objectives,

2. clearly separate either in space or time, the four principal categories of display material, ie,
   * reference or background information,
   * exposition material to which the user may be required to respond,
   * action (response) of the user, and
   * reward (reinforcement) received by the user as a result of action,
3. at any stage, where the user is presented with more than two alternatives, a menu should be displayed.

The rationale behind the above is based upon the 'information-processing' model of learning behaviour. The learner is assumed to be able to deal with only one input 'channel' at a time and only able to process information sequentially.

The 'demonstration' type, in which the user's only action may be to start, branch, or stop the program, can only be justified in comparison with a good textbook if it does something which a textbook cannot such as demonstrating dynamic behaviour. Such dynamic programs were produced in the 1970s by teachers at upper secondary and tertiary level education to illustrate mathematical and physical phenomena. Typical are the solutions of the Schrodinger equation, free fall with air resistance, and phasor diagrams (McKenzie et al,1978) and the behaviour of a standing wave (Miller,1983).

Both the drill and practice and the programmed learning modes are basically designed for individualized instruction. As they 'require' continuous user feedback for evaluation of the learning progress, they will normally only be efficient with one microcomputer per pupil.

The aim of many educational games is simply to provide drill and practice by introducing motivational material and competition. These can be used successfully with more than one pupil per micro.

Case studies require considerable time and special expertise to produce, usually require additional non-microcomputer educational material, and may have a limited market. Their costs usually reflect this. Good historical case study examples are Waterloo (Apple II) and Mary Rose (BBC micro). They will normally be more suitable for older pupils (10 plus) and can be readily structured for use with groups.

A simulation can be distinguished from a case study if it concentrates on certain elements relating to a real situation while ignoring others and therefore allowing the whole of the information relating to the simulation to be contained within the microcomputer program. Simulations which have appeared in many forms on different computers are:

* landing a space craft (often called LUNAR LANDER)
* governance of a village or town in the agricultural era for a number of years (various names such as HAMMURABI or KINGDOM).

As with case studies, there will usually be a minimum age below which the learning achieved from a particular simulation is less effective.

Exploratory programs include both those with an external goal (problem-solving) and those in which the user is given a basic minimum of ground rules and allowed to create anything desired within those rules. The latter might be a complete programming language. Gifted children from eight years upwards can learn to program in one of the simpler languages such as BASIC. Papert (1980) has described how, in developing the language LOGO, he created the 'turtle' to enable even younger and less gifted children to explore graphics as a stepping stone towards using more abstract ideas and symbols. Simpler exploratory programs of the latter type may concentrate on graphics or music creation only.

The main characteristic of exploratory programs is that users must devise their own procedures and may set their own objectives although guidance from teachers in the form of worksheets may be desirable in the preliminary stages. If a language framework is used, then the more users must use problem-solving skills to achieve their goals.

Some programs may contain elements of two or more of the categories in Table 1. If a modular approach with a menu is used, it is quite possible for a single program to contain a demonstration module, a drill and practice module, a tutorial module, and an educational game module. Even within one module, it may sometimes be difficult to distinguish between certain categories. For example, a program by Dethlefson and Moody (1982) to simulate neighbourhood segregation could apparently be categorized either as a demonstration or a simulation. If one uses the degree of control possible to the user during the course of one 'run' of the exercise as the criterion, then it would seem to be a demonstration since the program runs automatically to a conclusion after the user has set up the initial data.

SKILL-ENHANCEMENT AND SUBJECT-BASED LEARNING

There is probably a clear distinction to be drawn between the learning of general skills (ie, with symbolic information content such as speech and numeracy) and specific learning about 'real' things (eg, natural history). In general, the acquisition of skills requires a high degree of overlearning to ensure that the learner's performance does not suffer even after lengthy time periods without practice. Typical examples are spelling words, mutiplication tables, use of keyboard, and foreign language vocabulary.

Computer programs to promote the overlearning of skills - Steinberg (1984) uses the term 'automatization' - should preferably possess the following characteristics:

* fast cycle time
* immediate feedback
* field-tested criterion to specify the amount of overlearning required
* motivational material to reduce/prevent learner boredom

Such programs will usually be of the drill and practice category. The optimum number of learners per micro will be influenced by the number of micros available per classroom. The optimum type of motivational material will depend on the number of learners in the particular learning environment.

Most educationalists would accept that overlearning of all the curriculum (particularly that part defined above as subject-based learning) is impracticable. Hence the pass mark for many examinations is a mere 40 per cent! For such educational material presented through a microcomputer, a criterion of 95 to 100 per cent short-term learning would be expected even though only part of the learning may be retained in the long-term. Where subject-based material must be learned thoroughly (eg, as a precondition for further learning) the optimum strategy may be to insert remedial material if necessary in the later learning stages rather than use an overlearning strategy at its first introduction.

THEORIES OF LEARNING

In addition to the information-processing model for acquiring knowledge referred to above, four models of the learning process would seem to have particular relevance to analysing educational computer programs. These may be categorized as follows.

1. Learning as a product of acquiring skills. This approach is exemplified by the work of Skinner(1968).
2. Learning by the gradual development of more complex modes of learning. This differs from the 'skill' model in postulating a hierarchy of techniques gradually acquired by children in the course of their intellectual development. This model has been used by Gagné(1977) and, to a limited extent, by Piaget (Boden,1980). Many 'expert systems' have made use of this model.
3. Learning as a continual process of developing and modifying conceptual frameworks (or 'scripts'). This model has also been used by Piaget and is now being incorporated into work on 'artificial intelligence' (Schank,1982).
4. Learning as a feedback process in which the learner's responses are modified by perception of previous performance. This model has been adopted mainly by psychologists investigating sensory-motor skills involving timing.

THE SKILL MODEL

General skills are acquired in the development of those class of skills (abilities) recognized as making up general intelligence. Psychological theory indicates that many such skills are normally overlearned by most children in the normal course of their educational development. Additional practice (after overlearning has occurred) produces relatively little effect on their performance in IQ tests and accounts for the relative stability of IQ ratings. As Hebb(1949) has pointed out, 'innate potential for development (of the abilities contributing to intelligence) is not logically a guarantee that the development will occur... experience is essential'. This inevitably leads to the conclusion that for pupils to develop their full natural potential (Hebb's 'Intelligence A'), they should be encouraged to overlearn all the skills which contribute to 'intelligence'.

These general skills have been grouped by Thurstone(1938) into seven 'primary' abilities of perceptual speed, association memory, verbal comprehension, word fluency, number manipulation, space visualization, and logical reasoning. Many psychologists have suggested that this classification is too simplified. Burt(1955) has criticized Thurstone on the basis of his researches which seemed to indicate a much more complex pattern and Guildford(1959) has postulated a matrix of perhaps over 120 abilities. Many of these skills are acquired between the ages of four and ten although Burt and others have pointed out that logical reasoning skills are acquired over a much longer period.

The experimental work of the behavioural psychologist Skinner (1968) indicates that techniques for the precise control of reinforcing effects to control behaviour are now available. He has used these techniques to train animals to perform three or four well-defined responses in any experimental session and claims that these techniques can be used in human learning. His method is called 'operant conditioning' because the animal has to operate on the environment before obtaining a reward (provided externally). According to Skinner, if a new skill or element of knowledge required to be learned by a human being is followed by some preferred or rewarding activity (but only if the learning has been successfully achieved) then this is the basic prototype of learning. Also, a learner who begins with a liking for the 'reinforcement' will transfer this liking to the learning task.

While Skinner and his followers claim that his methods can apply to all forms of learning, it ignores the possibility of internal reinforcement. Nevertheless, the idea of reward for achievement has now become an integral part of educational thinking.

Failure to achieve the potential for particular abilities may occur due either to lack of opportunity to overlearn such skills (eg, gipsy children with very low school attendance records) or to lack of motivation (often due to the absence of any reward structure). In such cases, microcomputer-based instructional programs, particularly giving practice in the seven Thurstone skill areas, should be of considerable value. If, in addition, these are presented as educational games, motivation should not be a problem.

THE HIERARCHY MODEL

When operating in the real world, skills must be applied to specific situations or tasks. Understanding the context in which one operates requires subject-based learning. A clear line between general skills and subject-based learning may be impossible to draw because of the considerable overlap in such fields as numeracy and literacy. Nevertheless, in practice, one can define subject-based learning as learning which, whether absent or present, would have almost negligible effect on IQ ratings as measured by culture-free (eg, Cattell,1940) tests.

In constructing learning programs for subject-based material, Gagné's theory provides a useful basis. This postulates a hierarchy of learning processes from the simplest to the most complex including stimulus-response learning, chaining (memory association), discrimination, concept formation, rule learning, and problem solving. Gagné considers stimulus-response and chaining to be basic forms of learning and the others to be 'intellectual skills'. He defines discrimination learning as acquiring 'a response which differentiates (by name or otherwise) the stimulus features of a single member of a set from those of other members' or 'to distinguish several different members of a set, making a different response to each.' Discrimination must inevtably be involved in learning to classify different items under the same heading. The latter is one of the essential features of concept formation.

Two types of concept learning are distinguished by Gagné: concrete and defined. A simplified summary of the distinction might be that concrete concepts relate to the classification of perceived objects using discriminatory learning while defined concepts relate to abstract ideas or events which need to be classified according to rules. One method of defining a rule is by a statement such as: if concept A and concept B then concept C. This would be a relatively simple rule. A more complex rule might be: if concept D and concept E and not concept F then concept G else concept H.

The main justification for identifying what types of learning may be required in producing a teaching program are:

* to ensure that each item is suitably reinforced, usually by testing and feedback
* to more easily select the appropriate test criterion.

Examples of how to design appropriate instructional sequences using task analysis and Gagné's system are found in Principles of Instructional Design (Gagné and Briggs,1974).

THE FRAMEWORK MODEL

Research by Piaget and other educationalists strongly suggests that a real understanding of concepts and abstractions will only occur when the learner has reached a certain stage of intellectual development. The child must already possess a set of learning frameworks before new learning can be assimilated.

Schank(1982) has developed a theory of dynamic memory based on his work on computer artificial intelligence programs at MIT. His main contention is that memorizing by itself is not enough. The learner (ie, Schank's computer) must have a context into which to slot newly acquired information in order to make use of such information in an 'intelligent' way by responding sensible to questions. Schank refers to such frameworks as 'scripts' and suggest that human beings learn by reminding themselves of a previously acquired script, modifying it in accordance with the learning experience. His work is still at a relatively early stage but it has already affected the thinking behind the development of expert systems.

THE FEEDBACK MODEL

The idea of using feedback control systems as a model for a human operator was proposed by Craik(1948) and later elaborated by Hick and Bates(1950). At the same time, Wiener(1948) had been developing the concept of negative feedback in his theory of cybernetics. The latter was defined as the study of how self-regulation is applied to both physical and biological systems. This model seems to be of special application where the learner's responses produce actions which can be perceived as measurable on an analogue scale, ie, the degree or response error can vary from very small to very large (as distinct from simply right or wrong). Thus, acquiring a skill in controlling a physical action is a process of learning how to 'correct' responses in order to produce the required behaviour. It could be that the acquisition of early language makes use of this model.

APPLYING LEARNING THEORIES TO CONSTRUCTING PROGRAMS

Although human beings are still far more complex than any mechanical/electrical control system or computer, research by psychologists, computer scientists and other scientists is gradually resulting in a better understanding of how we learn. The application of models and theories as described above should allow educationalists to construct more efficient and relevant teaching programs. The skills model provides useful guidance in devising programs for learning simple skills from discrimination between shapes and symbols to spelling and arithmetic. A microcomputer can provide Skinnerian reinforcement in many ways ranging from a simple tick to colourful graphics or a tune. A typical example is Words,Words,Words (Stonier,1982) which produces moving graphic scenes following a series of successful recognitions of objects and their correct spelling via the keyboard. Skinner's theory would predict that the learner's liking for spelling tasks would increase after working through this program!

The hierarchy model is particularly applicable to programmed learning sequences in which the learned material is composed mainly of discrimination, concept formation and rule acquisition. The main task here is to correctly identify the type of learning required and ensure that the question to which the user responds tests that type of understanding. Some of the early teaching programs failed to do that. One of the common errors was to introduce a new concept by giving it a name and to ask the learner to fill in a blank in a partially complet statement - the missing word being the name just given. Such a test was really memory association rather than what should be really examined, ie, whether the learner really understands (by knowing how to apply) the concept. The testing does not necessarily have to be in the same mode as the material. For example, it is quite legitimate to use a discrimination test to assess the understanding of concepts or rules. The basic principle is to try to obtain a response which clearly distiguishes between learners with a full understanding and those with only partial or no understanding.

The frameworks model has implications for all levels of learning but particularly for the age range up to 12. It suggests that learning will be enhanced if a teaching program can start from a framework of knowledge with which the learner is already familiar. This framework can be enlarged by first reminding the learner of the existing knowledge, then showing parallels between this and some new material, and finally emphasizing the difference between the new material and the old.

Papert(1980) relates how, as a young child, he became fascinated with gears and applied his understanding of how gears meshed together to solve mathematical problems as he grew older. To provide a general 'facilitator' for children to learn, he developed the LOGO 'turtle' which draws as it moves across the screen in response to commands which an input of numbers to indicate either linear or angular movement. Another example is a computer teaching program which makes use of the concepts learned in obtaining the areas of rectangles to introduce the multiplication of algebraic expressions involving two variables, x and y.

The areas of learning where the feedback model may have practical value at present seem to be more limited. Sensory-motor learning involving negative feedback will be required in many arcade games but in very few explicitly educational games. In the cognitive area, an understanding of feedback processes may be acquired in both simulations and exploratory programs. One example of the latter is the use of the turtle in LOGO by pupils attempting to draw objects such as circles by trial and error.

Learner responses in the social sciences such as language communication and reactions to social situations may have a continuum of 'error'. Although few computer programs are available in such topics, some authors have already been experimenting with a feedback approach. The main pedagogical difficulty may lie in representing the degree of 'error' in the feedback to the learner. Indeed, in some social science areas, 'correct' responses may be governed by social norms which vary with time and culture. It may be that computer programs developed in these areas may eventually have more impact on educational thinking than the much larger number already constructed in science and technology.

RESEARCH IMPLICATIONS

Microcomputer programs with educational aims are now appearing in substantial numbers. Their technical quality is variable but unpublished research by the author has indicated that this can be evaluated with reasonable accuracy by experienced teachers. Their educational value is much more difficult to assess for the following reasons:

* difficulties in assessing what has really been learned (as opposed to merely memorized);
* different appropriate (efficient?) learning styles for different age/ability ranges;
* variations in the pre-knowledge of program users;
* variations in the educational environment in which the program may be used;
* cost-effectiveness of micromputer based learning relative to other modes of learning.

Research into the above should not only involve children in classroom situations but children at home, students in higher education, employed, unemployed, and retired adults. All these are potential users of educational microcomputer programs.

A number of specific questions need investigating if we are to develop computer-based learning to its full potential.

1. In the current educational environments throughout the world, at what ages do children develop different educational skills?
2. What are the optimum educational models and strategies to adopt in developing educational computer programs for different age ranges and different subject areas?
3. What criteria should be used to effectively and efficiently assess computer programs for their educational value? (Feasibility and cost-effectiveness are relevant here.)
4. To what extent can the particular characteristics of microcomputers accelerate the development of intellectual skills and learning? Particular areas of investigation might include (a) use of games and simulations, (b) use of teaching programming (eg, LOGO), (c) use of educational databases.
5. To what extent will attitudes towards, eg, technology, education, and society be affected amongst those who have used microcomputers passively (leisure and educational programs) and actively (writing programs, using databases through networks etc).

Microcomputer programs themselves provide the possibility of the adoption of new investigative techniques. Question 1 could be tackled by developing a series of games each with a different type or range of intellectual skills. These could then be rated by children of different age/abilty/culture on various criteria. Question 2 could be approached by using different models of learning to try and devise alternative educational programs. For example, alternative forms of a programmed learning style tutorial program could be produced - linear with short steps for the skills model, and branching mode for the feedback model. Responses in each program for each learner can readily be stored and evaluated later at leisure by the researcher.

The non-technological methodologies of social science research (eg, questionnaires, interviews, observation) will also play an important role in research such as described above. In particular, they are invaluable when investigating attitudes and conceptual frameworks used by the learner. All possible resources and all known investigative techniques must be used if we are to make the best possible use of the enormous educational potential which the microelectronic revolution provides for us all.

REFERENCES

Boden, M(1979) Piaget. Fontana, London.
Burt, C(1955) The evidence for the concept of intelligence. British Journal of Educational Psychology, 25, pp158-177.
Cattell, R B(1940) A culture-free intelligence test. Journal of Educational Psychology, 31, pp161-179.
Craik, K(1948) Theory of the human operator in control systems. British Journal of Psychology, 38, pp55-61 and 142-148.
Dethlefsen, E and Moody, C(1982) Simulating neighbourhood segregation. BYTE, 7, pp178-206
Gagné, R M(1977) The Conditions of Learning (3rd ed). Holt, Rinehart & Winston, New York.
Gagné, R M and Briggs, L J(1974) Priciples of Instructional Design. Holt, Rinehart and Winston, New York.
Guildford, J P(1959) Three faces of intellect. American Psychologist, 14, pp469-479
Hebb, D O(1949) The Organization of Behaviour. Wiley, New York.
Hick, W E and Bates, J A V(1950) The Human Operator of Control Mechanisms. Permanent Records of Research and Development No. 17, Ministry of Supply, HMSO, London.
Howe, J A and Du Boulay, B(1979) Microprocessor assisted learning: turning the clock back? Programmed Learning and Educational Technology, 16, 3, pp240-246.
Kemmis S, Atkin, R and Wright E(1977) How Do Students Learn? Centre for Applied Research in Education, University of East Anglia.
McKenzie, J, Elton L and Lewis R(1978) Interactive Computer Graphics in Science Teaching. Ellis Horwood, NJ.
Miller, D(1983) Studying standing wave formation via the Apple. Windfall, 2, pp69-71.
Papert, S(1980) Mindstorms. Harvester Press, London.
Schank, R C(1982) Dynamic Memory. Cambridge University Press.
Skinner, B F(1968) The Technology of Teaching. Appleton-Century-Crofts.
Steinberg, R J (1984) Towards a triarchic theory of intelligence. Behavioural and Brain Sciences, 7, 2, pp269-285.
Stonier, T T(1982) Words Words Words (Computer Program). Applied Systems Knowledge (ASK), London
Thurstone, L L (1938) Primary Mental Abilities. University of Chicago Press, Chicago.
Wiener, N(1948) Cybernetics. Wiley, New York.

1.6 The Theoretical Influences on the Design and Implementation of Computer-Mediated Learning

D F Sewell, R D Ward and D Rotheray
Educational Technology Research Group, Department of Psychology, Hull University

Abstract: The concept of microcomputer-based learning environments has been given particular pre-eminence by Papert's notion of microworlds (1980), a theme further developed by Lawler (1982). Essentially, a microworld is an artificial environment in which important things happen and there are important things to be learned. This definition draws significantly on the theoretical approach of Piaget in that it implies a belief in exploratory learning, rather than an approach based in a Skinnerian behaviourist mould. Additionally, the definition given above implies that microworlds should be constructed so that they possess both interactive and dynamic components, in that as the user 'explores' the environment under his or her own initiative, that environment changes as a result of the exploratory process. Thus, both LOGO and PROLOG can be seen as languages which promote such qualities. In addition, adventure games and simulations also promote the ideals of exploration and discovery. Although the 'designers' of such environments generally acknowledge the influence of Piaget in this sphere, additional cognitive models can be drawn upon. Of particular relevance here are the ideas normally associated with the developmental psychologist, Jerome Bruner. One of Bruner's central arguments has been that a better understanding of children's cognitive abilities can be obtained when children are placed in situations which have relevance for them, and when they are given the appropriate means of expressing such skills as they possess. The use of microcomputers and the associated concept of computer-based microworlds provides children with a new 'tool' with which to express their cognitive skills. Olson (1976) has argued that 'intelligence' has to be seen in a context of both cultural and technological influences, in that culture determines what is 'intelligence' (what 'powerful ideas' to put into the microworld), and that technological innovations can influence the development and expression of cognition (the effect of the microworld on the user). If computer-mediated education is to have the impact foreseen by many of its advocates, it is important to consider the rationale, manner and evaluation of its use in the light of the theoretical frameworks already available.

INTRODUCTION

Much has been said about the use of the microcomputer as an educational tool, but relatively little attempt has been made to place this use within particular models of cognitive developments. As Mills (1985) points out, not only can CAL be categorized according to the degree of user control permitted to the learner, but also particular implementations often reflect differing models of learning and, hence, of cognitive development. It must be said, however, that these models are rarely made explicit by the program designers.

ACTIVITY MODELS

A notable exception to this general trend has been the development of LOGO and its use as envisaged by Papert (1980). Papert's view of LOGO and its origins owes much to the influence of Piaget, an influence which can be also found in other areas of AI (Boden, 1981). These influences tend to draw on Piaget's view of children as epistemologists, rather than on his outline of cognitive development along well-defined stages. The acceptance by Papert of the former model of knowledge acquisition led him to an emphasis on 'discovery learning' via the medium of the microcomputer. We thus find in 'Mindstorms' an emphasis on children discovering knowledge through their exploration of 'computer microworlds', which Goldenberg (1982) has defined as 'a well-defined, but limited, learning environment in which interesting things happen and in which there are important ideas to be learned.' These 'important ideas' are analogous to Papert's 'powerful ideas' which are essentially cognitive skills valued by society. Papert emphasizes mathematical and physical concepts, and their discovery via the medium of LOGO. Other Logophiles emphasize problem solving (Harvey, 1982) or the acquisition of reading skills (Lawler,1982). The important linking feature of the learning of these particular cognitive abilities lies not so much in the fact that they have been emphasized in the context of LOGO but, more significantly, on the fact that they reflect an adherence to the particular model of cognitive growth emphasized by Piaget and by other cognitive theorists.

Broadly speaking this model has the central proposition that learning takes place via interaction with a learning environment which, in some sense, embodies what is to be learnt. As a result of the interaction, the learner constructs a set of internal hypotheses (or schemata) about the nature of the world. These schemata then act as 'a set of rules serving as instructions for producing a population prototype' (Evans,1967). Subsequent information is then processed within the existing schema which adjusts in order to cope with dissonant information. Although the schematic model of learning implied above is often associated with recent cognitive theorists, its origins can be traced to Piaget's ideas on assimilation and equilibration. For Piaget, assimilation was the integration of the experience of reality into an intellectual structure, and equilibration was the process of schema modification in order to compensate for the disturbances caused by novel information.

In the Piagetian model referred to above, development occurs as a progression through a series of stages, each characterized by its own form of equilibration. An essential element in this model is that learning is only possible if a complex structure is based on a simpler structure, a conclusion which finds echoes in Papert's discussion of 'powerful ideas'. This notion remains one of the most significant aspects to emerge from Piagetian theory, yet it seems that the Piagetians themselves seemed to overlook its significance for the design of their own observational studies. Piaget's stage theory generated a veritable mini-industry in psychological experiments examining the validity, or otherwise, of stage theory. The overall conclusion to emerge from a wealth of studies was that many Piagetians failed to take account of the child's current mental state, the child's 'world knowledge', or to pose questions that made sense to the child (ie could be processed within existing schemata). These failings resulted in an underestimation of children's mental abilities.

This research tradition, generally associated with Bruner's model of cognitive growth, has indicated that the claims made for the strict interpretation of stage theory have been unfounded, and that children are considerably less limited than originally supposed. In all cases, this re-interpretation of children's abilities has been based on studies which have presented tasks to children in a manner which either made sense to the child or removed unnecessary confusing elements in the testing procedure - see Donaldson(1978), for a review of such investigations.

Thus Piaget has made two important contributions to the present discussion, one positive and one negative. First, he laid the foundation stone of the constructivist, hierarchical model implicit in such approaches as LOGO. Second, by making striking claims about the cognitive limitations of children, a research tradition was generated which attacked those assertions by making explicit the limiting factors in the learning process. The work of Bruner and his followers has clearly demonstrated that the limiting factors have often been in the testing situation and task structure rather than within the learner.

Although Piagetian and Brunerian approaches are often considered to be at odds, there are essential similarities between the models. Both are basically hierarchical models in which cognitive growth is an ordered process from simple to complex. In both models, this development is based upon interactions with the environment, and the learner is presumed to be an active participant in the learning process. Nor is this hierarchical framework restricted to Piaget and Bruner. It is implicit in the work of many cognitive and AI theorists. Norman and Rumelhart (1975) categorized three modes of learning:

1. <u>Accretion</u> - the addition of new knowledge to existing schemata. The framework exists, but new data are entered.
2. <u>Structuring</u> - the formation of new conceptualizations when existing schemata will no longer suffice.

3. Tuning – the fine adjustment of knowledge to a task which occurs when the appropriate schemata exist and the necessary knowledge is within them, but they are inefficient for the task at hand because they are too general or not matched to the particular task.

In these terms, 'accretion', the most common form of learning, is equivalent to 'assimilation' and 'structuring' to 'accommodation'.

Schank (1982) developed a theory of dynamic memory based on his work in AI. His main point is that memorizing is not enough, but that the learner must have a context into which to place newly acquired information in order to make intelligent use of the incoming data. Schank refers to the existing frameworks as scripts, and argues that the most efficient learning takes place when we remind ourselves of a previous script and modify it in accordance with a new learning experience. There are close similarities here with Norman's statement (1982) that 'knowledge does not imply understanding.' The latter comes when the former is interpreted in the light of existing conceptual frameworks.

The direct implication of these views for the design of learning experiences is that they should begin with a framework of knowledge with which the learner is already familiar, and then show parallels between the existing framework and new material. Additionally, the learner should be able to explore the differences between new and old material, thereby allowing opportunity for conceptual restructuring. This is the basis of Papert's advocacy of LOGO. Turtle geometry is said to succeed because it can be related to 'body knowledge' (ie, a domain of experience with which the child is already familiar and to which the learner can relate). In the Piagetian scheme, 'knowing' an object consists of acting upon it, manipulating it and discovering its properties. Note, however, that the 'object' need not necessarily be a physical object, although in the early phases of cognitive growth it may well be. It can, for example, be a linguistic or conceptual 'object' in the sense that these can be manipulated and their functions explored. The turtle, physical or screen based, is an example of such a hypothesis-testing object, or object to think with. The turtle is fundamentally neutral (as is the microcomputer) in that its actions are dependent upon the input of the user, although this input is, in turn, constrained by the limits set by LOGO.

Gagné (1970,1975) referred to those objects which stimulated learning as 'objects of instruction' - ie stimuli from which concepts could be taught or derived. Although Gagné is a psychologist in the learning theory mould, his is an essentially hierarchical model of learning in which complex cognitive abilities are based upon the mastery of simpler skills. In this scheme, as in Piaget's and Bruner's, the components of cognitive growth are to be found in the child's environment and in the nature of the child's interactions with the environment. The environment, populated as it is with objects and people, provides the necessary raw material for cognitive explorations.

Children growing up in modern technological societies are increasingly placed in an environment in which the microcomputer is one of the 'objects of instruction' or, more flexibly, one of the objects to think with - along with people, toys, games, sand, water etc. Aaron Sloman (1978) has described the modern digital computer as 'perhaps the most complex toy ever created by man'. His choice of the word 'toy' is particularly apt. As outlined above, cognitive growth can be seen as a process which is dependent on the nature of our interactions with the environment. From early childhood on, many of these interactions can be viewed as 'play' activities in that they involve manipulations and explorations of the environment. Sloman points out that from infancy we need to play with toys 'be they bricks, dolls, construction kits, paint and brushes, words, nursery rhymes, stories, pencil and paper, mathematical problems, crossword puzzles, games like chess, musical instruments, theatres, scientific theories, and other people'. Out of these interactions comes understanding - ie, cognition. As implied earlier, the microcomputer is an essentially neutral 'toy'. Its efficiency as a provider of stimuli for encouraging cognitive growth depends significantly on how the computer-mediated learning experiences are structured - ie on how the microworlds are designed, the nature of the interactions they permit, and on which powerful ideas they incorporate. Lawler (1982) has, in fact, referred to the process of designing microworlds as 'cognitive engineering' and alludes to the designers of the computer learning environments as 'architects of inner space'.

LOGO AND PROLOG

Although the implications of the theoretical frameworks referred to above are readily perceived, it is worth considering the extent to which current educational software incorporates the principles of exploration, user freedom, active involvement etc. LOGO has already been implicated as a learning environment which owes its origins to ideas in developmental psychology. Although LOGO can be adapted for use in many ways (eg Howe's use of LOGO contains more imposed structure than does Papert's envisaged use), many of its proponents would maintain that 'pure' LOGO requires a commitment to exploratory learning. Additionally, LOGO allows users to impose their own structure on the environment. The user freedom inherent in the language permits the user to combine and recombine the LOGO primitives in such a way as to change the immediate environment within the limits of user and LOGO potentials. This considerable flexibility can be viewed as one of the major strengths of this particular language. Indeed, it can be argued that such an imposition of one's will upon the environment is a major component of normal cognitive growth. Halliday (1973,1975), in discussing the development of language, has argued that this is one of the major functions of language. Via the growth of communicative skills, the child comes to comprehend the nature of the environment and to explore his or her own cognitive abilities through language, by giving instructions, describing situations, reflecting on the past, speculating on the future, and imagining the unknown (the fantasy element so prevalent in children's literature). The communication made possible thus becomes, among other things, a vehicle for testing possibilities. In testing possibilities, whether via language, conventional play or through the medium of a microcomputer, we are basically exploring and developing our own cognitions or schemata. Through interactions with the environment these schemata can be examined, their implications and validity assessed, and the necessary modifications made – the processes of assimilation and equilibration referred to earlier.

In the context of microcomputer-based learning LOGO provides one such interactive possibility. In manipulating the turtle, using the features of turtle geometry or LOGO's list processing capacity (McDougall et al,1982), children are said to develop their own cognitive schemata and problem-solving strategies.

LOGO has been used as an example in this discussion not least because it is a well-known educational language (at least by reputation). However, more significantly, LOGO contains many of the elements already referred to. It is one of the few computer-based learning tools which claims a theoretical basis, and for which major cognitive claims have been made. It must be stated, however, that many of these claims have yet to be substantiated by sound objective data.

In the present context, a major feature of LOGO is that it permits users to impose their own cognitive structure on the environment – eg by the definition and combination of new user-defined procedures. A similar argument can be made for another current 'vogue' language, namely PROLOG. Although there has been some dispute about the relative merits of LOGO and PROLOG (Mellar,1983), it is significant that amongst the advantages claimed for PROLOG is that it enhances logical thinking, a claim not far removed from the argument that use of LOGO improves problem-solving strategies.

Although LOGO and PROLOG demonstrate significant differences – eg the former is best known for its graphics environment and for being a procedural language, whereas the latter is text based and declarative – both share the feature that their potential is best realized when the user is in control of the input, be it manipulating the turtle, or in constructing and querying a database. Ennals (1983) views an important feature of PROLOG as lying not in the fact that it is a programming language per se, but in that its use demands logical thinking. For Ennals and others associated with the relatively embryonic use of PROLOG in the classroom, the associations between logic, clarity of thought and many areas of the school curriculum are self evident. Ennals also reports that, notwithstanding criticisms about PROLOG's front end, nine-year-old children rapidly gain facility with its syntax. These criticisms are, to some extent, nullified by both the 'simple' front end, and by the 'Man In The Street Interface' (MITSI) currently being developed by Jonathon Briggs (Briggs, personal communication,1984).

To many classroom users of PROLOG, its attractions lie not in the claims that it may form the basis of the fifth generation languages, but in the nature of the cognitive skills that its use may promote. The development and expression of these abilities (ie those associated with logical thinking) are currently being explored through the use of PROLOG in the classroom.

It is no accident that its introduction in a classroom setting (see Ennals,1983) involves the construction of databases on material familiar to the users – eg football, friendship patterns, school meals, bus routes etc. As LOGO's turtle geometry is related to the child's 'body knowledge', so use of PROLOG is related to 'world knowledge'. In both cases the programming language is a medium through which children can express and explore the implications of their own understanding. These then become a route to the cognitive 'meta skills' which underpin many everyday activities.

MICROWORLDS

Bruner's contention that children's cognitive abilities are best examined in situations with which the child is familiar (ie is syntonic with their world knowledge) takes on an additional force when placed in the context of microcomputer-based learning environments which allow children to create their own personal microworlds.

This process of creation, which is analogous to the arguments presented earlier concerning the imposition of one's own cognitions on to the environment can also be found in apparently less powerful computer environments, although it is, of course, not restricted to computers. The program 'Animals' and its various derivatives (eg 'Tree of Knowledge') have been widely welcomed by both teachers and children. In such programs the user can develop a tree-structure which grows as more objects are inserted. The user is thus able to create a personal data tree. It is not even necessary that the items in the database are real 'animals', although this is often the first use. The database could be populated by orcs, goblins, dragons, giants, dwarves, elves etc. All that is necessary is that the child can cognitively identify the various items to be inserted and express their discriminating features. With each new addition the user has to provide a question which will discriminate between the new entry and one already included. In such a process, the user is not only required to reflect on possible salient discriminating features, but also to distinguish between a question enquiring about a difference and a statement declaring that difference. This latter procedure demands sophisticated linguistic and conceptual skills, as well as illustrating the close relationships which exist between thought and language.

The last 12 months have also seen a growing acceptance of a potential role for computer-based simulations and Adventure games in educational computing (Educational Computing, June and November, 1983). Although these are not creative environments in the same vein as LOGO and PROLOG they do allow users to impose their own strategies upon the task at hand. Thus, although the environments are essentially constrained, they do permit and, in fact, require exploration if their potentials are to be discovered. This limiting factor, however, may soon cease to be the case. The appearance of Adventure generators (eg, 'The Quill') allows individuals to construct their own adventure, and to insert their own characters, clues, problems etc. Such developments many well reflect a significant move in Adventure games towards environments which can be tailored towards particular educational objectives. This could well prove to be a powerful tool in the hands of imaginative teachers and children.

Simulations represent a further exploratory style of program. A wide variety of simulations exists including ones on archaeology, history, economics, politics, exploration, pollution control, evolution, flying and military battles. There are even games which simulate being a football manager. The essence of these simulations lies not so much in their accurate reflection of reality, although there are some very accurate simulations, but in their facility to allow the user to experience a set of problems and to see the consequences of various decisions. Simulations enable the user to adopt different strategies – eg in running an imaginary country or in adopting different battle tactics. In this process, the user is forming differing hypotheses (in order to solve the simulated problem) and in testing out these hypotheses. The richness of the potential hypothesis-testing ultimately depends on the quality of the simulation – ie on the quality of the microworld.

CONCLUSIONS

As argued earlier, hypothesis-testing forms an important component of cognitive growth. The hypotheses reflect internal schemata and allow exploration of the implication of those schemata. The returning data, in turn, allow modification or equilibration. Hypothesis-testing is inherent in simulation. It is also built into the computer-mediated learning environments described above. In Burton and Brown's Intelligent Tutoring System 'How the West was Won' (1982) the success of the computer tutor lay not simply in the quality of its intervention but in the fact that the users sought to 'psych' the coach ie to discover the situations which would result in the computer coach's intervention. In other words, hypotheses were formed about the way the tutor operated and those hypotheses were then tested. A significant potential of computer environments is that feedback about these hypotheses can be immediately apparent. Such a situation is not always to be found in the classroom.

This paper has argued that CAL can be examined in the context of models of cognitive development and, in particular, within the broad context of a hierarchical model of learning. Not only can styles of CAL be regarded in this light, but also it can be argued that developments in this field need to take into account our understanding of the factors known to influence cognitive growth. The framework provided by modern developmental and cognitive psychology provides such an opportunity. However, it does more. Not only can it provide guidelines for the development, implementation and assessment of CAL, but it can also benefit from the data on the nature of children's interactions with the new technology - ie our observations may result in a better understanding of cognitive growth.

Our conception of children's intellectual abilities is often clouded by preconceptions about those abilities, and by children's behaviour in environments which do not provide them with the opportunity to display sophisticated cognitive skills. Bruner's work has demonstrated the importance of providing children with the appropriate environment. Papert, coming from the Piagetian stable, has stated essentially the same thing. Olson (1976) argued that the expression of intellectual skills was critically influenced by the nature of the surrounding technology. The way in which we use the new technology and design the learning experiences may well have significant influences on the expression of intellectual skills.

REFERENCES

Boden, M A (1981) Minds and Mechanisms. Harvester, Brighton.
Briggs, J (1984) Personal communication.
Burton, R R and Brown, J S (1982) An investigation of computer coaching for informal learning. In Sleeman, D and Brown, J S. Intelligent Tutoring Systems. Academic Press, London.
Donaldson, M (1978) Children's Minds. Fontana/Collins, Glasgow.
Educational Computing (1983) June and November.
Ennals, J R (1983) Beginning micro-PROLOG. Ellis Horwood, Chichester.
Evans, S H (1967) A brief statement of schema theory. Psychonomic Science 8, pp 87-88.
Gagné, R M (1970) The Conditions of Learning. Holt, Rinehart and Winston, London.
Gagné, R M (1975) Essentials of Learning for Instruction. Dryden Press, Hinsdale.
Goldenberg, E P (1982) LOGO - a cultural glossary. Byte 7, 8, pp 163-193.
Halliday, M A K (1973) Explorations in the Functions of Language. Edward Arnold, London.
Halliday, M A K (1975) Learning How to Mean: Explorations in the Development of Language. Edward Arnold, London.
Harvey, B (1982) Why LOGO? Byte, 7, 8, pp 163-193.
Lawler, R W (1982) Designing computer-based microworlds. Byte, 7, 8, pp 138-160.
McDougall, A, Adams, T and Adams, P (1982) Learning Logo on the Apple II. Prentice-Hall, Australia.
Mellar, H (1983) Languages at logoheads. Soft, July, pp 82-106.
Mills, G M (1985) Categories of educational microcomputer programs: theories of learning and implications for future research. Aspects of Educational Technology XVIII. Kogan Page, London
Norman, D A (1982) Learning and Memory. W H Freeman, San Francisco.
Norman, D A and Rumelhart, D E (1975) Memory and knowledge. In Norman, D A et al, Explorations in Cognition. W H Freeman, San Francisco.
Olson, D R (1976) Culture, technology and intellect. In Resnick, L B The Nature of Intelligence. Lawrence Earlbaum Associates, Hillsdale.
Papert, S (1980) Mindstorms: Children, Computers and Powerful Ideas. Harvester, Brighton.
Schank, R C (1982) Dynamic Memory. Cambridge University Press, Cambridge.
Sloman, A (1978) The Computer Revolution in Philosophy. Harvester, Brighton.

Section 2:
Computer-Based Learning—
Systems Development
and Evaluation

2.1 Integrated Teaching Strategies Utilizing Computer-Based and Media-Based Materials

C F A Bryce and A M Stewart
Dundee College of Technology

Abstract: Examination of any textbook on teaching methods, particularly in higher education, will reveal a range of activities together with some description of the attributes of each. Similarly, examination of the various educational media available indicates propensities for the facilitating of particular educational objective achievement, and examintion of computer-assisted learning practices indicate different categories of learning activities. In this paper, the authors discuss an alternative paradigm for teaching methods and media utilization, and describe a project in which this paradigm is being implemented through the integration of media-based and computer-based learning.

DEFINITIONS

It seems to be fairly standard practice in degree course submissions to the Council for National Academic Awards (CNAA) to have a section on 'methods of teaching' and, in these, some sort of definition of each teaching method is attempted. For example, a degree in business studies submission included the following:

Lecture: a formal, one-hour presentation by a lecturer as part of a teaching programme with students required to undertake a limited amount of specified reading.

Seminar: a structured, small group activity which emphasizes student presentation and participation on the basis of wider study.

A degree in quantity surveying submission from the same college included:

Tutorial: Group of students engaged in discussion on topics related to academic studies or industrial practice. The items for discussion would be introduced by the students, college staff or guest speakers. The activity would encourage individual development and oral expression and stimulate cross fertilization of ideas.

Although such descriptions describe the physical structure of these teaching methods, they say little, if anything, about the kind of learning intended to be facilitated through them. The International Dictionary of Education (Page and Thomas, 1977) defines 'lecture' as: 'Teaching method in which facts of principles are presented orally to groups of students who take notes, have little or no participation in the learning, and experience passive rather than active learning. The lecturer may follow up his/her lecture with a seminar or tutorial.' (p 203)

'Seminar' is defined as either:

(a) 'Small-group discussion session, particularly one following the presentation of an essay or other work or a lead-lecture.
(b) Short course or conference of a number of sessions with a higher degree of participation and discussion between students and teacher or seminar leader.' (p 307)

'Tutorial' is defined as:

'Personal face-to-face teaching in a small tutorial group, the discussion between teacher or tutor and students often being based on written work by one or more of the students.' (p 348)

Again, little is said of what each method is meant to achieve, other than the reference to 'facts' and 'principles'. The Dictionary of Education (Good,1973) does little to help by defining 'lecture' as:

'a method of teaching by which the instructor gives an oral presentation of facts and principles, the class usually being responsible for taking notes; usually implies little or no class participation, such as questioning or discussion during the class period.'

It rather strangely defines 'lecture method' as:

'an instructional procedure by which the lecturer seeks to create interest, to influence, stimulate or mould opinion, to promote activity, to impart information, or to develop critical thinking, largely by the use of the verbal message, with a minimum of class participation.'

Probably few would disagree with the idea that the lecture is useful for 'facts and principles' but would readily agree with Kozma, Belle and Williams (1978) that, for content other than information, the lecture must be augmented. Macmillan and Powell (1973) state that, in general, discussion is useful for:

(a) refining and structuring concepts.
(b) Analysing procedures, organizations, and functions.
(c) Examining the applicability of general principles to particular circumstances.
(d) exposing, comparing and examining attitudes.

They suggest that it may complement other learning by following a lecture. In fact, they go on to suggest that lectures should generally be followed by seminars and tutorials or exercises in some form or another.

DISCUSSION

There appears to be general agreement that the lecture needs to be supplemented with other types of teaching activity if a range of cognitive objectives (ignoring affective objectives) is to be achieved. Entwistle (1981) points out that a versatility in the method of teaching is demanded to allow students of all cognitive styles to learn effectively. It could probably be further argued that versatility in the method of teaching is likewise demanded if learning at different levels, including higher cognitive levels, is to take place.

It seems artificial, however, to separate 'lectures' from 'tutorials' or 'discussion' or 'seminars' just as it is often artificial to separate cognitive and affective learning objectives, as Lessinger and Gillis (1976) have pointed out. In any topic or task there will always be a range of objectives requiring a range of teaching methods to facilitate their achievement. It becomes totally unrealistic to separate those methods in time as seems so often the case when examination of course proposals for CNAA indicates so many hours of lecture and so many hours of tutorial. What is needed is a range of teaching methods within the traditional teaching period of 50 minutes integrated to match the range of learning objectives identified in the task or topic analysis.

Perhaps the use of term 'lesson' deserves wider acceptance, particularly in higher education? MacMillan and Powell (1973) describe it as a session so planned that, at each stage of development, the method used is the one most likely to promote efficient learning. Yorke (1981) argues that colleagues in further education would claim that they teach lessons rather than give lectures, and that the difference lies in the nature of the interaction between the teacher and the class – an interaction which facilitates the achievement of a wider range of objectives. A parallel must be drawn between the need to integrate teaching methods in an interactive way and the possibility of integrating interactive media in learning.

INVESTIGATIONS

In an early investigation of the effectiveness of media in learning, Stewart (1973) describes how his students had to use tape-slide programmes for one part of the study, move on to film for another part, and then back to tape-slide for a final part. The attributes of tape-slide were not adequate to meet particular learning needs - film was much more appropriate.

The contribution which media makes to learning has frequently been discussed. Heidt (1978) identified more than 12 media classifications or taxonomies. He usefully reviewed the six most common but argued that they were deficient in their connection with theoretical models of teaching and learning, and that applicability to problems of media design and instruction are illusory. More recently, Reiser and Gagné (1983) looked at the characteristics of media selection models, identifying the factors in media selection as being:

a) Physical attrubutes of the media,
b) Learner, setting and task characteristics.
c) Practical factors.

They argued that proper identification of the media attributes necessary in a given situation is dependent upon consideration of the characteristics of the intended learners, the instructional setting, and the learning task.

Clark (1983) has argued that the most current summaries and meta-analysis of media comparison studies clearly suggest that media do not influence learning under any conditions, but that it is the method of instruction that leads more directly and powerfully to learning. He concludes that media are delivery methods for instruction and that it is what the teacher does - the teaching - that influences learning.

Faced with this apparent conflict of evidence, Bryce and Stewart (1981) have described a pragmatic approach which they adopted to try and develop a presentational system which incorporated the attributes of the available media and which, by requiring a variety of learning styles, could meet the learning characteristics of most learners and help to facilitate the achievement of a wide range of learning objectives.

In a series of investigations (Bryce and Stewart,1978,1979,1981,1982,1983), they progressed from systems which exploited the attributes of visual media to systems which coupled this exploitation with the additional attributes of computer-based learning. The computer was linked with random-access microfiche, random-access audio and random-access video so that the structuring was done via the computer which activated, where necessary, the presentational mode most appropriate for the content.

With the advent of videodisc and its successful interfacing by the authors to a BBC microcomputer in 1982, the challenge of integrating media-based and computer-based learning with a considerable degree of interactivity was accepted. It was no longer necessary to consider the attributes of the individual media or even the various attributes of computer-based learning such as 'drill and practice', 'tutorial', or 'simulation'. It was possible to bring all of these together and, in a pardigm similar to that already described in relation to 'lesson', to structure the learning experience to take account of the range of learning objectives identified by calling upon the various media/computer attributes as required.

CONCLUSION

Fields and Paris (1981) have claimed that hardware and software technology development is far in advance of instructional strategies development. They cite the fact that instructional strategies, which determine the educational effectiveness of CAL systems, have not shown any dramatic improvement over the past 20 years. The present authors would argue that the time has now come to show that instructional strategies are being developed which are likely to lead to improvement in instructional effectiveness. Certainly it was accepted that, if it was not worth writing on paper 20 years ago, it is certainly not worth putting on videodisc today. There are no excuses - the delivery system is there and the instructional developers must meet the challenge.

ACKNOWLEDGEMENT

The authors wish to acknowledge the financial support of the Scottish Education Department, Tyne Video Ltd, and Update Publications.

REFERENCES

Bryce, C F A and Stewart, A M (1978) Design and Production of Self-Instructional Learning
    Packages in Biochemistry using the Phillips PIP System. In Brook, D and Race, P (eds)
    Aspects of Educational Technology XII. Kogan Page, London.
Bryce, C F A and Stewart, A M (1979) The Application of Random-Access Back Projection in
    Computer-Assisted Instruction. In Page, G T and Whitlock, Q A (eds) Aspects of
    Educational Technology XIII. Kogan Page, London.
Bryce, C F A and Stewart, A M (1981) Multi-Media/Multi-Purpose: Is the Quality of the
    Learning Experience being well Served by the Use of Educational Media? In Percival, F
    and Ellington, H I (eds) Aspects of Educational Technology XV. Kogan Page, London.
Bryce, C F A and Stewart, A M (1982) Improving Computer-Aided Instruction by the Use of
    Interfaced Random-Access Audio-Visual Equipment. Report on Research Project No.
    P/24/1, Scottish Education Department.
Bryce, C F A and Stewart, A M (1983) Integrating Computer-Based and Media-Based
    Learning. Educational Media International 1983-84.
Clark, R B (1983) Reconsidering Research on Learning from Media. Review of Educational
    Research,53,4 pp445-459.
Entwistle, N (1981) Styles of Learning and Teaching. John Wiley & Son, New York.
Fields, C and Paris, J (1981) Hardware-Software. In O'Neill, H F (ed) Computer-Based
    Instruction: a State-of-the Art Assessment. Academic Press, New York.
Good, C V (1973) Dictionary of Education (3rd ed). McGraw-Hill, New York.
Heidt, E V (1978) Instructional media and the Individual Learner. Kogan Page, London.
Kozma, R B, Belle, L W and Williams, G W (1978) Instructional Techniques in Higher
    Education. Educational Technology Publications, Englewood Cliffs, New Jersey.
Lessinger, L M and Gillis, D (1976) Teaching as a Performing Art. Crescendo Publications.
MacMillan, P and Powell, L (1973) An Induction Course for Teaching in Further Education
    and Industry. Pitman Publishing, London.
Page, G T and Thomas, J B (1977) International Dictionary of Education. Kogan Page, London.
Reiser, R A and Gagné, R M (1983) Selecting Media for Instruction. Educational Technology
    Publications, Englewood Cliffs, New Jersey.
Stewart, A M (1973) An evaluation of the effectiveness of a self-instructional technique in
    chemical education. Unpublished MSc thesis, University of Dundee.
Yorke, D M (1981) Patterns of teaching. Council for Educational Technology, London.

2.2 The Design and Development of Computer-Aided Learning Systems for Industrial Applications

A K Kochar
Reader in Manufacturing Systems Engineering, University of Bradford
and J McLean
Senior Training Adviser, Engineering Industry Training Board

Abstract: Many computer-aided learning systems are available for use in the structured teaching environment, ie, schools, colleges and universities. In contrast, very few comprehensive computer-aided learning systems packages have been developed specifically for on or off the job training in an industrial environment. The vast majority of the existing industrial computer-aided learning packages are in the form of individual modules instead of an integrated set of modules. Comprehensive computer-aided learning packages to be used in an industrial environment, incorporating a number of modules all of which are related to a central theme, have to be very robust, easy to operate, and must include substantial back-up facilities. Based upon the experience of developing such packages, this paper descibes the facilities which should be incorporated in computer-aided learning systems designed for on the job training in industry.

SUMMARY

Educational institutions, the armed services and some large corporations have had computer-aided learning programs in their repertoires of learning for some time now. However, very little of industrial life has so far been touched by the use of the computer as a training aid.

The development and use of computer-aided learning requires resources and expertise that are not widely available; until recently it has required large computers for implementation. Also the costs of development are high with few companies having training functions of a size that can take on the required development. As a result most industrial companies have not been able to use computer-aided learning systems.

The concept of training material to be used at or close to the shop floor with little or no tutorial support is still more a dream than a reality. Apart from keyboard skills training and self-study packages on how to operate commercial software there is little available for the training manager in a medium-sized company. This is in spite of the increased availability and use of powerful low cost microcomputers.

As a result of collaboration between the University of Bradford and the Engineering Industry Training Board the authors were involved in the development of a computer-based learning package for use in industry. CALPICS (Computer Aided Learning of Production and Inventory Control Systems,1983) aims to promote more effective production control through an enhanced understanding of the principles involved. This paper reflects on some of the principles incorporated in the design of this training aid and other related learning material as well as insights and lessons derived from their own experiences.

It is suggested that computer-aided learning material for use in industry needs to be multi-purpose, flexible in use and modular in structure. It also needs to be simple to use, robust and at all times under the control of the learner.

THE LEARNING ENVIRONMENT

Much industrial training is carried out in an environment similar to that in a college. That is an environment of a planned and coherent programme aimed at clear and specific goals, for example, training in specific skills, product knowledge or procedures, first appointment training for various job categories. Such an environment is relatively structured.

However, a lot of industrial training is relatively unstructured. In many cases training aims are general and difficult if not impossible to specify with any great precision. 'Making managers more financially aware' or 'Improving relationships between departments' are typical of such broad training aims. A lack of precision does not imply that the required training is less important. Indeed it is arguable that this type of training is more important since it is often directly linked to some desired (or required) improvement in business performance.

Also, a considerable amount of training has to be planned and implemented in the context of rapid and radical change. Sudden changes in resources or organization structure resulting from redirection of the business; contraction and personnel change due to redundancy; absorption of personnel, products and processes following amalgamation. All these result in a wide range of training problems to which solutions have to be found, often in a short time.

Of necessity any training for an unstructured environment like this needs to be flexible and capable of being modified during implementation. However useful computers may be in a structured training situation, their use in an unstructured training environment is unlikely to include prescriptive individualized instruction, the type that accounts for the majority of applications at present.

COMPUTER-AIDED LEARNING IN AN INDUSTRIAL ENVIRONMENT

There are many reasons why the use of computers in industrial training could and should increase. With industrial contraction people have tended to broaden the scope of their responsibilities. New technology in many guises, together with more rapidly changing organizations has increased the range of training needed with fewer people filling similar roles. Training courses are less appropriate to satisfying individual needs. Costs of training courses, including travel and accommodation, are high and more difficult to justify in an austere economic climate. Possibly the most difficult issue is that of letting people attend training courses when they are scheduled the release problem. Conflicts between long-term or even urgent training needs and short-term business priorities and budget limitations are a constant headache for the industrial trainer. Increased use of open-learning training approaches, including the use of computers among training media, is a natural consequence.

On grounds of cost-effectiveness there is further support for this trend. There are cases where computer-assisted training programs have reduced training times by between 20 and 50 per cent and in some instances by as much as 60 per cent, four days for computer-based training against a 10-day traditional course. This course compression, even if the training was no more effective, could be a sufficient financial justification. That is if all the savings are not swallowed in development costs.

The cost of developing a programme of training based on a computer can be many times that of a more conventional programme. A rough comparison between the development times for different types of courseware is given in Table 1. This is based in part on information published by the Manpower Services Commission (1982).

Hours of development	Average	Range
Conventional course	5	2 - 10
Open learning study text	20	10 - 50
Computer-aided learning	150	50 - 250

Table 1   Hours to develop one hour of courseware

Computer-aided learning programs can be specific and individualized, as most of them are at present. It is perhaps ironic that they are also the most expensive. Cost effectiveness can be increased if the training material can be designed and used to satisfy a range of learning needs.

While development costs are high the cost of delivering training using a computer can be much lower if there is no need for a significant tutor involvement. Delivery costs per trainee can be less than one third of the delivery costs for a course with a full-time tutor.

If a reasonable assessment of development costs can be made it is possible to determine a break-even position, in terms of the number of trainees, at which a computer-aided learning program becomes more cost-effective. Development costs represent the fixed costs with delivery costs being the variable costs. On average figures this would mean that approximately 300 trainees would need to take a computer-based program before it was more economic than a conventional alternative. This figure would of course be reduced if the training time were shorter with computor-aided learning methods than with the alternative.

Experience has shown that the inclusion of a computer in a training program has an attraction in itself. Call it the novelty of the technology or whatever but it does seem to have a stimulating and motivating influence. Incidentally this seems to be more marked with groups than with individuals.

FLEXIBILITY OF COMPUTER-AIDED LEARNING

In spite of efforts by a number of agencies to provide a software information service it is not an easy matter to locate training software for a particular application. If the present trend continues, and what emerges is an increasing number of small packages for highly specific applications, the situation will get worse. In a few years the training managers are likely to experience problems of identifying and selecting training software comparable to those of identifying and selecting more general application software for microcomputers. If, on the other hand, training material were to develop in the form of substantial packages of related training modules the problems of selection will be easier and the material is likely to have a wider range of possible uses. There are additional reasons why flexibility of use is seen as an important principle. Experience has shown that the way material is used is not always the way it was designed to be used. It has also shown that it is possible to have training material that can be flexible in its use. There is a useful field of study open in examining how computer-aided learning training is used in practice as distinct from the way it is designed to be used. There are surely a number of useful lessons to be learned.

It can be a rewarding as well as a humbling experience to design training software with one aim in mind and find it used in an unexpected way. Two managers from a Sheffield tool company were intended to work through some training materials on the principles of production using a computer. After studying less than a third of the program, a heated discussion took place and the computer and its training material were abandonned. It emerged that having been stimulated, they were diverted into considering the production problems in their company. Later it emerged that a number of decisions were made resulting in substantial cost savings. The computer and its training material apparently acted as a catalyst. In these circumstances, to validate training effectiveness in terms of end test performance would be meaningless, particularly as the overall aim of the training was to aid and stimulate more effective production control.

From experiences like the one just quoted it seems there is a need for training software that can be used in a variety of ways and for a variety of purposes. The notion of flexible resource training material is fairly familiar in written form but it does not often apply when computers are involved. Training designers often seem to become much more prescriptive in this situation.

Some material has been deliberately prepared for use in different ways. A stimulating experience was to spend a day with the entire fourth year of a Stockton school, some 200 pupils, spread out over two adjoining sports halls. The purpose was to help develop an awareness of how business works and in particular the financial consequences of management decisions. This activity was supported by five microcomputers running a simultaneous business simulation. In a different context the same material has been used with mature business graduates and managers to illustrate the difference between profit and cash flow.

LEARNING STRATEGIES

In the excitement of applying the technology of computer-aided learning it is easy to overlook fundamental aspects of how people learn. Any training material is likely to reflect the assumptions by the designer of how people learn. Similarly the way training is implemented reflects assumptions by the tutor, teacher or trainer. In group training with a live tutor, issues about who is in charge of the learning process and how learning will be done can be aired if they are significant, and adjustments made.

With study texts the learner is free to study in any way he or she chooses, irrespective of any preconceived notions on the part of the designer. Study material produced by the Open University is often deliberately structured to enable students to adopt alternative patterns of study (Rowntree and Conors,1983).

The design of computer-aided learning does not leave scope for dialogue with a tutor, apart from disembodied messages to a comment file. Neither does the trainee have any study choices other than those inherent in the material, by accident or by design.

A lot of computer-aided learning material is based on the objectives-mastery model in which assumptions by the designer, perhaps unintentionally, can be conveyed to the trainee through the material itself.

> I know what you need
> I decide the training aims
> I decide the training content
> I decide the training sequence
> I decide how and when to test you
> I decide when you have learned

Subliminal messages implying a little more modesty would be more appropriate.

The objectives-mastery model of training is based on notions that training design is a systematic and linear process entirely under the control of the trainer. There is no shortage of advocates for this model which is probably appropriate to quite a lot of training (Davies,1971). However, a more cautious approach is necessary in other situations.

The nature of learning has been the subject of study for many years and efforts have been made to relate the theory of learning to the design of multi-media training materials (Gagné and Briggs,1979). Different perspectives and approaches of cognitive psychology have resulted in a range of useful insights but, so far, no unifying theory of the processes of learning. How an individual learns is a very private and mysterious activity which may never be fully understood.

What is fully understood is that different people have different ways of approaching the business of learning, different learning strategies, and that they vary in their effectiveness. Apparently individuals do not change their ways of learning easily or quickly. Neither are they good at understanding their own methods of learning. People learn less well when forced to adopt an unfamiliar learning strategy.

One conclusion from this is to ensure a degree of flexibility in how training material can be studied and thus allow learners choices of how to learn. This is not to argue that all training material should be designed on 'discovery learning' principles even though there is evidence that a guided discovery approach can be effective for some types of training and can reduce training times (Belbin,1969).

A free simulation exercise can be confusing and frustrating to learners who seek some direction or guidance. The same simulation with prompts, suggestions and help facilities could be effective with a wider range of learners.

Training material on a computer of the information-question-response type can be frustrating and ineffective if it is only possible to follow one or a small range of sequences through the topic, or if one cannot go forwards, backwards or opt at will to do something else. The same material with more options could be studied in a variety of ways.

It is often assumed that because a computer is capable of delivering individualized training that this should be its main use. This is an assumption that needs to be challenged. Spending a day or more at a learning centre and being the only person following a particular program can be a lonely and demotivating experience.

It has been interesting to observe how material, designed for individual use, seemed to be more effective when studied by small groups of two or three. The learning value of interaction with others is a dimension of computer-aided learning as much as any other form of training.

TRAINING DESIGN PRINCIPLES

There are a range of models seeking to summarize principles of courseware design. Sometimes, one suspects, there are as many models as there are designers. Most of these point to a linear process like the one shown below.

> Identify learning need
> Identify learning aims (learning map)
> Define objectives (hierarchy of objectives)
> Determine testing strategy
> Select training media
> Design structure

> Design content
> Implement design
> Test, validate and review
> Implement training
> Evaluate training

Some models join the two ends and make it a cycle. A cynical mind would conclude that designers construct models <u>post hoc</u>, to explain to themselves what they have done, or ought to have done. This is because these principles seem to be honoured more in the breach than in the observance.

No comment on computer-aided learning can be complete without reference to the need for documentation. User guides, course manuals and workbooks are a requirement of practically any computer-aided learning application. Hardly any training is effective in a single medium, whether it be lecture, text, exercise computer, or video. It is almost an axiom that all training is multi-media. Apart from questions about how suitable a computer implementation may be it is essential to answer the question, what will the trainee be left with on completion of the training? If the answer is nothing then it is time to think again.

Many course designers will probably agree that a linear approach rarely works in practice. At the least the elements of clarifying aims, determining content and specifying training activity are a cyclical or iterative process.

If the computer-aided learning material is to be suitable for study in a number of different ways it is necessary to build in multiple entry and exit points. This will usually mean a series of menus arranged in a hierarchical structure. It also means designing learning units that are relatively small so that choices are frequently available.

An important need for use where there is limited tutorial support is that of a single start-up routine with prompts directing the learner to the required area of study (which disks to insert where). This also means a menu approach is most likely.

Again, if the learner is to control his or her own progress through the material he or she will need access to records of what has been done already, with an indication of any test performance. Options of preview material, examine objectives or having unrestricted access to tests increase the range of learning options available. Some otherwise excellent computer-aided learning material is made almost unusable by the absence of such features, including some where the only way out of a particular activity is to switch off and start again.

Access to help facilities at any time and the ability to step backwards (and forwards) through a study topic are important requirements in any but the most trivial applications. It is felt essential to have a facility to absorb a current activity and immediately have a choice of what to do next. Some of these principles, based on seeing how people actually use computer-aided learning material, can be in conflict with preconceived notions of routing and branching logic. The issue is resolved only by having clear views about who is the best person to decide what to do - the designer or the learner. The authors prefer a balance in favour of the learner.

The use of computer-aided learning with naive computer users can lead to a number of keyboard related problems. Secure routines and input validation with clear error messages are obvious requirements. Less obvious are problems arising from multiple key stroke entries. The pace of learning can be slowed down considerably by learners having to hunt for a large number of keys before making progress. Keying time can be a crucial problem in situations where a number of people in a group are interacting with a computer as for example in a business simulation. Queues lead to frustration. For this among other reasons the authors are cautious about the use of free text entry and response matching. There are dangers in giving the impression to learners that a system is more clever than it really is. Encouraging this view is regarded as unhealthy.

SPECIFYING COMPUTER-AIDED LEARNING DESIGN

There are normally considered to be three skills required in the development of any form of computer-aided learning material: expertise in the subject matter, training design and in computing. These skills are rarely present in one individual.

If authoring systems are used, the computing element is less significant and the expertise can be acquired. Invariably this is a longer and more difficult process than claimed by the producers of such systems. Even if it is the most effective method there can be problems

with a team approach. Problems increase where individuals involved in a project are not
working as a team but through links between different functions of an organization.

Where the three elements of design are carried out by different organizations, either in
collaboration or on strictly commercial terms, the problems of communication can become
difficult. The main problem is in specifying what is needed. Experience has shown that
specifying learning requirements to a training designer is somewhat easier than a training
designer specifying requirements to a software writer. With screen layout details and precise
information on sequencing and control logic the specification for even a small training
application can be bulky. Preparation of a specification has been found to be far more time-
consuming than actually doing the training design.

CONCLUSIONS

Apart from a few one-off applications, comparatively few comprehensive computer-aided
learning packages are available for use in an unstructured industrial environment. In spite of
the availability of some authoring systems, the costs of developing the learning material
remain high and prohibitive. Furthermore comparatively few guidelines are available for the
development of material suitable for the unstructured industrial learning environment.

Experience of the development and subsequent use of the CALPICS package has shown that
best results are obtained by ensuring that the learning material is flexible with number of
entry and exit points. Other criteria for the development of effective learning material have
been specified.

The actual use of comprehensive computer-aided learning packages has shown that in many
situations, depending upon overall objectives, group learning can yield better results than
individualized learning.

REFERENCES

Belbin,R M (1969) The Discovery Method: An International Experiment in Re-training.
    OECD, Paris.
Davies,I K (1971) The Management of Learning. McGraw-Hill, London.
Engineering Industry Training Board (1983) Computer Aided Learning of Production and
    Inventory Control Systems (CALPICS) Publication V10.
Gagné,R M and Briggs,J L (1979) Principles of Instructional Design. Holt, Rinehart & Winston,
    New York.
Manpower Services Commission (1982) Computer Based Training.
Rowntree,D and Conors,B (1983) How to develop self-instructional material. Open University,
    Milton Keynes.

2.3 A Computer-Assisted Self-Instruction System for Teachers: The Present State of Development

H Nishinosono and K Nagano
Kyoto University of Education, Japan

Abstract: The rapid change of society requires teachers in service to learn ceaselessly and to improve their professional competence continuously. Although demands for refresher course from teachers are increasing, the number of educational institutions sufficient to satisfy them will not be met under the present financial constraints. One solution to this problem is to develop a computer system which can accommodate a vast body of knowledge and resources for self-instruction in a computer database. CASIST (Computer-Assisted Self-Instruction System for Teachers) currently being developed at the Centre for Education (Kyoto University of Education) is composed of four major susbsystems:

1. Instructional Resource Management Systems (IRMS).
2. Curriculum Management and Generation System (CUMGES).
3. Diagnosis, Analysis and Consultation System (DACS).
4. Educational Document Management and Retrieval System (EDMARS).

A conceptual framework representing a teacher facilitates the teachers participating in the developmental project of CASIST to collaborate efficiently in the construction of the system. A teacher, as a professional instructor, is hypothesized to consist of two groups of competence; those which can be trained through training courses or seminars, and those which do not show obvious effects from training. Skills for communicating with other teachers, specifying instructional objectives, constructing test items, analysing students' states and behaviours, and so on, would be greatly improved by exposing teachers to self-instruction or self-study programmes. Mini-APPER, one of the subsystems of DACS, has been implemented on a microcomputer, and has the potential for accumulating students' records in a database, extracting data from it and analysing it. In the subsystems of IRCS, instructional resources such as test items, educational objectives, and textbooks are being stored. In EDMARS, more than 50,000 documents of educational studies have been accumulated in a minicomputer which can be accessed through microcomputers. A diagnosis system is being studied in depth to accummulate knowledgeable propositions or statements concerning description of learners, instructional strategies, and teachers' judgement. The conceptual framework for constructing CASIST and the present state of development is discussed.

RATIONALE FOR SELF-INSTRUCTION IN TEACHER EDUCATION

Since teacher education in Japan was renovated after the last world war, teachers for elementary and secondary levels have been trained within the framework of university education rather than normal schools as previously. The 1970s was the decade for the current discussion on the assessment and improvement of the conventional teacher education regime. A number of studies and surveys have been conducted and reported by academic bodies, for instance, the Japanese Society for the Study of Education, Japan Comparative Education Society etc.

Three new universities (Hyogo, Jou-etsu and Naruto) have been established in the last five years and are mainly aimed at providing in-service teachers with the opportunity of refreshing and improving their professional careers. These three universities recruit students from in-service teachers for a two-year graduate course. After graduating from the universities, the teachers are expected to play a leading role among other teachers. However, the number of teachers who can enjoy the two year release from their workplace is very small. Other teachers continue learning efforts to refresh their professional competence by taking retraining courses at local educational institutions or joining study meetings of instruction sponsored by various organizations. Although the activities of these organizations are highly appreciated and participated in by many teachers, the participants do not enjoy any academic certificates or credits towards their promotion. Some universities besides the three mentioned above offer Master degree courses for in-service teachers but the number participating is not large. An entirely new concept and system is expected to emerge for in-service teacher education.

The terms self-instruction, self-learning, self-guided learning, self-directed learning, self-teaching, self-study, and various others are often synonomously used to describe recent trends in adult education. The self-learning efforts of teachers should be interlinked with the lifelong learning scheme of teacher education. Self-directed learning (Cropley,1981) or self-instruction (Hendrey,1979) is a potential solution for in-service teachers wishing to renew their knowledge and improve their professional skills. A high morale in continuous learning results from the awareness of, and inquiring into, appropriate problems at the workplace, and the self-confidence generated by the successful solving them by their own efforts.

In addition to the awareness of the need for continuous learning and the motivation of improving their professional competence, the skills necessary for self-learning are also a pre-requisite for success in lifelong learning. Cropley (1981) suggests the following six items for lifelong learning skills:

1. Capacity to set personal objectives in a realistic way.
2. Effectiveness in applying knowledge already possessed.
3. Efficiency in evaluating one's own learning.
4. Skill at locating information when it becomes apparent that there is need for it.
5. Effectiveness in using different learning strategies and in learning in different settings (such as in groups, or alone, with or without a teacher and so on).
6. Skill in using learning devices such as libraries or the media.

Needless to say, any citizen maintains the right to refuse to be involved in a lifelong education programme. However, self-instruction should be a leading framework for the teacher education of the future when financial and personal contraints force us to change conventional teacher education towards self-sustaining education systems free from these constraints. One possible solution may be to adopt new technologies, especially applied behavioural science, communication and computer technology in the scheme for future teacher education.

A CONCEPTUAL MODEL FOR DESIGNING A SELF-INSTRUCTIONAL SYSTEM

A conceptual model representing a teacher's learning can guide us in efficiently developing a computer-assisted system of self-instruction or self-improvement for teachers. The key notions in self-learning schemes are teachers skills, knowledge, attitudes, motivation, and values when improving their own daily work, especially classroom teaching. The model shown in Figure 1 represents a teacher who is involved in classroom teaching on one side, and is confronted with a variety of information sources in his or her professional activities on the other side. In this model these two sources are pre-eminent agents in the self-improvement scheme. A problem-solving approach is adopted in this model, that is teachers are expected to find and focus on their own problems in their teaching. To solve these problems, they have to specify the details of the problems, investigate the crucial points for improvement, identify the constraints, gather needed information, and elaborate a plan of action. For these activities, training programmes, information bank or databank, and data-processing facilities are needed. The recent development of computer technology facilitates the production of materials including editing and printing of instructional materials using a word-processor, accumulation of a vast quantity of information, fast and complicated analysis of data collected from the teacher's instructional experience. Another factor is the fact that the computer is now easily operated and widely used by teachers in their daily work. If we succed in organizing teachers' activities and computer facilities in such a way that the process of self-improvement of teachers correspond to the present principles and regulation for teacher education, the computer system may be approved as a potential facility for implementing self-instructional schemes in in-service teacher education.

The computer system cannot function separately from the human aspect of teachers. Their motivation and active involvement are indispensible for the continuous and appropriate development of any computer system. The computer is only a core station for the source of information, a tool of data-processing, editing, and printing of instructional materials, a retrieval system for documents, and a terminal for guided learning. It is the teachers who organize and integrate these facilities into a comprehensive information system for self-learning.

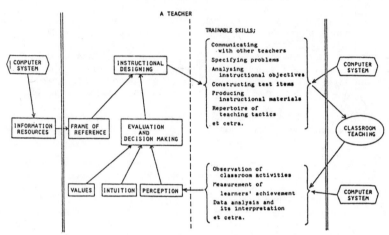

Figure 1   A conceptual model of a teacher

In the model shown in Figure 1, a teacher in charge of teaching is presumed to be composed of two aspects:

(a)   The objective ability to pinpoint problems, to conduct task analysis, to produce instructional materials, to analyse the recorded or observed teaching process and so on.

(b)   The subjective process of making decisions as well as the value system of the knowledge accumulated in the teacher.

The roles of a computer are assigned to these two aspects. The computer system is being developed to enhance these aspects and to facilitate the teacher's self-directed learning (Nishinosono, 1981).

THE PRESENT STATE OF THE SYSTEM UNDER DEVELOPMENT

In the conventional frame-oriented CAI, designers or authors have to develop whole sequences of materials to be studied by learners at terminals. This type of CAI requires a great amount of work to prepare. To overcome the need to spend such large amounts of time on any single CAI program within in-service teacher education, resources for learning can be collected from their own classroom teaching in the form of questionnaires, data on learner's responses, and transcripts of activities in the classroom. To release teachers from the burden of collecting instructional resources, textbooks and other materials including instructional objectives and test items are being stored in the system database. The present configuration of CASIST is being developed on the MELCOM COSMO-700S CPU 2MB, Disk 460MB at the Centre for Educational Research and Training of the Kyoto University of Education. It consists of four major subsystems and currently the major parts of these systems have been developed as a prototype.

1. Instructional Resource Management System (IRMS)

Instructional resources used for classroom teaching and individualized learning include statements of instructional aims or objectives, test items for evaluation, textbooks, teacher-made materials, and other instructional materials. These resources are being accumulated in the database of the computer. The following items should be taken into account to facilitate users of the system when referring to appropriate materials required for their instruction and when designing lesson plans for their pupils and students, not to mention considering the environmental conditions of instruction.

a) The contents and structure of instructional objectives, test items and elemental materials should be stored flexibly so that they can be easily modified to cope with changes in curricula or learners' needs.
b) The system is expected to be utilized widely by teachers of local schools, student teachers and educational researchers in universities. The language for prescribing the contents and the structure of instructional materials should be easily learned and used. The system should be easily operated by those who do not have any experience in using computers.
c) The items stored in the computer include statements written in Japanese characters, figures and diagrams. The stored items should be easily updated, revised and managed by the users.

A large part of the resources are statements of instructional objectives, test items, inventories of questionnaires and textbooks. These elemental components are separately stored as sub-items and given sequential numbers – used when looking for appropriate items later to be used for instructional designing. The structure and relationships of these sub-items are described using various short statements or key words selected from the items' contents. Describing structure separately from the whole content in this way facilitates the revison of, the editing and the construction of both objectives and test items (Nagano, Nishinosono et al,1977).

2 Curriculum Management and Generation System (CUMGES)

Curricula should be suited to local needs and individuals. It requires an incredible amount of time and labour for teachers to prepare the proper curriculum to satisfy the aims specific to their local situation, the teacher's abilities and, not least, the students' needs. The elemental instructional resources which are stored in the IRMS are rearranged and organized according to a structure given by the teacher-programmer. He or she can request the computer to generate a sequence of instructional objectives, instructional materials and test items for the evaluation of curriculum. This sequence of contents and objectives is described in a programming language according to the teacher's own interpretation of results obtained from the analysis of the collected data, and to his or her subjective hypothesis on the instructional process. Figure 2 shows the flow diagram of this subsystem. Data collected from the actual teaching are analysed and used for evaluating the hypothetical construction of the curriculum. The structure of the system

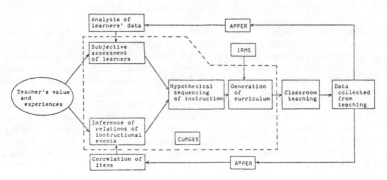

Figure 2   Diagram of CUMGES

reflects the importance of subjective judgement and inference by the teachers. One can easily give a network or a tree structure to the connection of the elemental components of the objectives, test items and instructional materials. The structure is also easily revised by modifying the program which describes it. A teacher's competence is expected to be improved through the objective analysis of classroom teaching. modification of the structure of the instructional objectives and by adjustment of the original curriculum to the student's needs and the local situation (Nagano,1982).

3 Diagnosis, Analysis and Consultation System (DACS)

At present, this system consists of two major subsystems:

* Analysing Programme Package for Educational Research (APPER).
* Computer synchronized Video Recorded Behaviour Analyser (VIRBA).

The systematic analysis of data gathered from classroom teaching is indispensible for the improvement of a teacher's competence. APPER is used for the analysis of numerical and nominal type data. The program package includes not only the programs for conventional statistical analysis, but also those for diagnostic and chronological analysis of individual learners whose data are accumulated systematically in a database of APPER. This system has been implemented on a microcomputer for use at local schools (Nishinosono and Nagano,1976; Nagano and Nishinosono,1981).

VIRBA has been developed for behaviour analysis of classroom teaching. A video player is fully synchronized with, and controlled by, a microcomputer. Category systems for interaction analysis are usually applied to investigate the details of the instructional process. The transcripts of verbal communication are also stored in the microcomputer and linked to the sequence of categorical data based on the analysis of observed behaviour. Teachers themselves can analyse their own teaching by using this facility. Sequences of categorical data of behaviour and transcripts are stored in a structured form in the database and used for later analysis. Any part of the recorded references can be accessed by specifying time, categories, or contents of transcripts. The data is stored in a form similar to the LISP language so that the structure of the instructional process can be analysed by using LISP (Nishinosono, Nagano et al,1984).

4 Educational Document Management and Retrieval System (EDMARS)

The documentation of books, research papers and other reference materials is one of the most urgent problems in Japanese educational circles. Japanese characters and the structure of sentences are the most serious obstacles to developments in the processing and retrieval of documents. However, the problem is being gradually overcome by recent developments in computer technology. More than 50,000 research paper titles in Japanese have been accumulated in computers through collaboration with the staff at the Curriculum Research and Development Centre of Gifu University. Reports on teaching written by local school teachers are being accumulated at the National Institute for Educational Research and a number of local education centres. A thesaurus for Japanese educational documentation is being developed by the staff of various universities and expected to be issued in the next few years.

Recent developments in microcomputers makes feasible the installation of terminals which can deal with numerals, the English alphabet, Japanese phonetic characters (katakana), and Japanese characters (kanji). Communications technology is opening up a new era of information exchange by means of networks spanning a wide area. Although terminals installed in local schools can be connected through ordinary telephone lines, the present speed of transferring information between microcomputers is insufficiently fast to maintain daily business. In the near future, this obstacle will be removed by the installation of optical fibre networks with a much higher speed of transferring information.

CONCLUSION

This action-oriented scheme of planning, implementing and evaluating instruction is expected to greatly motivate teachers towards self-learning projects on curriculum construction and improving their teaching skills. To implement this scheme, teachers have to be provided with:

* Instructional resources including instructional objectives.
* Test items and other teaching and learning materials.
* Facilities for analysing learners' reactions and behaviours.
* A flexible editor for revising the constructed curricula.
* A retrieval system for referring to the reports written by instructional researchers and other teachers.

The computer system CASIST is intended to provide in-service and pre-service teachers with these facilities. Although a great deal of further study is needed before the system is fully operational, the major part of the system has been completed as an experimental prototype in middle range computer connected to several microcomputers.

REFERENCES

Cropley, A J (1981) Lifelong Learning: A Rationale for Teacher Training. Journal of Education for Teaching, 7, 1.

Hendrey, A (1979) Towards the Self-Instruction for Teacher Education. mimeo, UNESCO.

Nagano, K, Nishinosono, H et al (1977) Computer management and Search of Instructional Objectives and Test Items. (in Japanese) Japan Journal of Educational Technology, 2, 4.

Nagano, K, Nishinosono, H et al (1981) Development of Data Processing System and an Operational Language II. (in Japanese) Japan Journal of Educational Technology, 6, 2.

Nagano, K (1982) An Application of Production System to Extracting Decision Rules for Evaluating Learner's Performance. (in Japanese) Journal of Computer Assisted Instruction, 2, 2.

Nishinosono, H and Nagano, K (1976) An Analysing Package for Educational Research (APPER). (in Japanese) Bulletin of Kyoto University of Education Series B, 48.

Nishinosono, H (1981) Process of Instruction. (in Japanese) Daiichi-Houki Shuppan, Tokyo.

Nishinosono, H, Nagano, K et al (1984) Developmental Research on Communication Analyser of Classroom Teaching. (in Japanese) Report of Grant-aided Project for Developmental Scientific Research of Ministry of Education Science and Culture. Project 57880047.

2.4 Computer Science in New School Culture

R M Bottino, P Forcheri and M T Molfino
Istituto per la Matematica Applicata del CNR, Genova, Italy

Abstract: The problems in introducing computer science concepts into the secondary school are being generally debated. In the current situation, it is necessary to reflect both on the cultural and professional modifications that such an introduction implies and to carry out a number of experiments to test the educational possibilities of different approaches. This paper describes a project aimed at introducing computer science basic concepts into secondary school mathematical courses. A characteristic of this project is the teaching of the fundamental concepts of computer science as part of a unitary work that students must develop step by step. We illustrate the aims, contents, and working methods stressed by this project, which consists of a set of work sheets for students in conjunction with a teacher's guide. The choice of the Pascal programming language will also be briefly discussed.

INTRODUCTION

The introduction of computer science as a teaching subject in all school courses is now being debated, at an operative level in Italy, notably during the proceedings of our 8th Congress on the Teaching of Mathematics (1983). An indication of the importance of this debate is a national experiment involving all levels of schools planned by the European Educational Centre (CEDE), an organ of the Italian Ministry of Education. This discussion on the introduction of computer science is based on causes both inside and outside the schools. The changed requirements of the business world, the mass introduction of cheap microcomputers, and publishes numerous enterprises are among the external causes which have led to a strong demand for qualification in the computer science field. Inside the school, the stimulus for new curricula arises from groups of teachers and students, from the results of experiments carried out by the Italian National Council for Research (CNR) and university research teams, and from the experience acquired through the introduction of courses for computer science experts and programmer-accountants (Boero, Furinghetti and Pedemonte,1982; Bottino,1983; Ferrari,Forcheri,Lemut and Molfino,1981; Provera,1980).

The main aspects of the problem are the school levels, the choice of content, the working methodology, the quality and type of teachers' educational training, and the follow-up courses required. This paper illustrates a project aimed to introduce computer science in the first two years of 'high secondary' schools (age from 14 to 16 years). We will point out the reasons and indicate the content and the working methods developed by this project, which consists of a set of work sheets supplemented by a teachers' guide. A characteristic of this project is the teaching of the fundamental concepts of computer science as part of a unitary work that students develop step by step.

THE PROJECT

Aims

The project is intended to test the possibilty of introducing computer science basic concepts in a secondary school mathematics course by placing them in a real context through problem solving activities. Students must play an active role in the learning process: for this reason, we believe that problem solving with computers is an interesting cognitive task - it makes it possible for problem-formulating and problem-solving skills to be brought together in a single environment.

Young students are usually more interested in obtaining the solution of problems than in finding methods to solve them. The ability to abstract concepts from a specific situation, to recognize the general ideas that the procedures are based upon, and to apply behaviour strategies in problem solving, are some of the central goals of a learning process. Another reason for introducing the learning of computer science concepts through solving a real problem was to give students some ideas about the technical possibilities, the constraints and the limitations of computing devices.

Contents

The project is focused on the problem of the computation of a telephone bill for a generic user (see Figure 1). Computer science concepts are introduced by developing this subject while different exercises are proposed to consolidate their learning. In our opinion, it is more instructive to write a single program of reasonable size that is correct, than spend the same time writing a number of programs which are unrealistically small or which do not work properly.

The telephone bill, payable every three months, consists of a fixed rate and a variable one. The variable rate depends on the number of 'unit calls' you make. The number of unit calls you make for each call depends on time and distance. The tables below are given to enable you to calculate the cost of fixed and variable rates.

FIXED RATE

CATEGORY	NETWORK 1 up to 500 subscribers	NETWORK 2 more than 500 subscribers
A (professional use)	37,500 lit	29,250 lit
B (private use)	15,810 lit	14,010 lit

VARIABLE RATE

CATEGORY	UNIT CALL NUMBER	UNIT COST
A	–	106 lit
B	up to 120	40 lit
	from 121 to 198	96 lit
	from 199 to 399	106 lit
	more than 399	113 lit

Figure 1 Telephone bill calculation

We chose the telephone bill problem for two reasons:

1. We wanted students to deal with a problem which is now really carried out in an automatic way. Also, we wanted to encourage students to look inside an ordinary problem to realize that expert knowledge, in some cases, can be made explicit and communicated. On the other hand, the main problem for a beginner is how to get started. The final solution requires the finding of a complex algorithm and learning a series of completely new techniques to implement it.
2. The problem allows different levels of simplification to be structured. For example, it is possible to begin with the problem of computing the telephone bill for a user who belongs to network 1 and category A (in which the unit calls cost does not change with number of calls). The resolution of this sub-problem leads to the introduction of basic computer science concepts such as program, data, input, output, identifiers, assignment, etc. The next steps consist of removing the constraints to be able to deal

with more general problems. This part requires the introduction of other computer science concepts such as decision and repetition. The complete program must also consider input errors - in fact, robustness is one of the most important characteristics or a program performing an effective task.

Computer outputs have an increasing importance as a means of communication. Therefore the ability to design them clearly and meaningfully is another basic skill to develop in an educational context. Hence students are asked to produce a final output of the program which should correspond to Figure 2.

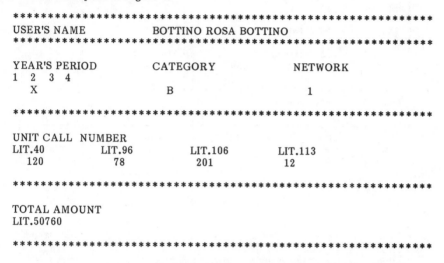

Figure 2 An example of a complete output

   Mathematical notions about finite arithmetics, approximation, scientific notation, logic operators and so on are introduced while developing the main problem. Moreover, the telephone bill problem allows characters to be manipulated as well as work with numerical data - in our opinion, another important educational aspect.
   The programming language chosen for use in this project is Pascal. This choice allows an implementation of the project which naturally corresponds with its educational aims. In fact, we deal with the telephone bill problem by dividing it into sub-problems corresponding to a series of procedures. The Pascal language is an excellent teaching tool which allows the coherent unification of the concepts both of structured programming and of top-down methodology, thus giving a hierarchical structure of programs by means of procedures. It allows the organization of a program according to the following classical equation (Wirth,1976):

   algorithms + data structure = programs

A structured programming language gives good habits in writing, debugging and modifying programs. Such habits are useful, not only for further subsequent study in the computer science field, but also as a general learning methodology.

WORK METHOD

The project is divided into four units according to the computer science concepts introduced and corresponding to different complexity levels of the problem under consideration (see Table 1). Each unit consists of a series of sheets that students must work with, filling in the blank spaces. Usually, in a unit, the new computer science concepts are introduced by means of a program that students are required to use and analyse, followed by a section focused to formalize the ideas previously seen. Then learners can deal with different problems whose solutions require the use of the preceeding concepts.

UNIT	TELEPHONE BILL PROBLEM	COMPUTER SCIENCE CONCEPTS	MATHEMATICAL NOTIONS	HOURS NUMBER class lab home
1	Introduction to the complete problem. A first simplification, network 1, category A.	Program, numerical data, assignment, I/O operations.	Variable, approximation, scientific notation, finite arithmetic.	3h 1h 30min
2	Category A without network limitation.	Decision, Boolean operators (AND/OR), alphanumeric data, procedures.	Expression handling, logic operations, truth tables.	3h 1h 30min
3	Input errors detection.	Repetition, termination condition.		3h 1.3h 30min
4	The complete program.	Program organization, array structure	Formulae construction, symbolic manipulation.	3h 1,3h 30min

Table 1 Project workplan

In this project, a number of hours are dedicated to laboratory activities where students use microcomputers to test and debug their programs. At the end of each unit, there is a test to verify the students' knowledge and a review section which summarizes in a brief and structured way the new concepts introduced. The development of each unit requires about five hours consisting of classroom work (about three hours), homework (about 30 minutes) and laboratory activities (one hour).

The teacher is provided with a guide which gives him or her detailed suggestions about the development of each unit. As the problem under consideration is different from the usual topics of school curricula, it is probably difficult for the instructor to have a global view of all the difficulties involved. The project also needs an organization differing from the usual in requiring strict links between class, laboratory and home activities.

CONCLUDING REMARKS

We have presented the main features of a project aimed at introducing in an operative way, the basic concepts of computer science during the resolution of an articulated problem. Problem-solving activities with a computer can play an important role in the new school culture as the organization and realization of computer programs is a good way of testing one's understanding of complex processes (Howe,O'Shea and Plam,1980).

Computer science in school should not be restricted to the use of computers but we believe that an awareness of the general concepts and language of computer science must start, for 14- to 15-year-old students, with the effective use of a machine. In Italian schools, it is now possible to experiment with short projects which do not require the introduction of a new subject or a change in the current organization of the school.

We have outlined a project which is intended to verify previous theoretical ideas. It presents a series of requisites that, in our opinion, are useful in enhancing the learning process. For example, they include the resolution of a real problem through a 'learning by doing' approach (Papert,1980), and the choice of a number of sub-goals so that the increasing difficulties act as a stimulus for students rather than a deterrence.

REFERENCES

Boero, P , Furinghetti, F and Pedemonte, O (1982) An introduction to programming for students in sciences. Computers and Education, 6.

Bottino, R M (1983) A course for secondary school teachers concerning the use of programmable pocket calculators. Computers and Education, 7.

Bottino, R M, Forcheri, P and Molfino, M T (1983) A workplan to test the educational opportunities for using small computer in secondary schools. In Trott, A, Strongman, H and Giddins, L (eds) Aspects of Educational Technology XVI. Kogan Page, London.

Ferrari, G , Forcheri, P , Lemut, E and Molfino, M T (1981) Introduction to co-ordinating programming concepts in university courses. Computers and Education, 5.

Howe, J A, O'Shea, T and Plam, F (1980) Teaching mathematics through Logo programming: an evaluation study. In Lewis, and Tagg, (eds) Computer-Assisted Learning,Scope, Progress,Limits. North-Holland.

Papert, S (1980) Mindstorms. Harvester Press, London.

Proceedings of 8th Congress on the Teaching of Mathematics, NUMI, Supplement No,3 (1983) (In Italian).

Provera, E (1980) Calcolatore tascabile e programmazione strutturata: due strumenti per la didattica. Diddatica delle Scienza, 89.

Wirth, N (1976) Algorithms + Data Structures = Programs. Prentice Hall, Englewood Cliffs, New Jersey.

2.5 How Impoverished is Existing Educational Software for Microcomputers?

R D Ward and D F Sewell

Educational Technology Research Group, Department of Psychology, Hull University

Abstract: Recent developments in educational software for microcomputers have been criticised for being of poor quality, based upon outdated technology and impoverished theories of learning, and reflecting little programming skill. It has been said that more thought needs to be directed towards developing a more formal basis for the design of learning experiences based upon the new information technology (Sage and Smith, 1983). Despite these criticisms commercial software if proliferating. While it is usually possible to identify some defects in most programs, there are positive aspects too. Some styles of program show considerable imagination, there have been some attempts to design software which reflects theories of cognitive development, technical quality is steadily improving and there is a readiness to invent and try out new learning situations.

At a time when teachers and home users are encumbered by 32K cassette-based systems, it may sound hopelessly optimistic to forecast cheap microcomputers with millions of bytes of main memory, connected to international networks. But when these machines do arrive, whether it be sooner or later, they will be accompanied by expert tutoring systems and complex learning environments which fully use the increased resources. There will be some very impressive software.

This does not have to mean that present efforts will be wasted. Future technology will be able to take what is good about existing programs, improve it and remedy its shortcomings. This process, this software evolution, is one aspect of the development of a more formal basis for the design of learning experiences.

This paper examines existing styles of educational software in order to begin to identify those positive aspects upon which building might take place. Some potentially useful learning situations are considered, their limitations discussed, and likely improvements suggested in the areas of computation, learning theory and program content. It should, however, be added that many suggestions are based on theory which remains to be experimentally validated in a computer-assisted learning context.

INTRODUCTION

We are trying to see a proliferation of educational software for microcomputers, marketed by an increasing number of commercial firms. Much of it is aimed at primary or pre-school children, particularly for use in the home, and the associated advertising materials widely claim that the software will help to develop children's language, thinking, problem solving, decision making, strategic numeracy or other skills. Syllabus-based software for older children is also set to appear. Clearly, a lot of effort, imagination and innovation is being directed towards the development of microcomputer-based learning experiences, and there is a readiness to experiment with new ideas.

Although the advertised claims are rarely supported by practical evidence, they may have some justification in theory. Bork (1984) suggests that the advantages of using computers in education can be subdivided into two main areas; interactivity and individualization. Certainly, the active participation of the learner in the learning process, and the adaptation of the learning process to the individual's level and needs, appear desirable in many theories of cognitive, developmental and educational psychology. Computers undoubtedly appear to possess educationally effective characteristics.

Despite all this, current educational software for microcomputers has been severely criticised. Sage and Smith(1983) consider that more thought should be devoted to the development of a more formal basis for the design of learning experiences based upon the new technology. They describe the current situation as one of 'theoretical impoverishment'. O'Shea and Self(1983) additionally criticize the technical quality of programs and the outdated technology upon which they are based. There appears to have been little attempt to consolidate the use of developed ideas and techniques, and the novelty of a program seems an important factor for its publication. It is still often said that no good educational software is yet available.

This paper attempts to reconcile these conflicting viewpoints by examining available programs with the above issues in mind. Software is discussed under three general headings between which there is considerable overlap. Within each area the origins, interactivity, adaptability to the needs of the pupil and some technological limitations are considered. The examples used are mainly from the areas of language and thinking skills software, as this reflects the author's interests, but many of the conclusions should be relevant to a wider range of topic area.

Possibly such issues avoid the question which, in the end, should be answered for every piece of software that is to be used: does it teach what it is supposed to teach? Perhaps this can only be answered, if at all, through long-term practical evaluation, the results of which should enlighten any theoretical perspective such as the one taken here. It is, however, believed that theoretical perspectives can be useful, particularly in the absence of hard experimental evidence. It is assumed that the software mentioned is 'bug-free', as published software does now seem to be faily good in this respect.

DRILL AND PRACTICE PROGRAMS

Several kinds of activity of the so called 'drill and practice' style originated early in the development of computer-assisted learning. For reading and language work these include sorting letters or words into alphabetical order; making new words from the letters of other words; pairing antonyms or synonyms; identifying words from their definitions; rearranging jumbled sentences, paragraphs, verses or sequences of operations; hangman games and cloze variations.

It seems likely that these techniques became common as much because of their suitability for mainframe computers with teletype terminals, and because they are easy to program, than because of their use in programmed learning. The fact that they are associated with programmed learning and its underlying behaviourist philosophy of education has led to them becoming unfashionable among many program developers and educationalists today. Usually the learner is highly constrained, questions being presented in an order beyond his or her control, each having only one 'right' answer. While there are ways of allowing the learner more freedom over his or her own learning in this type of program, more pupil-centred program styles with greater interactivity seem now to be in favour.

Low interactivity may not always be a bad thing. One advantage of constraining the learner is that attention (provided that the programs do not lose the learner's attention), is directed in an organized way towards particular aspects of the materials contained in the programs. This can be especially useful when the approach is used in conjunction with carefully researched and structured materials which have been selected according to individual levels of attainment, allowing teachers to prescribe particular activities using particular materials for particular pupils. Alternatively pupils might be able to choose to suit their own requirements. 'Drill and practice' software has a high potential for the individualization of learning, and the materials are of as much importance as the programs themselves. It is a pity that so little software makes use of the large amounts of materials developed without computers in mind, but which are suitable for use with computers.

There are however exceptions, for example Wiltshire(1982) has developed computerized sight reading exercises based upon the Dolch vocabulary (Dolch,1951), Candy and Edmonds (1982) report a project which draws upon Peters'(1981) approach to the remediation of spelling, and Rostron and Sewell(1984) are collecting and developing materials based upon the LARSP analysis of linguistic development (Crystal et al,1976). There are also a number of analytic programs (eg, Readamatics) which can calculate the readability of texts, and these can be helpful when producing passages for use with cloze type programs. Perhaps the most common use of structured materials occurs in arithmetical drill and practice programs where problems are often of graded difficulty, but this is easy to implement on a microcomputer.

Also, it is recognized that unstructured, natural materials are sometimes used deliberately (Moores,1978), and therefore nursery rhymes or proverbs may occasionally be preferred to graded texts.

Although microcomputers now used in schools have relatively few limitations with respect to the simple human-computer interfaces in these programs, problems do arise because of limited memory capacity. For example the jumbled sentence reorganization task in 'Word Sequencing' (Wills and Wills,1982), is accompanied by only three files, 35 unstructured sentences, 25 nursery rhyme titles and 28 proverbs. Teachers may not have the time or the desire to construct their own supplementary materials. In comparison, Rostron and Sewell's LARSP-based jumble programs is associated with thousands of structured sentences occupying four 100k disks. This amount of material could not be simultaneously contained in memory, and run-time access would involve impracticably long loading times if used with a cassette based machine. Mass market publishers are therefore as yet reluctant to take packages of this size (setting aside the high price of multi-disc packages). Future technology with higher capacity main memory and better peripherals for storing and downloading files will be able to cope more flexibly with large organizations of materials, and to take some initiative in its presentation.

ENVIRONMENTS FOR EXPLORATION

In 'drill and practice' programs the learner tends to perform exercises rather than participate in inherently meaningful activities. The activity of exploring computer-based microworlds is therefore usually presented as an opposite to 'drill and practice'. In terms of the learner freedom-constraint dimension this can be true, as seen for example in Papert's conception of Logo (Papert,1980), but it is possible to introduce constraints into the environment, as demonstrated in Logo for example by Howe and Ross(1981) and Lawler (1982). Howe and Ross report the use of work sheets and example programs for teaching mathematical concepts through Logo turtlegraphics, and Lawler designed a BEACH microworld in which pictures of objects could be produced and manipulated, for teaching elementary word recognition skills. Thus, although at face value the environmental approach adheres to the Piagetian viewpoint that the learner should be in control of his or her own learning, it is often thought desirable to limit the learner's freedom, either by imposing external directions, goals and demands, or by limiting the environment in some way. The freedom-constraint dimension is a continuous one.

From Papert's account it appears that much of Logo genuinely did originate out of Piagetian philosophy, but there are microworlds other than Logo, with different origins. (In fact microworlds are not necessarily computer based at all.) Educational adventures were developed from computer games such as Dungeons and Dragons, and their potential in the development of problem solving and language skills was recognized later. Simulations such as 'Spanish Main' (CET/MEP,1983) may too have origins in computer games. There are also various smaller microworlds with miscellaneous roots, for example in mathematics teaching schemes such as Dienes blocks (Hewett,1983), or in psycho-linguistic theory and deaf children's language (Ward et al,1983,1984). However, it is probably true that most program designs, to some extent at least, were achieved by reflecting on what the computer's abilities are, and how these can be applied.

Computer-based microworlds face one major difficulty, particularly when implemented on microcomputers: that of the user interface. Lawler's BEACH microworld for example (1982), consists of about 20 objects such as 'bird' and 'boat', and a similar number of actions such as 'move down' and 'paint green'. Each object and each action corresponds to a Logo procedure, and by typing procedure names, a child can construct graphics scenes and become familiar with reading and writing the words involved. The program does not however accept input that is more complex than individual procedure names, and Lawler acknowledges that more sophisticated programming would be necessary to do so. Sharples (1983) is using Logo to design exploratory tools with a higher level of linguistic complexity.

Adventures have similar limitations. These are environments which set inbuilt tasks for the user to achieve, such as finding and collecting hidden treasure (Kilworth,1982), or taking the role of a detective assigned to discover the identity of a murderer (Jackson,1983). It is argued that such programs require substantial and purposeful use of language within 'real' situations, and demand skills of concept formation, hypothesis testing, rule formation, planning, manipulating information and many other functions of ordinary language. Unfortunately the user's linguistic activity is usually more receptive than expressive; he or she is presented with complex and wordy descriptions of imaginery surroundings and companions, and with lists of portable objects, but is permitted only terse imperatives such as 'South', 'Take lamp' and 'Lamp on'.

The interfaces for the smaller microworlds too tend to be limited. Vennkids (CET/MEP, 1983) displays three overlapping Venn diagrams representing the concepts of red hair, fat faces and big boots, with numbers randomly assigned to the various possible simple and compound categories. The user must then answer questions such as:

* How many children have fat faces and big boots but not red hair?
* How many children have red hair but not fat faces or big boots?

The user's response is limited to the entry of numbers, and there is no facility for altering the number of members in any particular subset, or for putting questions to the computer.

Some microworlds require even simpler responses. For example in some of Hewett's programs (1983) the learner simply has to press the space bar when a moving cursor reaches the position at which a given Dienes block fits into a given sequence or arrangement. This seems acceptable when the programs are used with the five- to eight-year-old children for which they are designed, but the interface might be too limiting for, say, older children using more complex versions of these learning experiences. Nevertheless, such programs demand complex thought processes.

There is a more positive aspect to the interactive qualities of microworlds which goes beyond dialogues between human and computer. Adventures and simulations can promote group discussion and co-operative problem-solving activities away from the computer (Stewart,1983). Coburn et al(1982) describe an adventure game called Snooper Troops which small groups of pupils start with a dossier of photographs, newspaper clippings and lists of telephone numbers. Different groups can have different sources, but by using clues obtained from the computer they are able to raid others' sources, tap files and discover new sources of information, and this would appear to contain elements of real world problem solving. Spanish Main (CET/MEP,1983) is also designed as a team activity, and in this program a team of treasure hunters must sail their ship by grid-based co-ordinates, to various treasure islands, while a team of pirates attempt to apprehend them by sailing onto the same grid square. So although interactions between human and computer may be quite limited, software can promote rich interpersonal activities.

Used in an exploratory way, with a complete lack of constraint, environmental programs are almost by definition exactly compatible with the needs of the learner. More realistically, environments may be adapted to the needs of particular pupils by constraint or by structure. Provided that the learner's achievements are not greater than the highest allowed by any environment, then the learner is able to improve in some way, but the upper limit in many environments is a function of the user interface, and therefore certain approaches, for example the BEACH microworld, are suited only to pupils learning basic skills. As with 'drill and practice' programs, the development of microworld techniques is not being followed up by the development of structured materials geared to the needs of particular pupils. For example, adventure games with language graded for specific reading ages would be useful in primary and remedial education, but such programs would be costly to produce, and might not be best sellers. This approach has, however, been applied in foreign language teaching: an adventure has been written which requires the pupil to catch a French train and book into a French hotel, in French of course (Roberts, 1983).

In the future, interfaces clearly must be improved, and improvements are computationally possible, even in the immediate future. For example, although few existing microcomputer adventures allow the user to interact in anything like ordinary language, Jackson (1983) describes a game which can deal with commands such as:

* 'Walk around the house and knock on the door, then take out the revolver.'
* 'Say Hello and then go North.'
* 'Drop the magazine and the rose.'

A commercial database package now on the market, Ramis II (Mathematica Products Group, 1983), allows the user to ask questions such as:

* 'Give me the total units sold to each customer.'
* 'What were the average units also? Include the maximum and minimum units as well.'

Also the authors (Ward et al,1983,1984) have developed several environments in which the learner can discuss and manipulate displayed objects using subsets of written language, with either the user or the computer taking the initiative in the dialogue. A typical exchange might be:

* User: Is my blue cross taller than your green diamond?
* Computer: No, your blue cross is the same height as my green diamond.
* User: Make my blue cross taller.

This now needs to be followed up by the development of a scheme of environments graded in both linguistic and conceptual complexity. Of course looking further ahead, more powerful natural language interfaces have already been developed for large computers, and will eventually become available on smaller machines.

Bigger microcomputers will enrich microworlds considerably by allowing extensions to both content and to the facilities for manipulating that content. The software system Smalltalk (see O'Shea and Self,1983, pp200-215), which has this kind of potential, cannot be run on today's small machines. O'Shea and Self suggest that problem-solving environments and dialogue systems will be important to the future of computer-assisted learning mainly because, when considered in the light of future technology, their limitations are at present unclear.

Finally, there appear to be some interesting possibilities for microworlds on networks. When software like Spanish Main is run on a single machine, each team must use the computer out of sight of the other team. A network implementation would avoid this problem and could involve more than two ships, be played in real time rather than taking turns, and be between geographically separated teams. Adventure games on networks could involve many participants, and presumably any two or more participants, in any one location at the same time, would be able to communicate directly to exchange information or 'misinformation'. Certain obstacles might be passable only with knowledge obtained from other people, or be passed only by co-operating individuals. Competing teams might be directed by leaders, with individual team members being assigned particular roles. Bartle (1983) has some interesting ideas in this context.

DATABASE ACTIVITIES

In the above two categories of program, the learner is required to acquire or explore information that is pre-contained in the software. Database programs allow the learner to store, manipulate and retrieve information that has been collected by himself or herself. This approach can therefore allow considerable individuality. These programs might perhaps be seen as having their origins in computer science and business applications where the efficient handling of data is of great importance. Examples of software used in education are Animals, Factfile, word-processing and Prolog. Again there is some overlap between the categories adopted in this paper; Prolog in particular can be used as environmental software.

The Animals type of program was developed originally by Luehrmann at Dartmouth College (Ahl,1978), and so called because it contained knowledge about differences between animals. However, items other than animals may be contained, and versions have been enthusiastically received in primary education (eg, Futcher,1983). The program is a game in which the computer attempts to discover the name of an item which the user has in mind. It does this by working through a data tree of questions such as 'Can it fly?', and on reaching a terminal branch of the tree, it suggests that the item corresponding to that branch is the one the user has in mind. If this is incorrect, the user must add to the tree the name of the new item, plus a question which will distinguish it from the incorrect suggestion. If therefore the program starts with an empty data tree, it allows the user to create a new tree from scratch. Chandler (1984) in discussing its value in language development describes how users are forced to ask more and more suitable questions which make increasingly nice distinctions. In the process they need to obtain information from many sources and shape it into yes/no questions.

Despite its interactivity, and the high levels of cognitive activity required particularly in tree building, the game has limitations which are sometimes overlooked. In its inability to 'understand' the language it handles, it suffers from the same problems as the programs mentioned in the last section, and this limits its interactive facilities. Biscoe-Taylor (1982), for example, provides a facility for the user to attempt to guess which item the computer has in mind, ie the normal situation is reversed. This proceeds with the computer making a statement such as:

The answer to the question
Does it have feathers?
is NO.
Your guess is ?

The user then attempts to guess the name of the item. This symmetry of initiative between the user and the program is interesting, but it would be more elegant if the computer made statements in a more direct, non-convoluted form such as 'It has feathers'. Bartram (1983a) has written a version which achieves this through simple character string manipulation, although sometimes this does produce peculiarities such as 'It normallies fly'. This could be improved by using more rules in the program: quite small programs can handle many of the exceptions to particular morphological rules, as Johns has demonstrated (see Higgins,1982). Bartram's main interest was to provide additional dialogue facilities, such as some degree of nesting and the option to compare items. Nesting can occur when the user at any time refers to an item unknown to the program, whereupon the computer asks questions to define the new item, and then returns to the original topic. Comparisons are made by making statements about the branch in the data tree where two items diverge, for example that a blackbird has feathers whereas a goldfish does not.

This comparison is not quite the same thing as saying that a blackbird has feathers whereas a goldfish has scales. Nor does the computer allow the user to make guesses by asking direct questions about the properties of items, such as 'Can it swim?'. Also, when the user has guessed wrongly the computer responds inappropriately in a random way; it does not for example respond to the guess 'Is it a blackbird?' with 'No, it cannot fly'. All these facilities effectively need knowledge stored in more sophisticated data structures than trees, for example in relational databases, or Prolog clauses.

Factfile is not really a stand-alone program, but needs to be integrated into other work where facts are stored and sifted (Moss,1984; Hill,1984). It is easy to use and has many applications, and unlike Animals can store ordinal, interval and ratio data. However, memory space is again a limiting factor: it has a total capacity of only 63, 10-field records, or 239, 2-field records. There are also constraints of input and output dialogue. First, file creation is menu driven, and filenames, field headings and the data for each entry must be input as directed. Second, being a formated database, it cannot answer unanticipated questions; a more sophisticated structure would be required to do so.

Prolog databases can cope with unanticipated questions, as Prolog, among other things, is an open-ended query language. The cost of this flexibility is that, at present, the syntax of input and output can be very convoluted, eg, from Ennals (1983):

x is taller than y if x has height x and y has height Y and Y is less than x.
Which (x occupation y) x sex Male and x age z and 20 LESS z and condition Unmarried and occupation y.

For the future more friendly front ends are being developed. It may be that learning to use Prolog improves children's skills of language and logic as Latin was said to do (Kowalski, 1983), but more subtle criticisms have been made of Prolog's power to represent knowledge. Barwise and Perry (1983) argue that logic languages lack the necessary logical sophistication to handle many natural concepts, for example they do not take into consideration the situations in which statements apply. They believe that a theory of situation semantics is required. Dialogues do not consist simply of exchanged 'messages'; they occur within a complicated context which includes assumptions about other participants, general knowledge about the topic area and implicit forward or backward reference. Bartram (1983b) points out that these things give dialogues an overall cohesion in the sense of Halliday and Hasan (1976), and that cohesion is just as essential for human-computer dialogues as for human-human ones.

Developments in both hardware and software technology can contribute to the facilities available in microcomputer database programs. In education this can only increase the possibilities for highly interactive activities tailored to needs of particular children.

CONCLUSIONS

The evolution of computer-assisted learning (CAL) might idealistically be seen as a process in which numerous disconnected ideas and innovations are gradually brought together into practically effective and theoretically unified methods of education. In this light, the diverse range of program origins would seem to be a good thing: programmed learning, the practicable qualities of computers, games, methods and theories of psychology and education, business and computer science have all been mentioned. But Sage and Smith (1983) are probably correct that many approaches have been developed in an unplanned way, and perhaps now would seem an appropriate time to begin to integrate the different approaches and techniques into a single theoretical framework, although perhaps a loose framework would be best at first.

CAL has here been discussed within a working framework in which on one dimension, the knowledge contained in a program is considered to be either static and provided by the author or teacher, or dynamically provided by the learner. A second dimension is the degree of initiative allowed, and the facilities provided for the user to manipulate that information. This is only a rough guide because software may lie in almost any position along these dimensions, but of the headings adopted, 'drill and practice' tends to have static information with low learner initiative, exploratory environments tend to have static information with greater learner initiave and databased approaches contain dynamic information with various degrees of learner initiative.

Classificational frameworks of this kind seem useful for considering issues which relate to computer-assisted learning generally. More extensive ones have been constructed; eg, Rushby(1984) is correct in incorporating a place for the mentor into his model. When the software itself possesses some degree of initiative for interacting with the user, it partially assumes the role of mentor. Thus a possible third, unmentioned, dimension is the degree of initiative residing in the computer. Exising microcomputers are not yet capable of entering this area, but Sleeman and Brown (1981) have put together a collection of papers about intelligent tutoring systems which may have considerable future influence.

Other pieces should fit into the framework. New developments in hardware will enable more sophisticated software techniques to be applied, permitting greater quality, quantity and complexity of both static and dynamic information, and more powerful facilities by which both the user and the computer may manipulate this knowledge. The use of graphics, windows, multi-tasking and mice are all relevant. This will extend the interactive qualities of CAL.

Theoretical approaches too should become part of the framework, and the emergence of programs based in educational and psychological theory seems particularly encouraging. Non computer teaching schemes (eg, Moyle,1968; Fletcher,1970) can be applied to the organization of CAL materials. Cognitive and developmental psychology contains examples of skills which are needed by human beings in order to function successfully in the world (eg, Donaldson, 1978; Feuerstein, 1980), and computers appear to have a potential for developing such cognitive skills. Malone (1981) has examined motivational factors in computer games and in CAL. Finlayson(1983) is investigating the mathematical concepts present in Logo environments. These are only some of the approaches which should extend the individual qualities of CAL.

Some aspects of current CAL may be wanting, but it appears not as impoverished as some would claim. Work to date perhaps forms just the groundwork for the future when powerful microcomputers will overcome many existing software limitations in some of the ways discussed. Use is being made of the computer's individual and interactive qualities in educationally successful ways, and some understanding of the reasons for this success for this seems feasible. A stock of techniques is being assembled. If the various approaches could be brought together, it would not be too optimistic to talk about the emergence of a new discipline.

REFERENCES

Ahl, D H(1978) Basic Computer Games (Microcomputer ed). Workman Publishing, New York.
Bartle, R(1983) A voice from the dungeon. Practical Computing, Dec 1983, pp126-130.
Bartram, D(1983a) Unpublished Program for the Almarc Spirit 2. Department of Psychology, Hull University.
Bartram, D(1983b) EDAS: An Interactive Expert System for Experimental Design Analysis. Paper presented at the Ergonomics Society Conference, Leicester UK, September 1983.

Barwise, J and Perry, J(1983) Situations and Attitudes. MIT Press, Boston, US.

Biscoe-Taylor, M(1982) Tree of Knowledge (Computer Program). Acornsoft, Cambridge.

Bork, A(1984) The fourth revolution - computers and learning. In Terry, C (ed) Using Microcomputers in Schools. Croom Helm, London.

Candy, L and Edmonds, E A(1982) A study in the use of a computer as an aid to English teaching. International Journal of Man-Machine Studies, 16, pp333-339.

CET/MEP (1983) Micro Primer Packs I to IV (Computer Programs). Council for Educational Technology, London.

Chandler, D(1984) Microcomputers and the English teacher. In Terry, C (ed) Using Microcomputers in Schools. Croom Helm, London

Coburn, P, Kelman, P, Roberts, R, Snyder, T, Watt, D and Weiner, C(1982) Practical Guide to Computers in Education. Addison-Wesley, Reading, Massachussets.

Crystal, D, Fletcher, P and Garman, M(1976) The grammatical analysis of language disability: a procedure for assessment and remediation. Studies in Language Disability and Remediation I. Edward Arnold, London.

Dolch, E W(1951) Psychology and the Teaching of Reading. Garrard Press.

Donaldsen, M(1978) Children's Minds. Fontana/Collins, Glasgow.

Ennals, J R(1983) Beginning Micro-Prolog. Ellis Horwood, Chichester.

Feuerstein, R(1980) Instrumental Enrichment. An intervention program for cognitive modifiability. University Park Press, Baltimore.

Finlayson, H(1983) The development of mathematical thinking through Logo in primary schools. In Greater Manchester Primary Contact Special Issue 2: Microcomputers. Didsbury Scool of Education, Manchester Polytechnic.

Fletcher, H(1970) Mathematics for Schools Level 1 - Teachers Resource Book. Addison-Wesley, London.

Futcher, D(1983) An interactive experience. Educational Computing, 4, 5, p12.

Halliday, M A K and Hasan, R(1976) Cohesion in English. Longmans, Harlow, Essex.

Hewett, I V(1983) Launching Logic. Shiva Publishing Ltd, Nantwich, Cheshire.

Higgins, J(1982) The use of the computer in English language teaching. In Davies, G and Higgins, J, Computers, Language, and Language Learning. Centre for Information on Language Teaching and Research, London.

Hill, M(1984) Fairweather freind. Acorn User, 20,

Howe, J A M and Ross, P(1981) Moving Logo into a mathematics classroom. In Howe, J A M and Ross, P (eds) Microcomputers in Secondary Education: Issues and Techniques. Kogan Page, London.

Jackson, P(1983) Deadline. Soft, July 1983, pp61-62.

Kilworth, P(1982) Philosopher's Quest (Computer Program). Acornsoft, Cambridge.

Kowalski, R(1983) Foreword to Ennals, J R, Beginning Micro-Prolog. Ellis Horwood, Chichester.

Lawler, R W(1982) Designing computer-based microworlds. Byte, 7, 8, pp138-160.

Malone, T W(1981) Towards a theory of intrinsically motivating instruction. Cognitive Science, 4, pp333-370.

Mathematics Product Group(1983) Ramis II: Rapid Access Management Information System. Princeton, New Jersey.

Moores, B F(1978) Educating the Deaf. Houghton Mifflin, Boston.

Moss, S(1984) Databases. Educational Computing, January 1984, p25.

Moyle, D(1968) The Teaching of Reading. Ward Lock, London.

O'Shea, T and Self, J(1983) Learning and Teaching with Computers: Artificial Intelligence in Education. Harvester Press, Brighton.

Papert, S(1980) Mindstorms. Harvester Press, Brighton.

Peters, M L(1981) Spelling: Caught or Taught? Routledge and Kegan Paul, London.

Roberts, G(1983) M.E.P. Newsletter for Wales, 4, February 1983.

Rostron, A B and Sewell, D F(1984) Microtechnology in Special Education. Croom Helm, London.

Rushby, N(1984) Styles of computer based learning. In Terry, C(ed) Using Microcomputers in Schools. Croom Helm, London.

Sage, M W and Smith, D J(1983) Microcomputers in Education: a framework for research. Social Science Research Council, London.

Sharples, M(1983) A construction kit for language. In Chandler, D(ed) Exploring English with Microcomputers. M.E.P. Readers I, Council for Educational Technology, London.

Sleeman, D and Brown, D S(1981) Intelligent Tutoring Systems. Academic Press, London.

Stewart, J(1983) Does the use of the microcomputer inhibit the development of language in children? In Chandler, D(ed) Exploring English with Microcomputers. M.E.P. Readers I, Council for Educational Technology, London.

Ward, R D, Sewell, D F, Rostron, A B and Phillips, R J(1983) Interactive computer-assisted learning for the classroom: problems and principles. Programmed Learning and Educational Technology, 20, 4, pp269-275.

Ward, R D, Phillips, R J, Sewell, D F and Rostron, A B(in press) Language and Thought. Acornsoft, Cambridge.

Wills, A and Wills, R(1982) Word Sequencing (Computer Program). E.S.M., Wisbech and Acornsoft, Cambridgeshire.

Wiltshire, A(1982) Dolch (Computer Program). E.S.M., Wisbech, Cambridgeshire.

2.6 Educational Technology, Information Technology and the Resourcer's Apprentice

J A Gilman
Durham County Council

Abstract: The impact of microelectronics-based technology upon society is destined to create revolutionary changes within the latter. As a consequence, it must undergo not a mere change of gear but a veritable quantum leap into a new educational dimension if our educational provision is to prove capable of meeting these new demands. Fortunately, the apparatus and techniques of information technology provide schools with the means of achieving this revolution. However, two conditions must be met: the instruments of this 'new technology' (for example microcomputer hardware and software) must be efficiently orgaized within the school for efficient use in implementing the school curriculum; the latter must also, itself, be restructured to meet the new demands of society. A neutral school agency, independent of subject departments and manned by staff possessing the skills of resource organization and management needs to be established for the efficient control of micro-resources. These resources need to be co-ordinated with the school's existing traditional resources – human, book, audiovisual – within the framework of a single information resources collection. The staff member in control ('resourcer' with his apprentice, the microcomputer) would be responsible for access to the whole of the school's information sources and resources. In this role of 'school information manager', he or she should become one of the most influential members of the school community. At the same time, the school curriculum must be critically reviewed to deal with both the rapidly changing needs of society and the new and increasingly powerful range of resources becoming available for use by teachers and students. The aim must be the adoption of a new curricular perspective within which both content and methodology are transformed in the light of the school's new objectives, a process in which the school information manager will have a major role to play.

BACKGROUND

The fact that this conference is an International Conference on Educational Technology and the 18th in an annual series seems to prove that educational technology (ET) is alive and kicking in a considerable section of the overall spectrum of educational provision and in many parts of the world. However, I have to report that within the secondary education sector in the UK, ET as an agent of revolutionary change has proved to be a myth –unable to survive the rigours of its passage across the Atlantic, its progenitors. Most of us may remember the promises held out by ET in the 1960s to hard-pressed teachers in the then newly established comprehensive schools. It was going to open up a bright new era of educational provision tailored to meet the needs of a newly emerging technological society –in which the educational stage of our own schooldays (with outdated props of teachers, rows of pupils, textbooks) was to be transformed instantly into an Aladdin's cave of technological gadgetry – where individual learners would move happily from study carrel to TV seminar, harvesting knowledge against a background buzz of audiovisual equipment.

There was nothing wrong, or inappropriate, about the vision itself. Our society was experiencing change in the 1960s and at a rate which could scarcely be managed within the traditional teaching environment, curriculum, and methodology. An educational revolution was required, appeared imminent, but it never materialized. Instead, most of our schools continued in the traditional ways.

Two things went wrong, I would suggest.

First, the educational aspect of ET was submerged under its educational trimmings. The range and novelty of audiovisual hardware and software created excitement among those attracted by its potential to add a new dimension to their teaching strategy, but also created apprehension among those who perceived in ET a threat to the peacefulness of their existing well-ordered and trouble-free professional rut. Such stirrings tended to obscure the other aspect – a new educational philosophy. The latter was based on a concept of meeting pupils' actual educational needs rather than the artificial, often irrelevant requirements of examiners; and of equipping these pupils with both the capability and the desire to continue educating themeselves long after leaving school. Other radically new educational objectives included:

* Stressing the learning situation rather than the teaching procedure.
* Educating pupils as individuals, each possessing unique needs, and capable of unique responses, rather than as elements of an omnipresent class group within which individuality dissolves into anonymity and momentum becomes drift.
* Stimulating pupils' interest and imagination through the use, in conjunction with the traditional medium of print, of a wide range of auditory and graphical resource material and information sources.
* Encouraging pupils to create their own original resource items, as constituting an indispensible part of the learning process, in addition to making use of existing, readily available resource material.
* Adopting a structured approach towards the realization of defined learning objectives, as opposed to making an erratic progress from one lesson to the next along an ill-defined path of intuitive response.

Such a new concept of education required, for its implementation, the provision of a wide range of alternative and complementary teaching and learning resources for use by pupils as well as teachers. The agency for the organization and administration of these resources was to be the school library resource centre, designed to combine the stock of a multi-media library with the creative facilities of a reprographics unit and providing, on the one hand, an extensive hardware loans service to staff while meeting, on the other hand, the self-education needs of pupils. Library resource centres, of a kind, were established in a number of secondary schools but these seldom stimulated any significant revision of their respective schools' curriculum, let alone an educational revolution. How could they? There was never any real awareness in the schools of the existence of a philosophical dimension to ET, no realization that the role of the library resource centre was primarily that of supporting the pursuit of specific ET objectives by the school. Instead, its existence was viewed as an end in itself, readily accommodated within the framework of the existing school curriculum, requiring only the minimum expenditure of financial resources and staff time, and which certainly carried with it no revolutionary connotations.

Second, even if a school did subscribe to the revolutionary ethos and the educational objectives of ET, such a school which failed to achieve the efficient organization and effective exploitation of its various collections of teaching and learning resources was in no position to realize such aims. If the effective implementation of ET requires a properly equipped, staffed, and supported resource centre, few schools even today possess an agency of such a calibre.

With the majority of our secondary schools possessing neither an adequate appreciation of the aims and objectives of ET, nor an effective system for resources control capable of implementing them, the lack of impact appears inevitable in retrospect. Most schools never realized that their classrooms had been earmarked by educational strategists as a revolutionary background.

THE NEED FOR REVOLUTION

What relevance has the above history to the world of computers and information technology (IT) - the world of the 21st century? The answer is quite simple: if an educational revolution was needed in the 1960s and 1970s to equip the young for the new technological age, how much more urgent is the need to equip them for tomorrow's microelectronics age? If today's world is very different to that of our fathers, tommorrow's is likely to be unrecognizable. Society is being sucked into a maelstrom of technological innovation so destructive of the traditional institutions, concepts and practices which governed the lives of earlier generations as to constitute not a mere socio-economic revolution but a quantum leap into a totally new environmental dimension.

Our schools may have muddled through the last two decades in a typically British fashion without the benefit of an ET-generated educational revolution. But we can hardly claim that the average school-leaver of this period has been equipped, as a consequence of his or her educational expertise, to even comprehend, let alone resolve, the complex political, economic and social problems which have combined to deny him or her a satisfying, creative and constructive role in Great Britain in 1984. To have survived as well as we have into the 1980s has been undeservedly fortunate. To depend on the same good fortune to transform our present generation into school-leavers equipped to meet the challge of 21st century life would be as irresponsible as it would be disastrous.

Our assurance of a continued, let alone prosperous, future as a leading nation and a civilized society depends on our success in developing and implementing a totally new curricular perspective within a similarly redefined educational environment which is capable of accommodating whatever further changes the even more distant future may demand. Change of this dimension requires, not an evolutionary digression, but a revolutionary explosion.

Fortunately for us, IT offers both the tools and techniques for the creation of such a revolution. Indeed this revolution is already under way with thousands of teachers being introduced to the operation and use of microcomputers - now standard equipment in virtually every school in the UK. If the IT revolution is to succeed where the ET revolution failed, the reasons for this failure must be identified, existing parallels with the present stage of the IT revolution drawn, and an appropriate response initiated. Otherwise, the vehicle of the new revolution will inevitably become embedded in the same ruts which diverted its predecessor from its curriculum-oriented goals. This identification and its appropriate responses will now be examined in detail.

WHY THE ET REVOLUTION FAILED

We have identified the two main causes of the failure of the ET revolution as lack of awareness by schools of the aims and objectives of ET, together an accompanying lack of the effective system of resources control necessary for its implementation. The remedy for the first of these lay in the education of teachers to understand the existence and nature of the philosophy of ET so that they not only understood its essence but actively supported it by being willing to revise their own teaching strategies accordingly. The solution to the second required the setting up of the kind of library resource centre recommended by theorists as being indispensible to the achievement of their aims.

Similar problems now threaten the successful outcome of the coming IT revolution in schools. The impact of the new technology together with the many problems raised by its applications within the curriculum has tended to obscure the fact that, as with ET, the technology is not an end in itself but can support and implement a particular philosophy of education. Again, no effective system has yet been devised for the efficient organization and administration of the computer-based resources which constitute the apparatus of IT to allow its effective use across the entire spectrum of the school curriculum.

Of course, new electronic playthings will continue to proliferate within schools delighting us with their tricks or trimmings, whether we resolve these problems or not. However, without their successful resolution, it is clear that we will never achieve the seminal revolution of our education system which IT alone has the capability to realize, and which represents our only hope for the future.

Such an approach will naturally take full cognizance of the applicability of microcomputing systems within the educational process itself, both as a means of teaching pupils the operation and use of these systems, and also as teaching and learning resources throughout the curriculum. It will also acknowledge the fact that microcomputers have an increasingly important role to play in the administration of a school's information sources and resources -a role which will add considerably to the effectiveness of the latter within the context of the school curriculum.

INITIATING THE REVOLUTION

The mere utilization of microcomputers within a school will not bring about curricular reform. Traditional lessons taught on traditional lines and occasionally enlivened by a program will no more modify the overall educational experience than a filmstrip on African wildlife in place of textbook illustrations. Curricular reform need to be instituted primarily on the basis of a deliberate acceptance by the school community of the need for a totally new kind of educational programme. In support of this, the apparatus of IT will have an important, but not exclusive, role to play. Such a programme will naturally have to be designed in the light of an informed knowledge, and experience of the unique contribution which the microcomputer can make to the educational experience of the young who are living in an increasingly computer-dominated society. But the nature and scope of this programme must not be dictated by the quantity and characteristics of microcomputing hardware and software available in school. Other resources – human, book, audiovisual – have an equally important part to play. Computers should supplement and not supplant the school's existing collection of educational resources.

The restructuring of the school curriculum to accomodate the requirements of the information era will require the following:

* Redefinition of subject areas.
* Revision of syllabuses.
* Identification of resources of all kinds: their acquisition or production, and their subsequent organization for use.
* Teaching of new skills in information retrieval and in operating a wide range of technological equipment.
* Devising of new administrative procedures, both within subject departments and as part of the management structure of the school.
* Adoption of new strategies and methodologies by teaching staff appropriate to the revised content of the curriculum.

The latter, particularly, will need to take into account the inevitable changes that will occur in the community's (and hence the pupil's) attitudes towards educational provision and their consequent expectations of what the school should make available.

This philosophical aspect if IT, together with the various practical curricular developments to which it gives rise, needs to be discussed thoroughly with school teaching staff at all levels. Their acceptance must be obtained for the aims and objectives of IT, the application of this within their own school, together with the implications that this will have for their own professional activities. Crucial elements in the success or failure of the IT revolution will be the readiness of the teacher to re-examine the theoretical foundations of their individual teaching programmes, coupled with a complete re-appraisal of syllabus content, teaching methodology employed hitherto, and learning strategies that they have devised for their pupils.

It was this failure of many teachers to ensure acceptance of the principle and lack of readiness to accommodate the personal consequences of re-examination and re-appraisal which was one of the principal causes of the failure of ET to effect a revolution in our educational system. We cannot afford the same mistake again and yet this aspect of IT is still to be seriously considered, let alone implemented, in the great majority of those schools currently promoting the use of the technology of IT.

Once the curriculum has been restructured, its successful implementation will depend on the competent organization of a school's microcomputing hardware and software resources and their effective redeployment and exploitation across the curriculum as a whole. This aspect also has received minimal consideration to date. Its neglect will lead to any potential revolutionary momentum being engulfed in that morass of inter-departmental politicking which constitutes the traditional approach to resources availability in most secondary-level schools. For example, on the introduction of microcomputers, it was natural that they should be based in the science or mathematics department. Initially used almost solely for teaching computer studies, it was taken for granted that only teachers with expertise in electronics or mathematics would possess the inclination (and ability) to operate the equipment and teach about its use.

With the greater sophistication of microcomputers today, teachers of every subject are now being encouraged to experiment with them in the teaching of their subject areas and courses for all teachers are being provided in the UK by MEP and by local authorities. It is now accepted that microcomputer hardware and software should constitute merely another category of educational software material which, in its potential for applications in every area of the curriculum, is no different from the school's complementary collections of audiovisual resources and library bookstock. Such a concept is indispensible to the whole strategy of an educational revolution fuelled by IT. But, given such acceptance, and with a role destined to increase dramatically with the proliferation of educational software, one must question the desirability of the responsibility for the acquisition and organization of a school's microcomputer resources being solely in the hands of mathematics or science staff. This could be a barrier to the full and effective exploitation of these resources throughout the curriculum.

The successful management of microcomputer resources calls for an expertise in establishing and overseeing efficient storage, indexing, and loans procedures for their use, rather than computing. Such skills (which are conspicuously absent from the training and expertise of the majority of subject specialists, whatever their discipline), need to be complemented by an awareness of the potential applications of microcomputer resources in subject areas outside those directly associated with the sciences, such as music, art, commerce, English, and religious education. Furthermore, those concerned with the encouragement of the use of microcomputer resources throughout the school must be aware of, and capable of reassuring, the anxieties experienced by microelectronics-illiterate teaching colleagues confronted for the first time by an 'alien' technology.

The kind of services and facilities which a school, seeking to exploit the potential of IT throughout its community, will experience the need for have been outlined by the author (1983) and include the following:

1. The provision of a microcomputing information service, for the benefit of staff, pupils and members of the local community interested in acquiring and using a micro at school, or in the home.
2. Liaison with appropriate bodies outside the school, including the Microelectronics Education Programme, and LEA institutions such as teachers' centre, colleges etc.
3. The selection and acquisition of microcomputer hardware.
4. The training of staff and pupils in the use of this hardware.
5. Its deployment throughout the school, and its timetabling for use.
6. The selection and acquisition of microcomputer software.
7. The checking and assessment of this software.
8. The provision of facilities for the school-based production of software.
9. The efficient organization of software for storage and retrieval (including its proper classification and cataloguing).
10. The integration of software with the school's book and audiovisual resource collections, forming a unified collection of teaching and learning resource material.
11. The provision of facilities for accessing teletext and viewdata information systems.
12. The creation of a 'model' database, for use in school in the training of pupils and staff in information retrieval skills and techniques.
13. The provision of training in these skills and techniques.
14. The provision of training and practice in the downloading, storage, and the use of telesoftware.
15. The creation of school-based links with external computerized information networks (on a local, LEA-wide, regional, national and ultimately international, basis).
16. The establishment, in conjunction with primary 'feeder' schools, of a computer-based 'information consortium'. In due course, this would be the first stage in the setting-up of an LEA-wide information network (see 15 above).

Few mathematics or science teachers are likely to be able to afford the time (or possess the inclination) to become involved in such a range of activities. Yet these are all areas which will need to be catered for, to some extent, in the computer-oriented school of tomorrow. Therefore, the advantages inherent in placing the overall responsibility for the management of some central, neutral agency, manned by staff competent in the skills of resource organization, sympathetic to the needs of non-computer specialists, and free of ties with (and consequent obligation to) any particular department within the school appear to be both self-evident and indisputable. It must also be apparent that the skills and the duties of such staff would be identical with those of the staff both of the school's resource centre and the school library. Efficient management suggests that the functions of all three agencies should be combined within one centre, perhaps designated the school information resources centre. Apart from the potential improvement in efficiency possible within such a system, it would also be possible for the totality of the school's information sources and resources, irrespective of format or origin, to be co-ordinated within the framework of a unified, integrated collection of teaching and learning resources with tremendous benefits for the implementation of an IT-inspired curriculum.

The full potential of microcomputers, in respect of their contribution to the teaching and learning processes within a school, will never be realized while micro-resources are kept separate from other resources. However well-designed and produced, no software package exists which can provide a better educational experience when used in isolation from, rather than linked to or co-ordinated with, additional resource material.

CO-ORDINATING RESOURCES

A microcomputer program might well be complemented by a cine film or a video recording which isolates one particular aspect of the program and, by enlarging on this, enables the user to escape the restraints imposed upon his or her understanding of the wider aspects of the subject by the limitations of the VDU display. The same program may also be complemented by a book which can take the user on a philosophical exploration of a problem whose physical dimensions have been established by the microcomputer. Book, computer program, film, or video are alternative formats which allow exploration of different elements or aspects of the same problem. Each such resource item relates to others in the school's collection and it is to the school's advantage to provide an organizational framework within which each can be identified and linked to those others with which it shares some common element of theme, content or format. By including all these items within one information centre, it also becomes possible to stress the interrelationship of all forms of resource materials instead of accentuating their differences.

The nature of the training and expertise of the staff of such an information/resources centre must include skills and techniques of resources organization and administration – not usually associated with the education and training of teachers. Such skills and techniques are identical, however, to those required for the successful administration of a library and are precisely those received by professionally trained librarians. This points to a school librarian as the most suitable person to manage such an agency. Given the minimum educational role accorded to librarians in many secondary schools, this proposal may appear unsupportable on first consideration. However, the lowly status of such librarians is often a reflection of the lack of demands made upon them and support afforded them by school committees, rather than any lack of capability and potential. Although information has been traditionally stored in books and management of this information by librarians has therefore primarily involved them with books as physical objects, it is really information itself, and not its physical container, with which both librarian and library user are essential concerned. Librarianship has, in fact, been defined as constituting the management of information, so that librarians are, by definition, information managers.

Librarians have, for some time, been engaged in the management of non-book resources whose control requires the exercise of exactly the same skills and techniques as does that of book stock. In training, they receive much more instruction and practice in the application of microcomputers to their professional tasks, together with the management and use of microcomputer resources, than do students currently undergoing training for the teaching profession. For example, an increasing number of school librarians are involved in the management of audiovisual resources and becoming interested in the use of computerized databases as information sources. They are coming to recognize in IT the new face of their profession.

UK government-appointed bodies such as CET and MEP are agreed on the validity of this new role for school librarians in the IT era and have published (1983) recommendations for the provision of appropriate courses and other forms of support that will enable them to carry out such a role successfully. The transformation of roles has already begun. Within the school context, the term 'resourcerer' has been coined, half-seriously, to distinguish such an information manager from the still prevalent idea of a librarian as a book curator. With its connotation of 'hi-tech' wizardry, and with the microcomputer fulfilling the role of the 'resourcerer's apprentice' (possessed as was the sorcerer's apprentice, of power to wreak darmatic and unforeseen changes on the environment according to its master's design), 'resourcerer' seems an appropriate title for someone whose potential role encompasses the creation, maintenance and exploitation of the totality of his or her school's information sources and resources.

CONCLUSION

The appointment of the school librarian as a school's information manager with overall responsibility for the integration of microcomputer resources with the school's other educational resources bring with it an additional benefit not to be underestimated. The fear has sometimes been expressed that the advent of IT in our educational system will have a detrimental effect on the human and humane elements of that system. It is suggested that the computer and its needs will come to assume a greater importance within the school community than the needs of individual pupils and teachers, hence distorting the nature of that community so that it no longer represents the best interests of its human members. Such a possibility is a very real concern to many parents and teachers as well as to educationalists in general.

However, society still subscribes to certain concepts of civilized values, concepts which it tends to link with the world of literature in whose products such values were first expressed. Librarians, although no longer engaged exclusively in the custodianship of books, are nevertheless still viewed by the general public as possessing some degree of responsibility for the preservation and transmission of these values. School librarians themselves, with their innate love of literature would, I am sure, have no wish to disassociate themselves from this kind of responsibility. The school librarian is concerned with ensuring a balanced view by bringing to his or her work a concept of an educational information service in which no one resource medium is regarded as being superior to any other – each is complementary to the other. More than any other organizational framework that might be devised for the management of the school's resources, their containment within this conept of balanced equality will help to ensure that the resourcerer's apprentice – education's latest but most potent revolutionary agent – is kept firmly in its place as the servant, and not the master, of the educational system to whose service it has been harnessed. In this lies our best guarantee that civilized human values will continue to prevail in the computerized society we are now beginning to build for posterity.

REFERENCES

Gilman, J A (1983) Information Technology & the School Library Resource Centre. Occasional Paper No 11. Council for Educational Technology, London.
MEP / Library Association (1983) Information Technology: Guidelines for the School Librarian. Microelectronics in Education Programme, Newcastle (in association with the Library Association).

2.7 A Guide to Evaluating Methods — A Manual for Microtechnology Innovation

N D C Harris and R M Strachan
University of Bath

Abstract: The expectations in relation to software for microcomputers may have been exaggerated. Problems to date appear to relate to poor transfer of printed materials to the microcomputer as a page turner (cf teaching machines), and strategies which fail to use their facilities. The focus of the model for evaluation is primarily on the educational use rather than the sophistication of the software. The framework proposed suggests seven areas for consideration which are elaborated upon. Currently the information given to teachers about software omits many of the features of these area topics. In addition, because of pressure from publishers and limited funds in MEP (Microelectronics in Education Programme), much software is being produced which has limited evaluation. MEP has funded GEMS (Guide to Evaluation Methods – A Manual for Microtechnology Innovation) to enable software and other curriculum innovations in microtechnology to be evaluated during development. An outline of GEMS and the ideas behind it is given.

INTRODUCTION

The pace of innovation on the development of teaching and learning materials has speeded up with the advent of microtechnology to such an extent that evaluation is often in danger of being reduced to an afterthought. In the early stages of the introduction of a new technology into schools, a major problem is the poor educational quality. The technology has often been developed for another context (such as 16mm film entertainment, TV entertainment, business microcomputer software or home entertainment). Teachers have to choose appropriate software from a bewildering range with little help from the associated literature which often looks exciting but usually gives little information about effectiveness or problems in a classroom. Much reviewing concentrates on the sophistication of the program rather than the educational value of the resources. There is a need for more information about the educational value of published resources to enable teachers to make a better choice in spending. In a previous article (Harris,1980) the following suggestions were made as a basis for evaluation:

* user friendly
* style
* cost
* teacher reaction
* kids reaction
* management
* technical

It was clear to MEP that much of the material that was being generated was not being considered for its educational value. During its development, the key aims had been sophisticated programming and marketing as soon as possible. It was felt that some help was needed for developers of curriculum materials who had little or no experience of formative evaluation. 'A Guide to Evaluating Methods' (GEMS - Strachan,1983) was produced to encourage the questioning for the educational value of resources during the stages of design, development and dissemination of MEP projects, but also during their wider classroom use.

THE USERS

In one sense, GEMS is a 'recipe book of techniques' for evaluating, and chosen because they are uncomplicated, capable of providing quick feedback and, most importantly, they are grounded in the everyday experience of evaluating carried out by teachers. In his introduction to GEM, John Anderson stressed the practical nature of evaluating as being:

'The commonsense activity of thinking critically, in a self-examining way, about the usefulness and value of all new developments.'

What followed from this (and from reactions to early drafts) was the feeling was that there was a wider group of users than just teachers seconded to MEP. It was felt that GEMS could provide a set of 'tools for evaluating' to be left behind in the wake of MEP innovations; or it could be a useful starting point for teachers and lecturers who wanted to improve the quality of their work in a systematic, planned fashion.

ISSUES ON EVALUATING

In GEMS, and more particularly the workshops for MEP project directors based on it, a number of fundamental issue were raised about evaluating. An ideal definition of it would stress:

'the collection and provision of evidence on the basis of which decisions can be taken about the feasibility, effectiveness and educational value of curricula.' (Cooper,1976)

The ideal is seldom achieved and the reality of evaluating is more often a process for determining what works and what does not, and revising that which does not. At its worst, evaluating can end up as something which is usually and unfortunately inserted after a programme or project has been implemented.

REASONS FOR EVALUATING

There are a variety of reasons for carrying out an evaluation. The most obvious is that is a requirement of a funding body such as MEP or of a higher management. It may help to justify the choice of curricula and materials or assist in the identification of learning problems and their remedies. A sense of heightened professional self-awareness and confidence will lead to improved performance and increased professional satisfaction.

It may be necessary for those working on institutional and curriculum development to clarify and justify their intentions, making them explicit within a wider social framework. A more painful reason for evaluating may be that, in a period of recession and educational cutback, it may be necessary to provide evidence of 'value for money' to justify the allocation of scarce resources.

A PROCESS VIEW

The process of evaluating can be seen in Figure 1 as being cyclical and endless. Stages in the spiral include the identification of issues of interest in problems which become the focal points for evaluation. Information collected about these issues need to be sorted out and analysed so that judgements can be made about possible changes. The implementation of such changes will be monitored and judged, lead to further issues and so on. These stages are often clearly related and may be carried out simultaneously.

Before and during this cycle of evaluating it is important to consider who will be doing the evaluation. For example, will it involve people from inside the project or institution or from outside? Also, who will be the audience during the evaluation – insiders or outsiders? These questions will have a bearing on the writing and presentation of reports. The main focal points of a process of evaluating, whether in the area of microtechnology or other kinds of educational development, are the learners, the teachers, and the materials (software and hardware). Clearly these focal points cannot be considered in isolation either from each other or from social and political contexts.

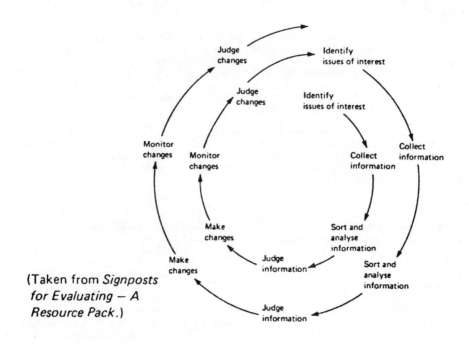

(Taken from *Signposts for Evaluating — A Resource Pack*.)

Figure 1   A cycle of evaluating

THE STRUCTURE AND CONTENT OF GEMS

As a 'recipe book' GEMS owed much of its material, ideas and techniques to earlier Bath University productions, particularly the 'Evaluation Resource Pack' (Harris and Bailey,1981) and 'Signposts for Evaluating' (Harris,Carter and Bell,1981). It was designed to be a little red book, convenient in size and comprehensible in range.
   Feedback from teachers and colleagues in the early stages of writing indicated a need for something which could be used quickly, and dipped into for an appropriate 'recipe'. But it was also felt that wider issues in evaluating should not be lost. Therefore, as well as methods, GEMS contains some case studies which give a broader picture of evaluating.
   GEMS has two main parts. Part One has three sections each containing a range of uncomplicated methods for collecting and analysing information. Section 1 deals with methods based on conversations, interviews and discussions under the title 'Talking and Listening Methods'. Section 2, 'Summarizing and Reporting Methods' includes the kinds of instruments used in the case studies. Also included were some practical hints on using hand-written notes to record information quickly and an outline of the potential and methods of organizing teleconferencing. Section 3 deals with 'Observing and Recording Methods'. Part Two contains case studies and appendices.

INNOVATING AND EVALUATING

GEMS was originally intended as a manual which MEP project directors could leave with teachers seconded to a project. It soon became clear that many MEP projects have been initiated and carried out by schools-based teachers. It was for those teachers and for those involved in microtechnology innovation in their classrooms on their own initiative or sposored by other local authorities that GEMS was written. This was stressed during the workshops which were designed as a model to be used by curriculum developers in MEP.
   The process view of evaluating is one which generates and supports continued critical reflection and development at the level of the classroom. Some major curriculum innovations of recent years have appeared as something wonderful brought down from on high to the

'lonely' classroom teacher. Too many unrealistic hopes have been raised – and dashed – and, like some some educational cargo cults, only relics remain of the original intention and enthusiasm. With the disappearance or the experts such innovations falter and degenerate under the pressures of time, energy, finace and examinations. If the innovation of microtechnology is to live up to its promise, then questions of educational value need to be kept in mind. GEMS was put together with the harassed and hard-pressed teacher in mind as a recipe book of methods which would help to keep microtechnology innovation cooking or at least simmering quietly.

ACKNOWLEDGEMENTS

We would like to thank MEP who funded this project and John Anderson and Brian Richards for their encouragement and contribution respectively.

REFERENCES

Cooper, K (1976) Curriculum evaluation – definition and boundaries. In Tawney, D (ed) Curriculum Evaluation Today: Trends and Implications. Macmillan Education, London.

Harris, N D C (1980) Expectation and realities: evaluation of computer software. Times Educational Supplement 12 Nov. Also CAL News, 21, pp4-6.

Harris, N D C and Bailey, J (1981) Evaluation Resource Pack. Council for Educational Technology, London.

Harris, N D C, Bell, C D and Carter, J E H (1981) Signposts for Evaluating: A Resource Pack. Council for Educational Technology/Schools Council, London.

Strachan, R M and Harris, N D C (1983) Guide to Evaluating Methods: A Manual for Microtechnology Innovation. National Extension College for Microelectronics Education Programme, Cambridge.

Section 3:
Computer-Based Learning—
Techniques

3.1 Databases in Education and Training: Concerns for the Educational Technologist

L MacDonald and R F Windsor
Council for Educational Technology, London

Abstract: The collection and dissemination of information has always been an important element in all education and training programmes. It has not, however, always been possible to afford or otherwise easily obtain suitable up-to-date information. For a number of reasons, chiefly the development of cheap and powerful microcomputers, that situation is changing rapidly. Teachers and trainers are using information from various sources. On-line access to databases is growing as well as the trend to micro-based databases. Information is now available for professional self-development to use with, or make available to, learners. The problems associated with all this activity are growing too, both for the 'creators' and the users of the information. This paper looks at what those problems are from the point of view both of the creator and the user. Training in a number of areas coupled with standardization can alleviate some of the problems outlined above.

INFORMATION

'Education is concerned to a large extent with obtaining, appraising, and conveying information.' (Thompson et al,1982)
'Office work is about getting hold of information and then using it.' (WHICH Computer? September 1983)

These definitions are contemporary but information has been important ever since, and perhaps before, man discovered fire. However, our ability to store and use it has never changed as dramatically as it has in the last few years.

Even developments using the printed word only enabled us to create vast filing cabinets, boxes or everyday piles of paper. This depended on someone creating a system that was an aid to memory. Such systems are passive and, if you have ever tried to find one reference from a heap of papers on someone's desk or look in someone else's filing cabinet, you will recognize the idiosyncratic problems associated with that task. Information technology (IT) has changed that. However, ironically, the wider uses of IT have problems of their own which can lead to less, not more, useful bits of information being available. This paper attempts to outline some of those problems and to encourage educational technologists to consider and debate the issues. Implicit in this aim is a belief that educational technology has a major role to play in co-operation with information specialists and computer technologists in order to achieve the best results for education and training. Indeed the evidence suggests that this is already beginning to happen; people in education and training are becoming aware of these changes in data-handling techniques and are taking action directly to explore their potential.

We are therefore going to examine some of these changes and their implication for the learning process. We will the consider some of the training, design, and research issues for the education and training sectors, and finally we will consider some of the emerging solutions.

INFORMATION STORAGE

Adding to the brain's ability to store and recall information is obviously not new. Over 100 years ago, Jules Verne had 20,000 cards and excerpts in a well-organized collection covering such fields as geography, science and technology. He could, of course, dip in and locate something - a fact or several similar references. If Jules Verne were alive today, might he consider electronic storage?

Undoubtedly he would. A reasonable justification is the decreasing real costs of storing and manipulating information, while the speed of communicating the results of searches for items increases. David Fairburn, Director of the National Computer Centre, stated at a CET conference in 1982 that the cost of storing information is likely to move in favour of electronic systems rather than paper-based systems around 1985. Furthermore, Fairburn predicted that by 1990, electronic storage will be the cheapest way to accommodate full colour and offer random access and motion. The cost in 1982 of holding 300 to 400 words on paper in a conventional filing system is approximately 25p. Compare this to the costs (Table 1) of holding the same information in a computer storage and of accessing it directly on-line.

	In main memory £	on-line direct access £
1950	1,000,000	−
1960	30,000	5,000
1970	5,100	1,000
1975	1,000	100
1980	100	6
1983	30	1
1985	3	0.3
1990	0.5	0.05

Table 1 Cost of holding 300 to 400 words of text electronically

This has meant many people moving to electronic storage in answer to the growing need to store and hold large amounts of information and the increasing cost of paper storage.

INFORMATION ACCESS

However, costs do not necessarily motivate people to use such technology: even when they do, the costs of storage are not the only ones to be taken into account. The costs of learning a new system, of getting hold of the information, of reproducing it, of manipulating it into useful forms, and of communicating it to others are all in need of consideration. Methods of direct comparison may not be so readily available. How many of us bother to cost the time it now takes us to satisfy information needs with telephone calls or library visits? To perform this thoroughly, one would need to cost not only petrol and parking charges but also the opportunity costs of one's own time.

'Information' is a free commodity to many people. It is much like air; you do not value it until it gets difficult to obtain. But it is a new and attractive proposition to have rapid access to a detail from among vast stores of information, to be able to manipulate in various ways, to combine it with the results of many other unrelated searches and to communicate it in many forms to anywhere in the world. This realization of IT has led to a stimulation of many new sources of information and a more widely informed populace. The latest figures indicate that 11 per cent of homes now own a microcomputer; we are also told that 80 per cent of these are used only for computer games but the software sales suggest that users are now beginning to move into other areas of interest. There are now thousands of Micronet subscribers who, even though they have joined initially only to gain access to yet more computer games, are now gaining awareness and experience of an electronic database. This sort of process has stimulated further information generation thus perpetuating an upward spiral of quantity. Quality is a different matter!

INFORMATION HANDLING

There is also, it appears, a gradual re-appraisal and questioning of society's assessment of 'expertise' and 'intellectual excellence'. 'We no longer need to assess these qualities on the basis of ability to remember information' (J Duke, in a study commissioned by CET on Educational Environments for the 1990s). Rather, people and judgements will be assessed by the amount of appropriate information used and the processes involved in arriving at their conclusions. Students are now examined on their enhanced abilities using the aid of a calculator in a similar fashion.

DATABASES

We have seen that people need no longer rely on headfuls of data supplemented by filing cabinets, indexes, catalogues, directories and whole libraries. We are beginning to find it more economical and expedient to rely on diskfuls of data manipulated by computer software. This sort of information collection, when organized electronically, is known as a database. (A purist will distinguish between a database which contains bibliographic reference and a databank which contains factual information requiring no further reference but we are not purists and feel that database is a generally understood and accepted term.)

There are three main types of database in operation in education and training:

1 Databases available on-line from database suppliers or operators eg, BLAISE-LINE LOCKHEED DIALOG.
2 Databases available through database operators - mediated by 'professionals' eg, ECCTIS, MARIS.
3 Databases disseminated on disk, microfiche or paper for direct user operation eg, BUFVC HELPIS file.

The historical origins of a database have implications for its accessibility. Many databases have developed from manual information systems serving special interest groups and the information may later be made more widely available at a price. Databases like BLAISE or Prestel are more unusual in that they were set up as a public service right from the start. Recently, several databases have been set up to give information on a whole range of further education courses such as ECTIS and Guildford Educational Service's PICKUP database.

These databases all store information electronically; however, they do not all disseminate it electronically. A range of media and methods is available for dissemination; each has its own advantages and disadvantages for user accessibility. For instance, one user may find it more convenient to make his or her own searches; another may prefer to rely upon the mediation of professionals. This raises questions which deserve a fuller consideration than can be given here.

PROBLEMS

We are concerned because both creators and users are faced with a number of problems each with a range of solutions. As soon as choices are made then some information is locked within a system where it may not be available to others for a variety of reasons. The creator may, in fact, wish it to be widely available but this may become impossible once his or her choices have been made. We do not include in our concerns private information or information for a closed group. Access to this is quite rightly restricted and procedures exist for this to be made quite safe.

PROBLEMS FOR CREATORS

To explain our concerns, let us look at what the choices might imply using a more straightforward example such as that involved in selecting a video system. Supposing that we have decided to buy a video-cassette recorder, we have to choose between three formats while bearing in mind a number of other considerations such as portability or special recording features. Having made a choice of format, we have to accept that we may lose access to potentially useful material presented in another format. Choosing a cheaper option, we may lose out on special facilities. If we decide now to make video materials and make them available to others, there is an effect upon our market because of the choices we made or those made by potential users.

With information storage, the issues are wider and more complicated. As a creator of a database, the problems we face include:

* Who is the audience?
* Where are they located?

* What is the possible maximum and minimum capacity neede to store the data (information) now or in a few years?
* How many people might be likely to use the database at the same time?
* Is there a budget - can we/ do we want to sell our information?

Other issues that a user may ask are laid out in the Appendix but conclusions from such issues may lead the creator to the following alternatives:

* Use existing hardware and software.
* Design from scratch.
* Put information in someone else's database.

PROBLEMS FOR USERS

Information can thus be stored in different ways and retrieved in different ways. For example, we have mentioned Prestel which is a viewdata system with advantages such as easy accessibility and use, but a disadvantage inherent in its tree structure. The structure of the database is, however, only one level of choice or difficulty. Familiarity with one database in no way suggests that the user will be instantly successful with another which may have a completely different structure and need a completely different search technique.

The user is faced with additional issues besides the hardware and software. As a potential user or seeker for information, how can I locate relevant sources for my needs? How can I check that the information displayed is up-to-date? How can I get help in searching your system? Without getting into your database, and therefore spending money, how can I get a good idea of what is available? Compare this with other media: videos have previews, books have contents pages and indexes. How can I learn to 'drive' your system (BLAISE courses last from two to three days, POLIS courses are two days and cost extra)? How can I find my way round the complicated conceptual rabbit warrens of your command structure? Spatial awareness can be lost and this has been compared to word blindness.

SOME SOLUTIONS

All these issues affect the cost/benefit for the user and may put off people who might otherwise enjoy this aspect of IT. CET's work so far leads us to suggest that there are some solutions. In this section, we hope to outline how we believe the issues raised above can be tackled in both the short and long term.

Free text searching is available on large database systems. One such database system uses only the term 'GET' to locate any word in the database from among its 100 million words. This total is being added to at the rate of 200,000 words per day. The result of the search takes a few seconds. This can be used or refined by selecting a further term using 'PICK' to narrow down the search. It is designed to be used by journalists using BBC material plus articles from the Guardian and Economist.

Details of the system and how to use it are contained on four sides of A4 paper folded to pocket size. Other information is contained within the system. However, the software is flexible and offers the user a number of alternatives. For instance, a 'menu' structure can be created and this can be used to find identical information by using 'GET' and 'PICK'. The menu merely 'lies' on top of the normal search procedures and aids users for their first search or as many times as necessary in their searches on the database. This brings 'training' down to a two-hour session on the potential of the system, and an introduction to the system's search techniques. Other features include:

* Microcomputer-based system compatible with the mainframe system so that searches are prepared in advance thus using precisely the same terms, achieving savings on telephone costs and avoiding training in a number of different techniques.
* The ability to 'take down' pieces of the databases for local searching or use in other forms such as hard copy.
* Synonym rings can be set up so that the creator, and users, can be involved in building terms that can be used as alternatives. For instance, an American article may use computer-aided instruction, computer-based instruction, computer-managed training, computer-aided learning all to mean computer-based training or computer-based learning. The synonym ring once established search for all these terms automatically.

* Because the database can handle vast amounts of data and store it cheaply (a typical cost for 30 million characters is £2,000), journal articles, reviews, abstracts, and other wordy text can be stored cheaply but searched quickly. Reviews, particularly for software, are seen as increasingly important.

The major problem related earlier of the lack of common or similar search techniques can be eliminated by such software. At other levels, for software and hardware, technical issues remain, some of which are now being tackled. For example, John Coll of MEP is attempting to get some basic agreements on fundamentals among the microcomputer-based systems. If this gains acceptance, this will go some way towards lessening problems. We feel that there is an important step that could help to overcome this and some of the other issues.

In America, there is an 'umbrella' database called 'source'. For the cost of a telephone call which is slightly above the long distance rates in the UK, you can search on-line for an hour for the additional cost of $5. The database covers 60 areas and is, in effect, 60 specialist areas but with a common main index, common structures, command language and thesaurus.

The UK training and education sectors need such a database. This would enable organizations and institutions, even individuals, to buy in 'chunks' of storage and 'sell off' or give away their information. As a user, we would want to know that the answer to our search is comprehensive and up-to-date. We do not want to have to search several databases in different ways and then take further time to compare the results. If we are paying for information (and publicly funded databases are expected to become self-financing in the near future), we will demand a high standard of service. Why should people have patience with an inconvenient and unco-ordinated complex of incompatible systems?

THE ROLE OF EDUCATIONAL TECHNOLOGY

We will certainly look to educational technologists for advice and awareness of the issues we have outlined here. Who is better placed to consider the information needs of education and training, to take into account all the issues as outlined here and arrive at a general overview? Who else is to tackle the problems we have outlined here so that more information does not get locked away inside technological filing cabinets? We feel that these are properly the concerns of educational technologists, and we hope that they would be pressing for work on standards for storage, retrieval and transfer, as well as an umbrella education and training database within the United Kingdom.

REFERENCES

Duke, J (in preparation) Educational Environments for the 1990s. Council for Educational Technology, London.
Thompson, Knowles et al (1982) In Owen,K (ed) Videotex in Education. CET, London
WHICH Computer? (1983) September.

APPENDIX: Questions to consider when reviewing electronic database systems.

When considering database systems there are a number of general issues to consider. In addition to these, there are specific issue related to stand-alone systems or on-line systems. Definitions of stand-alone and on-line systems are given below.

General points related to all electronic databases

* Who is using this system already and for what purposes?
* When retrieving information from the database, what is the full procedure, and is this written down anywhere eg, how is a question asked of the system?
* What search facilities are available both during the search and outside the database eg, a comprehensive readable manual or telephone support?
* What hardware and software is needed to use the database?
* What are the costs of the hardware and software and are there other costs in using the database?
* What is the response time on this database?

* How is information put into the database?
* What training is required to use the system? Are there courses available and how much do they cost?
* Is it possible to save searches and print out the records retrieved?
* How easily and quickly can I formulate records on this system for my specific purposes?

Stand-alone system eg, a database on a microcomputer

* What is the size of memory available for use on the database once the program has been loaded, and how many records would that allow?
* Are there any limitations to the record structure?
* How easy is it to update, change or re-organize the data?

On-line system eg, a large mini or mainframe computer accessed by a terminal via the telephone system

* How many simultaneous users does the system allow for?
* What hardware is needed to use the system eg, what terminal is required or can a microcomputer with special software be used?
* At what speed is the database accessed eg, 300/300, 1200/75, 1200/1200? Is there a choice of speeds? (This has consequences for the costs and choice of modems.)

3.2 Face Robot with Response Analyser in the Classroom

K Nagaoka
Kobe University, Japan

Abstract: This paper reports on the Face Robot system, the purpose of which is the pacemaking of simultaneous group instruction. The principle of the system consists of pacemaking theory with analysis of the response curve and dynamic representation of the face method. Response curves can be obtained by monitoring the learner's time required to do an exercise using a response analyser. The face method has been adopted as a man-machine interface between the microromputer and the teacher. The outline and function of the system is shown just in a simulation mode in order to research the relation between the response curve and the face to ascertain the feasibility of the system.

INSTRUCTION

Educational technology contributes to two formats of instructional process: individual type and group type. There has been recently a great number of applications of microcomputers in education. But the majority of them aim at individual instruction (learning) like CAI (CAL). However, the most popular instructional format in schools in Japan and other countries today is the lecture, or group instruction. The Face Robot system described in this paper should be used for group instruction in the classroom. It thus appears very useful in the field of classroom instruction at the present time.

The system consists of a response analyser (RA) and a microcomputer. The main purpose of the system is simultaneous pacemaking of instruction in the classroom by acquiring the response time of the learners. Particularly, the dynamic representation of the face method is used as a man-machine interface in this system.

SYSTEM CONSTRUCTION

The system construction is shown in Figure 1. The Face Robot system is divided into three subsystems as shown in the upper part of Figure 1. They are:

1. Data acquisition
2. Data analysis
3. Face display

The data acquisition subsystem faces the learners to acquire data. But it can be any educational object which can serve as a source of time data in general instead of the leaners' responses. The acquired data are analysed by means of calculation of indices and estimation of parameters with probability model in the data analysis subsystem. In the face display subsystem the face, as an expression of the learning process of the learners, is represented on the CRT. Some rule must be set up to assign the calculated indexes to the factors of expression in the face. The rule can be set up at will by the user.

Some performance modes of the system can be supposed as shown in Figure 1. They are:

1. Practical mode
2. Simulation mode
3. General mode

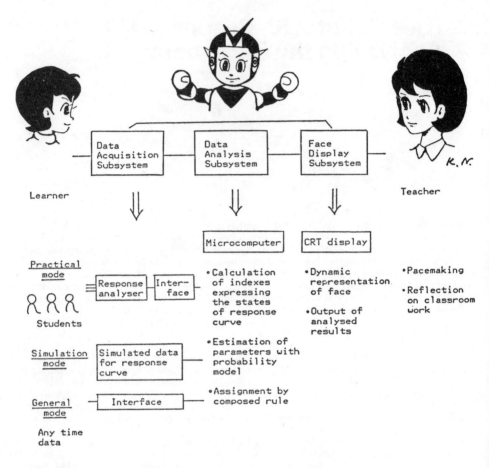

Fig. 1   <u>System   Construction</u>

In the practical mode, the data acquisition subsystem consists of an RA, which is ordinarily composed of a device on the teacher's desk with a meter to indicate the response rate and a button provided on each learner's desk for him or her to operate, in addition to an interface that connects the RA and a microcomputer. The data are acquired when the student in the actual classroom operates the button in this mode.

In the simulation mode, the data are acquired by means of generation of random variables with the probability model stored in the microcomputer. The discussion in this paper is on this mode.

In the general mode, the system can deal with any data of time series.

RESPONSE CURVE

The situation is supposed to be that the teacher shows an exercise and gives instructions to the learners who are to respond by operating the RA button in the classroom when they have finished the exercise. If the RA buttons are of multiple-choice type, the learners' responses are to select an alternative that they think is correct.

In that case, a response curve that indicates a transition of response rate with time is obtained and shown in Figure 2. The notation used for the response curve is also indicated in Figure 2. The symbols are:

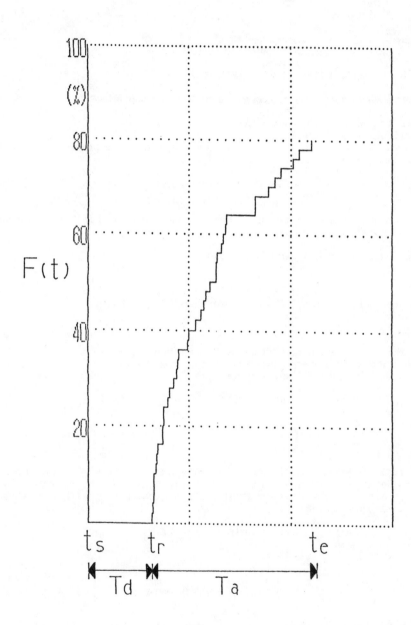

Figure 2 <u>Notation</u>

ts : time of start
tr : time of start of response
te : time of end
T_d : time interval of no response (dead time)
T_a : time interval of response   (answering time)

THEORETICAL DISTRIBUTION OF RESPONSE TIME

The simplest assumptions for the response time model of a group of learners are:

1. There is a physically mimimum response time of the learners.
2. There is also a mean response time.
3. The group is homogeneous thus the theoretical distribution of response time maximizes its own entropy, ie,

$$\int \int_{t_0}^{\alpha} f(t) \log f(t) dt \ ---> \text{maximum}$$

If the above assumption is made, the cumulative exponential curve will be derived by means of calculus of variations as follows:

(response density) $f(t) = (1/\mu) \exp(-(t-t_0)/\mu),$ $t >= t_0$
                   zero $t < t_0$

(response curve) $F(t) = \int_{t_0}^{t} f(t) \, dt = 1 - \exp(-(t-t_0)/\mu),$ $t >= t_0$
                   zero $t < t_0$

where μ is the mean value and t_0 is the physically minumum response time required, or the theoretical no-response time. Let $t_0 = 0$ for the sake of simplicity, then $f(t)$ and $F(t)$ are rewritten to:

     $f(t) =$ $(1/\mu) \exp(-t/\mu)$ $t >= 0$
                     zero $t < 0$ (1)

     $F(t) =$ $1 - \exp(-t/\mu)$ $t >= 0$
                     zero $t < 0$ (2)

These (1) and (2) are the essential formulae in the following. In the case of an exercise that includes n-subordinate factors that are independent of one another and the response curves of which have the same the response density $f_n(t)$ will be n-1 convolutions of (1), or the Gamma distribution with parameter n:

     $f_n(t) =$ $1/(n-1)! \ (t^{n-1}/\mu^n) \exp(-t/\mu)$ (3)

and then:

     $F_n(t) =$ $\displaystyle 1 - \sum_{i=1}^{n} 1/(n-i)! \ (t^{n-i}/\mu^{n-i}) \exp(-t/\mu)$ (4)

The formula (4) increases more slowly than (2) at first and become S-shaped according to the value of n.

   On the other hand, in the case of n-subordinate factors that are dependent on one another, and the μ of which are the same:

     $f_n(t) =$ $(1/n\mu) \exp(-t/n\mu)$ (5)

     $F_n(t) =$ $1 - \exp(-t/n\mu)$ (6)

The shapes of the curve in the above case are the same as those of (1) and (2), but elongated n times.

It is supposed that the response curve (4) corresponds to an exercise which consists of multiplex contents, and (6) corresponds to simply increased but homogeneous contents. This result is useful for observing the response curves.

PACEMAKING WITH RESPONSE CURVE

The pacemaking behaviour of the teacher in the learner's exercise or problem–solving process explained above is limited here, as follows:

(a) When should the teacher let the learners stop the exercise (or which exercise should be given next, or which instruction should be given)?
(b) When should the teacher give a hint to the learners (and how should it be given)?

It has been known from actual experiences that the points to be noted in pacemaking by observing a response curve are as follows:

1. To end when the response rate has arrived at an appropriate level, not too low and not too high. The level is often set at 80 per cent.
2. To end when an appropriate length of time has passed, not too soon and not too late. The time is often set at T_a between two and three times T_d.
3. To give a hint when the response rate does not increase for a while, or the response curve becomes flat.
4. To consider the items given in parentheses in a) and b) according to the shape of response curve and its estimated parameters that will be introduced in the next section.

SIMULATION MODE

In this paper, the outline and function of the system is expressed in the simulation mode as mentioned before, so all the discussions in the following sections will relate to this mode.

The generation of a response curve with random variables by the microcomputer is based on the Gamma distribution derived as formulae (3) and (4). When the number of responding learners is N, random variables Xi,i=1,...,N having a Gamma density with the parameters T and n are generated.

$$Xi = -\mu \log \prod_{j=1}^{n} rj, \quad i = 1...N,$$

where r_j is a random variable with uniform density in the interval (0,1).

With respect to the analysis of response curves to estimate the parameters, the probability model may be anything and not resticted to the one used in this system. It is subject to the user's preference. The Weibull distribution function is preferred here, because the parameters of the Gamma distribution is hard to estimate whereas the Weibull parameters are easier to estimate and there are some previous results on the fitting of the Weibull distribution model to response curves (Fujita,1975). The Weibull distribution is:

$$F(t) = \begin{array}{ll} 1 - \exp(-(t-t_o)^m/\mu) & t >= t_o \\ zero & t < t_o \end{array}$$

and it is one of the generalizations of the exponential distribution. The parameters are as follows:

1. m: shape parameter. As the value of m is greater than one, it corresponds to the multiplex contents like parameter n of the Gamma distribution.
2. μ: scale parameter. It corresponds to increased contents as with the Gamma distribution.
3. t_o: location parameter. It is estimated from the whole data, so not always equal to T_d, the time interval between the start and the first response.

REPRESENTATION OF FACE

It is important to arrange a sophisticated man-machine interface between the information of the response curve and the observation of the teacher, because the teacher, during instruction in the classroom, does not have the time to evaluate quickly various numerical results from the microcomputer. For this need the face method was adopted and the Face Display subsystem was organized. In the system, the face is represented not statically but dynamically.

The face method was proposed by Chernoff (1973) for a multivariate classification and has recently been applied in many fields of statistics. It is very difficult to set up a rule that assigns the indexes of the response curve to the factors of expression of the face if the emotional factors are to be considered. Although this problem is essentially important in the Face Robot system and is going to be studied technologically in the near future, the face represented on the CRT should be, at present, regarded just as a multivariate graphic indicator.

Five examples of the face currently adopted are shown in Figure 3. The face has seven factors of expression and the outline of the face is changeable according to the user's preference. The seven factors and the corresponding indexes are indicated in $T_a$ble 1. This correspondence is based on the current rule.

In Table 1, t is the current time, ti is the time of last response (i-th response), t(i-4) is the time of the (i-4)th response, T_a80 is the estimated time for 80% responses, and INT( ) is the integer function.

The assigned indexes are quantized into nine graded discrete values, so that the smoothness of the face's motion is not sufficient. Because of that the ability of calculation and display speed of the microcomputer at present is not enough for a numerically exact display of the factors of expression on the CRT. In the near future, however, this problem will be solved.

The grade of values was translated from the values of indexes. The translation formulae are also shown in Table 1. The seven values are expressed as a vector (xl, x2,...,x7), where xl is the value of the factor i that is the factor number in Table 1. In Figure 3, the face A is all-nine expression (9,9,9,9,9,9,9), B is all-one (1,1,1,1,1,1,1), C is the mean (5,5,5,5,5,5,5), D is an example of puzzled expression (3,1,1,9,1,2,5), and E is an example of joyful expression (9,9,9,7,5,9,5).

No. of Factor	Factors of Expression	Indexes of Response Curve	Translation Formula	Means of Indexes
1	Shape of mouth	Response rate	$INT(F(t))+1$	Performance of responses
2	Distance between eyes and eyebrows	Estimated Weibull shape paramater m	$INT(9(m-1))+1$	Degree of multiplexity
3	Distance between both eyebrows	Length of plateau	$INT(\dfrac{t-ti}{Td/40})+1$	Evaluation of plateau of learning(absolute)
4	Distance between nose and mouth	Change of response curve	$INT(\dfrac{4(t-ti)}{t-t(i-4)})+1$	Evaluation of plateau of learning(relative)
5	Shape of eyebrows	Estimated time for 80% response	$INT(Ta80/2)+1$	Prediction of performance
6	Shape of eyes	Normalized estimated time for 80% response	$INT(\dfrac{Ta80+Td}{t/9})+1$	Normalized predictive performance
7	Distance between both eyes	Time normalized with Td	$INT(9t/5Td)$	Time scale normalized with no-response time

Table 1. Factors of Expression and Indexes

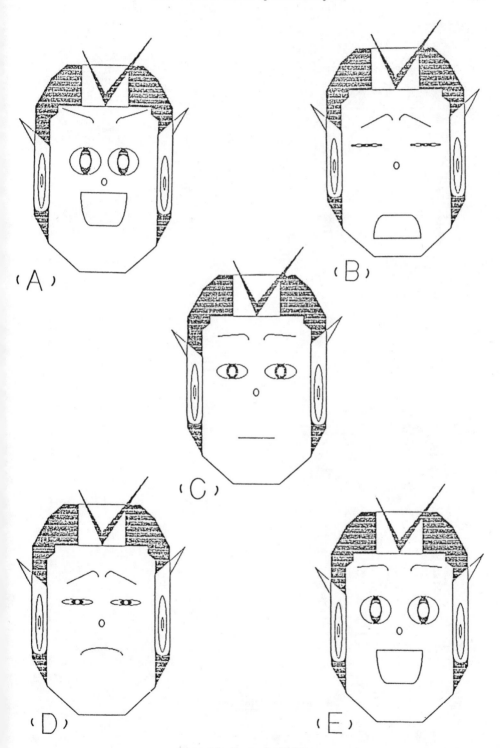

Figure 3   Example of face

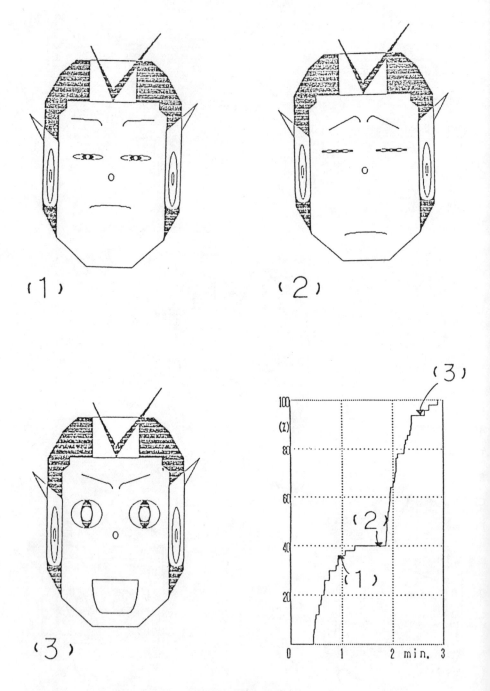

Figure 4   <u>Motion of face</u>

FACE ROBOT

Let an example of the face robot motion be shown in Figure 4. The successive motions of face can be depicted corresponding to the dynamic changes of response curve. The data shown in Figure 4 are generated as an example of the response curve having the teacher's hint. Three faces were represented at three different time points (1) (3). The first response(t=ts) occurred at about 30 seconds after start (t=tr); T_d=30 seconds. The response rate increased quickly approaching the time point (1) and after one minute, gradually began to change slowly. There came presently a plateau the length of which was about 37 seconds. Then the curve suddenly rose again immediately after the time point (2) as if the teacher had given a hint for the learners who had not finished the exercise yet and the learners had become responsive with the timely hint. At the time point (3), the response rate rose fairly high. It is supposed to be possible to identify the three faces from one another corresponding to each state of the response curve.

CONCLUSIONS

The present report merely concerns itself with the simulation mode and aims at relating the theory of pacemaking with respose curves and the face method. The next step is naturally the use of the practical mode with students and a teacher in an actual classroom situation. Considering such situations, the name Face Robot has been adopted so that this system will not seem to be just a machine which rigidly controls the learners, but a friendly aid which expresses the state of their learning process. The study is progressing on the following points:

1. Constructing the hardware system including the interface between RA and microcomputer in the practical mode.
2. Researching how to use this system effectively in the actual classroom.
3. Using the system as a training tool for the skill of pacemaking.
4. Improving the rule that assigns the indices of the response curve to the factors of expression of face by a multivariate analysis like multi-dimensional scaling.
5. Applying the system to a group CAL system requiring the automatic judgement capability for pacemaking.

ACKNOWLEDGEMENT

The author thanks Kazuo Seko for his helpful assistance.

REFERENCES

Chernoff, H (1973) The Use of Faces to Represent Points in k-Dimensional Space Graphically. Journal of American Statistical Association, 68, pp361-368.
Fujita, H (1975) Educational Informatics. Shohkohdoh, Tokyo. (in Japanese)

3.3 Appropriate Uses for Medium Resolution Colour Graphics in Computer-Aided Learning

G M Boyd
Concordia University, Montreal, Canada

Abstract: Medium resolution graphics enable quasi-animated colour-cued directed graph explanations of problem solving techniques to be presented. They also enable the equivalent of strip cartoon presentations of problem situations. These techniques, together with conventional presentations and input treatment, provide a powerful new approach to teaching problem solving skills in complex coupled system situations. Design and development considerations, including choice of languages and equipment are discussed. Sample graphics sequences were shown during the conference. Preliminary results or trials are presented.

INTRODUCTION

The currently available personal computers have severe limitations on resolution, colour quality, and simultaneous presentation space when compared to slides, films and books. On the other hand, they offer dynamic interactive characteristics far exceeding those available in any other audiovisual medium. Judging from the currently available studyware (this term is preferred to courseware as being less restrictive), there is a great need to develop the aesthetic sensibilities and imaginative skills of producers to exploit the new possibilities and to circumvent the constraints of the new medium.

A somewhat adventurous approach is required now because it will take many years to do enough detailed controlled research to establish the optimal design rules for particular classes of learner, subject matter, and educational aims to make production scientifically sound. The best that we can do at present is to combine what little has been established by researchers (mainly results on learning from pictures and text) with some aesthetic heuristics derived from the experience and the tacit knowledge of effective artists, musicians and teachers. A little help may also come from some of the philosophers writing on aesthetics who, as poets of sorts, cannot afford to be totally blind to what is attractive, potentially didactic, and memorable.

Among the latter, I have found it worthwhile reading some work of Findlay (1967) on 'the perspicuous and the poignant' as primary aesthetic qualities, and the essays of Santayana (1896) on why particular forms are delightful and satisfying while others are uninteresting. However, most of what has been published on aesthetics is utterly useless to people confronted with choosing the forms, motions and sounds most likely to help certain learners learn certain skills. Whitehead's (1929) three-phase categorization of learning (first, romance; second, precision; third, generalization) is indeed germane because the form that our presentations should take differs greatly depending on which of those phases of learning is to be supported at a given moment.

The sorts of images and sounds needed to captivate in the romance phase of learning constitute distractions (or 'noise') in the precision phase. The kinds of visual tools needed for definition and precision may sometimes also serve for generalization but both these phases require spare, formally powerful images, unlike the romance phase which, in general, needs more florid, surprising and humanly fascinating displays. In these latter phases, intrinsic motivation takes over so that the illustrative explication of structure and process then becomes the whole job.

Kaleidoscope, video-game sorts of graphics have a place in the romance phase of learning under circumstances where intrinsic motivation is not high. There is a current tendency to over-indulge in pyrotechnics for marketing reasons which is especially harmful to the definition and generalization phases of learning.

MEDIUM RESOLUTION GRAPHICS

Here 'medium resolution' graphics are defined as those which can be displayed on an ordinary colour television type monitor or inexpensive RGB monitor. This implies about 200 to 400 pixels horizontally and between 150 and 300 pixels vertically ('pixel' means picture element). Typically, between four and 32 colours and from two to 16 levels of brightness are available on such moderately priced computer systems as Apple II, Spectrum, BBC/Acorn, and Commodore64.

What is available for education and training purposes is largely determined by what is saleable in the entertainment and office equipment markets. At present, they provide us with the options of:

* low resolution colour at a very low price
* medium resolution colour of about colour-TV quality at an appreciable price
* higher resolution (600by400 or 600by1200 pixels) monochrome word-processing and 'business-graphics' displays.

Recently, Lamberski and Dwyer (1983) have found experimentally that 'color coding is found to be an important instructional variable in improving student information acquisition under specific conditions', and Stone (1983) found that 'for simple cognitive tasks a chromatic presentation seems to elicit more verbal responses than an achromatic version' (of a film). Unless there are contra-indications, colour is now experimentally verified as being the normally preferred display mode capability. One disadvantage is that colour printers are appreciably more expensive to use while current research indicates that it is valuable to provide learners with print-outs of the detailed sequences of their own work (Boyd et al, 1983). However monochrome print-outs of colour material are quite usable.

LIMITATIONS OF ECONOMICAL DISPLAY SYSTEMS

The limitations imposed by an artist's medium can be used to develop distinctly memorable styles of art (as with the strong and direct woodcuts of Albrecht Durer). It is in this spirit that we should approach the design of medium resolution graphics for the support of learning. There is, however, a caveat also to be drawn from art history: attempts to impose some vision unsuited to a medium have produced most singularly unmemorable results.

The educationally serious limitations of computers with medium resolution colour displays (even with pixel mapped type displays) are:

1. Only a very limited amount of detail can be shown while at the same time maintaining the global picture.
2. Only one page/screen can be viewed at a time.
3. Colour display is subject to severe distortion of both hue and saturation as well as brightness depending on the condition and adjustment of each learner's machine.
4. The number of colours, and number of brightness are few.
5. Diagonal and curved lines are subject to 'jagging' (stairstep effect).
6. A quite limited number of totally different frames can be stored on an ordinary (floppy) disk or its equivalents unless NAPLPS code is used; even then the limitations are much more severe than with animated film etc.
7. The edges of a display may be cut off by maladjusted CRT units.

Most of these limitations are not likely to be overcome quickly at affordable cost. Videodisk technology can supply a lot of fairly high-quality television type images but only at quite considerable expense. Unfortunately Direct Read and Write (DRAW) videodisk systems are significantly more expensive again.

What these limitations mean is that a premium is placed on the repetitive use of a comparatively small number of image elements (sprites, pictographs, schematic symbols etc) which can be moved and re-combined to give enough images to teach what is to be learned. For example, the Latin fable of Philemon and Baucus has been turned into an animated low resolution colour graphics lesson by G. Marussi at Concordia University by using a very limited number of forms which re-combine to exhibit a house, a temple and an old couple being tranformed into trees. Telidon/NAPLPS encoding permits about 20 times as many frames to be stored on a given disk or tape than for medium resolution graphics.

Bearing these limitations in mind, the graphic designer can go ahead to exploit the advantage of this medium. Many of the limitations are familiar to those who have already worked with 8mm film or with TV. Novices will find such classic manuals as the Thames and Hudson Manual of Television Graphics (Hurrell,1973) and the very comprehensive book on applied media aesthetics Sight Sound Motion (Zettl,1973) to be invaluable for this kind of work.

OPPORTUNTIES INHERENT IN MEDIUM RESOLUTION COMPUTER GRAPHICS SYSTEMS

Medium resolution pixel-mapped colour displays do offer a number of outstanding advantages of their own to the instructional materials developer as follows:

1. Animation of selected parts or objects (including moving, blinking, fading in and out, windowing and zooming in) is readily achieved.
2. Intense brilliant colour for attention cueing etc is possible.
3. The forced simplicity is a virtue. Between three and seven 'chunks' is all that anyone should be expected to take in at one time.
4. Blank space for emphasis etc costs nothing to display and almost nothing to store (unlike any other audiovisual medium).
5. Text may be oriented easily in at least four directions.
6. Many type fonts (providing only that there is not too much difference between thick and thin line widths and not too much complexity) can be used.
7. Audio tones can be used to indicate that something has changed on the screen etc.
8. It is becoming very easy to skip back and forth among frames.

There is a rich variety of possibilities now available; the question remains how to choose and use them for maximal educative benefit.

Nygard and Ranganathan (1983) give seven ways to use computer graphics to enhance educational effectiveness:

* develop labels for new concepts
* establish and reinforce associations with previously learned concepts
* illustrate rules, procedures and problem solving techniques
* illustrate and summarize material learned earlier
* suggest the nature of phenomena which have not yet been completely described
* provide a source of data
* retain interest.

Some research evidence exists to support all these uses. Such evidence is difficult to obtain and more difficult to generalize because we have so few good measures for the quality of images.

An excellent review of the research in the field of instructional illustration is by Levie and Lentz (1982). Some of their general conclusions are:

'Illustrations can help learners understand what they read, can help learners remember what they read, and can sometimes be used as effective and efficient substitutes for words, or as providers of extralinguistic information.'

'Learner generated imaginal adjuncts are generally less helpful than provided illustrations.'

AESTHETICS HEURISTICS AS A MEANS TO EFFECTIVE GRAPHICS

The central question in aesthetics is what qualities make a pattern contagious? What qualities tend to make people want to remember and pass on a pattern? In particular, which of these qualities are both effective and fairly universal? Only graphics with these qualities will teach effectively.

How many categories is it convenient to work with? If we establish too few categories, then the process of relating them to each particular instance is too long and complicated. If too many categories are used, they will not be remembered, and complex relations among categories need to be invoked.

I find three categories or evaluative dimensions most useful in deciding what to do to improve illustrations for the romance phase of learning:

1. Rhythmic formal power
2. Surprising juxtaposition
3. Human-interest identification.

f a pattern is lacking in any one of these qualities, its addition will make the pattern more memorable. A graph for plotting these variables is shown in Figure 1.

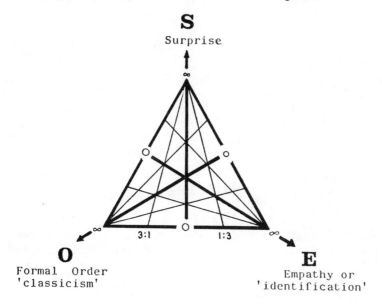

Fig. 1.   The Aesthetic Value triangle , exhibiting three
          independent classes of heuristics for design.

* <u>Formal power</u> has to do with economy of means and repetitive re-combination of a few forms or colours or notes etc to make complex but rhythmically intelligible patterns. Because formal power is lost when simplicity is replaced by excessive variety, a demand for formal power limits the amount of both other categoric qualities which can be packed into a work.

* <u>Surprising juxtaposition</u> has to do with requisite variety and with jolting people out of the syndrome of recognition followed by immediate naming followed by immediate ignoring, which we so frequently apply to deny the magic of the moment in favour of getting on with business. 'Information' is, by definition, unexpected pattern which then reduces our uncertainty somewhat about what to expect in the future. If a picture or musical phrase etc is to be informative, it must be somewhat surprising.

* <u>Human-interest identification</u> has to do with our propensity to model our behaviour upon that of others whom we judge to be like ourselves. Bandura's (1971) work on the way children emulate the behaviour of those children they see on TV whom they judge to be like themselves is perhaps most germane here. Identification is also an important factor in adult learning. Much of the effectiveness of comic strip cartoons depends on identification with person or animal protagonists.

A given image sequence can be shown to several judges each of whom touches the point on the aesthetic triangle-space which seems to characterize the image sequence. The correlation among raters and the rater consistency can be examined in this way with a computer touchscreen arrangement. Our preliminary trials indicate that fairly good agreement is obtainable.

Another approach to the characterization of image quality is to use Osgood's semantic differential technique to obtain factor loading for the three key factors, potency, activity and value. This is probably complementary to the above technique because the activity dimension (rhythm repetition delay) is under-represented by the aesthetic triangle scheme.

Several ways in which medium resolution graphics can be effectively used have been presented. A method for appraising the quality of such graphics apart from empirical investigation with learners (which does not generalize readily) has been presented in the expectation that this will be useful to developers of computer aided learning materials.

REFERENCES

Bandura, A (1971) Psychological Modelling: Conflicting Theories. Aldine Atherton, Chicago.
Boyd, G M, Douglas, L and Lebel, C (1983) Learner support options in computer assisted learning. In National Research Council of Canada, Proceedings of the Fourth Canadian Symposium on Instructional Technology. Ottawa.
Findlay, J N (1967) The perspicuous and the poignant. British Journal of Aesthetics, 7, 1, pp3-19.
Hurrell, R (1973) The Thames and Hudson Manual of Television Graphics. Thames and Hudson, London.
Lamberski, R J and Dwyer, F M (1983) The instructional effect of coding (colour and black and white) on information acquisition and retrieval. Educational Communications and Technology Journal, 31, 1, pp9-22.
Levie, W H and Lentz, R (1982) Effects of text illustrations, a review of research. Educational Communications and Technology Journal, 30, 4, pp195-232.
Nygard, K E and Ranganathan, B (1983) A system for generating instructional computer graphics. AEDS Journal, 16, 3, pp177-187.
Santayana, G (1961) The Sense of Beauty (originally pubished 1896). Collier, New York.
Stone, V L (1983) Effects of colour in filmed behaviour sequences on description and elaboration by Liberian schoolboys. Educational Communications and Technology Journal, 31, 1, pp33-45.
Whitehead, A N (1929) The Aims of Education. Cambridge University Press, Cambridge.
Zettl, H (1973) SIGHT SOUND MOTION Applied Media Aesthetics. Wadsworth, Belmont Ca.

3.4 Workshop: LOGO — A Tool for Thinking

S Gascoigne
Author and Teacher, Bradford

Abstract: Programming in schools today usually means learning a language, that is, acquiring a skill. However, another aspect of programming is teaching children to think. In this respect the computer is seen in terms of a tool for problem-solving and creativity. LOGO was developed from LISP, the main language of computational theories in artificial intelligence, as a language particularly suitable for children. It is versatile - dealing with complex graphics, simple databases, and allowing sophisticated interactive conversations. It has a user-friendly syntax and is based on 'procedures' as building blocks for writing programs.

REPORT

Although the workshop was planned for no more than 24 participants, it attracted some 40 delegates. Despite this excess number, everyone managed to gain some 'hands-on' experience. There were two major themes:

1. The ever-growing involvement of artificial intelligence (AI) concepts in education.
2. Programming as a tool for thinking.

AI, through such languages as LISP, LOGO, and PROLOG, is becoming an important science in education and industrial training. Although well established for a number of years in reserach institutions, AI is finally making its appearance in the classroom both at school level and in further education. So far, the main trends in the development of computer-based learning have been along the lines suggested by behavioural psychology in which the learner is 'conditioned' or 'programmed' to learn certain facts or skills. Thus we have a plethora of learning situations, from programmed learning, linear/branching programs to sophisticated authoring systems such as PILOT. However, as microcomputer technology develops towards 'intelligent' machines, there is an urgent need to concentrate on ideas from cognitive psychology in which the learner is not programmed but, on the contrary, is in control of the learning situation. The learner uses the microcomputer as an aid in investigations and problem-solving. The computer is seen as a tool for controlling the learning environment and one way to do this, to control the computer, is to program it.

Programming in schools today usually means learning a language such as BASIC or PASCAL as part of the curriculum called computer science. Children learn the basic skills of programming in the hope that it will equip them for the computerized society of the future. Programming is thus seen as a skill, similar to an engineering skill or learning a foreign language. However, another aspect of programming is teaching the learner to think. In this respect, the computer is seen in terms of problem-solving and creativity. The originators of LOGO - researchers in AI - first saw learning and thinking in terms of computation. These researchers looked at models from cognitive psychology and came up with what they called computational metaphors. For example, the way we think can be expressed in terms of programming. From this computational theory of learning, LISP was developed. LOGO in turn was developed from LISP, to be a language for everyone.

Although written originally for children, LOGO can be used at any level. It can be used for simple screen doodling or for investigating spirolaterals, or Newtonian physics. It can be used to teach children or adults problem-solving or computer literacy. The workshop was based on the 'turtle graphics' part of LOGO as this aspect is more geared towards intuitive learning and creativity than the 'list processing' part of LOGO. Through the use of visual imagery, turtle graphics is more immediate and identifiable by learners who may not be familiar with computers.

Members of the workshop were asked to place themselves in the situation of learner looking at LOGO for the first time. Since LOGO is a language for exploration, members were asked to experiment by using only four basic commands to move the screen turtle: FORWARD, BACKWARD, RIGHT, and LEFT. Each command was followed by a number to indicate the number of steps or degrees to move the turtle. After a short period of screen doodling, members went on to draw specific shapes such as a square, triangle, and circle. Having done this, they wrote a procedure to draw a shape and then experiment with that shape, using it as a sub-procedure to a main procedure with a new name such as PATTERN or SHAPE.

The majority of members wrote programs such as:

```
TO PATTERN
SQUARE
LEFT 45
SQUARE
LEFT 45
SQUARE
```

in which SQUARE was a sub-procedure of PATTERN.

Admittedly the content of these programs was not very sophisticated, but we were looking at how a learner can use the computer to create familiar things and ideas. There tends to be a considerable gap between what the learner already knows and what is demanded by our educational system and the rapidly expanding technological society. The leap from the commonplace to the realm of abstract thought is, for many learners, an enormous leap into the unknown.

LOGO is based on the learner's own experience. It is not imposed from above but is developed by the learner him or herself. Such powerful ideas as recursion and variable stepping are introduced gradually in response to a demand by the learner for more sophisticated programs. As an example of recursion, the following program was produced:

```
TO BUBBLES
REPEAT RANDOM 30 (OCTO)
BUBBLES
END
```

This program uses OCTO as a sub-procedure and employs recursion to create a new program each time. The program (or procedure) for OCTO was:

```
TO OCTO
MAKE "TURN RANDOM 20
REPEAT 10 (FD :TURN LEFT 45)
END
```

This as well as other programs in the workshop are taken from the book Microchild (1984).

Due to time shortage, the workshop could only offer a brief introduction to programming as a tool for thinking. It was not the intention of the presenter to run the workshop as a crash course on LOGO but rather to demonstrate an intuitive and creative approach to the use of computers in education. Certainly, members of the workshop enjoyed themselves. One may ask if constructive learning can really be fun? Is LOGO only for younger children? Looking at the work produced by members at the workshop, the answer to the last question clearly indicated that this is not the case. LOGO can be used at any stage or level of learning as a stimulating tool for problem-solving and thinking.

QUESTIONS AND DISCUSSION

Mr Preston from the Education and Library Board in Northern Ireland asked how one might introduce LOGO to teachers. The answer was that teachers of LOGO must themselves be problem-solvers. Like members of the workshop, they need to be encouraged to explore and experiment with the screen turtle rather than learn a prescribed package of ready-made procedures. They should, ideally, be seen to learn alongside the learner. LOGO should not be formalized. An authoritarian approach should be avoided. The teacher of LOGO is seen in terms of a manager of knowledge rather than an authority on how one should program.

Dr Rushby from Imperial College asked if LOGO and PROLOG were compatible. The answer given was that both are valid languages in education. However, they are different. LOGO is procedural while PROLOG is declarative. PROLOG is a database language and a logic-based programming language. Both provide the learner with a personal learning experience. Like LOGO, PROLOG can be used at any age or level. In the presenter's work in schools, both LOGO and PROLOG are used as tools for thinking and creativity.

Professor Stonier of Bradford University suggested that perhaps LOGO might be used for biological simulations, an approach already tried by the presenter with children. This involved simulating the behaviour of a unicellular organism which demonstrated stimulus-bound behaviour. Professor Stonier asked if LOGO had ever been used for more advanced applications. The presenter had no knowledge of such work but could see no reason why it could not be used for research into, for example, some areas of cytology.

After the workshop, there was a brief discussion about the use of LOGO in general for computer training with adults. The presenter pointed out that it had already been used successfully in the Third World for developing human resources. Perhaps LOGO could be a useful aid to intellectual stimulation not only in formal education but also as a leisure activity.

REFERENCE

Gascoigne, S (1984) Microchild - Learning through LOGO. Macmillan, London & Basingstoke.

3.5 Workshop: New Computer-Assisted Learning Material from Homerton College

F Daly
Homerton College, Cambridge

The workshop began with a short talk and demonstration to introduce some of the computer-assisted learning (CAL) material developed at Homerton College. This was followed by a period in which participants used the software for themselves. The materials are drawn from modern languages, the sciences and geometry. The following is a brief description of some of the features of the software:

Quelle Tête and Kopfjager

(for learners in their second or third year of second language learning)
The learner selects a number of facial features given in the foreign language and uses them to build up an identikit of an imaginary person. Having chosen a feature, a learner is able to refine it by reference to its size, shape, length etc. The outcome of each selection is an immediate drawing which may be erased, retained, or altered as desired.

Jeu des Ménages and Umziehen

(for learners at the end of their first year or in their second year of language learning)
Confronted with the task of furnishing a house, the learner has to respond to questions in a foreign language. The computer asks where a number of items of furniture are to be placed and the learner is expected to respond. The programs make use of attractive graphics to show the pieces of furniture placed in the room. The computer accepts unusual rooms for each item but may, after a while, become a little careless and position some at strange angles such as upside down or on its side. When this happens, it asks in the foreign language if this is acceptable to the learner. If the learner chooses not to accept the position, the object is re-arranged in a more orthodox way.

Chemical Collisions

This program simulates a reaction system in which two species of molecules, which are shown in different colours moving around on screen, are mixed together and make random collisions. Many of the collisions are elastic and do not result in chemical change. Some of the collisions are more energetic than others and these result in the formation of product molecules which are shown in a third colour. The program has many options to show graphs and bar charts which describe the state and behaviour of the system in detail.

Lift

This computer program features a miniature person called Mabel who stands on some scales in a lift shaft. Her weight pulls her down on to the scales and the learner (or teacher) can move the scales up and down the lift shaft. There are options within the program so that the user may zoom in on the scales and see how its reading is affected by the motion of the system. Also, there are options to display vectors, numbers and graphs to describe the displacement, velocity, and acceleration of Mabel and the scales.

Floater

The program is about a small particle in a square box. The movement of the particle is controlled in two dimensions with a joystick. The path of the particle is unimpeded by friction and, when it reaches the side of the box, it bounces with perfect elasticity. Unless the joystick is used to influence the motion of the particle, it will continue indefinitely in a state of rest or uniform motion. The system can be thought of as having a number of measuring instruments built in. The displacement, velocity, and acceleration of the particle are constantly monitored. These quantities can be displayed numerically with vectors, and on graphs plotted against time. They can be displayed separately, in groups, or all at once.

Tessellations

This is a program which breaks new ground in CAL and school geometry. It is already being used in infant and junior schools and in higher education. It can be used as an extension of practical work and to generate material for work with pencil, ruler and paper. It can be used as part of a course in traditional school geometry and to introduce ideas that are outside many syllabuses. It is quite 'open-ended'. The problems that it deals with can be approached in a variety of ways and at many different levels. Tessellations can be used to generate tiles which always fit together so that they can be tessellated across the plane of the screen. Depending on the artistic skill of the user, the program will generate beautiful coloured patterns.

From a mathematical point of view, plane patterns can be classified into 17 groups. We have programmed into Tessellations the underlying rules of these 17 geometrical symmetry groups. This means that, within the limitations of the resolution and colour of the computer, any pattern from the Islamic, Chinese, Celtic, or Japanese cultures can be drawn. Because of its mathematical completeness, not only will Tessellations draw every plane pattern that has previously been drawn, but also it can make every plane pattern that can ever be thought of!

We have had interest expressed in Tessellations from mathematicians, artists, physicists, chemists, crystallographers, home economists and many others who are interested in designing patterns.

Tessellations supports an extensive library facility so that shapes can be stored, retrieved, and erased in an easy and consistent manner. Any pattern produced on the screen can be transferred to the printer at the touch of a single button. The pattern is retained on the screen and the design process can be continued from where it left off. It is possible to zoom in and zoom out from the pattern by altering the scaling factor. The pattern can also be rotated and distorted in all the ways that are mathematically possible for plane patterns.

Section 4:
Training Design

4.1 Keynote Address on Training: New Training Initiatives

P Keen

Head of Training, Manpower Services Commission, Sheffield

SUMMARY

A common theme today is the ever increasing pace of change. This is reflected in the changing economic structure as follows:

* Traditional industries - particularly heavy industries - in decline.
* Growth in the service sector and in high technology jobs.
* The changing nature of jobs and the need for new skills as technology advances.

What does all this mean for people and their training needs? First they need an effective foundation - through education and initial training. Second, they need to be able to adapt and change. This means that we need to provide an adequate educational/training base together with the means by which people can subsequently retrain and extend their skills. This is the purpose of the 'New Training Initiative', comprising in detail:

* An initial foundation through the Youth Training Scheme (YTS) or at school (for example, CPVE or TVEI).
* More effective initial occupational training either with YTS or subsequently.
* Wider opportunities for adults to train and retrain.

In particular, it is reflected in the efforts to improve access to training by:

* Removing barriers to entry.
* Establishing recognized standards of competence to replace time-serving.
* Enabling people to build upon existing skills and knowledge, and attain the necessary standard of competence to do a job.
* Developing more flexible delivery systems (for example, Open Tech, CBI, non-flexible modular training arrangements).
* Generally improving the cost-effectiveness of training so that it is a more attractive investment.

Where does all this lead to? I suggest:

* A more adaptive society better able to respond to a changing world.
* A better trained workforce.
* A more effective utilization of human resource.

But it is a large menu. Change on this scale demands substantial commitment and management.

4.2 Seven Steps Towards Establishing a National Network of Open Learning for Managers in the Hotel and Catering Industry

P Critten
Hotel and Catering Training Board, Wembley, London

Abstract: A recent survey has shown that only a minority of supervisors and managers in the hotel and catering industry have had an opportunity to gain an appropriate professional qualification. Technology change is beginning to make an impact on the industry, creating a requirement for older, established managers to update their skills. Despite the recession, a substantial growth in employment in the hotel and catering industry is expected. This poses the problem of how to increase the supply of qualified and skilled staff to meet existing demands on the industry and also to provide for the demands created by future growth. The dispersed nature of the industry and its structure create barriers to the use of traditional vocational education routes. An approach is therefore needed which can provide the necessary opportunities for managers and supervisors to enhance their skills oustide a formal teaching situation. Against this background, the Hotel and Catering Industry Training Board, working in conjunction with the Manpower Services Commission, set out in 1983 to develop an Open Tech system for hotel and catering managers and supervisors. This is intended to provide a route for professional study and recognition through open learning incorporating distance learning materials which, until now, have not been available. This paper concentrates on the practicalities of setting up an innovative system. It takes the form of a progress report highlighting the problems and pitfalls encountered and discusses how they were overcome. It should provide some useful guidelines for the establishment of such schemes in the future.

ESTABLISHING AN IDENTITY

By this, we mean both an identity that is immediately recognizable and also the intention to follow a distinctive approach to learning. To achieve this, we designed a brochure with a distinctive logo, and outlined an approach to learning based on the manager's own place of work

One drawback with issuing the brochure was that it suggested that the scheme was already launched whereas we were still at a draft stage. However, it did confirm that there was a demand and a market for the product. Our market is the manager or department head who perhaps left college some 15 to 20 years ago with a craft qualification. He/she sees open learning as an ideal way of updating skills without having to spend time at college.

EVOLVING A HOUSE STYLE

The next step was to produce the learning material. So far we have mainly used established college lecturers who have subject matter expertise in the various fields. Our criteria for selecting contributors has tended to be to look for people who want to experiment with their material; not those who will simply regurgitate lecture notes or use the exercise to produce copy for their next book. No-one yet has had previous experience of writing distance material. I would regard this as an advantage. It means that we can evolve our own house-style specific to the kind of students that the lecturers know are typical of our market in the industry.

One weekend workshop was organized for us by John Coffey and OTTSU. Out of this workshop emerged our own house-style. I must admit that it reflects what has been a strong influence on me – programmed learning – but only in that we have encouraged contributors to follow such basic rules as:

1. Try to use just one A4 page to convey an idea, give an example, and finish with some kind of activity or question to which the student has to respond and which is then discussed on the following page.
2. Work from EXAMPLE to RULE – never the other way round. (Lecturers find this particularly difficult at first!)

We also encourage the use of authentic case–study material; but the best case study is the one that the student prepares from his/her own experience which is encouraged by the use of a diary.

DECIDING ON AN APPROPRIATE METHOD OF DELIVERY

Our criteria for deciding on an appropriate format for delivering material were:

1. It should allow for easy access and amendment.
2. It should accommodate up to four audiocassettes; we wanted to explore the use of audiotape to present case studies and to enable students and tutors to feed back responses to each other (also to provide an alternative for those students who found it difficult to write an account of their responses).

To meet these criteria, we had designed a loose–leaf binder with a plastic insert for audio–cassettes. One of the problems that we have encountered is that students are intimidated by having all of the material presented to them in this way all at once. We are therefore looking at alternative ways to make delivery of material more acceptable.

PROVIDING SUPPORT FACILITIES

From the outset, we had decided on two key support facilities:

1. Access to a local tutor who would initially introduce the material and be available to answer queries, discuss issues as required, and assess work.
2. To provide technology appropriate to the subjects being covered. As one of the first units to be covered was Information Technology, it was important to provide students with hands-on experience of a microcomputer. Manpower Services Commission agreed to the purchase of 24 BBC/Acorn microcomputers (Model B) for them to be loaned to students for this purpose. We have also linked the students into Micronet and hope to explore the use of electronic mail facilities. The students receive self–instructional material which takes them step–by–step through a range of software packages adapted to hotel and catering operations.

Finally, before students received their unit from their tutor, it was important that they were helped to orient themselves to open learning. Therefore, we produced a Student Handbook. Depending on what unit they are working through, the students are required at the end of the handbook to ask themselves a series of questions related to their work which the forthcoming unit will help them to resolve.

PROVIDING ADEQUATE FEEDBACK

There are three levels of feedback from the tutor to the student:

1. 'Self-assessment questions' (as shown in the Appendix) to which the student receives immediate feedback on the next page.
2. Tutor Marked Assignments which come at the end of each module of each unit (see example in the Appendix). This requires the student to respond in writing to the tutor who, in turn, makes an assessment of how well the student has responded. We are also exploring the possibility of using audio-response and feedback, and we will be experimenting with the NEC 'MAIL' computer package which is based on multiple choice questions which, depending on the choice made by the student, provides a personal letter to the student giving appropriate feedback.

3. A project which is to be completed at the end of each unit, assessed by agreement between student, employer and tutor.

THE ORGANIZATION OF NATIONAL DISTRIBUTION AND PUBLICITY

So far we have piloted the units in four geographical regions – Brighton, Newcastle, Coventry and Norwich. But, if the scheme is to be a credible alternative to a further education course, it must be made available on a national basis.

In order to get our message across, we have produced a brochure and will shortly be circulating a leaflet and poster to all colleges offering catering courses and to companies alerting them to future opportunities. To provide up-to-date information on units' availability, we have put 30 pages of information on Prestel. From this facility, we can also get feedback from potential students about additional units they would be interested in studying.

ESTABLISHING LINKS WITH OTHER LEARNING NETWORKS

Finally, it is important that any student working through our network is also linked in to other networks that will extend opportunities for self-development. One of the factors leading to the relative demise of programmed learning was that it was too self-contained; by its very nature, it was not easily integrated into more conventional teaching systems. On the other hand, a characteristic of open learning is that it should encourage collaboration between different systems and achievement in one system should lead to progress within another.

Thus, we hope that our students will have a link into the facilities offered by the computer-based National Catering Business Game, based at Stafford College of Further Education. We also hope that professional bodies like NEBSS, B/TEC and the professional management body of our industry, the Hotel, Catering and Institutional Management Association (HCIMA) will consider awarding credits in recognition of what students have achieved on successfully completing each unit's project.

APPENDIX

First Page of a Pamphlet issued by HCIMA Open Tech

The Hotel and Catering Industry is a growth industry; and yet it is estimated that there are 300,000 supervisors and managers who are unable to acquire management skills and qualifications by the more traditional vocational educational routes. It was in this context that the Hotel and Catering Industry Training Board applied for funds under the MSC's Open Tech scheme to develop open learning material for supervisors and managers in the industry. In the first year of funding, two open learning units have been produced:

'Getting the Job Done' (covering target setting, communications and motivation)
'Using Technology to Aid Management Decision Making' (providing hands-on experience of computers for managers)

These units are currently being piloted on 46 students. The inside pages of this pamphlet illustrates how the student is introduced to the material and the back page gives an example of the material and the kind of assignment that is set.
In the coming year of funding (84/85) a further eight units will be developed:

* Accommodation Management   * Industrial Relations
* Marketing   * Financial Control
* Quality Control   * Planning a Profitable Business
* Managing Staff Effectively   * Food and Beverage Management

Sample Page from 'Getting the Job Done'

ANSWER TO S.A.Q. 1.5
Your answer should have included the following:

Finance: working within buget, buying from nominated suppliers
Markets: providing client with the standards of food and service expected by the client
Products and Services: maintaining standards of food and service,
                   buying supplies of specified quality
Personnel: appointment of staff
           staff induction
           staff meetings
           staff training

In looking at the above answer, you will see that Stephen Waites' supervisory duties are well balanced and that his efforts are concerned with helping his employers (the contract catering company) to achieve their goals and, equally importantly, to ensure that the client's goals also are achieved. Stephen Waites has clearly identified responsibilities under the four key headings:

     Financial
     Markets
     Products and Services
     Personnel

Note that the first three are primarily concerned with achieving the employer's main goals and we shall call these 'target achievement' duties. The last, the Personnel duties, are those concerned with building the team of staff necessary to achieve the employer's goals. These we call 'team building' duties.
Read the case study again carefully and you will see that Stephen Waites is a good supervisor because he achieves a good balance between these different types of duties. Could he achieve his client's satisfaction (made up of finance and marketing tasks) if he did not also concern himself with the quality of the products (product and service duties) or the induction and welfare of his staff (personnel duties).
In your Diary over the next few days, identify which of your duties are 'target achievement' duties and which are 'team building'.

Sample Tutor Marked Assignment

Spend about four hours on this

TMA 2

This TMA marks the end of module 1 of this course. It is designed to give you a clear understanding of what targets consist of and how to specify them clearly.

Part I

Select four supervisory tasks for which you are responsible and prepare clear targets. Two of the targets are to be concerned with target achievement and the other two with team building.

Training Design

Task	Standard of Performance	Time
Target Achievement 1		
Target Achievement 2		
Team Building 1		
Team Building 2		

4.3 The Background, Development and Piloting of a Youth Trainer's Course

J Hills
Coventry Technical College

Abstract: When the New Training Initiative (NTI) was announced in 1981 by the Manpower Services Commission (MSC), it quickly became apparent that the Youth Training Scheme (YTS) was to be given a high priority and was to be off the ground in September 1983. The MSC's proposals for a broad based staff training for the YTS included establishing 55 Accredited Centres. These are to be the local focal points for YTS staff training. A central priority was the devising of 'a recognized course of study and appropriate assessment' leading to a nationally recognized staff training qualification. The author is an educational technologist working in the curriculum development team responsible for this new course development. The new course appears to follow a popular and quite traditional approach including objectives, a modular and integrated approach, and negotiated coursework assignments. However, for any new course to be successful, careful monitoring is essential. To this end, a team of experienced assessors have been appointed to oversee the establishment of the providing centres and the operating of the course on a pilot basis. Already the classic educational technology (systematic) approach has helped the team avoid some pitfalls. There are one or two outstanding problems yet to be solved and they include the problem of a wide target population who need to be subjected to a variety of assessment methods. The current spread of course members are already demanding further training and, by implication, that of a higher level.

BACKGROUND

The NTI (MSC,1981) is designed to improve and modernize training opportunities across the whole of the potential workforce. Three interrelated objectives for training in the 1980s were set out in the consultative document, 'A New Training Initiative', issued in May 1981 and are as follows:

1   We must develop skill training including apprenticeship in such a way as to enable young people entering at different ages and with different educational attainment to acquire agreed standards of skill appropriate to the jobs available and to provide them with a basis for progression through further learning.
2   We must move towards a position where all young people under the age of 18 have the opportunity either of continuing in full-time education or of entering a period of planned work experience combined with work related training and education.
3   We must open up widespread opportunities for adults, whether employed, unemployed or returning to work, to acquire, increase or update their skills and knowledge during the course of their working life.

Objective 2 is being realized in the form of the MSC's Youth Training Scheme.

YTS STAFF TRAINING

The YTS is intended primarily to be work-based. The many agencies concerned with the delivery of YTS will be expected to work collaboratively to ensure the integration of the elements of the YTS programme.

The target group for staff training for YTS is very wide and includes employees, the education sector, and MSC staff. The training needs will be equally varied and range from YTS awareness for senior management through planning and organizational needs at intermediate level to the individual needs of instructors, teachers and supervisors. To meet this enormous training need, Accredited Centres have been set up in each of 55 MSC areas to operate as a focus for staff training and development activity. Centres have been identified from various agencies and will liaise with MSC local offices to plan and execute training events. The main feature of a centre will be the array of training modules it offers to cover the elements of the YTS staff programme. It has become necessary to annex other establishments to accredited centres in order to give the necessary resource capability and provide the full range of the necessary expertise.

The success of YTS depends in large measure upon the quality of its trainers. Efficient first-in-line trainers/supervisors can enable trainees to benefit even from a poorly designed scheme. On the other hand, poor trainers/supervisors can unwittingly have an adverse effect on trainess even in the best designed scheme. Therefore, it is necessary to determine at an early stage the training needs of front line trainers/supervisors and an effective strategy for providing the necessary training.

A NEW COURSE TO MEET THE NEEDS

Thus a need developed for a new course to meet the perceived and actual needs of YTS staff and to provide it with a framework suitable for the MSC accredited centres (and their annexes) to deliver. Following discussions with MSC officers, staff training co-ordinators of accredited centres and appointed officers of the City and Guilds of London Institute (CGLI), priority was given to 'the development of a recognized course of study and appropriate assessment leading to the C & G Course No. 924 Youth Trainers' Award'. The course aims are given in the Appendix.

CRITERIA AND LIMITATIONS

The proposed scheme, to be offered on a pilot basis, will need to meet the criteria and limitations set by MSC and also the criteria set by CGLI for an award-bearing course. These are as follows:

1. The course content needs to be organized in such a way that it may be delivered as an integrated course of approximately 90 hours, or in modular format.
2. The format must be flexible enough to allow for multi-discipline, multi-agency entry, eg personnel and training staff from industry and commerce, further education staff, careers officers, and first-in-line instructors and supervisors.
3. It may be expected that certain modules will be mandatory, eg YTS introduction, but that some course participants, depending on their previous qualifications and experience, will not need to attend the full course of study to be able successfully to complete the course assessment requirements.
4. The assessment procedures must:
   * satisfy CGLI standards
   * be cost effective for both the accredited centres to run and for CGLI to moderate
   * accommodate
      (a) assessment of knowledge and skill for all modules which may be achieved by all course participants, and also
      (b) well qualified and experienced personnel who may be exempted from agreed parts of the course
   * be flexible in regard to the time taken to complete all the modules,
   * measure the ability to organize training in the five YTS core areas, ie
         numeracy and its application
         communication
         problem solving and planning
         manual dexterity
         computer literacy/ information technology
   * test the ability to
      (a) analyse the tasks applicable to a range of occupations in a company/industry
      (b) identify the key skills necessary to perform those tasks

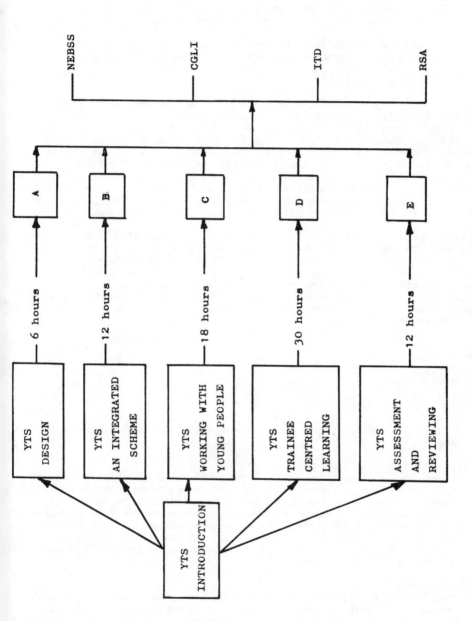

Figure 1   A framework for progression

      (c) relate the core areas to the tasks in the form of practical, work-based training assignments

  5. The content of the syllabus must:
* meet the requirements of MSC
* provide a well balanced course justifying an award from CGLI
* provide a suitable basis for progression to further study (see Figure 1).

Bearing in mind the criteria and limitations stated above, the CGLI offer a total of 21 course objectives plus appropriate assessment procedures as the basis for their award.

THE ACHIEVEMENT CHECKLIST

The achievement checklist which is issued to every candidate who registers for the award is the means of recording a youth trainer's attainment of the objectives of the '924 scheme'. The checklist contains the objectives for the scheme in the same order in which they are presented in the syllabus, but it is stressed that neither the checklist nor the syllabus is intended as a teaching programme. Centres which provide the course are free to organize the objectives into teaching programmes to suit their own and their students' needs.

    The layout of the checklist is also significant in that it should provide a quick reference for course members to check which areas they have covered, are covering, and have yet to cover. The checklist is also intended where possible to be used as a vehicle for negotiation between tutor and course member, and serve both as a 'formative' document and a 'summative' document.

    The achievement checklist layout consists of three columns as shown in Figure 2. In the first column, the course objectives and key objectives for each module are listed. Adjacent to them, in the second column, are listed enabling objectives which help to determine the criteria to be met in achieving the course objectives. The third column entitled 'How achieved', is subdivided into two further columns marked 'Method' and 'Comments'. In the method column, initials should be inserted to show the type of activity undertaken to provide evidence of achievement of the particular module objectives. The sort of activity offered for assessment would be as follows:

	initial
previous activity	PA
course activity	CA
work base activity	WBA
module assignment	MA
course project	CP

Course tutors and assessors are given the following guidelines by way of explanation of the five activities:

  1. previous activity
This is where a candidate has previous experience either of a practical training nature or by virtue of a demonstrated ability whilst attending a previous training event. This experience or training can be clearly seen by the candidate and the tutor to have covered particular '924' objectives. Reference should be made on the checklist to this experience and, where possible, evidence should be examined by the tutor to back up the reference. For example, for objective 21, a candidate has previously produced a range of learning/training events for his/her trainees and has produced the appropriate resources used for the sessions.

  2. course activity
This is where, during the attendance part of the course, the candidate has successfully completed an activity in front of his peers. This activity could cover one or more of the objectives. For example, for objective 6 (integrated scheme), the candidate may be asked to describe to the group, his or her ideas of integration within the YTS.

  3. work based activity
This could be where a candidate operates a successful training session at his own YTS centre. For example, if this session was on communication, this might cover objective

SYLLABUS OBJECTIVE	ENABLING OBJECTIVES	HOW ACHIEVED	
		METHOD	COMMENTS
Key Objective – Demonstrate the ability to design learning opportunities/training assignments appropriate to his/her area of work.			
4. Describe the role of his/her part of the scheme in the integrated provision of training opportunities for young people.	4.1 can explain the integrated nature and arrangement of own scheme provision.		
	4.2 can show the relationship of own training function to other elements in the scheme		
	4.3 can describe own role and place in overall provision		
5. Plan and organise work-based projects within his/her area of work to enable trainees to be effectively occupied in both a vocational and occupational sense.	5.1 can organise a work-based project by breaking down content into a logical sequence and structure		
	5.2 can allocate work-based project content to the six Learning Opportunities.		
	5.3 can demonstrate that she/he is using a wide range of work-based projects in training		
	5.4 can demonstrate how the skills used in a work-based project can be transferred to other contexts		

Figure 2 Achievement checklist – YTS an integrated scheme

7. This sort of work based activity would normally need to be observed by a course tutor from the providing centre. Another example could be where the youth trainer has planned a systematic training programme by the use of task analysis. This could satisfy objective 18. It would be essential for the course tutor to obtain a copy of the programme as evidence of achievement.

4. module assignment

This is where the candidate youth trainer and the '924' course tutor jointly agree on an assignment covering all the objectives of one of the course modules. The modules that could be covered in this way are:

YTS as an integrated scheme
YTS working with young people
YTS assessing and reviewing
YTS trainee centred learning

For example, a module assignment on working with young people may be designed to cover negotiating with a group of young people to identify their needs, ie objective 8. From this negotiation, the trainer could plan and operate a session on communications, which is objective 7. To operate such a communications session, one may use objective 9 which looks at the world of non-employment as a vehicle for communication. This, in turn, may lead to an involvement with objectives 10, 11 and 12 to complete the module assignment. The supervising tutor would need to observe some or all of the discussion/training session with the young people to ascertain that the objectives of the training session had been met.

5. course project

This is where the youth trainer and the course tutor jointly agree on a project covering objectives from more than one module. For example, a youth trainer may negotiate with trainees to identify their training needs, objective 8, which may lead to a need to plan and organize training assignments for the young people to enable them to be effective in both a vocational and occupational sense, objective 5. This may involve the use of assessment methods, objective 14, which, in turn, may lead to the need to demonstrate different communication methods, objective 23.

There can be no definite time guidelines as to how long a module assignment or course project should take as this will depend upon the scope of the assignment itself and the previous experience of the youth trainer. However, as an approximate guide, a module assignment would not normally be expected to take more than one day to complete.

THE '926' EXPERIENCE

The CGLI course no. 926 Instructor-Supervisor Award (Hills,1980) was offered to meet the urgent training needs of instructors and supervisors who were generally skilled craftsmen taken off the unemployment register and amongst whom there is a wide range of technical skills. They had little or no experience of training roles, no pedagogical starting point, little idea of the overall Youth Opportunities Programme (YOP) concept, and needed guidance on the motivation and counselling of the young unemployed.

The scheme was devised on the assumption that the course member would pursue a course attached to an appropriate establishment of further education or other approved centre for approximately 80 hours plus a similar amount of time in related on-the-job practice, at least 10 hours of which was supervised by a course tutor.

The scheme was devised to provide the trainee instructor with competence in five basic areas of skill:

* instructional skill
* communication skill
* caring and guidance skill
* evaluation skill
* job skill

The course assessment in profile form measures the students' achievement in the five areas of skill as listed above and is carried out by the course tutor. The profile is intended to be used as a guide to progress during the course (formative), and as a record of attainment at the end of the course (summative). The intention was to produce a flexible course aimed at taking into account the diverse backgrounds of the course members. These could range from newly qualified graduates to those recently working in a variety of occupations and who were last involved in their own training/education several years ago.

Much experience has been gained by the CGLI and, indeed, by those operating course no. 926. It is deemed worthwhile to make a comparison between the nature of '926' and the emergent '924' course.

It must be stated that '924' is not intended to be a 'beefed-up' course no. 926. However, the range of course members who will eventually benefit from '924' will be very similar to those previously working on the YOP schemes. '926' and its five skill areas has a lot to offer instructors and supervisors in the development of their role and function when working with unemployed young people in a wide variety of settings. There is obviously some strong 'carry-over' from the philosophical underpinning of '926'.

Course no. 926 offered a quite unique opportunity or 'role-led' staff development. With the expertise gained in the five skill areas, the course members were equipped to perform their various roles whatever type of youth programme they worked on. The MSC-directed change of philosophy and curriculum in youth training via the YTS demands that training staff have to undertake additional roles which makes the '924' very much a curriculum-led staff development.

While the principles and process of the value-laden profile assessment worked very well for '926', it has become inappropriate for '924'. The profile relied for its 'formative' use on the 'on-the-job' supervision element of '926'. As this element is not available to the same extent in '924', due to the discrete allocation of funds, alternative methods of assessment and record of achievement become necessary. Obviously, a major influence on the form of '924' has been the role of the accredited centres, particularly with strict control of funds. As previously mentioned, there is a noticeable lack of funds for a significant amount of supervision and coaching at the workplace. Instead of funding up to 10 hours per individual, only two hours funding is available. This has caused the demise of the 'formative' profile found to be so beneficial with '926'.

While YTS includes a wider range of client, now to include industrial training staff, FE staff, careers officers, etc, the main course participants will still be drawn from 'first-in-line' instructors and supervisors. There is a very noticeable lack of take-up of '924' by industrial/commercial trainers (from Mode A sponsors). Although '924' is seen to be a qualification in its own right, there is now a positive move based on an original MSC proposal to make '924' part of 'progressive training'. This is generally welcomed by CGLI and the majority of course members.

The Youth Training Scheme embodies many new concepts to trainers, eg occupational training families, core skills, integration, and occupationally and vocationally based training. These items are included in the main course objectives. To facilitate a better understanding of the '924' objectives, enabling objectives have been prepared which expand on the main course objectives. Whilst it is hoped that these enabling objectives are not prescriptive, it is expected that course tutors will rely heavily on them, particularly during the pilot period (see Figure 2).

ROLE OF THE EDUCATIONAL TECHNOLOGIST

The educational technologist working in a curriculum development team is supporting four main elements:

* establishing educational purposes or goals
* selecting educational experiences that are most likely to lead to goal achievement
* organizing these experiences to make them readily available and deliverable to learners
* determining the extent to which the goals are attained.

More specifically, the educational technologist for course no. 924 was concerned directly with the following:

1   Writing/editing objectives for the course.
2   Identifying problems likely to affect the course operation.

3 Advising on modes of operation.
4 Checking possible sequences of learning experiences.
5 Deciding areas of responsibility.
6 Advising on the role of pilot course assessors.

Whilst a basic systematic approach was used for designing this course, the speed with which it had to be ready for delivery meant cutting many corners. Some of the unsolved difficulties are now beginning to emerge during the pilot period and include the following:

1. Attempting to offer the course on both an integrated and modular basis from the same providing centre.
2. Using a range of experiential learning methods where appropriate with adults who are not familiar with such methods.
3. Adopting a new form of assessment and recording device, ie the achievement checklist (although not ideal it appears to be gaining credibility and may turn out to be the only workable system of assessment and recording of attainment, given the diversity of the course).
4. The general problems of adult learners:
   * requiring sensitive teaching/learning methods
   * having some learning and study difficulties
   * the fears and anxieties of adults returning to learn.
5. Resolving the dilemma of offering a role-led, staff-development requirement through a course that is ostensibly offering curriculum-led staff-development.
6. Managing within the time constraints imposed by the distribution of funds, viz on-the-job supervision at the course member's workplace.

SUMMARY

The take-up of this new course has been gradual. Eventually, all 55 accredited centres will offer training events, either integrated or modular, which will lead to the '924' award. Several hundred course members have been registered with CGLI for the award but relatively few to date have successfully fulfilled all the requirement to gain it. The pilot period is being closely monitored by a team of CGLI Regional Assessors. It is hoped that their feedback will provide sufficient evidence for the '924' course to be adopted and be fully operational by September 1984.

REFERENCES

Hills, J E (1980) Educational technology helps the unemployed. In Winterburn, R and Evans, L (eds) Aspects of Educational Technology XIV. Kogan Page, London.
MSC (1981) A New Training Initiative. Manpower Services Commision, Sheffield.
MSC (1982) Youth Task Group Report. Manpower Services Commision, Sheffield.

APPENDIX

Course Aims

By the end of the prescribed modules, the trainee instructor/supervisor/responsible officer should be able to:
1. Understand the purpose and organization of YTS and its relationship with the three objectives of the New Training Initiative.
2. Understand the concepts of, and methods of training in:
   * basic tranferrable skills
   * core skills
   * occupational training families.
3. Know how to use assessment, recording, and reviewing methods appropriate to YTS trainee's needs.
4. Understand his or her role in integrated on-the-job and off-the-job training or education.

5. Understand his or her role in guidance and support of trainees.
6. Understand his/her role in planning work experience, including induction.
7. Understand his or her responsibilities in the context of the management and administration framework of his or her Scheme.

4.4 Workshop: Towards Industrial Understanding in the Context of Training

H I Ellington
Robert Gordon's Institute of Technology, Aberdeen
J K Sinclair
Association for Educational and Training Technology, Stirling
and B S Alloway
University of Bradford

Abstract: The three presenters in this workshop each have a concern for the greater understanding of industry from the perspectives of activities in schools, designing and utilizing educational packages, and the ways in which young people learn about the industries in which they take up employment. The team were involved in a series of meetings sponsored by AETT during 1983 and have looked at a number of approaches to 'industrial understanding' and the ways in which further developments need to take place. In the climate of economic and industrial change in the United Kingdom, it is especially important to explore as many approaches as possible and the team intended to share their experiences, using case studies, with others of a similar concern.

BACKGROUND

This workshop stemmed from a paper given at ETIC82 (Ellington et al,1983). Following that presentation, it was decided to form an AETT working party to explore possible developments. The three members leading the workshop met several times during 1983 and examined over 20 schemes.

THE PERSPECTIVES

Each member brought his area of concern to the meetings and this led to three perspectives as follows:

Considerations on the educational side

It seems almost axiomatic that teachers need to know about:

* Industry in their area.
* The short-term and long-term employment prospects for school-leavers.
* Patterns of training opportunities.
* The further education provision in their area.

There should ideally be a mechanism to ensure that people from education can regularly meet with people from industry to share ideas and expertise. It is a bonus if teachers have personal experience of work in industry. Teachers should know that resource material is available in a variety of media, should know where to obtain it, and should have opportunities to preview it before including it as an integral part of the teaching programme.

Considerations on the design and utilization of media packages

Included in the work examined were packages/simulations/games on the following themes:

1 The Ekofisk Oil Field resource materials.
2 The Project Scotia competition.
3 The Ile de Performance Management Training exercise.
4 The Dounreay tape-slide programmes.

A significant amount of expertise, time, finance and enthusiasm had evidently gone into these projects, and it became obvious that any future commitments would require similar support resources.

Considerations on training related to changing industrial needs

The relationship between local industry and training needs to be under constant observation, especially in relation to the massive changes in emphasis dictated by world recession, our own economic situation in Britain, the move towards microprocessor technology, and the emergence of very small and very large industrial organisations. Traditional forms of training through apprenticeship have become much less a significant method of preparation for work. New initiatives through such bodies as the Manpower Services Commission need to be understood by all who are concerned with the provision of training. The publicity methods used by a society to present its industrial products, methods and organization influence the degree of understanding of the importance of industry. This understanding is vital for young people who need to make choices on specific training related to meaningful and realistic employment within a community.

DISCUSSION

The workshop attracted some 20 delegates who joined in with a wide-ranging discussion after the three brief presentations. Issues raised included the following:

* Establishing new subjects in schools that aimed at a specific understanding of local industry.
* Using new technologies for the presentation of 'industrial understanding' information.
* The plight of communities where much industry had closed.
* Creating appropriate new training methods for the 1980s.
* A comparison with training approaches in overseas countries.

Following the workshop report presented to the AETT Council, it has been agreed that the working party should continue to examine this area in relation to the significance of educational technology.

REFERENCE

Ellington, H I, Addinall, E and Langton, N H (1983) Forming links between education and industry: how educational technologists can help. In Trott, A et al (eds) <u>Aspects of Educational Technology XVI</u>. Kogan Page, London.

4.5 Organizational Entry/Transitional Training

R L Miller

Human Resources Research Organization, New York

SUMMARY

The process of entry into an organization is quite important since behaviours initially acquired shape subsequent learning and, in fact, often persist unless special circumstances provide for their extinction. Similarly, organizational transition is often a critical process since:

1. The transitioning worker is not a functioning member of a cohesive, supportive social group and thus may be more accepting of information based influence.
2. The acquired expectations which shape future behaviour are the most open to diverse sources.

The replacement of soldiers in the US Army in Europe (USAREUR) is a system which combines both organizational entry and transition. Most soldiers come to USAREUR from a stateside training programme. Thus, the USAREUR assignment is a transition between Army assignments and an entry into the soldier's first operational job.

The purpose of the presentation was to describe the development, implementation, and evaluation of a three stage training programme designed to provide realistic expectations regarding a USAREUR tour, initial in-processing with a minimum of personnel disruption, and adjustment into a functioning military unit.

Initial orientation was designed to take place at two locations – the stateside military installation, and the point of embarkation for USAREUR. Research indicated that the prime time for influencing expectations was immediately after a soldier received orders for USAREUR. Conversely, information was less readily retained when provided at the point of embarkation.

Community Based In-Processing was designed to provide a centralized two week programme which would cover all essential areas prior to the soldier reporting for full-time assignment to his/her job. This system was more effective than the previous method which required half-time work / half-time in-processing during the first month in USAREUR.

Unit entry was significantly enhanced by a system of 'learner controlled' briefings which provided for more active participation on the part of the new assignee. The evaluation of this sub-system indicated that the organizational socialization of the soldier was accomplished more quickly and effectively using this approach.

Section 5:
Professional Training

5.1 Building Experiential Learning into an In-Service Training Course for Middle Managers

H I Ellington and E Addinall

Robert Gordon's Institute of Technology, Aberdeen

Abstract: This paper describes how the authors helped to develop an in-service training course for middle managers working at the Nuclear Power Development Establishment at Dounreay in Scotland (DNPDE) operated by the United Kingdom Atomic Energy Authority (UKAEA). In recent years, DNPDE has been moving towards further consolidation of its longstanding 'corporate management' policy, in which managerial and supervisory staff at all levels are made to feel personally involved in the overall management process. As part of this development, it was decided early in 1983, to run a one-week in-service course for scientific, engineering and management staff working in the 'middle management' layer of the Dounreay hierarchy, who would undertake the course in batches of 16. The main subject areas to be covered in the course were identified and, after this had been done, the authors were asked to help build an element of 'experiential learning' into the course structure. This paper describes how the work was carried out, dealing first with the overall planning of the course and then with the design of the various participative exercises that were incorporated therein. It concludes by describing the first running of the course, which took place in March 1984.

THE ORIGINS OF THE COURSE

DNPDE, which is located several miles west of Thurso on the northernmost coast of the Scottish mainland, is the UKAEA's main fast reactor development centre. It employs over 2,200 people of whom 1,000 are scientific, engineering and administrative staff.

In recent years, DNPDE has been moving towards further consolidation of its longstanding 'corporate management' policy with the aim of making managerial and supervisory staff at all levels feel personally involved in the overall management process. As part of this programme, it was decided early in 1983 to develop a one-week in-service training course for scientific (scientists working at Senior Scientific Officer level), engineering (engineers working at Professional and Technology Officer level 1), and management (administrators working at Senior Executive Officer level) staff working in Dounreay - approximately 160 people. The course, which it was intended would eventually be undertaken by all such staff in batches of 16, would have the following broad aims:

1. To improve two-way communication within the Dounreay management hierarchy.
2. To provide the participants with experience of making management decisions and being accountable for their actions.

would deal with topics like the function and structure of UKAEA, two important 'resources' at Dounreay (money and staff), and the role of management in the operation of the site.

HOW WE BECAME INVOLVED IN THE PLANNING OF THE COURSE

In April 1982, a representative of Dounreay's Fast Reactor Training Centre (FRTC), which was to be responsible for the planning, organization, and operation of the above course, visited us in Aberdeen in order to discuss the course structure. We had previously carried out a considerable amount of consultancy work for the UKAEA in the field of instructional design (Ellington, Addinall and Langton,1982; Ellington and Addinall,1983), and had also run a number of our simulation exercises in earlier FRTC courses. Thus, it was hoped that we would be able to develop a 'custom-built' exercise, based on some aspect(s) of FRTC's work at Dounreay, suitable for incorporation in the course. We agreed to visit Dounreay in June in order to discuss the matter further.

In the course of the subsequent visit, we spent two full days discussing the proposed course with senior members of the staff of FRTC and other members of the DNPDE staff, including staff training representatives from the seven divisions into which Dounreay is divided. We also spoke to the Assistant Director (Engineering and Safety), who was to have overall responsibility for the proposed course. As a result of these discussions, we recommended that the course should be completely re-organized in order to accommodate a whole series of participative exercises, each of which would be designed to complement a specific aspect of the 'conventional lecture' content. This, we felt, would be a much better way of building in a participative element into the course than devoting two days to a single large-scale simulation exercise, as had originally been planned. This suggestion was taken on board by the FRTC, who asked us to produce a revised structure for the course incorporating such exercises.

HOW THE OVERALL PLAN FOR THE COURSE WAS DECIDED

In deciding on the type of participation exercises that should be built into the course, we were greatly helped by the discussions that had taken place with the divisional training representatives during our June visit. At this meeting, which we ran in the form of a structured brainstorming session, we first invited the training representatives to identify the specific skills that they would like to see developed in the course and give us some idea of the relative importance that they attached to those. The resulting list, together with the 'importance' ratings (on a zero to 10 scale) was as follows:

* man-management skills: 10
* decision-making skills: 10
* skills related to the conduct of meetings: 9
* communication skills: 8
* interpersonal skills: 8
* skills related to handling disciplinary problems: 7
* skills related to preparing expenditure proposals: 5

Armed with this list, we then discussed with the training representatives some basic ideas for exercises that would enable these various skills to be developed in simulated situations that the course participants would perceive as being relevant to their job situations at Dounreay. (This was a key consideration, since the training representatives were virtually unanimous in strongly opposing the idea of running a 'conventional' management course. A number of them had attended such courses outside Dounreay and felt that most of what had gone on was largely irrelevant to the somewhat specialized needs of DNPDE staff.) These discussions were extremely useful in clarifying our own ideas as to what was required, and enabled us to produce a provisional list of exercises that appeared to be suitable for use in the course.

The third and final stage in the overall design of the course involved devising a structure that:

1. Incorporated all the lecture content wanted by our FRIC colleagues.
2. Incorporated as many as possible of the exercises that had emerged from our brainstorming session with the staff representatives.
3. Satisfied the contsraints imposed by the overall timetable within which the course would have to be run (the Dounreay working week).
4. Constituted a balanced course with a suitable mixture of passive and participative components.

The final structure that we came up with is shown in Figure 1.

HOW THE INDIVIDUAL EXERCISES WERE DEVELOPED

Once the overall structure of the course had been agreed upon, we were able to start work on the next part of the development work – converting the basic ideas for exercises shown in

Time	Monday	Tuesday	Wednesday	Thursday	Friday
0830	ICEBREAKER (A buzz group session on the course objectives) —0915	LECTURE 4 "The first resource – staff" —0930	EXERCISE 4 (A role-playing simulation exercise based on the handling and conduct of a safety meeting)	EXERCISE 6 (An extended simulated case study involving planning an agreed overall response to an imposed Policy change)	EXERCISE 7 (A series of buzz group sessions based on the handling of different emergency situations)
0915	LECTURE 1 "An overview of the UKAEA; its tasks; its sister organization"	EXERCISE 2 (A simulated case study based on Personnel selection)			
1030	COFFEE	COFFEE	COFFEE	COFFEE	COFFEE
1100	LECTURE 2 "The second resource – money"	EXERCISE 3 (A simulated case study based on the handling of a disciplinary situation)	LECTURE 6 "Administration services"	EXERCISE 6 (continued)	PREPARATION FOR PANEL SESSION (A flexible discussion session)
1215	LUNCH	LUNCH	LUNCH	LUNCH	LUNCH
1315	LECTURE 3 "Using the second resource – practical budget management"	LECTURE 5 "Management as a corporate function"	EXERCISE 5 (A role-playing simulation exercise based on the handling of a crisis situation)	EXERCISE 6 (continued)	PANEL SESSION (A panel discussion session involving senior DNPDE staff)
1430	TEA	TEA	TEA (during meeting)	TEA	TEA
1500	EXERCISE 1 (A simulated case study on the preparation of a capital expenditure proposal)	DISCUSSION (Review of work of course so far)		EXERCISE 6 (continued)	DEBRIEFING SESSION (Discussion of outcomes of course with organisers) —1600 END OF COURSE
1615					

Figure 1 : the overall structure of the DNPDE Middle-Management Training Course

Figure 1 into packages of resource materials that could actually be used to run the exercises in the course. One of our primary design aims was to produce each exercise in the form a completely self-contained self-supportive package so that the course could eventually be run by FRTC staff without our assistance. This made it necessary for us to produce a comprehensive 'organizer's manual' for each exercise in addition to all the various resource materials that would be used by the course participants.

Continuing with our policy of making the maximum possible use of DNPDE staff in developing our ideas for the course, we arranged a second visit to Dounreay in order to hold further discussions. This visit, which took place in August 1983, lasted for a full week, and consisted of a series of interviews with 12 different staff training representatives and specialists in areas such as finance, personnel, health and safety, and contracts and stores. These interviews were interspersed with regular progress meetings and brainstorming sessions with the course organizers. Such was the co-operation we received from everyone that, by the end of the week, we had:

* been able to agree on basic scenarios and structures for all the exercises that were to be incorporated in the course;
* enlisted the help of appropriate area specialists in obtaining the detailed information that we needed in order to write the resource materials for the different exercises;
* enlisted the promised help of several of these specialists in actually running the different exercises (a representative of the Finance Section in running exercise 1; a representative of the Personnel Section in running exercises 2 and 3; and so on).

The actual writing of the exercises was carried out in Aberdeen during the following six months, in close collaboration with our colleagues in Dounreay, and the work was completed in time for the first running of the new course to be held at the end of March 1984, as planned. Details of the various exercises are given below, together with information on how they fit into the overall context of the course.

The 'Icebreaker'

This is a 'buzz group' session in which the participants (working in pairs) draw up lists of their perceived objectives for the course, ranked in order of importance; these are then discussed and collated in a plenary session, the outcome of which is (hopefully) an agreed list of objectives for the course. The 'Icebreaker' has three main functions:

1. To set the scene for the whole course by involving the participants right from the start.
2. To help create an informal atmosphere of co-operation among the participants by getting them to talk to one another.
3. To help the participants to identify their perceived objectives for the course (as opposed to the objectives perceived by the course organizers).

The agreed list of objectives that is generated by the 'Icebreaker' is used as the starting point of the debriefing session at the very end of the course.

Exercise 1

This is designed as a follow-up to Lecture 3, which deals with practical budget management. It gives the participants practical experience of preparing a capital expenditure proposal, and involves writing the investment appraisal (justification of the proposed expenditure in terms of cost effectiveness) that is such an important part of all such proposals. The exercise is built round a simulated scenario that involves making a case for the purchase of a hydraulic hoist system – a scenario that is based on an actual situation that occurred at Dounreay recently. The participants carry out the work in small groups (four in each).

Exercises 2 and 3

Exercise 2 and 3 are both designed as follow-ups to Lecture 4, which deals with the handling of relationships with subordinate staff. Both are built round simulated scenarios that are closely based on the real-life job situations of the course participants. The first involves drawing up a short list of four from 15 applicants for a junior clerical post, the participants again working in groups of four. The second is a 'fishbowl' exercise in which some of the participants act out roles in a scenario that involves handling a typical disciplinary situation, with the remainder observing and then criticizing; the participants work in two groups of eight, each carrying out the same exercise (in different rooms).

Exercise 4

This is a highly-structured role-playing simulation exercise that is designed to give the course participants practical experience of how to conduct themselves at formal meetings. It is built round a realistic scenario based on a typical safety meeting. As in Exercise 3, the participants work in two groups of eight, each carrying out exactly the same exercise. Like all the later exercises in the course, Exercise 4 is not designed as a follow-up to any specific element of the lecture content, but as a general vehicle for achieving the overall aims of the course (development of managerial, decision-making, interpersonal, communication and other skills).

Exercise 5

This is an extended simulation exercise based on the handling of a crisis situation by two teams representing two of the main divisions at Dounreay (those responsible for the operation of Dounreay's prototype fast reactor and those responsible for the reprocessing of fast reactor fuel). The two teams (each of eight people) start the exercise in separate rooms, but are allowed to alter this arrangement later if they wish. The exercise is based on the hypothesis that all supplies of bottled and bulk gases (argon, nitrogen, oxygen etc) are shortly to be cut off due to external industrial action. Since such gases are essential to Dounreay's operations, the participants have to consider the implications of the cut-off and draw up contingency plans - something that requires close inter-divisional collaboration.

Exercise 6

In this, the pivotal exercise in the course, the participants are confronted with another situation that requires close intra- and inter-divisional co-operation. It is built round a scenario in which the participants have to respond to a major policy decision that has implications for all divisions at Dounreay. This is presented to them in the form of a 'memorandum from the Directorate', the object of the exercise being to consider the implications of the memorandum and establish an agreed overall policy for its implementation throughout DNPDE. The exercise starts as a plenary session, but the participants are free to organize their later work in any way that they wish.

Exercise 7

This is, in fact, a series of 'buzz group' exercises in which the participants (working in pairs) have to decide how they would handle different types of emergency situation, each buzz group session being followed by a plenary debriefing session. The exercise is completely flexible and open-ended, with the participants working through as many different scenarios as possible in the time available.

The 'Panel Session'

This is a conventional panel session in which the participants have the opportunity to discuss with senior members of staff any matters that interest or concern them (the course, their work situations, the general situation at Dounreay, the role of the UKAEA etc).

The 'Debriefing Session

This is intended to round off the course by re-examining the list of agreed objectives generated by the opening 'Icebreaker' session and discussing the extent to which the participants feel that these have been achieved. It also gives the participants an ooportunity to suggest ways in which the course could be improved.

HOW THE COURSE WAS RUN

The first running of the new course took place from March 26th to 30th 1984 in the FRTC at Dounreay. As planned, we played a major role in the running of the course, acting as organizers of all the participant exercises. This served the double function of:

1. Enabling us to field trial the exercises that we had written in the actual situation in which they were to be used.
2. Enabling the FRTC staff who were to run the exercises in later courses to see how this should be done.

In the event, the course proved extremely successful and no major design flaws in any of the exercises were revealed. Thus, after the inevitable fine tuning and minor alterations have been carried out, it is planned to run it with further groups of middle managers at regular intervals over the next few years, as originally envisaged.

CONCLUSION

One of the recurrent themes at recent ETIC conferences has been the need for meaningful and constructive collaboration between education and industry. At ETIC82, we presented a general case for collaboration of this type, arguing that educational technologists working in the higher education sector are particularly well placed to play an important role in forging such links (Ellington and Addinall,1983). Last year, we described a specific example of collaboration of this type, showing how we had been able to help develop a distance learning course for use with offshore oil personnel (Ellington, Addinall and Blood,1984). The present paper describes a further example of such collaboration, and also demonstrates how standard group learning techniques can be adapted for use in industrial training situations. Thus, we again hope that it will prove of interest to colleagues on both sides of the education/industry 'divide'.

REFERENCES

Ellington, H I, Addinall, E and Langton, N H L (1982) How technologicall-based simulation exercises can be used in management training. In Gray, L and Waitt, I (eds) Perspectives on Academic Gaming and Simulation 7. Kogan Page, London.
Ellington, H I and Addinall, E (1983) Forming links between education and industry – how educationeˉ technologists can help. In Trott, A, Strongman, H and Giddons, L (eds) Aspects of Educational Technology XVI. Kogan Page, London.
Ellington, H I, Addinall, E and Blood, J (1984) Providing extension training for offshore personnel – an educational technology-based approach. In Shaw, K (ed) Aspects of Educational Technology XVII. Kogan Page, London.

5.2 The Development of a Computer-Based Training Project within the Staff Training Branch of the Manpower Services Commission

A S Henney and D E Timms
Manpower Services Commission, Sheffield

Abstract: During the past two years, the Staff Training Branch of the Manpower Services Commission has been engaged in a project in computer based training. This paper describes the project, including its organization, topics chosen for computer based presentation, and the way in which the packages have been evaluated. The paper ends with a section showing how the project has acted as a base for further developments.

INTRODUCTION

The Manpower Services Commission (MSC) is the organization within the Civil Service whose task it is to provide a national training and employment service. It employs just over 20,000 people, most of whom work in the regions. Its head office is in Sheffield.

The Staff Training Branch of the MSC is also based in Sheffield at Ranmoor Hall. Its function is to ensure that all the people who work within the MSC are properly trained to carry out their duties. Staff at management level are trained at Ranmoor Hall while clerical staff are trained within their own regions. There are nine such regions, each of which covers a wide geographical area as is indicated by their titles, for example Scotland, or Wales and the South West.

Computer based training (CBT) is of great interest to the MSC's Staff Training Branch since it seems to offer a number of potential advantages. In particular, staff should be able to learn subjects at the time required at an office near their home; they should be able to go through the training at their own pace and learn relatively quickly.

This potential was examined about three years ago in a small study which was aimed at training staff to carry out cashier duties. The CBT package was tested on a group of 10 people. Some learning gain was shown and this method of providing training proved acceptable to the staff using it.

It was then decided to carry out a more broadly based project using more packages and more microcomputers over a wide geographical area. Thus the Midlands CBT project, known as MIDCAL, was developed. This was formally launched in June 1982.

ORGANIZATION

The day-to-day work of the project is carried out centrally at Ranmoor Hall by a group of three - the project manager whose main role is that of co-ordinator, and two others whose tasks include courseware design and programming. Some of the courseware design has also been carried out by trainers in the Midlands. Their designs have usually been programmed at Ranmoor Hall, but some staff in the regions have also acquired programming skills and are able to produce complete packages in the Midlands. However, irrespective of the place in which the package has been produced, efforts are made to ensure that all of them meet explicit standards of presentation and documentation.

The central team operates by reporting to a National Steering Group which meets quarterly. It also works in co-ordination with a small regional working group and, through this, with the regional staff trainers.

TECHNICAL BACKGROUND

The CBT material is presented through microcomputers. These consist of a central processor with VDU (Commodore PET 8032), a disk drive (8050), and a line printer (4022P). The microcomputer has 32k of random access memory (RAM), and the VDU has an 80 column screen. This particular equipment was chosen not so much because it was ideal for CBT but because it was widely used within the Civil Service so that when and if the project came to an end, the equipment would find a ready use elsewhere.

In fact, the equipment has proved quite satisfactory for the task. It does not display colour (except that the VDU shows characters in green on black or vice versa), and the graphics are rudimentary. On the other hand, the courses developed require neither colour nor advanced graphics so that this potential disadvantage is unimportant.

In order to make the packages available to as many staff as possible, 14 of the microcomputers have been placed in the Midlands area at MSC offices in the larger towns such as Birmingham, Coventry, Leicester and Nottingham. At each of the offices, a member of staff has responsibility for setting up the machine when somebody wants to use it, and for the general administration attached to the running of the project.

The programming language originally used for the project was BASIC. However, it was soon found that this language was inadequate as a means for developing CBT programs. CBT requires a language which readily handles text, examines user input, and manipulates characters on the VDU. BASIC cannot easily do these things and so it was time consuming and therefore expensive to use. Instead, the project adopted PILOT, a high level language related to BASIC but which possesses the necessary text matching and file handling capabilities. The particular form of PILOT used is MSCPILOT. This is an adaptation to make it easier to use by those programming and to provide options (including certain printing facilities) which make the courses more interesting and effective for the students.

CHOICE OF SUBJECT

During the project, the choice of subject to be converted into a CBT package has been to a large extent a compromise. It was recognized that one of the advantages of CBT over other forms of non-tutorial learning was that it could be interactive. In this way, a student could be made to think about his or her responses and the program would respond to the particular typed input by branching into different parts. If the student chose correct responses in a multiple-choice situation or typed in appropriate sentences in a constructed response mode, then the program could move forward quickly. If he or she experienced difficulty with the material, then the program would move down remedial paths or include extra sections. It was considered that material which offered little scope for interaction (ie which was simply page-turning - presenting text with few questions) was not really using the computer to its best advantage.

The other side of the situation was that the region, through the staff trainers, had certain priorities about the subjects which should be covered. It was decided by the Steering Group that the most immediate priority was to involve the trainers in what they saw as a regional training need which could be ameliorated by CBT. Thus, because of this priority, and because of the inexperience of the people involved as to what could be considered suitable material, some of the earlier programs involved more text presentation, and less interaction, than was later considered desirable.

The project has now been running for almost two years. During that time, 16 packages have been produced. These cover a wide range of tasks. Many are about clerical topics, since it is with these that regional staff trainers are mainly concerned. Other packages cover such areas as taking job vacancies by telephone from an employer, drawing up statistical tables, and staff assessment. Two action mazes have been developed, which exercise managers' skills in supervising staff and in delegating responsibility.

EVALUATION OF PACKAGES

In evaluating the packages, two main issues have been addressed - the extent to which they result in a learning gain, and the extent to which they are acceptable to staff.

The learning aspect has been approached by producing, for some of the earlier packages, pre- and post-course tests and comparing the results. In the case of one package (the taking of reports of vacancies by telephone), it also proved possible to organize a control group. The results of such testing demonstrated a satisfactory learning gain.

The investigation of the acceptability to staff of CBT has included the use of structured interviewing and informal discussion. However, staff views have been gathered mainly by questionnaire. The first questionnaires completed by staff were on paper but these are now presented by VDU at the end of each course by requiring the student to type in responses.

The views of four groups have been gathered – the students themselves, supervisors, managers, and staff trainers. Students clearly like CBT as a method and, in particular, its ability to adapt to their own need for pace of presentation and revision. They also believe that the training has benefited them. This does not necessarily mean that they would all like to see it take over other forms of training. Some see it as a supplement to desk training from colleagues or training from tutors, particularly when they want deeper information on specific details.

Staff trainers also regard it as a useful technique. They continue to suggest topics for development as computer based courses. In those cases where a CBT course covers the same ground as a tutorial course and where it can handle the numbers involved, the original conventional course has been cancelled. Supervisors consider CBT courses to be reasonably effective. Regional managers continue to press for further subjects to be covered by computer methods.

FUTURE DEVELOPMENTS

The project has demonstrated that CBT has a useful role to play in the delivery of staff training within the MSC. There are two main ways in which its contribution will shortly be enhanced.

Firstly, it is hoped that the improvement in authoring languages (particularly in frame generators such as Microtext), will mean that staff trainers themselves will be able to develop CBT materials without having to turn to other specialists. Consequently computer-based materials might be developed in an immediate and flexible way to suit a specific training need.

Secondly, it is planned to establish a number of learning resource centres, each of which will contain microcomputers as well as other forms of equipment and instructional material. Initially, it is planned to establish one in each of three regions. If they prove successful, the other six regions will also be given such a facility. These will be integrated within the regional staff training operation and, while they will not exist exclusively to promote CBT, they will be able to provide computer based courses such as are appropriate.

5.3 NUMINE for Nurses

P Pleasance
Charles Frears School of Nursing, Leicester

Abstract: Generally speaking, nurse education has not been an enthusiastic receiver of the products of educational technology. Despite the papers presented at past ETIC conferences, the overall uptake of good, high-quality, educational technology has proved disappointingly low. Probably every one of the 187 schools of nursing in England and Wales now possesses its own sophisticated audio-visual hardware, but generally promise has been far ahead of progress. With the advent of the computer revolution, small desk-top microcomputers are appearing in the schools of nursing. Purchased from non-recurrent sources of funding, these are being enthusiastically used for a multitude of tasks in an ad hoc and unguided way. In 1982, the International Medical Informatics Association held a two-day International Working Conference (followed by a week's closed workshop), focussing on 'the impact of computers on nursing'. Prior to this event, staff from the National Health Service (NHS) Learning Resources Unit in Sheffield and the Nightingale School of Nursing in London had independently suggested the formation of a user-group to support this new enthusiasm, and NUMINE, the Network of Users of Microcomputers in Nurse Education, was launched in September 1982. Having a current membership of 180, NUMINE is the only peer-group which caters solely for nurse education. This paper discusses its formation, activities and future hopes as well as providing a view of nursing's present knowledge about computer-assisted learning. It will also identify major areas of difficulty and suggest ways in which these can be overcome.

INTRODUCTION

Much of what is reported here will not be new to the world of education in general, but it is innovative and in some ways revolutionary when it is applied to the education and training of nurses. Some of the comments in this paper may sound like criticism of fellow nurse tutors. This is not intended; neither is it supposed in any way to sound like a grousing session. However it is apparent that in many ways we face an uphill struggle if we are to achieve our ultimate objective - that is to see computer assisted learning included in the curriculum of the school of nursing.

It may be of value to provide some background information about nurse training. There are at present two grades of qualification - the Enrolled and the Registered Nurse. The course for Enrolment takes two years to complete, that for Registration three years. The training is shared between theoretical study blocks within the school or college of nursing, alternating with ward allocations where the practical nursing skills are gained. The Registered Nurse will thus have spent some 26 weeks (six months) of her three-year training in the school of nursing divided into one- or two-week blocks interspersed throughout the course.

The past five or so years have seen many changes in the curriculum of nurse education. There is a move away from what may be called the medical or disease oriented model, towards the patient centred/patient's problem approach. This seemingly irrelevant point may well prove to be one of the main reasons why CAL will find a vital role within the programme. Namely that, because of the ethical/moral issues associated with experimentation - ie 'What happens to the patient if I don't carry out this piece of nursing care, or if I do this instead of that?' - it is very difficult for some nurse learners to be innovative or research oriented in their thoughts about nursing practice. As yet computer simulations of patients on which the nurse can 'try out' her ideas appear to be the only real way of developing these skills. Huckabay et al(1979) showed in their research that student nurses taught by patient simulation models were able to transfer their learning to the clinical setting significantly better than students not taught by CAL. Murray et al(1978) argued the same effect in their work with medical undergraduates. Use of this technology also overcomes the problem of the varying experiences that students may receive during their ward allocations. Meadows (1977) states: 'Computer simulations...put into every student's hand, the same quality experience.'

Nurse tutors, working within the school of nursing are responsible for the implementation of the syllabuses for nurse training. Each school of nursing has relative autonomy in the way the curriculum is developed (although approval of these schemes is obtained from the statutory bodies which control nursing). A nurse tutor is firstly a qualified registered nurse who has gained a sufficiently wide experience of clinical practice. After achieving 'evidence of further study' such as the Diploma of Nursing, they may apply to one of the polytechnics or universities that run Certificate of Education (or equivalent) courses which have been approved as acceptable to allow registration as a nurse tutor with the United Kingdom Central Council for Nurses, Midwives and Health Visitors. It is interesting to note that in 1983 it was reported that throughout the United Kingdom there were some 1,900 vacancies for nurse teachers if the desired teacher/student ratio were to be achieved. In addition to this a letter dated 15 March 1984 from the Chief Executive of the English National Board stated that as of the summer of 1984 there would be a 25 per cent reduction in the funds available to support entrants to full-time tutor training courses. (Details of these cuts are available at the time or writing.) It is not implied that an even greater lack of tutors is an excuse to use computers in their place. These facts point to two rather disturbing areas:

1. Since the reductions are due to financial cutbacks, it is likely to mean that funds will be even more difficult to find for the purchase of hardware and software.
2. It is likely that tutors already in post will have less and less time to develop this new area of the curriculum.

THE BIRTH OF NUMINE

Nursing in the UK may have been aware of the potential of the computer as a professional practical tool for some years now, but it has only been in the past three years that it has been aware of this potential in educational terms.

Early in 1982 several articles about computers started to appear in the nursing press. This in itself demonstrated the rising interest. Staff from the NHS Learning Resources Unit in Sheffield and the Nightingale School of Nursing in London independently suggested the formation of a user group to support this new enthusiasm. Part of the remit of the NHS Learning Resources Unit (NHSLRU) when it was set up in 1972/3 by the Department of Health, was to encourage the use of all aspects of educational technology in nursing, and Mr Ian Townsend was by this time concentrating on the new microtechnology.

Out of suggestions from both these sources, NUMINE held its inaugural meeting in October 1982 at which the following main aims were defined:

1. To provide constant interchange of information amongst the membership on current developmental work, and established methods and techniques.
2. To make available to others, information shared between members.
3. To encourage exchange between members and colleagues in other countries.
4. To maintain an up to date position vis a vis CAL by holding regional meetings and conferences; and reporting these either in a quarterly newsletter or an occasional paper.
5. To evaluate current and future software.
6. To act as an informed, specialist pressure group.

Since that time, membership of the network has increased rapidly. Bi-monthly meetings are held at various centres around the country. These meetings range from opportunities to simply meet and freely swap ideas, to more structured sessions featuring talks from leading lights in the movement. One particularly memorable such occasion was held here at Bradford University where Professor Stonier was the main speaker. Several contributions have also been made during this time to the nursing press (Pleasance et al,1983; Norman and Townsend,1983a,1983b,1983c,1983d).

WHY NUMINE?

NUMINE is doing a much needed job; with a total membership (March 1984) of over 200, its members are involved in the few major nurse education computer initiatives that have been sponsored. It was considered that another way of achieving our aims was to perform an analysis of our active membership of 150. Thus in the survey which was recently completed, the following picture emerged:

* 77 per cent have access to a computer either at home or at work.
* 45 per cent have their own computer at home. Of these, the most popular models are:
  BBC Model B (17%)
  Sinclair - both ZX81s and Spectrums (20%)
  Commodore - both VIC 20s and 64s (4%)

The most popular language used is BASIC (53 per cent) with others scoring very low. Of the schools of nursing represented by our membership, 60 per cent did have a computer. These are mainly Commodore Machines (17 per cent) and BBC Model B (19 per cent). The remainder cover a broad spectrum with various machines being represented in small numbers.

Only a relatively small proportion of the use of these computers lies on the administrative side of education eg the allocation of learners to the appropriate wards (15 per cent), record-keeping (14 per cent) and word processing (7 per cent). Other uses are given as indexing/filing systems (library or audiovisual aids), CAL, and the storage and retrieval of multiple choice objective test items used in the assessment of learners.

It was surprising that many schools did possess quite sophisticated equipment in terms of a full range of peripheral hardware. However the picture that emerges is one of under-utilization. The following answers were obtained to the question 'What do you intend to use your equipment for?': 25 per cent of the users intend to develop CAL programs; another 13 per cent are looking to using the computer for the manipulation of MCQ data; another 4 per cent (each) want to use it for word processing, allocations and general record keeping. The main reason given for possessing the computer is using, or developing CAL (27 per cent). Unfortunately however, the fact remains that many members do not truly understand the significance of what this entails - a subject which will be addressed later in this paper.

No member of NUMINE has received professional training in computer related subjects (other than very short courses), although many are exploring the possibilities of undertaking long-term, part-time courses of study of their own volition.

FUTURE DEVELOPMENTS

As to future developments, NUMINE is now actively involved in various projects aimed at furthering the cause of CAL in nurse education:

1. A central Software Library has just been set up at the Charles Frears School of Nursing, Leicester. There are now various individuals and one or two commercial organizations starting to produce CAL packages. By maintaining this library, it will be possible to monitor the quality of the sofware that comes onto the market. It is also envisaged that any person who is involved in nurse education could borrow programs in order to carry out their own evaluation so as to ensure that it fulfils their particular need before making any commitment. A regularly updated catalogue of the library stock will be issued with NUMINE Notes, giving details both of program content and machine application (Pleasance, 1984).

2. Evaluation. As and when programs are produced, NUMINE will publish an evaluation. Secondly, within this category, a large number of book publishers have been, and are being contacted. Our request is that any texts that are relevant to our field be made available for review and, if possible, held in a lending library for the use of members.

3. In addition to the previously mentioned regular meetings, the King Edward's Hospital Fund for London (King's Fund) are organizing a one day conference on our behalf entitled 'Using Computers - The Next Step'. It is considered by NUMINE that, in this venture, we have an opportunity to be heard by a wider and perhaps more influential audience than ever before. A varied and stimulating programme of very eminent speakers has been arranged and the occasion is awaited with eager anticipation.

4. Preliminary negotiations are taking place at the present time with a company which

has developed an authoring system dedicated to educational software development. The hope is that if nurse tutors can utilize such a system, then the first truly valid nursing courseware in this country may be produced.

5. NUMINE, through its assosciation with the NHS Learning Resources Unit has been able to be of assistance as a source of information to the Nurses Computer Liason Group set up by the chief area nursing officers in Scotland. This group recommended to the Scottish National Board that a joint project between nurse teachers and the Scottish Microelectronics Development Project (SMDP), be commisioned to:

*   Develop and distribute sound, well documented software for use, initially in several project centres, but eventually nationally.
*   Standardize purchase of hardware and promote computer awareness in colleges of nursing.
*   Evaluate and test the outcome of CAL in nurse education.

The exciting news is that the Board accepted these recommendations and is now setting up the project. NUMINE watches on with more than a little interest, and the prayer that on this occasion at least, the authorities in England will not allow our colleagues north of the border to get too far ahead.

PROBLEMS AND DIFFICULTIES

Generally speaking, nurse education has not been an enthusiastic receiver of the products of educational technology. Despite the papers presented at the past ETIC conferences, the overall uptake of good, high quality educational technology has been disappointingly low. There are schools of nursing that still possess Bristol Tutors (lying unused and forgotten in a small corner of the library); nevertheless many schools possess linear printed programmed texts - and use them frequently. Probably every one of the 187 schools of nursing in England and Wales now has its own fairly sophisticated audiovisual hardware, but all in all, promise has been far ahead of progress.

Centralized guidance and advice is still awaited. Such august bodies as the NHS Computer Policy Committee and the Health Services Information Steering Group have yet to address the question of education in the NHS, especially where nurses are concerned. The DHSS and the statutory bodies controlling nursing, likewise have given no real direction. The director of nurse education in each school of nursing is entitled to make an independent selection of audiovisual hardware, but what is likely to happen where computers are concerned is that, either every centre will end up with its own system (probably incompatible with other schools in the region) or whilst awaiting a definite decision, nursing will once again miss the boat, and will end up with nothing.

There is then the problem of who is going to write the software. There appears to be inadequate funding for outside, commercial programmers, and the possibility of full-time nurse tutors undertaking the role is fraught with difficulties. There is just not the time available for them to write the kind of software that is most effective and useful - that is patient simulation. Simple programmed learning and page-turning programs are easy to write, but unfortunately of limited value: in most cases a book, or even a lecture would do it just as well. The argument that 'something is better than nothing' lacks substance when viewed from the angle that unless the quality is good, then not only will it not be used once the novelty has worn off, but the reputation of CAL as a whole will suffer, and the computer will disappear as a teaching tool in nurse education. Frenzel (1980), as well as many others, identified the situation well in relation to general education.

Because of the relative newness of the subject, not many of the courses for the preparation of nurse teachers can give their students an in-depth appreciation of and training in the techniques of CAL. To date (apart from the efforts of NUMINE) there have been few imperatives at national level to support the in-service education of tutorial staff in this subject. Following the impetus derived from a conference in 1982 entitled 'The Impact of Computers on Nursing', the DHSS hosted a number of short seminars on CBT-related sujects, but not specifically for nurse educators. In the 18 months since then, there has been no concerted support for in-service education, apart, that is, from the bi-monthly meetings hosted by NUMINE members for interested parties.

SUMMARY

It is very difficult to sum up the long term aims of NUMINE without referring back to the objectives of the Scottish Joint Project mentioned earlier. There will have to be some central initiative and guidance in England so that it will be possible to:

* Develop and distribute sound, well documented software
* Standardize hardware purchases
* Evaluate and test the outcome of CAL in nurse education.

It may sound, having read this paper, that there prevails an aura of gloom and despondency. This is not the case. There is a great deal of interest and even enthusiasm amongst a very large number of nurse teachers. NUMINE is doing all that it can to support this enthusiasm, and to channel it in the most appropriate direction.

What is a cause for concern is the fact that up to now, no software of the quality that is sought, has appeared on the market. Until this happens it may prove difficult to maintain the impetus that has so far been achieved. Also until that software appears, it is impossible to test out the theories on the person who matters most - the student; and finally, there is a great need to carry out thorough empirical research in order to attempt to prove what NUMINE believes - that there is a place for the computer in the curriculum of nurse training.

When that program arrives, NUMINE will be waiting for it....

REFERENCES

Frenzel, L (1980) The personal computer - last chance for CAI. Byte, July, pp86-96.

Huckabay, L M D, Anderson, N and Holn, D M (1979) Cognitive, affective, and transfer of learning consequences of CAI. Nursing Research, 28, 4, pp228-233.

Meadows, L S (1977) Nursing education in crisis: a computer alternative. Journal of Nursing Education, 16, 5, pp13-21

Murray, T S, Barber, J H, and Dunn W R (1978) Attitudes of medical undergraduates to CAL. Medical Education, 12, pp6-9.

Norman, S and Townsend, I (1983a) COMPUTERS 2: introducing CAL. Nursing Mirror, 156, 6, pp40-41.

Norman, S and Townsend, I (1983b) COMPUTERS 3: looking for CAL and the model. Nursing Mirror, 156, 7, pp23-24.

Norman, S and Townsend, I (1983c) COMPUTERS 4: priority is the keyword. Nursing Mirror, 156, 8, pp36-38.

Norman, S and Townsend, I (1983) Computers in the curriculum. Nursing Times, 79, 39, pp12-14.

Olivier, P and Sweeney, M A (1980) Evaluation of clinical learning by computer. Nurse Educator, 5, 4, pp26-31.

Pleasance, P I (1984) NUMINE software library. In Townsend, I (ed) NUMINE Notes for January - March 1984. NHSLRU-NUMINE, Sheffield.

Pleasance, P I, Norman, S and Townsend, I (1983) COMPUTERS 1: learning with CAL and PLATO. Nursing Mirror, 156, 5, pp36-38.

Townsend, I (1983) News from Scotland. In Townsend I (ed) NUMINE Notes for September-December 1983. NHSLRU-NUMINE, Sheffield.

5.4 The Justification for CBT in the Provident Financial Group PLC

A Roebuck

Provident Financial Group PLC, Bradford

Abstract: Provident's training organization, like many others, has the problem of providing a wide range of training services from a limited budget. This paper looks at the justification for CBT within a general training context in a climate of reducing overheads and ever increasing need for efficiency. It will concentrate on the factors which enable CBT to provide an ever increasing proportion of the direct training effort. The initial commitment section shows how pilot activity commenced in the organization. It looks at the level of involvement, the aims, and the resourcing in terms of manpower and equipment required. The returns to date attempt to quantify the successes and failures over the last five years and how these are constructively used as arguments for and against the wider adoption of facilities and the development of training materials. In the light of experience, it is possible to outline general guidelines which are now being adopted within the organization to aid in the development and use of CBT, the investment required, and the organization and the people involved.

THE INITIAL COMMITMENT

Table 1 shows the build-up over seven years of CBT resources. The year 1982 was atypical due to parallel activities involved in converting from on-line terminals to microcomputers. See Appendices 1 - 5 for examples of branch staff training over this period.

year	staff	VDU	cost x £1000	% budget
1977	1	1	7	–
1978	2	2	11	–
1979	3	3	22	4
1980	5	5	38	8
1981	5	5	43	9
1982	5	12	80	16 (conversion)
1983	5	10	60	12
1984	7	24	90	13

Table 1 . The initial commitment of Provident Financial Group PLC to CBT

THE RETURNS TO DATE

The initial argument for CBT was based on the nationwide adoption of a computer network. This computer network evolved over a number of sizeable pilot activities which were eventually curtailed leaving the CBT element with little factual evidence of its true validity. A similar situation arose with pilot EPR (Enhanced Payment Records). This system has, however, been adopted by one company in the group and CBT has played an extremely effective role in all branch staff training.

The successes are sufficiently evident in terms of accurate form filling (customer debt

insurance and keyboard training.   ABM (assistant branch manager) induction is an
administration and assessment programme moving from a successful pilot to nationwide
adoption and pointing the way forward for CBT in the group. It is used to reduce the
involvement of branch or area managers in producing competent new assistant branch
managers (see Appendix 6). Recruitment is a contentious area but the CBT activity is
expected to save a great deal of staff time and improve staff competency (Treece,1985).

DEVELOPMENT IN THE LIGHT OF EXPERIENCE

Several tools have been produced to help with deciding on the validity of CBT as a solution to
a specific training problem (Appendix 7). If development is justified, can objectives be set
and achieved by using CBT (Appendix 8)? If we can design and present the training, then
certain management/administrative facilities are required, eg delegate session report
(Appendix 9).

REFERENCE

Treece, G (1985) Computer-based training: a management tool. In Mills, G M and
        Alloway, B S (eds) Aspects of Educational Technology XVIII. Kogan Page, London.

APPENDIX 1

Mentor Lessons for June 1981

from Field Personnel and Training Officer /Branch premises:

LESSON NAME	FOR	NO. OF STUDENTS
Use of System 80 Information	Branch Staff	12
Disciplinary Interview: Case Study	Branch Staff	17
Consumer Credit Act	Branch Staff	2
Sales Techniques Revision	Branch Staff	13
Employment Legislation (1)	Branch Staff	24
Employment Legislation (2)	Branch Staff	7
Sales Techniques Case Study	Branch Staff	1
Training Agents in Sales Techniques	Branch Staff	9
Introduction to Provident Fin Group	Branch Staff	21
from Unicredit, Metrochange House		
Use of the Credit Scoring System (1)	Unicredit Staff	16
Use of the Credit Scoring System (2)	Unicredit Staff	16
from PMSL, Mixenden		
Key Operation – Numeric	Key Operators	2
Key Operation – Alpha	Key Operators	2
from Training Centre, St. Blaise House		
Introduction to Computers (1)	Group Staff	3
Introduction to Computers (2)	Group Staff	3
Sales Techniques Revision	Group Staff	2
Sales Techniques Case Study	Group Staff	2
TP80 Management Information	Group Staff	1
TP80 Management Inf Case Study	Group Staff	1

APPENDIX 2

Mentor one-day courses for groups of four staff (30 November to 9 December 1982)

Timetable

9.00am	Group leader attends Area Office to link up the 'Terminal' under instruction from Mr Paul Curzon (Medway West).
9.30am	Branch Manager only: LESSON ELI – Employment legislation on dismissal: Time approximately 60 min.
10.30am	Remainder of the group arrive. 1st lesson – CDISYS – Maintenance of an effective debt insurance branch control system: Time approximately 30 min. 2nd lesson – CDIP – Procedures for handling customer debt insurance claims, including a case study: Time approximately 75 min.
12.30pm	Lunch
1.30pm	Group participation: 3rd lesson – CONSUME – Standards and practice of 'the Consumer Credit Act': Time approximately 30 min. 4th lesson – TRAG – Introduction to the training of agents in sales. Time approximately 30 min.
2.30pm	Group discussion, attended if possible by Mr. W Choufot – FPTO. Time approximately 1 hour.
3.30pm	Branch Manager only: LESSON – JOEB – Management decision making. Time span from 5 to 45 min.

The attending Branch Manager will be the group leader and he should encourage each member of his group to take turns at operating the keyboard.

APPENDIX 3

Memo from	F W Forfar FPTO	
to	A S Roebuck, MENTOR manager	Date 12 October 1982

Subject: MENTOR

The following is report on MENTOR for the month of September.
Total number of delegates 30. Total number of lessons 75.
Breakdown of lessons:

PROVFG	5	CDIP	2
ABMINTRO	5	CDISYS	3
CONSUME	4	PHONE	4
TIME	14	SELFASSESSMENT	9
JOEB	10	INTERVIEW	1
TRAG	9	ELI	2
STREV	5	P.A.C.	2

No serious breakdowns except Wednesday, 23rd September due to major failure at Mixenden. MENTOR system was ver well received by all concerned and recognized as having an important role to play in future training plans.
MENTOR proved to be very portable. The system was operated from 10 different locations, covering an area of approximately 200 miles, and was used on most occasions without any back-up telephones. PMSL, Mr John Walsh in particular, proved very useful and helpful during sign-on and in solving any minor problems.
Overall a very successful month, giving wide coverage to staff.
Roll on March 1983....HAVE MENTOR....WILL TRAVEL

APPENDIX 4

Memo from	W F Chouffot	
to	R Aylett	Date: 7 January 1983

Subject: MENTOR use 1 Nov to 9 Dec 1982

Having set out to create as much student coverage as possible with travel being kept to a minimum, I am satisfied that with prior planning this was achieved.

However, at the end of an exercise like this, I am left wondering if the cost factor is commensurate with the benefits, such as more/ better informed/ educated staff, things which are hard to quantify. Certainly in terms of a PR job, then visibly/conversationally this MENTOR schedule has been a resounding success.

MENTOR SCHEDULE ANALYSIS

LESSON	TIMES USED	TIME – HOURS
TIME	7	$5\frac{1}{4}$
BE4	4	$4\frac{1}{2}$
JOEB	11	$8\frac{1}{4}$
BE2	1	1
EL1	9	$9\frac{3}{4}$
EL2	3	3
CDISYS	12	$7\frac{3}{4}$
TRAG	12	$7\frac{1}{2}$
CDIP	11	10
CONSUME	9	$5\frac{1}{2}$
BE3	1	1
total	$\overline{80}$	$\overline{63\frac{1}{2}}$

The total number of students was 49.
Time lost (through line failure faults) was approximately 3 hours.

APPENDIX 5

MENTOR programme Areas 18 & 19 Jan – Feb 1983

PROGRAMME		students	PLANNED USAGE lessons	time (hours)
Jan				
10/11	Londonderry West	6	14	$7\frac{1}{4}$
12/13	Londonderry North	5	13	$6\frac{3}{4}$
14/17	Waterside	5	11	$5\frac{3}{4}$
18/19	Coleraine	3	9	$4\frac{3}{4}$
20/21	Ballymena	5	13	$6\frac{3}{4}$
24/25	Craigavon	6	14	$7\frac{1}{4}$
26/27	Belfast North	7	15	$8\frac{1}{2}$
28/31	Belfast South	7	15	$8\frac{1}{2}$
Feb				
1/2	Belfast West	7	15	$7\frac{1}{4}$
3/4	Carrickfergus	6	14	$7\frac{1}{2}$
7/8	Lisburn	4	10	$5\frac{1}{4}$
9/10	Newtonwards	7	15	$7\frac{1}{2}$
		$\overline{68}$	$\overline{158}$	$\overline{83}$

APPENDIX 6

PROVIDENT FINANCIAL GROUP PLC   TRAINEE CENTRED LEARNING

The aim of this paper is to show how trainee–centred learning has been used by the Provident Group as a means of helping to solve the problem of training in small, dispersed units and relieve the branch mangers of the necessity of spending an increasing amount of time on training.
Prepared by the Provident Group Training Department.

1.   The Need for Trainee-Centred Learning

Due to the increasing day-to-day pressures of a rapidly growing business in recent years, branch managers have felt that they did not have enough time to train staff properly – particularly new employees. Because a manager could not devote enough time to staff training, he spent too much of his time correcting their mistakes which left him less time to devote to staff training. Because he could not devote enough time to staff training ....

2.   The Induction Training Programme

To break the never-ending circle, and to improve the effectiveness of induction training without overloading the branch manager, a trainee-centred learning package was developed. The result is a self-pacing Induction Training Programme which takes two to four weeks to complete depending on the trainee.

(a) System

The Training Programme is based on a system of do-it-yourself learning. During the training period, the manager gives the trainee a series of assignments, each of which is designed to help him find out information for himself with a minimum of supervision. Before carrying out an assignment the trainee is briefed by the manager as to the requirements of that assignment and, on completion, the trainee is de-briefed by the manager to discuss the implications of what has been learned and answer any queries. The notes made by the trainee whilst carrying out an assignment are filed in the training binder.

(b) Training Methods

The overall training method places a large emphasis on the trainee learning by doing in order to achieve specific objectives. Each assignment is broken down into three parts:

(i)   The objectives to be achieved on completion of the assignment.
(ii)   The training method which could be any one or a combination of:
* Programmed learning texts
* Computer-based training, eg MENTOR II
* Case studies and exercises
* 'Discovery learning'
* Practical experience.

The programmed texts, case studies and exercises and other reference material are all included in the package as appendices.

(iii)   The briefing section, giving a list of materials required and detailed instructions as to how each part of the assignment is carried out.

(c) The Branch Manager's Role

Whilst one of the main objectives of the induction programme is to reduce the time involvement of the branch manager, his role of controlling and administering the programme is still vitally important. It was decided, therefore, to select a training branch per area (consisting of eight to 10 branches) in which all new recruits would undergo their induction training. The criteria for the selection of training branches are:

(i)   The branch should be fully staffed, thus allowing the manager some time for the briefing and de-briefing sessions.
(ii)   The branch should be physically large enough to allow the trainee to study where necessary in relative peace and quiet.
(iii)   The manager should be enthusiastic towards the training function.

Whilst the use of training branches is the ideal arrangement, there have been many occasions when, for various reasons, trainees have successfully undergone their induction training in the 'home' branch.

Included in the package is a detailed guide for the branch manager covering such items as the sequencing and planning of assignments and checklists for the briefing and de-briefing sessions.

3 Introduction of Trainee-Centred Learning to Branch Managers

As the success or failure of the induction training programme depended to a large extent on its acceptance by branch managers, a series of courses for branch managers was run throughout the country by Guardian Business Service Ltd. The basic aim of the course was to explain the concept of trainee-centred learning and also to convince managers that trainees would actually learn something by carrying out an assignment. One of the main features of the course was the way in which managers responded to the learning effectiveness of assignments by carrying out assignments specially designed to increase their knowledge. During the course, emphasis was placed on the skills required in the briefing and de-briefing sessions.

4 Conclusions

Reports from the managers of training branches indicate that the programme is easy to administer, their time involvement is greatly reduced, and the trainees have greater knowledge in less time than before.
   Inherent advantages of the training programme have proved to be:
   a   It is time saving for the branch manager.
   b   The training is carried out in a 'real life' situation. The trainee is involved from the outset in the 'climate' and day-to-day work of a branch office.
   c   The trainee immediately feels a sense of achievement and is quickly able to contribute to the work of the branch office by practising what he has learned from an assignment.
   d   The concept of trainee-centred learning simulates the trained assistant's job in that he is normally allocated daily work by his manager in the form of 'field' visits. In carrying out these visists, he is working totally on his own initiative and reports on his results to the manager at the end of the day.
   e   All new recruits throughout the country are receiving exactly the same level of induction training, hence there is a standardization throughout the company in procedures and office methods.

APPENDIX 7

Training Application

Factor to be considered	Rating	Score (0-4)	Value £
Different initial levels and learning speeds	Few-many		
Amount of complex calculation/simulation	None-majority		
Number of personnel to be trained	10-1000		
Difficulty in ensuring a consistent course content/standard	Difficulty		
Need to update portions	Occurrences		
Need for training to be at a precise time	Ease of supply		
Need to present training at many locations at the same time	Difficulty		
Difficulty in achieving cost-effective delegate/trainer ratios	Difficulty		
Need to provide precise evaluation/feedback	Difficulty		
Difficulty in providing effective control of training	Difficulty		
Difficulty of training administration	Difficulty		
Quantity of training staff required	Few-many		
Need for training to be on an individual basis	Low-high		
Need to minimize training time	Low-high		
Value of time absent	Low-high		
Cost of travelling, accommodation, subsistence	Low-high		
Difficulty in releasing staff for training	Difficulty		
Need for on-job-training	Low-high		
Difficulty in providing trainer	Difficulty		

Estimated development time ___ hours @ £ _____ = _____
Estimated number of delegates ____
Estimated development cost per delegate _____
Add machine costs plus software costs _____

Total cost per delegate _____
Deduct tangible saving _____
Net cost per delegate _____

APPENDIX 8

Behavioural/Training Objectives

Objective classification	Action verb which may enable objective measurement				
Knowledge	alter	answer	underline	reply	define
	write	select	cite	state	recall
	reproduce	specify	list	recognize	measure
	relate	name	label	spell	
Comprehension	translate	solve	prove	describe	identify
	illustrate	explain	modify	justify	represent
	judge	categorize	select	name	contrast
	divide	indicate	formulate	classify	convert
Application	predict	make	fit	obtain	select
	choose	construct	join	assess	find
	compute	calculate	explain	show	use
	prepare	produce	perform	maintain	demonstrate
	help	carry out	weigh	cause	
Analysis	diagnose	check	isolate	locate	analyse
	select	pick	identify	separate	distinguish
	justify	solve	conclude	compare	differentiate
	resolve	verify	contrast	extract	break–down
Synthesis	combine	draw	select	test	restate
	argue	relate	complete	discuss	summarize
	precis	organize	conclude	calculate	generalize
	derive	finish			
Evaluation	judge	defend	identify	support	evaluate
	attack	avoid	readjust	determine	criticize
	select	mark	recognize	adjust	choose
Motor	file	mainitain	remove	operate	hold
	position	take	assemble	lower	raise
	press	perform	lift	recover	turn
	demonstrate				
Attitudinal	be confident		be enthusiastic		

APPENDIX 9

DELEGATE SESSION REPORT

Delegate (name)   Location (branch name)

Course (course name)
Session (session name)

Unanticipated answer:	(unanticipated answer)
Response time:	(time in seconds)
Question:	(summary of question)
Correct answer:	(expected correct answer)

(Format is repeated for every unanticipated answer in a given session)

5.5 Computer-Based Training: A Management Tool

G Treece
Provident Financial Group PLC, Bradford

Abstract: This paper deals with the use of a computer–based training (CBT) package as a management tool. The areas covered include aiding recruitment and managerial assessment/development within the Provident Financial Group PLC. The author has particular responsibility for management training.

INTRODUCTION

This paper reports on the investigation by one company into the major reasons for ineffective management. It discusses the subsequent measures being taken to reduce that ineffectiveness using the resource of computer based training as a management tool.

BACKGROUND

Provident Personal Credit (PPC) is the major operating subsidiary of the Provident Financial group, contributing 80 per cent of the turnover (£300 million in 1983). PPC deals in weekly credit with self-employed agents collecting instalments from customers' homes. There are 480 branches throughout the UK, each having one manager and two or three assistant managers. This gives a total of approximately 1500 managers.

Recent group diversification has accelerated the broadening of the customer base. However, it is economically essential that a high degree of effectiveness is maintained by these 1500 managers.

HISTORY OF CBT

The company has a long history of involvement with computer based training. It is several years since CBT was identified as the most effective, quick and easy way to reach the large number of people concerned, given their geographically dispersed locations. The commitment by the group in this field has resulted in the establishment of PMSL MENTOR Ltd, a subsidiary company marketing CBT software.

INVESTIGATION INTO MANAGEMENT EFFECTIVENESS

The list below indicates the reasons why managers may be ineffective in their job.

1. Wrong person selected for the job.
2. Individuals' weaknesses not identified or corrected.
3. Not enough management training.
4. Training insufficiently thorough.
5. Breakdown in relationships.

Wrong Person for the Job

No company likes to admit ever employing the wrong person. However, investigations show that this is a problem for many companies.

Within PPC, some regions experience a turnover of managers in excess of 30 per cent per year. These figures may indicate that some selections are wrong. As with any job, there are certain 'types' of people who are most likely to carry it out successfully. External consultants were brought in to define the personality profile that is most able to accomplish the job and to devise a method of assessing whether an applicant fits the criteria of this profile. The consultants produced a profile that checks for three specific personality traits plus verbal intelligence in measuring an applicant's suitability. A sequence of tests was then formulated to identify whether an applicant falls into the accepted profile (see Appendix 1).

Computer based training material has been developed to incorporate these tests in order to simplify the screening of applicants. The advantages of using CBT are:

(a) standardized invigilation
(b) impartial interpretation, error free
(c) quick to assess and provide results (yes or no)
(d) resolves problems of needing specialists to interpret results
(e) needs minimum supervision.

For an outline of benefits, see Appendix 2. Note that the costs of the system have not been shown as they are found to be negligible. No extra machines need be bought as the workflow dictates that training material is not used on Mondays or Tuesdays; therefore, they can be used during these days with no additional overheads.

Individuals' Weaknesses

The problem here is related to existing staff who obviously did not undergo the screening process when recruited, and newly appointed staff who, though generally acceptable, may still have some weak areas which can cause ineffectiveness. There are two requirements:

1. To identify the weak areas of a member of staff.
    Many standard tests which are designed to measure personality profiles are available. These can be incorporated into a CBT package which is then used to assess individuals in the shortest possible time, regardless of geographical location. The results are then returned to head office in the form of a diskette or via a letter to be processed and analysed by a suitably qualified expert. It is neither legally nor practically acceptable for interpretation to be carried out in the branch offices.
2. To arrange a corrective course of action.
    Following interpretation of the test, a corrective course of action can be planned and implemented for individuals. This is followed up by the setting of another similar personality assessment test at a later date to indicate the effectiveness of the corrective action taken (see later).

Not Enough Management Training

With 1,500 managers to train, it is easy to fall into a situation where trainers are spending the majority of their time delivering information, ie giving courses and thereby reducing the time available for research, design, and writing the much needed new material. It is essential that training meets the following requirements:

*   time out of office minimized
*   training available at 'off-peak' times
*   subjects covered to include, induction, thorough knowledge, assessment, summary, reference, case studies.

CBT is eminently suitable to meet the above criteria and, therefore, the quantity of available training can be increased within the smallest possible time.

Training Insufficiently Thorough

The problem here is that existing courses could not be followed up or validated because of lack of resources. CBT can solve this by:

* providing results on effectiveness of training given
* providing follow-up training at very little extra cost.

Quality will always be maintained as CBT is standardized, never varying because of an 'off' day.

Communications Breakdown

The problem of management ineffectiveness may often be rooted not in selection or training but in communication breakdown. It is accepted that two people are required to form any kind of communication, and also to cause any breakdown of communication. One cause of a breakdown is that individuals' expectations of each other do not match. CBT can be used to analyse a person's expectations of others and is a powerful tool for identifying clashes of expectations. Following the analysis, an 'expert' is required to advise on action to reduce the gap between expectations. The 'expectations' approach was instigated by the University of Durham. It is currently being developed as a pilot system.

NOTE

No definition of CBT has been given in this paper. This is intentional as, by giving a strict, narrow definition to a term, we are restricted in our use of the technology by the definition we have given. Some may argue that the advantages listed above as a, b, and e fall outside their understanding of the term CBT. Does this necessitate the invention of even more unfriendly jargon? Or, are we to ignore all the other uses of computers and their impact on training and education?

APPENDIX 1

Stages of screening

	Applicants (20)	
(20min)	Intelligence	Reject (10)
(50min)	Personality	Reject (6)
	Interview	Reject (3)
	Accept (1)	

APPENDIX 2

Outline of Benefits

	Current % OK	% OK after screening	Improvement
Region A	50	75	25
Region B	70	91	21

Calculated improvement nationwide = 22%

Savings = Turnover of staff x Improvement in employing a 'good' manager
x Cost of hiring a 'bad' manager

1. Assuming cost = £1000 per year, savings = 300 x 22% x £1000 = £66,000 per year

2. Assuming cost = £2000 per year, savings = 300 x 22% x £2000 = £132,000 per year.

Section 6:
Communication and
Diffusion

6.1 Strategy Cueing for Activating Students' Use of Illustrations in Text: A Report of Two Studies

R M Bernard
Concordia University, Montreal, Canada

Abstract: In recent years a number of authors have suggested that instructional text could be improved if designers would consider the intended function of pictures and illustrations relative to the content of the prose. As many as ten functions have been proposed, including motivation, explication, retention and comprehension. However, if the student user is not aware that a particular function is being employed, especially if it is an instructional function like retention or comprehension, then the exercise may be in jeopardy despite the good intentions of the designer. As Rigney(1978) has pointed out, materials alone do not always cue students to the most appropriate and productive learning strategy. Such is the case with visuals of all kinds and in particular illustrations in text that are intended to fulfil a particular role. Often students need to be informed as to the nature of the learning task and to the most profitable strategy to apply to a class of instructional content.

The purpose of this paper is to describe two studies that were designed to assess the viability of providing instructional strategies in text as a means of improving the use of illustrations as retentional aids. Two types of strategies were tested, embedded strategies and detached. The paper details the nature of these experiments and the results that were achieved.

INTRODUCTION

During the last several decades, a substantial research effort has been directed towards identifying those characteristics of instructional materials that lead to optimal learning results. Initially, research questions such as 'Is material (or medium) X better than material (or medium) Y?' (Salomon and Clark,1977) were asked, but in recent years gross comparisons between materials have been replaced by more refined queries. Typically, such questions are focused upon the attributes of a particular material or medium that improve learning performance. Researchers interested in verbal processing and print-based materials have been particularly active in this regard, and there now exists a substantial literature on instructional text. Adjuncts to text such as advance organizers; overviews and summaries, organizational and typographical cueing and pictures and illustrations, to name a few, have been extensively scrutinized, and yet, the conclusion reached in integrative reviews of these variables (see Shimmerlik,1978; Luiten, Akerson and Ames, 1980; Reder,1980; Levie and Lentz,1982; Moore and Readance,1983) suggests that textual adjuncts, at best, are but modestly effective in enhancing recall and comprehension of verbal content.

One of the underlying assumptions of much of this research is that student-subjects are both willing and able to use a particular adjunct that is under investigation. A typical research design involves the comparison of at least two conditions; one in which an adjunct is present and one in which an adjunct is absent. Subjects are often not informed of the presence of the adjunct nor told what advantages might accrue from conscientiously employing it. Similarly, explanations of how to best use adjuncts are seldom included and training is rarely provided. Weinstein's (1978) comment about the paucity of strategy training in the schools, 'We tell our students what to learn, but say nothing about how to go about learning. The assumption that the abilities involved in learning are either innate or naturally acquired is probably fallacious.' (p 32), appears to apply as well to many of the studies that have been done in the area of textual design.

Admittedly, much of the work that my research teams and I have done with illustrations in text is open to the above criticism. We have investigated a wide range of diagrams and illustrations without seriously considering whether our subjects were aware of the designer's intentions or able to profit from the adjunct illustrations that were provided. The net return has been disappointingly low, prompting us to conclude that illustrations in text contribute only minimally to a learner's retention and understanding of textual content. In retrospect, however, we surmise that, because of the relative complexity of the illustrations and their presumed retentional function (Duchastel,1981), strategy conditions would have enhanced their effectiveness. Recently, we have begun to explore ways of encouraging students to take fuller advantage of illustrations in text. The studies reported here are our initial attempts to assess the effects of supplying strategy instructions or prompting conditions in textbook-like materials.

Rigney's (1978) work in the area of instructional strategies provided a framework for this research. Rigney divides instructional strategies, aimed at affecting cognitive strategies that a learner applies to a given instructional task, into two categories. Embedded strategies, as the name implies, are designed into the body of the instructional content and are often intended to compensate for a student's lack of strategy development. Inserted post-questions in text (Rothkopf,1970) exemplify an embedded strategy designed to facilitate interaction with the content but, because they are embedded in the text, retention of the content that is specifically addressed (ie, often referred to as intentional recall) tends to be increased while recall of the content that is not specifically addressed (ie, incidental recall) tends to be depressed (Glynn,1978). Detached strategies, on the other hand, are more general in nature and are, at least in principle, adaptable to a wider range of tasks and contents. Aptitude-by-treatment-intereaction research on detached strategies, however, points to conflicting results. In some studies (eg, Winn,1981) only high ability students have profited from this strategy, while other studies (Salomon,1974; Dean and Kulhavy, 1981) have found the detached strategy useful only to lower ability students who presumably do not bring a cogent strategy to the instructional setting. Differences in task and strategy requirements may eventually be found to account for these contradictory findings.

The two studies reported here were designed to assess the effectiveness of strategy conditions included in textbook-like materials. Both involve the testing of detached strategies, but in Study 1 we investigated embedded strategies as well. Our interest in both cases was to affect student utilization of illustrations that appear within a textual format. In Study 1 the illustrations were similar to those found in standard text, while in Study 2, the illustration might be more aptly referred to as a graphic organizer.

STUDY 1

Introduction

In the first study we were interested in determining if students naturally attempt to interpret and remember the overall purpose and the details of illustrations in text during the course of reading. Most importantly, we wanted to assess how detached, embedded and a combination of both kinds of strategies would affect this natural recall pattern. The strategies were designed to aid students in translating the illustrations into memorable verbal sequences. Such translation may be necessary for the logical connections and sequentially coded elements in the illustrations to become apparent (Winn,1982). More superficial processing of the illustrations might lead to high recognition of physical properties (eg, patterns) but lower recall of the substantive content. We hypothesized that both embedded and detached strategies would promote this translation, resulting in higher recall scores for the illustrated content in these conditions. An initial pilot study provided encouraging support for the effectiveness of the embedded strategy, but little evidence that the detached strategy affected student behavior. Subsequently, the detached strategy was redesigned (a sample of the final design appears in Figure 1) for the main experiment.

Method

Subjects The subjects for the main experiment in this study were 143 students at a college in Ontario, Canada. They ranged in age from 18 to 21 years and were tested in a normal classroom setting.
Design The experimental design was a 2 x 3 factorial in which all comparisons were between-

groups. The first independent variable, embedded strategy, had two levels: (1) embedded strategy present, and (2) embedded strategy absent. The second, detached strategy, had three levels: (1) detached strategy present with illustrations, (2) detached strategy absent with illustrations, and (3) detached strategy absent without illustrations. This latter condition was included so that the effects of the embedded strategy without the illustration present could be compared with the other embedded strategy conditions in which the illustration was present. One condition, 'without embedded strategy and without illustration' was included to complete the factorial design and to determine if test items could be answered successfully without the presence of either the illustration or the embedded strategy.

<u>Materials</u> The passage used in this study was derived from a self-instructional unit developed by a research assistant entitled 'The Nature of Pain'. The topic was chosen because it was visual in nature and because it was deemed to be of general appeal. The content was factually based and was submitted to and approved by a physician at the Pain Management Unit at the Royal Victoria Hospital.

Study the diagram carefully. Locate and name the main parts of the nervous system included in the illustration. Next, trace the pain process represented step-by-step in the direction of the arrows. While you trace the route, describe it in your own words to help you remember it.

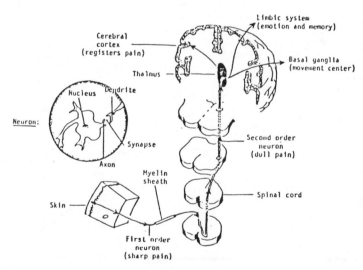

Figure 2: The 'pathway' of pain

The <u>neuron</u> consists of cell body, a nucleus, axons and dendrites. <u>Dendrites</u> register the impulses - they are the 'receivers', if you like. The <u>axons</u> conduct the impulses across the <u>synapse</u> (the gap between the neurons) to other parts of the nervous system - the 'senders'. The sheath which surrounds the axon contains a substance, <u>myelin</u>, which effects the speed at which the electrical impulses can be conducted. <u>First-order neu-ons</u> with a thick myelin sheath carry information about sharp

Figure 1. <u>Sample illustration with Detached Strategy (above) and Embedded Strategy (below)</u>.

The learning strategies were operationalized as additional textual paragraphs which were intended to provoke processing of the information contained in the illustrations. The detached strategy condition consisted of a series of four embedded paragraphs, each of which appeared within the text just prior to the relevant illustration. These paragraphs simply directed the reader's attention to the illustration and suggested how one might proceed to 'read' it (see Figure 1). The format of the embedded strategy was similar to that for the detached strategy except that the paragraphs were positioned after the illustration. One major difference was that the embedded strategy led the reader through the illustration step by step, detailing significant features and describing the relationship among important elements (see Figure 1).

Four different illustrations were designed by a research assistant and positioned near the relevant content in the passage. The first and second illustrations were similar to those that appear in standard text. The third was modelled after Holliday's (1976) work-block diagram and the fourth was a compare–contrast diagram depicting the characteristics of the three types of pain detailed in the text. These illustrations appeared in four of the six cells of the design.

A 30-item recognition test was devised as a mix of pictorial and textually-based items. Seventeen items came from the illustrated content and the remainder came from the verbal text. For the purpose of testing, the items were randomly mixed and afterwards the items from the illustrated and verbal contents were separated into two scales.

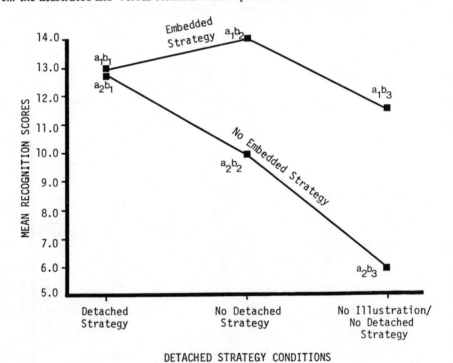

Figure 2. Interaction of Detached, Embedded and No Illustration Conditions.

Procedure The experimental materials were administered to eight intact classes. Since random assignment of subjects to conditions was clearly impossible, conditions were randomly assigned to subjects. This is possible when subjects are to work independently. Before the subjects began working, the Nelson-Denny Reading Test was administered. Reading level was assessed because of its potential usefulness as a covariate in the subsequent analysis. After completing the reading test, subjects were directed to read and study the text. Study time was approximately 30 minutes. When everyone had finished, subjects completed a short mathematics quiz to reduce rote memorization of the content. Subjects were then directed to complete the recognition test. When they had completed this task, they were thanked for their co-operation and the experimental session ended.

Results Before analysing the design using analysis of covariance, a test of homogeneity of regression was conducted to determine whether there was a covariate by treatment interaction that would invalidate the use of ANCOVA. The test was not significant indicating that the Nelson-Denny Reading Test could be used to remove otherwise unexplained variation due to individual reading level differences. The analysis of covariance indicated a significant main effect for the factor detached strategy, $F (1,138) = 14.32$, p less than .001, and a main effect for embedded strategy, $F (2,138) = 25.94$, p less than .001. The interaction of detached and embedded strategies was also significant, $F (2,138) = 5.02$, p less than .01. Because of the interaction, post hoc analysis of the simple main effects was conducted. Post hoc tests revealed the following difference among pairs and combinations of means (refer to Figure 2):

1. Embedded strategy with detached strategy was not different than no embedded strategy with detached strategy (a_1b_1 vs. a_1b_2).
2. Embedded strategy with detached strategy was not different than no embedded strategy with detached strategy (a_1b_1 vs. a_2b_1).
3. Detached strategy with no embedded strategy was different than no detached and no embedded strategy (a_2b_1 vs. a_2b_2).
4. Embedded strategy with no detached strategy was different than no detached and no embedded strategy (a_1b_2 vs. a_2b_2).
5. The combination of embedded and detached (a_1b_1) and embedded without detached (a_1b_2) was different than the embedded without illustration condition (a_1b_3).

These results will be discussed later in combination with Study 2.

STUDY 2

Introduction

The purpose of Study 2 was to determine if strategy conditions would assist learners in using a graphic organizer as a prompt to recalling the verbal contents of the text. Past research Moore & Readance,1983) on this specialized kind of illustration has indicated little effect on the recall of passage contents. We argued that an illustration of this type which graphically depicts the structure of the superordinate concepts contained in the text would prove effective if students were told how to use it and if textual cueing (headings and subheadings) were present to indicate the location of the concepts. A pilot study was conducted in which strategy and no strategy conditions were present but textual cueing was absent. Results indicated that the detached strategy was modestly effective. Several modifications were made to the materials as a result of this pilot study.

Method

Subjects Subjects for the main experiment in Study 2 were 158 students enrolled in the first year of a hotel management course at an Ontario college. Their ages ranged from 18 to 21 years and they were all native English speakers.

Design The design was a 2 x 2 factorial in which both factors were between-group. The independent variables were strategy (with strategy and without strategy) and textual cueing (with cueing and without cueing). The dependent measure was recall as assessed by a cued recall test.

Materials The passage used in this experiment was an actual textual selection taken from a supplementary textbook used in the hotel management curriculum. Subjects, however, had not previously been exposed to this material and the topic had not been covered in classes. The passage was rewritten and completely re-formatted to reflect the purposes of the experiment. A multi-level cueing system was added to two of the conditions (ie, cueing present). Information in the text addressed the kinds of budgets used in the hotel and restaurant industry, the advantages and disadvantages of budgeting, the purposes of budgeting, and explained in detail the budget cycle and the persons and groups who are normally involved in budget preparation.

The instructional strategy described how to match systematically the structure of the graphic organizer to the structure of the passage and how to visualize the graphic organizer

and its components so that it could be remembered more clearly. The graphic organizer
itself was a flow diagram with six superordinate and 17 subordinate topics. It depicted, in
sequential order, the major idea units in the text. All subjects in the experiment, unlike
Study 1, received the graphic organizer.

Subjects in the No Strategy condition received a 'placebo' strategy (ie, a short description
of the goals of the hotel industry) which was formated to appear the same as the strategy
condition. A short statement was included at the end of the 'placebo strategy' which pointed
to the presence of the graphic organizer, but did not mention how to use it. This statement
was included in an attempt to provide promptings to this condition so that any differences
between it and the strategy conditions would more likely be the result of subjects' use of the
strategy.

The dependent measure was a 40-item cued recall test which was scored 'blind' by two
raters. The interrater reliability for these raters was .95. The Nelson-Denny Test was also
administered to subjects in this experiment for the same purpose as in Study 1.
Procedure The procedure for Study 2 was essentially the same as for Study 1. Materials
were randomly assigned to subjects and no time limits were imposed for either the study or
the testing phases of the experiment.

Results

As in the case of Study 1, the first step in the analysis was to test for homogeneity of
regression to determine if the Nelson-Denny Test was a suitable covariate. Results of this
test, unlike Study 1, indicated a treatments by covariate interaction involving both of the
independent variables. The Nelson-Denny by cueing by strategy interaction was significant, F
(1,147) = 5.17, p less than .02, suggesting that subjects at different levels of reading ability

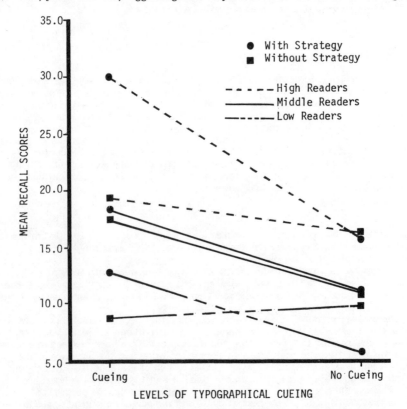

Figure 3. Interaction of Cueing, Detached Strategy
and Levels of Reading.

performed differently depending upon which combination of strategy and cueing they received. This interaction invalidated the use of the reading measure as a covariate, but opened up the possibility of meaningful interpretation. Cronbach and Snow(1977) argue that aptitude-treatment-interactions that are detected in the course of testing regression assumptions should be investigated using either step-wise regression with dummy coding or post hoc blocking on the aptitude variable. The latter approach was chosen.

Scores on the reading measure were divided into three categories: high, medium and low, to serve as the levels of the aptitude variable. Since post hoc blocking involves a redistribution of subjects across the new design, disproportionate cell frequencies and standard deviations often result. A test of homogeneity of variance, Cochran's C = .14, p less than .05, revealed no differences in the intra-cell variances.

The newly formed design was a three levels of aptitude by two levels of cueing by two levels of strategy factorial. The strategy main effect was not significant, but both cueing, F (1,147) = 21.28, p less than .001, and aptitude, F (1,147) = 22.43, p less than .001, were. None of the two-way interactions were significant, but the three-way interaction was significant, F (2,147) = 4.44, p = .013. This was the same interaction between the three variables that was detected in testing for homogeneity of regression. The cell means are shown in Figure 3.

Post hoc analysis of the simple main effects of the design revealed the following differences (refer to Figure 3):

1. For low readers, there were no significant differences - strategy and cueing.
2. For middle readers, there was a significant difference between levels of cueing, but there were no differences between levels of strategy.
3. For high readers, there was a difference in both strategy and cueing. Those who received both cueing and strategy outperformed all other combinations

These results will be discussed in the following section.

DISCUSSION

In both studies reported herein, there is evidence that the strategy conditions enhanced recall of the relevant content (ie, pictorial content in Study 1 and verbal content in Study 2). The studies differ, however, in regard to the nature of this effectiveness. Subjects in both the embedded and detached strategy conditions and their combination (Study 1) outperformed subjects in the no strategy and no strategy/no illustration conditions, while only higher level readers (Study 2) profited from the detached strategy and then, only in the presence of typographical cueing. The differential patterns noted here may be attributable to differences in the cognitive tasks that were required of subjects in complying with the strategy instructions. Study 1 strategies attempted to direct subjects to relevant information that could be translated and recalled in terms of verbal strings, whereas the strategy in Study 2 requested that students relate the spatial organizational features of the graphic organizer to the organizational structure of the passage. Since this structure was most apparent when typographical cueing was present, this combination produced the greatest mean recall. The latter is apparently a more formidable cognitive task than the former, since only the upper one-third of the sample in Study 2 were able to perform it.

In addition, differences were found (Study 1) between embedded strategy conditions in which the illustrations were present and absent. This attests to the usefulness of the non-verbal elements and labelling contained in the illustrations. This difference argues in favour of the inclusion of illustrations in text. However, these results also indicate that either a detached or embedded strategy will likely help students make fuller use of the illustrations. A similar claim may be made for the inclusion of typographical cueing (Study 2) in text, if the full effects of a graphic organizer or possibly other forms of organizational illustrations are to be realized. One particularly interesting finding in Study 1 involves the similarity in the conditions that received detached strategies, embedded strategies and their combination (ie, both). The fact that the combined condition did not promote additional and more dramatic recall results than either strategy condition alone may be the result of the outcome similarity of the two strategies. The detached strategy laid out a plan of attack for students while the embedded strategy provided the explicit outcomes of that plan. In other words, if students in the combined condition conscientiously followed the detached instructions, then the embedded strategy encountered later was redundant and probably unnecessary. Based on these findings, a textual designer would not need to include both kinds of strategies in order to affect recall performance.

The following recommendations appear to be warranted as a result of Study 1:

1. If illustrations that are to be included in text containing information that supplements, but is not explicitly covered in the text, the detached strategy appears to be more appropriate.

2. If the illustration provides a complementary function (ie, depicting that which is explicitly described), the relationship between illustration and description should be made explicit. This could be achieved through extended captions which describe what the student should attend to or carefully specified references to particular elements or relationships in the illustrations.

At first glance, the results of Study 2 appear to contradict the prior research (Dean and Kulhavy,1981; Mayer,1980) on detached strategies that has suggested a beneficial result for lower rather than higher level students and support the opposite. However, a simple discovery causes us to question this conclusion. When we compared the scores of our 'high level readers' with the norms of the Nelson-Denny Test we found that, according to this standardized scale, our subjects were more like low to middle readers. Using this new interpretation, the results of Study 2 seem to support previous research that found that strategy instructions benefited only the low ability students. However, since relatively few high level readers participated in our study, it is impossible to settle this issue using the current data. Future work, with a better distribution of readers at all levels of ability, will be necessary before the situation can be clarified.

The studies reported in this paper indicate tentatively that greater concern for the strategy that a student uses while in the process of reading instructional text may be warranted and that relatively simple adjunct strategy instructions can improve student involvement in the content. Whether or not these results will generalize to standard classroom settings is not known, however they appear to justify additional field studies of these variables. Other questions, relating to alternative forms of strategy instructions, their placement in text, their effect upon levels of instructional outcomes and their interactive relationship with these and other learner characteristics, remain open as well. For the moment, we can only safely conclude that a modest effort on the part of print-based designers can alter the approach that a learner takes toward both the verbal and non-verbal contents of instructional text resulting in more effective learning performance.

REFERENCES

Cronbach, L J and Snow, R C (1977) Aptitudes and instructional methods. Irvington Publishers, New York.

Dean, R S and Kulhavy, R W (1981) Influence of spatial organization in prose learning. Journal of Educational Psychology, 73, pp57-64.

Duchastel, P C (1981) Reseach on illustrations in text: Issues and perspectives. Educational Communication and Technology Journal, 28, pp283-287.

Glynn, S M (1978) Capturing readers' attention by means of typographical cueing. Educational Technology, 18, pp7-12.

Holliday, W G (1976) Teaching verbal chains using flow diagrams and text. Audiovisual Communication Review, 24, pp63-78.

Levie, W H and Lentz, R (1982) Effect of text illustrations: A review of the research. Educational Communication and Technology Journal, 30, pp195-232.

Luiten, J, Ames, W and Akerson, G (1980) A meta-analysis of the effects of advance organizers on learning and retention. American Educational Research Journal, 17, pp211-218.

Mayer, E R (1980) Elaboration techniques that increase meaningfulness of technical text. Journal of Educational Psychology, 72, pp770-784.

Moore, D and Readance, J (1983) A quantitative and qualitative review of graphic organizer research. Paper presented at the annual meeting of the American Educational Research Association, Montreal, Canada.

Reder, L M (1980) The role of elaboration in the comprehension and retention of prose: A critical review. Review of Educational Research, 50, pp5-53.

Rigney, J W (1978) Learning Strategies: A theoretical perspective. In O'Neil H F Jr (Ed) Learning strategies. Academic Press, New York.

Rothkopf, E Z (1970) The concept of mathemagenic activities. Review of Educational Research, 40, pp325-336.

Salomon, G (1974) Can we affect cognitive skills through visual media? An hypothesis and initial findings. Audiovisual Communication Review, 20, pp401-422.

Salomon, G and Clark, R E (1977) Re-examining the methodology of research on media and technology in education. Review of Educational Research, 47, pp99-120.

Shimmerlik, S M (1978) Organization theory and memory for prose: A review of the literature. Review of Educational Research, 48, pp103-140.

Weinstein, C E (1978) Elaboration skills as a learning strategy. In O'Neill, H F Jr (Ed) Learning Strategies. Academic Press, New York.

Winn, W (1981) Effect of attribute highlighting and diagramatic organization in identification and classification. Journal of Research in Science Teaching, 18, pp23-32.

Winn, W (1982) Visualization in learning and instruction: A cognitive approach. Educational Communication and Technology Journal, 30, pp3-25.

6.2 The Application of a Systems Approach to Conduct a Personal Contact Programme in Distance Education

K Sharma

Himachal Pradesh University, India

Abstract: This paper presents a description of the systems approach to conduct personal contact programmes for students of Master of Education (M Ed) enrolled with the Directorate of Correspondence Courses of Himachal Pradesh University, Simla, India. Himachal Pradesh University is the first university in India to offer M Ed courses through distance education. In order to maintain good academic standards, it is obligatory for students to attend a 15-day personal contact programme once every semester. This is organized at various venues to facilitate participation of the students. It is used for both supplementing instructional material provided in the form of lessons and to discuss and solve various difficulties of academic nature.

A systems approach was used to make these contact programmes effective and useful. The total task was studies in two phases – administrative and academic. Elements were identified for these two phases and the interrelationships of various elements established. These were finally developed into a structure of the system, which was envisaged in having five stages: planning, preparation, execution, assessment and winding up. The system thus developed was applied in real situations and assessment of the system was made to obtain the necessary feedback. Comparison was also made with personal contact programs organized on traditional lines and the systems approach found to be much superior to it in terms of programme effectiveness and student satisfaction.

INTRODUCTION

Distance Education has emerged as a very effective channel of non-formal education in India. During the last 20 years, a large number of universities have set up institutions of distance education in order to meet the ever increasing demand of higher education. Himachal Pradesh University, Shimla, was the first in the country to introduce postgraduate courses including professional courses like Master of Education, through distance education. The Directorate of Correspondence Courses of Himachal Pradesh University has been using a systems approach to make the academic programmes more effective. Three different systems have been developed in the areas of course material design, conduct of personal contact programme and handling of response sheets. Sharma and Sharma (1976) developed a system of the conduct of personal contact programme which was implemented and subsequently modified. The present paper outlines this project.

The term 'system' has been used in a technical sense and referes to 'a dynamic organization of mutually related components in a meaningful pattern'. Taking any problem according to this approach is known as the systems approach which consists of four main activities. These are:

1. Analysis of the system's components and interrelationships.
2. Synthesis of these elements together with those previously unrelated.
3. Model building to show the structure and relationships with a view to possible quantification.
4. Simulation of the system prior to implementation in real life and modification of the model, where necessary, in the light of the evaluation.

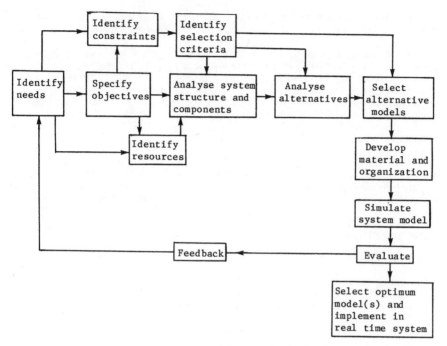

Figure 1   The systems approach to education

Like all other channels of education, distance education too considers the teacher as the pivot of all educational activities. But unlike other channels, here the exposure of the teacher to his or her students is partly in person and partly through lessons. To provide the former mode of exposure, all institutions of distance education have considered personal contact programmes almost a necessity. It is mainly for two purposes: to supplement the instructional material provided for the students in the form of lessons and, second, to remove difficulties of an academic nature with the help of direct contact with teachers.

OBJECTIVES

The objects of this project were:

(a)   To isolate different components of the contact programme.
(b)   To analyse the system's components and establish their interrelationships.
(c)   To develop a system of personal contact programme showing the structure and relationships among various elements.

To arrive finally at a system for the conduct of personal contact programme, the investigator started with a questionnaire pertaining to duration, mode of conduct, number of working hours per day, desired nature of instructions, problems and suggestions upon them etc. The questionnaire was circulated among 500 correspondence students of an M Ed class enrolled in Himachal Pradesh University for the year 1975-76. The questionnaire was returned by 120 of them, out of these 120 students, 108 were male and 12 female. The responses of the students to these questions were collected and classified for each question separately.

As revealed by the investigation, the preferred duration of the personal contact programme was found to be 14 days. A majority of the students (78 per cent) thought it better to keep the personal contact programme compulsory. On the issue of the content covered, during the contact programme, preference of total coverage and coverage of selected topics was favoured by an almost comparable number of the students. About the suitable strategy of instruction, the group under investigation suggested the use of lectures followed by structured discussions or learning exercises - whatever fits the nature of the lectures. Some students recommended the use of audiovisual material, programmed learning material, continuous evaluation, library work, individual guidance and distribution of a synopsis of the lectures.

In addition to these suggestions, the group felt strongly for the need of boarding and lodging arrangements to be made by the university during personal contact programmes. They explicitly mentioned that daily working hours should not exceed five. The size of the class should be reduced to some number below 50. Problems of response sheets should be discussed by the teachers concerned during the contact programme. Achievement tests should be administered at the end of the contact programme.

FUNCTIONAL ELEMENTS

With the help of the information gathered through the questionnaire, a thorough analysis of the task of conducting a personal contact programme was made. The investigator decided to analyse the task for its functional elements. The total task was studied in two phases: first administrative, and second academic. Thus the task of conducting a personal contact programme, as it should be, was analysed for its functional elements of administrative and academic phases separately.

The following elements were identified for the two phases:

Elements at the Administrative phase

1. Deciding about the venue of the personal contact programmes.
2. Inviting students' preferences for a venue of the personal contact programme.
3. Selecting and deputing the co-ordinator and teachers from the Director.
4. Inviting experts.
5. Sending reference books and other material to the venue of the personal contact programme.
6. Course preparation of instructional objectives.
7. Preparing a battery of tests to be administered to the students during the personal contact programme.
8. Setting up a classroom.
9. Arranging students' lodging.
10. Preparing time schedule.
11. Setting up a temporary library.
12. Appointing subordinate staff.
13. Issuing attendance slips.
14. Making payments to the staff.
15. Submitting accounts.
16. Submitting report to the university about the conduct of personal contact programme.

Elements at the Academic phase

1. Informal meeting .
2. Distribution of written statements of instruction objectives.
3. Administering a battery of tests on all the courses the students are going to take up.
4. Distribution of time schedule.
5. Lectures preceded by synopsis.
6. Generating discussion.
7. Organisation of seminars.
8. Ensuring the use of library by the students.
9. Individual guidance.
10. Assessment of the students' performance.
11. Evaluation of the personal contact programme.

STRUCTURE OF THE SYSTEM

For maintaining connections among various elements, Robert Glaser's (1967) model of teaching was followed as a guideline. The model is considered to be a simple teaching model which provides an uncomplicated yet fairly adequate conceptualization of the teaching process. It has four components:

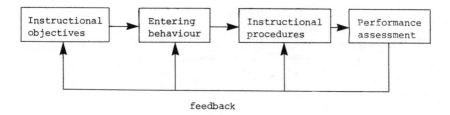

feedback

Figure 2   Glaser's Model of Teaching

Figure 2 shows the major sequence of events in the instructional process.

The investigator visualized the development of a system of personal contact programme as the end product of this study. For this purpose the analysis of the systems' components was followed by establishing the interrelationships of different components and finally arriving at a structure of the system (see Figure 3).

In order to place the structure into Glaser's model of teaching, all the elements were classified into five classes according to the sequential development of the constituent elements. These are:

1. Planning at the Directorate level.
2. Preparation of the personal contact programme at the selected venue.
3. Execution of the courses.
4. Performance assessment.
5. Winding up the contact programme.

Planning at the Directorate Level

The planning starts with the decision about the venues of the contact programmes. This is exclusively a decision taken by the Directorate. The main criteria of selecting a venue are the density of the students in a given area and the availability of physical facilities for organizing personal contact programme at that place.

The students are informed of the venues of the personal contact programmes and their preference for the same are invited. Simultaneously the following important decisions have also to be taken:

(a)   Deputing co-ordinator.
(b)   Deputing teachers from the Directorate.
(c)   Inviting guest speakers and other experts from other institutions.
(d)   Preparation of attendance register and other material.
(e)   Acquisition of books from the library for the contact programme.

A committee of the teachers of the Directorate prepares the instructional objectives in each course and evolves tools to be used as pretests and post-tests in the contact programme.

Planning at the venue of the contact programme

The second stage of the preparation for the contact programme starts at the venue of the contact programme. This preparation is made in two phases: first phase covers all physical arrangements pertaining to classroom, students' lodging, setting up of a library, appointing subordinate staff and framing a time schedule of the personal contact programme. The second phase concerns the distribution of the instructional objectives, administering a battery of tests and distribution of time schedule. This is done in a meeting on the very first day of the contact programme.

At this stage, the students are exposed to actual instruction. The strategy as suggested by the group under study runs in the following sequence:

(a)   lectures preceded by distribution of synopsis and followed by discussion;
(b)   seminars;

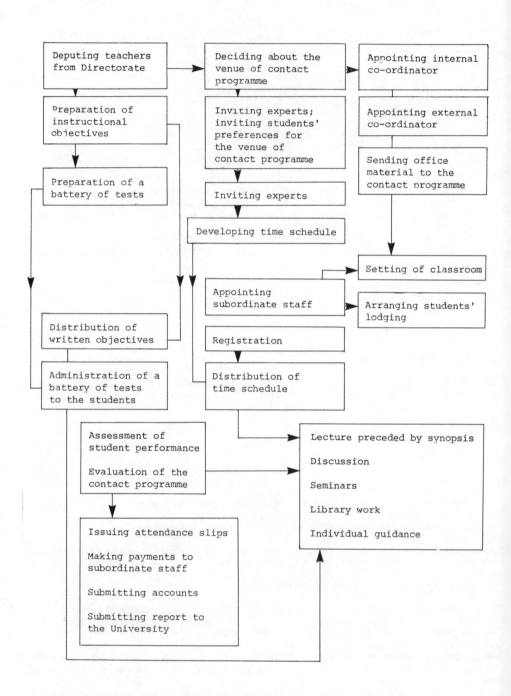

Figure 3   Systems Approach to the Conduct of Personal
Contact Programme (Sharma,1983)

(c) library work;
(d) individual work (individual guidance).

Evaluation

The fourth stage of the model pertains to evaluation aspect. Evaluation of students' performance as well as of the personal contact programme is done simultaneously towards the end of the programme. The scores of the evaluation sheets are used on the one hand, as a feedback for the instructional procedures and on the other a feedback for planning at the Directorate level and at the venue of the personal contact programme.

This is followed by the last stage of winding up the programme. It is a stage which directly relates to the office of the Directorate. This involves: issuing of attendance slips, making payments to the temporary staff employed during the contact programme, and submitting a report and accounts of the contact programme to the university.

In 1982–83, this system was modified in the light of comments and suggestions given by the students and teachers. The major changes made in the system are as under:

1. The students' preference for the venue of the personal contact programme is invited at the time of the submission of the admission form by them in the beginning of the semester in order to save time and postal expenses.
2. The practice of sending books and other reference material to the venue of the contact programme is discontinued as the books got damaged during transit and their transportation involved heavy expenses. Instead, the institution, where the contact programmes are held, are requested to allow the students of the Directorate an access to their library.
3. Instead of one co-ordinator, two co-ordinators are appointed: one from the Directorate of Correspondence Courses (internal co-ordinator) and the other from the institution in which the personal contact programme is being organized.
4. The daily working hours have been increased from five to six.
5. Instead of preparing the time schedule at the venue of the contact programme, it is now prepared tentatively in the Directorate well in advance by the faculty subject to slight modifications later on.
6. The payment to the external experts and other subordinate staff engaged temporarily are made by the accountant of the Directorate instead of the internal co-ordinator. This has helped in reducing the work load of the internal co-ordinator and also in the proper maintenance of the accounts.

Results achieved with the implementation of the system's approach

Though no exact statistical quantification has so far been worked out, the approach is estimated to have yielded the following results:

1. With the streamlining of the programme, it has added to the efficiency on the part of the organizers.
2. Achievement of greater economy on the exchequer.
3. The entire programme being basically examination–oriented, there has been a steady and definite improvement in the examination results.
4. The employment of external experts, and the exposure of students to debates, seminars, discussions and individual guidance has proved to be very effective both academically and administratively.

REFERENCES

Clarke, J (1969) A Systems Approach to Aspects of Primary Education. In Mann, A P and Brunstrom, C K (eds) Aspects of Educational Technology III. Pitman, London.
Cook, C J and Walker, D (1970) The Development: of an Integral Learning System in Higher Education. In Mann, A P and Brunstrom, C K (eds) Aspects of Educational Technology III. Pitman, London.
Glaser, R (1967) Psychology and Instructional Technology. In Glaser, R (ed) Training, Research and Education. University of Pittsburgh Press, Pittsburgh.

Hawkins, P F and Hawkins, R E (1973) The Application of the Systems Approach to Training in Royal Naval School. In Budgett, R and Leedham, J F (eds) Aspects of Educational Technology VII. Pitman, London.

Hodge, P (1970) Systems, Structures and Strategies for a Technology of Education. In Bajpai, A C and Leedham, J F (eds) Aspects of Educational Technology IV. Pitman, London.

Sharma, K and Sharma, A B (1976) Systems Approach to Conduct Contact Programmes in a Correspondence Courses Education System. Directorate of Correspondence Courses, Himachal Pradesh University, Shimla, India.

6.3 Transition to a Team Approach in Patient Education

S C Driver and G A Shearer
University of Melbourne, Australia

Abstract: This paper reports on a three-year-old project concerned with the systematic development and validation of learning materials for renal dialysis patients. No single individual had all the knowledge and skills necessary; therefore a two-tiered team approach was essential. A small team of four (an educational technologist, an educational psychologist, a physician, and a dialysis nurse) were in constant daily communication about the development and mofication of instructional material. A second team of about a dozen people, drawn from disciplines as diverse as philosophy, theology, and nutritional science, met at monthly intervals to provide a wider perspective and valuable feedback to the project. An educational technology approach was adopted from the outset - an initial emphasis on the specification of objectives, and later the use of small scale trials with repeated modifications. Learner characteristics were particularly varied with some migrant patients having difficulty with printed passages in the English language. On another dimension, attitudinal and emotional problems were as significant as the cognitive domain. Learning material were developed across a broad spectrum of media-print, audio and television. In addition, a wide variety of approaches were utilized, eg personal and small-group tutorials, peer tutoring and games in various formats (crosswords and snakes and ladders). A condition of the grant was that the final materials, when developed, should be made available at cost to the Renal Units in hospitals throughout Australia and New Zealand. This has now occurred.

INTRODUCTION

Every year, 30 to 40 people under 60 years of age, out of each million in the Western world are diagnosed with terminal renal failure and require the use of an artificial kidney machine ie, renal dialysis. This may be either on a permanent basis or as an interim measure before renal transplantation. The choice will depend on patient needs and preferences as well as a supply of suitable cadaveric kidneys. Fortunately, as shown in Table 1, there is a considerable margin of safety in renal functioning. A normal life-style may be enjoyed if the kidneys function at 15 per cent or more of capacity.

% renal function remaining	Effect on life-style
100 – 15	Normal life
15 – 5	Restricted diet and life-style
5 – 0	Require renal dialysis 3 times per week

TABLE 1 <u>EFFECT OF RENAL DISEASE ON LIFE-STYLE</u>

It is important to be aware that most patients on renal dialysis need to continue dialysing for the remainder of their lives. Therefore, the actual number of patients on artificial kidney machines at any one time will be considerably higher than the annual rate mentioned above.

The current Australian cost for an in-patient on permanent hospital dialysis is $30,000 pa This may be compared with $12,000 pa for a patient on permanent self-dialysis (or home-dialysis). There is, therefore, a considerable economic saving in the development and implementation of an effective dialysis training programme. Apart from this economic aspect, there is also considerable benefit to the patient who gains in independence, confidence and self-esteem by becoming competent in self-dialysis. Indeed, with sufficient advance planning, some patients have made successful journeys interstate and overseas – far removed from the restrictions and dependence of the permanent hospital in-patient. Table 2 indicates the principal developmental stages through which the renal patient passes in developing autonomy. We must use both skill and patience in assisting the gradual transformation to autonomy. We will encounter individuals who appear permanently 'frozen' at a stage of the evolving sequence.

Stage	Manifestation	Effect on learning/living
1 Rejection	Unrealistic fear, despair and denial of renal problem. Why has this happened to me? (anger).	Unco-operative. Lacks motivation. Patient overwhelmed with the magnitude of setting-up and operating the dialysing equipment.
2 Developing self-awareness	Gradual development of knowledge and skills, producing frequent attitudinal changes.	Realization that time taken to dialyse interferes with previous life-style.
3 Re-organization	Diligent effort to succeed. Towards the end of the training period the patient obtains increasing reinforcement from his growing competence.	Gradual development of self-esteem in efforts to become self-reliant in complex tasks. Often assisted by contact with fellow sufferers.
4 Resolution	Development of competence and the overcoming of initial fears, anxieties and feelings of inadequacy.	Sufficient self-confidence to attempt home-dialysis management under supervision.
5 Identity change	A new life-style is established – supported by feeling of mastery and self-esteem. Now fully adjusted to life on dialysis.	Complete confidence in ability to self-dialyse. Autonomy achieved.

TABLE 2   DEVELOPMENTAL STAGES OF THE RENAL PATIENT

We now begin to understand the complexity of the training task. It involves adaptation and change to attitudes, values and motivation in addition to understanding medical and technical information. We can readily appreciate that no individual possesses the necessary knowledge and skills to develop, validate and implement an effective training programme. Only when a small team, comprising at least a renal physician, a renal nursing sister-in-charge, an educational technologist and an educational psychologist, pool their abilities and work together in a harmonious and integrated manner towards agreed aims and objectives, can there be reasonable hope of success. Today, the renal physician who presents his or her patient with a few pages of typescript, perhaps in semi-medical jargon, and expects full patient compliance and co-operation, is seen as unrealistic. To follow an apparently simple regimen, such as a weight-reduction diet, presents major problems to most obese patients.

Long-established habits cannot be readily changed, motivation may be insufficient, knowledge of nutrition may be inadequate and, of course, the way to hell remains paved with good intentions.

A major shift in the treatment of renal disease occurred with the institution of haemodialysis (and, later, peritoneal dialysis), in the home of the patient. Successful adjustment to home dialysis is almost wholly dependent on the quality of training for the management of the patient's chronic disability at home. Thus, effective instruction of the patient plays a vital part in the optimal rehabilitation of the patient, and prevents a patient in a renal centre becoming emotionally dependent on the staff at the centre.

In the United States of America, it has been claimed that the success of the training of renal patients is evidenced by the fact that more than 85 per cent of patients are rehabilitated, returning to full-time employment, school or household duties (Blagg et al, 1970). This is made possible by overnight haemodialysis which allows for minimal interference with personal and family life. There has been steadily increased interest in the training of suitable renal patients to undertake home dialysis, with considerable cost reduction in terms of bed usage and in the time required of medical and nursing staff.

This article discusses inter alia the difficulties encountered, the implications of a team approach and the effectiveness of the use of multi-media for self-instruction. It also touches on the cost-effectiveness of using self-instructional materials for patients of diverse background.

Haemodialysis in the patient's home is possible only when the patient has acquired the knowledge, skills and self-confidence to be able to manage his or her diet, to cope with a complex machine and to be able to conduct safety tests for a number of operations in the haemodialysis process. Errors could be fatal. Manufacturers have developed dialysis equipment to high performance standards. Many are engrossed with engineering innovation rather than ergonomic efficiency and simplicity of operation, desirable for the patient. There has been insufficient effort to develop the patient's knowledge and skills in parallel to the advance of technology. Nevertheless, this project attempted to use the principles of educational technology in a systematic approach to home dialysis.

ANALYSIS OF PATIENT TRAINING NEEDS

Although all patients ultimately need to master the same skills and to develop attitudes conducive to effective home dialysis, they commence from widely differing points. This is undoubtedly one of the greatest problems encountered in any attempt to develop a satisfactory educational programme for all dialysis patients. Reflect for a moment on the wide spectrum of abilities, interests, capacities, educational experience and socio-economic levels, and it will become evident that perhaps the major common experience of this diverse group is renal failure. At many of our major metropolitan teaching hospitals these problems are further compounded by a sketchy knowledge of English. The presence of immigrants without adequate fluency and lacking ability in the written word should cause us to make greater use of audiotapes and visual material.

A similar situation was encountered a few years ago in the course of devising a series of teaching programmes for diabetic patients. The design team resolved the communication problem by utilizing the three familiar colours of traffic signals and linking them to foods which the diabetic may eat in normal quantities, in measured quantities, and foods which are dangerous for the patient and must never be eaten. The linking of familiar colours to normal quantities, in measured quantities, and foods which are dangerous for the patient and must never be eaten. The linking of familiar colours to unknown food categories, apart from being a creative solution to a recurrent problem, was also highly successful as far as interest, understanding and retention of the material was concerned.

ANALYSIS OF PROBLEMS ENCOUNTERED

The training of patients for home dialysis presents unique problems. These problems are those of a patient learning a large and complex repertoire of skills and knowledge. This learning task is compounded by the chronic ill-health of the patient, which is usually sufficient to inhibit learning.

The very magnitude of the learning task often creates a stress with consequent learning blocks. In such a situation it is desirable to remove stress from the learning situation by presenting the material in the best possible learning format and, where possible, arrange for the learner to achieve success in the material presented. Since most of the learning modules designed were self-instructional, they could be structured for a high success rate. Without this patients quickly become discouraged and lose interest. The wide variation among patients suggests a strong case for replicated material, presented in more than one medium.

The development of positive attitudes is often a prerequisite for learning the various tasks faced by dialysis patients. These attitudinal factors have also been noted by Blagg et al (1970) when they wrote 'Successful home dialysis depends on a therapeutic philosophy that emphasizes self-confidence and independence ... both physical and psychological dependence on family and professional staff must be minimized'. The training programme is a more complex process than most other educationand training activities.

From the medical practitioner's viewpoint, there is the legal and moral responsibility for the patient. The physician-in-charge must be certain that a patient has the capability to undertake the management of diet, be able to monitor blood pressure and body weight, to access quickly and accurately a critical situation when a fault occurs in the dialysis process, together with a proven practical ablity to use those skills required for either haemodialysis or peritoneal dialysis.

The programme writer needs to be constantly aware of both the style and nature of the language he or she uses. Material which includes unfamiliar language or medical terminology will have little appeal to the patient - indeed it may be a foreign language to him or her. A frequent difficulty may occur in programme trials when patients seek to oblige the staff and are often unwilling to criticize material or reveal their ignorance. Consequently we need to encourage genuine responses and to use tests which probe more deeply and provide a valid measure of patient knowledge and skills.

A further difficulty which became apparent during the course of the project was the bridging of the gap between the medical practitioner's educational background, which naturally colours his or her viewpoint on learning and training, and that of his or her patient. There is, moreover, a tendency for physicians to equate patient learning with their own experience. The medical profession is recruited from a selective group of students with a scientific bias. In many cases they are drawn from élite schools. Medical training is rigorous, obtained to a large extent from listening to lectures and by extensive note-taking. It is natural for medical practitioners to view patient learning as being simply a diluted form of medical teaching, for example, the mini lecture replaces the formal lecture.

Furthermore, the motivation which carried the medical student through to his or her licence to practise is, and had to be, very intense and powerful. The patient, on the other hand, does not have a bright future, and knows that the disease is often terminal. The extensive demands of home dialysis may produce rejection of learning or antipathy towards home dialysis, perhaps partly due to the patient's acceptance of the security of the hospital ward and its care.

The teaching sisters in the home training unit found the repetition of the training material to slow learners irksome and time-consuming. The introduction of replicated material in various forms relieved them of a major part of a difficult task, thus giving them an opportunity to concentrate on remedial teaching and on instruction in skills which often had to be repeated a number of times. The teaching sisters shared to some degree the doctors' views about the patient's ability to learn.

To summarize, the effective training of patients for home dialysis presents the following special problems:

1. patients' chronic ill-health may inhibit learning;
2. wide variation in socio-economic background and in educational standards;
3. special difficulties faced by immigrants who speak and/or understand little English, or who may not be literate in any language;
4. the psychological effects on the mental outlook of many patients with renal failure;
5. the geriatric group who require more intensive training;
6. training in positive attitudes is necessary;
7. high quality of training is necessary because faulty performance may have lethal effects.

The above factors indicate a need for replicated material of a self-instructional nature because of the special characteristics of the learning problems. A satisfactory programme must permit patients to repeat particular learning sequences as often as necessary. With replicated material, they can work on it without delay and without occupying the time of the staff of the Renal Unit. Ultimately, this means a greater number of patients can be trained in a given period of time. Of course, in addition to replicated material, face-to-face instruction of both individuals and small groups remain an essential part of the overall training programme.

The wide variation of problem areas mentioned in the summary above, suggests a strong case for material to be presented in more than one form, for example, an audiocassette may be preferred to print. The use of suitable self-instructional material can build up self-confidence, self-esteem and thereby tends to motivate the learner.

PROCEDURE

As is common in all fields of human endeavour, communication was the greatest difficulty in this project. The pilot study soon revealed difficulty of communication between divergent groups of patients and physicians from the Renal Unit.

The sisters in the Dialysis Home Training Unit were the principal teachers of the patients. When given the opportunity, they became the 'sounding board' for the team's attempts to communicate the minimum knowledge, skills and attitudes necessary for the patients to become competent and self-reliant in the home dialysis situation.

The primary teaching problem was to eliminate medical jargon from the programmes, and yet provide the patient with an adequate understanding of renal disease, home dietary regimen and the technology of the dialysis equipment. Questions that arose in the early stages of the project were largely related to communication. Every patient presented a unique learning problem. What was the level of understanding of the patient when he or she entered the programme? Did he or she understand English and at what level? What depth of understanding is necessary for a patient in order to perform dialysis safely and effectively? To what extent do patients need to know the function of the heart, kidneys, or the circulatory system? Such were the questions in the minds of the team initially. The physicians expected the educationists to know the levels of understanding necessary for a patient's assessment as competent to perform home dialysis. In the long term this became very much a team decision, but initially there was no other way to evaluate a patient's capability for home dialysis than subjective judgement by sisters and phsicians providing opinions based on practical observation of the patient during training.

The initial flow of material was, as may be seen from Diagram 1, from the small team. The four members of this team came from diverse disciplines as shown in the flow diagram. This small team was the nucleus of the entire project and they met two or three times a week to review progress.

The larger team, again shown on Diagram 1, was designed to bring a breadth of perspective and experience to the project. The group held meetings every month or two and included such unlikely specialists as a philosopher, an evaluator, a psychiatrist, a hospital chaplain and an administrator. With the benefit of hindsight it may have been beneficial to include also a representative of renal patients in the main group. Not only would this person have brought a patient perspective to the deliberations but it would have assisted the introduction, validation and adoption of the programmes. However, the latter was not a problem in this project, although it is conceivable that this could be an area of difficulty in some projects.

The inclusion of a university philosopher and an evaluator was almost by accident. However, the individuals concerned made a useful contribution to discussions by asking some penetrating questions which others had not even considered. It is easy to be so familiar with a project that certain leading issues may entirely escape one's attention. In writing about their role in the project team they described them in these words, 'The intrinsic interest of the project for us had largely to do with what have come to be called "coping problems" or "the affective domain" in patient training, and their relation to teaching materials, procedures and acquired patient competence. That line of interest is also a preliminary evaluative criterion for any educational project'. (Fallon et al 1975)

The final test is how would we now design the study if we were repeating it. Without doubt we would adopt the same two-team approach - a small specialist team meeting every day or two, and a large diverse team, representing widespread interests, meeting at less frequent intervals. It now appears to the writers that in this matter both the fine detail and the broad issues can be adequately addressed.

Small team (Physicians, Renal Sister-in-Charge, Educational
Technologist and Educationist)
develop aims/objectives of the programme
↓
Physicians, Nursing Staff, Dietitians
contribute medical material
↓
Educationist, Graphic Designer and Educational Technologist
modify material and decide on media/format
↓
Prototype material
↓
Meeting of main team:
(Director of Renal Unit, Renal Physicians,
Senior Dialysis Technician, Sister-in-Charge Renal
Home Training Unit, Dietitian, Other Specialists,
Educational Technologist, Educationists, Graphic Designer)
↓
Small team re-drafts material
↓
Review by main team
↓
Small pilot trial
↓
Small team discusses and evaluates trial
↓
Final modifications by Educationists and Graphic Designer
↓
Approval by Renal Physicians
↓
Reproduce in trial form
↓
Re-check by Renal Staff
↓
Main trial
↓
Summative evaluation, final discussion
and modifications by main team
↓
Production, National distribution and implementation

DIAGRAM 1   <u>PROGRAMME DEVELOPMENT</u>

PATIENT COMPLIANCE

An important factor in successful training of patients for home dialysis is that of patient
compliance. Since the first conference, in 1976, on patient counselling in Amsterdam, there
has been a growing awareness in the medical profession of the importance of training in all
areas where patient compliance is relevant (White et al,1980; Pool,1980). This is now seen as
fundamental for successful palliative treatment, for example, adherence to regular drug
regimens for hypertensive patients. Similarly, the renal patient's responsibility for
monitoring and controlling diet, weight gain, blood pressure and restricted intake of fluids, all
require a high degree of patient compliance. Adequate patient training can make a

significant contribution to effective treatment. Indeed, in America, patient education is now regarded by some as being a legal obligation. The current situation has been described in these words, 'Patient education is no longer just a good idea. It is a legal obligation, especially with respect to self-care instruction, informed discharge, and follow-up care. The benefits to the well-being of patients cannot be questioned, although patient education is not a panacea for procuring well-being'. (McCaughrin,1979)

In the Home Training Unit a positive approach on the part of the staff leads to the gradual development of the self-confidence of the patient. The workload of the staff does not permit the full teaching time to be directed towards one patient and there is accordingly ample opportunity for self-instructional programmes. It is the opinion of the educationists working on the project that many more self-instructional programmes could have been used, were it not that the team had in many cases their normal workload to consider. Ideally, there would have been a much larger number of programmes provided for patients and many others provided in alternate form, had not time and cost factors precluded this.

EFFECTIVENESS OF THE OVERALL PROGRAMME

This project has required a new and critical look at the teaching/learning process in relation to the renal dialysis patient. In any learning situation the designer of material for self-instruction must take into account the application of learning principles and theories applicable to self-instructional material. However, in training patients for home dialysis there were certain areas in which face-to-face contact with the nursing sisters (who were the trainers) was indispensable in the teaching of skills of a psycho-motor nature. Perhaps this was best exemplified by fistula puncturing for the insertion of arterial or venous needles in haemodialysis. This, of course, raised the question of attitudinal change, because this skill was best achieved by the sister teaching such a skill. A skill of this kind was taught 'live' in a situation where the tutoring sister could shape the learning process, encourage better attempts and reinforce the fumbling attempts present in early stages of learning.

The importance of the tutorial staff in assisting patients with the adoption of positive attitudes cannot be overemphasized, because it is very difficult to attempt this in any self-instructional mode. The renal patient, often suffering from various degrees of malaise resulting from the illness, and also from the change in life-style, has often developed psychological problems. In some cases he or she has even lost interest in life and attempted suicide is not unknown. The regime of restricted diet, restricted social activity, as well as the lengthy time spent in going, dialysing and coming off dialysis, as well as maintaining the machine according to standards of scrupulous sterility, all add to the burden.

The project had a positive effect on the teaching staff. Two nursing sisters on the staff attended a course in learning theory and the preparation of mediated material, as well as a short course in the teaching of skills. The importance of skill teaching lies not only in acquiring specific skills, but also developing correct attitudes and confidence in the patient's ability to master his or her situation.

With the steady growth of a diversity of self-instructional modules, mostly in the form of print, the patient was able to build up progressively a manual to which he or she could refer. For example, patients used a manual setting out sequential procedural steps, and the related tests which occur sequentially. Should a fault occur in the dialysing equipment (triggering off an alarm), the patient could then refer to a fault finder to help in analysing and rectifying the fault. This was of substantial value to a patient who awakened to a terrifying situation in the early hours of the morning, by an alarm indicating that a blood leak was occurring.

The initial request of the medical staff, before this project commenced, was for a film or videotape as a means of teaching dialysis patients and medical students. Yet when the aims and objectives were clarified and the needs of patients investigated an entirely different product emerged. Learning materials in the final package ranged from printed protocols through diagrams and illustrations to audiotapes, simulated games (eg, snakes and ladders with a renal bias!) and crossword puzzles, based on essential knowledge required by the renal patient. A printed patient manual, complete with marginal notes and diagrams has also been published and widely distributed (Parer et al,1983). Patient response has been most encouraging and, above all, renal patients now achieve full autonomy and home dialysis in a shorter period of time. A condition of the initial funding was that the final teaching/learning materials should be made available to renal units throughout Australia and New Zealand and this has now occurred.

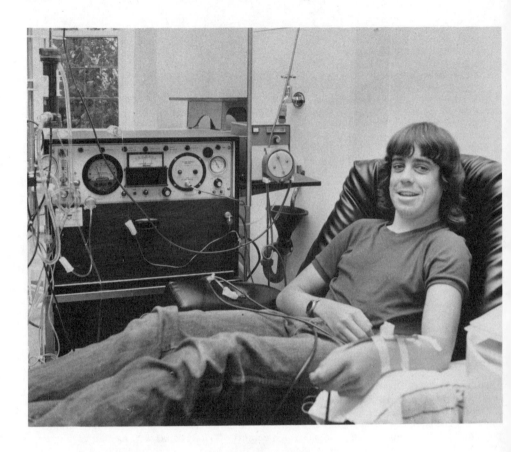

Patient under dialysis

ACKNOWLEDGEMENTS

We gratefully acknowledge the ready co-operation and assistance, throughout the entire project, of the patients and staff of the Renal Unit, Austin Hospital, Melbourne, Australia.
    The major funding of this project, including salaries, equipment and materials, was provided by the Clive and Vera Ramaciotti Foundation, Sydney, Australia. We thank the Foundation for their generous support.

REFERENCES

Blagg, C R, Daly, S M, Rosenquist, B J, Jensen, W M and Eachback, J W (1970) The Importance of Patient Training in Home Haemodialysis. Annals of Internal Medicine 73, 5, p 842.
Fallon, B J and Orton, T (1975) Statement to Ramaciotti project. Unpublished report.
McCaughrin, W C (1979) Legal Precedents in American Law for Patient Education. Patient Counselling and Health Education, 1, 4, p141.
Parer, M S, Driver, S C et al (1983) Living With Kidney Failure. Deakin University Press, Geelong, Victoria.
Pool, J J (1980) Expected and Actual Knowledge of Hospital Patients. Patient Counselling and Health Education, 3, 3, p111.
White, C W, Lemon, D K and Albanese, M A (1980) Efficacy of Health Education Efforts on Hospitalized Patients with Serious Cardiovascular Diseases. Patient Counselling and Health Education, 3, 4, p189.

6.4 Human Resource Development: Path Towards Socio-Economic Improvement in Third World Nations

E B Awotua-Efebo
Burroughs Corporation, Detroit, USA

Abstract: In developing nations, a vicious cycle exists: the inability of their people to improve their socio-economic conditions due to the fact that they are poor. Yet most of these nations are endowed with an abundance of mineral and human resources. Trying to break the vicious cycles, leaders of these nations embarked on economic and native-building primarily through industrialization. These leaders have not been successful.

This paper suggests developing and using the abundant human resources to break the vicious cycle. The topics explored include: means of developing human resources, technological choice and acquisition, problems facing developing nations, the need for a systems approach to human resource development.

INTRODUCTION

'Shirtless and barefoot in the relentless morning sun, Armando Ortiz swings a machete through the knee-high weeds around his goat pen to clear land for a new mud house. It is boring, backbreaking work, but that is all anyone in this rural mountain village (Union Y Libertad, Mexico) of 300 poor souls expects out of life. In this entire country, hardly anything has changed here; except the coming of electricity.'

This is how Karen Elliott-House and Steve Frazier described the life style of a typical family in rural parts of most Third World Nations. They continue:

'Some 400 miles to the north, on the fringes of Mexico City, Mr. Ortiz's cousin, Eugenio, spends his morning looking for a job without success. Eugenio left this quiet green village (Union Y Libertad) two years ago for what he thought would be a better life. Instead, he found only the smog and dust of an urban slum. Now, most afternoons, he sits dejectedly, amid the squalor of his aunt's ramshackle shanty in the slums. At 22 years of age, Eugenio faces a choice of poverty in the country or poverty in the city.'

The picture of Ortiz's family graphically illustrates the plight of millions of people in what is now referred to as the Third World. The majority of these people are unskilled and underdeveloped, causing a vicious cycle - rural poverty leading to flight to urban areas where unemployment leads to increased poverty.

The theme of this paper - the development of human resources as a means for socio-economic improvement - should be of particular interest to those leaders of the Third World nations and anyone, for that matter, who is interested in breaking the vicious cycle of poverty illustrated by the Ortiz family.

Socio-economic improvement is viewed as a process which is primarily directed towards:

1. the satisfaction of basic human needs (starting with the needs of the neediest, viz, the urban and rural poor);
2. endogenous self-reliance through social participation and control;
3. harmony with the environment to ensure the long-term sustainability of this development process (Reddy, 1979).

Now, more than ever before, the Third World nations are faced with mounting problems of unemployment and poverty. It is now clear that these nations will not be able to meet the basic needs of their millions of people before the turn of the century if the present status quo development strategies are continued (status quo in terms of spending more on the modern sector at the expense of increased productivity and incomes in the traditional rural and informal urban sectors where the majority of the population eke out a living).

This author feels strongly that the focus of any new development strategies in these nations should be on the abundant human resources, both in the rural and urban settings. The systems approach, if it is used correctly for developing the human resources, can be a vehicle for alleviating the socio-economic problems that now exist.

THIRD WORLD NATIONS: WHO ARE THEY?

In less than a score of years, the terms 'Third World' and 'developing nations' have come to be part of the vocabulary of politicians and academics. There is a tendency for some to think that all the nations grouped under the label 'Third World' are alike. This is far from the truth.

The countries generally covered by the term 'Third World' range from the oil-rich and rapidly industrializing nations of OPEC to mid-range developing countries with per capita incomes usually exceeding $900 per year with favorable growth prospects, on to the world's poorest countries in which annual per capita incomes fall below $200 and the industrial base is quite narrow and growth prospects are, at best, uncertain.

The Third World nations are concentrated in Africa, Central and South America, South Asia, the Middle East, and the Caribbean region. In contrast, 'developed nations' (the distinctions of 'first' and 'second' world nations remain undefined) is the term applied to the rich countries of western Europe, North America, and Australia.

To interpret conditions and events that affect human resource development in these nations, we must understand what the Third World is and is not.

CHARACTERISTICS OF THIRD WORLD NATIONS

Despite the fact that the Third World nations span the globe and have different cultures, histories, and pastoral life, they do have certain characteristics in common. Table 1 illustrates some of their characteristics as compared to those of the developed nations.

What the table shows is the presence of poverty, disease, and ignorance under Column II, 'Third World Nations,' and the absence of these in 'Developed Nations,' Column I. While basic problems still exist in developed nations, there is still a perception that the great difference between developed nations and Third World nations is that developed nations have solved their basic problems while Third World nations have failed (Davidson,1974).

MYTHS ABOUT THE THIRD WORLD NATIONS

It is necessary at this point to comment on and dispel some of the myths about why Third World nations have failed, so far, to solve their basic problems, why they lack skilled human resources and remain in a state of underdevelopment. Since the author is from Africa and is more familiar with that continent, he will discourse the myths that prevail about Africa.

This does not mean that the continents of Asia, Central and South America, and the Caribbean regions are free of myths that need to be dispelled. After all, the majority of Third World nations are within the tropical zone which is supposed to have jungles and wild animals and very hot climate that is unbearable.

One myth which relates to the development of human resources in Africa concerns tropical environment and the effect it has upon people. Most people who have never been in the tropics picture inordinately hot weather, a jungle with very tall trees and thick undergrowth, poisonous snakes hanging from each tree, and docile 'tribes' of men and women who are lazy and live off the bounty of nature. Novels and movies have helped to reinforce these myths, especially in the developed nations of the west. It is not difficult to see how these myths started.

Long before the Europeans arrived in and colonized Africa, they assumed that, as one went southward, the climate became warmer and the people who lived in these places became darker in complexion. Since people knew of the extreme heat of the Sahara desert, they concluded that the temperature further south was even hotter than that of the Sahara, that people would be roasted and ships would burn. These extreme beliefs were modified as exploration and colonization of the continent progressed.

Characteristics	Column I Developed Nations	Column II Third World Nations
Economy	Highly developed; sophisticated	Low-level development; simplistic
Literacy	High percentage	Low percentage (5-50%)
Labor force	Large percentage technicians, specialists, and highly industrialized community, efficiency	Peasant and agrarian; poor organization
Income	High per capita income	Very low per capita income
Birth rate	Low	Very high
Mortality rate	Low mortality rate; preventive health program	High mortality rate; disease, squalor
Government	Self-rule for many years	Recently autonomous or still colonial
Politics	Well organized and fairly stable political system	Transitional political stage; political system fairly unstable
Citizens' rights	People recognize their rights and obligations	Transitional stage; many do not know their rights and obligations
Education	Geared to the needs of the people and country	Inherited system from the colonial era with little or no relevance to nation
Production	Manufacturers	Consumers
Living style	Masses, by the large scientifically oriented, less superstitious, and generally efficient	Masses, largely superstitious, scientifically illiterate, and have not acquired technical efficiency

SOURCE: Fafunwa, 1969.

Table 1

Contrast Between Developed and Third World Nations

Recent technological advancements have made the world 'shrink', and modern communication techniques are helping to resolve some of the most absurd myths. However, the fact remains that many subtropical areas, such as the Sahara or some parts of California in the western United States of America, have recorded significantly higher temperatures than any ever recorded in the tropics. While many subtropical areas regularly record 120° Farenheit, the temperature in the tropics rarely exceeds 90° Farenheit. There are many factors that explain this disparity:

1. The rays of the sun are filtered by the humid atmosphere which lowers the temperature considerably.
2. The frequent canopy of clouds further filters the rays and also contributes to lowering the temperature.
3. Surface temperature is affected by the length of time the sun continually shines on an area.

In the tropics, with only slight seasonal variations, the sun shines for only 12 hours each day. In the subtropics and temperate zones, the 12-hour day occurs twice a year at the equinoxes. Half the year, it shines for more than 12 hours a day.

Another myth that continues to linger is that of the jungle, where tall trees and thick undergrowth make penetration and development of the land difficult. This myth probably came about because explorers followed the rivers. The edges of the tropical rain forest have a thick undergrowth since light abundantly reaches these areas. Within the forest, however, there is a different situation. The tall trees form a canopy that allows very little light to reach the ground, thereby reducing the energy for photosynthesis. The forest offers few hindrances to walking. The major hindrances are generally man-made. The African method for farming is to set fire to a plot, clear it, cultivate it; then, after three to four years of usage, the plot is abandoned and a new plot is located. This method can give rise to a secondary forest with considerable undergrowth.

Another myth about the tropics that should be dispelled is that its climate is unhealthful and inhospitable, at least to westerners. Tropical West Africa, for example, was once called the 'white man's grave.' It was not explained how the Africans could live and work in the tropics while the white man could not. While it is true that many Europeans died in the early times, there are reasons other than climate that account for the deaths. Many sailors died of scurvy and beriberi as a result of dietary deficiencies. Many also contacted diseases to which the African population was relatively immune.

Another cause of the early Europeans' difficulties was their unpreparedness for adapting to a new climate. Most of them had tight-fitting clothes. As Briggs(1960) indicates, 'adjustment to a hot climate involves a whole pattern of living, including type of clothing, style of walking and foods'. When the early Europeans attempted to adapt to the tropics, they often did so according to their misconceptions and not to the reality of the tropics.

It is necessary to take a more realistic view of Africa and the Third World nations. It is not the attempt of this author to paint Africa or any part of the Third World as a paradise on earth. Most parts of tropical Africa and the Third World nations are disease-ridden and unhealthy by western standards. The living conditions for most of the population are deplorable. However, this does not mean that the climate is unhealthful, nor the people imbeciles. The problems reflect the underdeveloped state of the human resources and their limited implementation. The benefit from past development strategies with emphasis on the modern sector has been disappointing. Due to the unexpectedly slow economic growth rate that has occurred--an average of 5 per cent, sustained over many years--these benefits have not filtered down to the majority of the people, but have remained concentrated in the hands of a few (Pyatt & Thorbecke,1976).

HUMAN RESOURCE DEVELOPMENT - A NEW DIRECTION

As stated earlier, most of the strategies proposed and adapted for improving the socio-economic condition in Third World nations (spending more on the modern sector at the expense of rural areas) are satisfying on aesthetic grounds. However, when thorough scrutiny discloses how the masses in these nations use inanimate sources of power and/or tools to multiply the effects of their efforts to create a better living condition, it becomes clear that such strategies are ludicrous in practice.

Human resource development is often considered to be synonymous with educational planning. As used here, human resource development has a wider domain than educational planning. The latter covers the arrangement and ordering of the school programs and the more formally managed in-service training centres. The former – human resource development – covers the establishment of standards that relieve morbidity and mortality to levels where the population can use whatever education and training it has to produce. Human resource development enables people to learn and adapt more effectively. To learn is to increase one's efficiency and effectiveness over time under constant conditions. To adapt is to maintain or increase one's efficiency or effectiveness over time under changing conditions. In short, human resource development can cover all of the institutional and individual ways in which a population acquires and improves knowledge and skill for social, political, and economic development. Much of this goes on privately, in the minds and hearts of men, women, and children, away from observation, characterization, and control. Formal education is a large part of human resource development – but not all. In planning, one will often involve the other, but not in all cases.

DEPENDENCY: STATE OF THIRD WORLD NATIONS

The fundamental dilemma of the Third World nations is that their abundant human resources are unskilled, underdeveloped, and in a continuing state of dependency. Because of this dependency, the majority of these nations are vulnerable, their vulnerability being the inability of a collectivity to determine a nation's responsibility to socio-economic forces within and outside its borders.

Programs for socio-economic improvement are built around organizations. Organizations, whether for profit, service, or fun, have purposes. As a result they also have needs. One of those needs is for the human resources within them to engage effectively in activities that lead toward accomplishing the organizations' purposes.

If the human resources within an organization cannot engage effectively, then the organization will turn to outside help in an attempt to accomplish its purposes. The providers of outside help (foreign aids from developed nations to Third World nations) may have needs and purposes of their own. When they take the responsibility of serving the organization's needs, they are at the same time attempting to serve their own. Conflicts between these two sets of needs often arise.

For example, in reviewing the worldwide use of educational television in Third World nations, Arnove(1975) found that educational television has not been aimed at reaching the most disadvantaged population – the rural poor and the urban unemployed. In the cases where programs are directed to the disadvantaged population, the program content is often inappropriate and represents models of behavior and values foreign to this group. He notes that in some cases educators and communicators who develop these programs are unconsious of their biases.

With abundant natural resources, independence in the majority of the Third World nations was intended to open up ways to mitigate their misery. In many cases, things are worse today than they were under colonial rule. Programmes like Point Four, the Marshall Plan, AID, UNESCO, The Peace Corps, and SS Hope have not worked as expected.

The problem with these programmes is one in which a foreigner (including western-trained nationals of Third World nations who carry the traditional disdain of the upper-class bureaucrats) from a developed nation, who is competent and knows the techniques of improved farming, administration, better sanitation etc, stands among people from less affluent Third World nations and attempts to communicate new ideas, such as advanced ways of farming, latest technology of education (ETV, CBT etc), best style of government, new ideology of cooperation etc. It is on this rock of inter-cultural communication that these programmes, though with good intentions, fail (Davidson,1974).

Downs (1971) points out that most foreign aid failures can be placed in two categories which are not mutually exclusive:

1. There is often a failure to understand the nature of fruitful change with resultant attempts to create projects in [Third World] nations which are inconsistent with the stage or level of the country's development – the model city gradually fills up with slum dwellers, the airline growing less efficient daily; the complex of hospital and health centres standing unused, serving only to remind the populace of the failure of government programmes.
2. The failures, or at least incomplete successes, may result partly from poor planning, but they reflect primarily the inability of those charged with introducing new technical knowledge to communicate ideas and practices effectively.

What Downs' statement implies is that aid programmes have sometimes tried to transplant the skills instead of going back to the fundamentals that may have accounted for the success of developing such strategies in the developed nations. The result for the Third World nations is that they are asked to copy rather than to be responsible for time-consuming development.

The degree to which a nation is vulnerable is directly related to the level of development of its human resources and on its socio-economic level. The more vulnerable a nation is, the more it depends on other nations to supply the basic needs for its survival and growth. The interaction between dependency (D) on the one hand and human resource development (HRD) and socio-economic level (SEL) on the other hand can be represented thus:

$D = F$ (HRD,SEL) where F is a factor that determines degree of dependency (1)

Since, in any society, the socio-economic level is related to the state of development of its human resources, then

$SEL = (K)(HRD)$ where K is a factor that determines the socio-economic level (2)

It becomes clear then (from 1 and 2 above) that

$D = F [K(HRD)]$

If we represent the compound factors caused by F and K as J, then the factor J is what needs to be investigated in order to diminish the dependency state of Third World nations. One way to investigate this is through the systems approach.

SYSTEMS APPROACH TO HUMAN RESOURCE DEVELOPMENT

Just as Third World nations are plagued with problems today, the developed nations, especially the United States military, were faced with challenges during the Second World War. In response to the challenges, civilians from various professions and military personnel were brought together to formulate and design strategies to solve eminent problems; thus, the systems approach was instituted. After the war, the systems approach was adopted by businesses, local and federal government agencies, and recently by educational institutions of the developed nations.

The systems approach can be defined as a planned and sustained effort to apply scientific methodology in a holistic way for improving all the means for organization development. It involves using self-analytic methods.

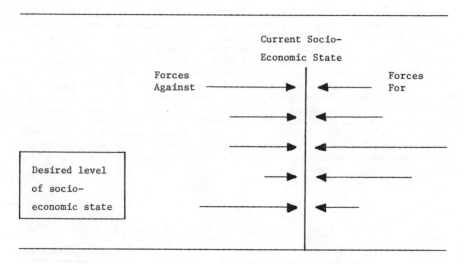

Figure 1:   Force-Field Analysis

The emphasis for Third World nations in applying the systems approach should be to identify the ends and means for socio-economic improvement, ie, investigate factor J rather than an individual as a target of change. Factor J should reveal if an important part of the means—human resource development—should be an entire organization or a subject.

The systems approach as proposed here should involve members of Third World nations themselves in the assessment, diagnosis, and transformation of their organization, rather than simply accepting diagnosis and prescriptions from an outside 'technocratic' expert. The members with assistance from outside consultants should examine current difficulties and their causes, and participate actively in the reformation of goals, the development of new group-process skills, the design of structures for achieving the goals, the alteration of the working climate, and the assessment of results.

The process of force-field analysis can be used as a tool to investigate factor J. The current socio-economic situation can be assessed by delineating the forces for and against movement toward an improved state (the desired level of socio-economic state). The present situation exists because of a balance determined by these forces (Fig. 1).

If we can determine and increase the forces which push toward the desired level of socio-economic state and/or decrease the forces pushing away from the desired state, then we can move toward the desired level of improvement in the socio-economic state. The key to achieving this is in developing the abundant human resources of these nations to become less dependent by learning to use and adapt inanimate sources of power and/or use of tools to multiply the effects of their efforts.

MEANS OF DEVELOPING HUMAN RESOURCES

Though inadequate to respond to the needs of their societies, the educational systems have been the sole means of human resource development in Third World nations. The educational systems in these nations are primarily organizations and many, if not most, efforts at educational reform have collapsed or have been absorbed without effect. This is caused by the limited attention given to the organizations context in which the reforms have been attempted (Carnoy & Levin,1976). Any major innovation in curriculum or instructional technique implies a change in the 'culture' of the educational system. For example, when educational television was introduced in El Salvador, there was a change in the behavior of the teachers (Mayo et al,1976). Changes in attitude due to educational reform or innovation have been reported in India (Mody,1978), and Japan (Nishimoto,1969).

Real improvement in developing the abundant human resources of Third World nations is to be determined not so much by the adaptation of new technology and specific educational practices, as by the modification of organizational conservation (evidenced by self-contained classrooms, civil service examinations in large cities, the 'tyranny of the schedule,' and the practice of ability grouping) and organizational pathology (school/community paranoia, mistrust, powerlessness and alienation in teachers, and repressive management of students' lives) inherited from colonial eras. The focus of human resource development should be on using the brain to create and innovate, instead of using it for storing and repeating.

Human resource development should not rely solely on the realm of formal educational institutions. With proliferation of technology for instruction, it is possible to develop human resources as defined earlier. Since a nation cannot use all known and available technology of instruction, the systems approach can be used in aiding the choice of the available appropriate technology.

A cube (like that shown in Figure 2) can be used in deciding on what actions to take. On the left is a list of the forces for and/or against what needs to be increased and/or decreased. This has been determined earlier through force-field analysis. The diagonal edge of the cube identifies the focus of attention. The focus of attention may be in adult education (both rural and urban), formal education, development of skills, citizens' rights, national obligations etc.

The technology of instruction is all those technologies known and available to the nation developing its human resources.

Applying the systems approach does not mean the destruction of traditional cultures and structures although, in some cases, these may be forces against the strategies adopted for human resource development. The systems approach must not encourage 'scientific' thinking that eliminates values and meaning, which are the life substance of culture. Rather, the systems approach should be used within the framework of the priceless moral and artistic values, ethical codes, and way of life of the people in these nations.

The rationale for this is simple. Human resource development to be successful can never

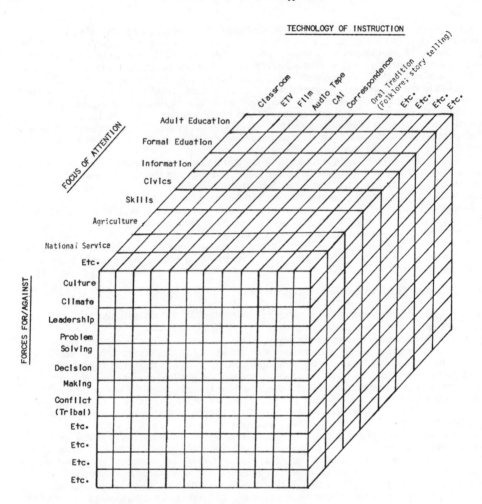

Figure 2: <u>SCHEME FOR HUMAN RESOURCE DEVELOPMENT</u>

be culture-free. Man is part of the culture in which he was born, has lived, and has become socialized. He is the carrier and disseminator as well as the producer of additions to it.

The culture of one society cannot be substituted for another – it can only be changed. In this process some of its elements are exposed more than others, and it is these which are utilized in new action. Culture is not static. Inherently or under exogenous inducement, it continuously changes, yet it remains the most constant element that one considers in developing human resources for socio-economic improvement.

CONCLUSION

The one essential need to improve the socio-economic state of Third World nations is the development of its abundant human resources. The general development strategies of the past two decades emphasized investing heavily in the modern industrial sector of the economy and concentrating government expenditures on 'economic' rather than 'social' overhead projects like human resource development. They expected the gain to 'trickle down' to the entire population in the form of growing per capita income. In the majority of these nations, not only has the standard of living fallen in the past decade, it has made them more vulnerable due to dependency on foreign aid.

The systems approach, used within the framework of the culture of these nations, has been suggested for human resource development. Force-field analysis is seen as a possible tool for determining the forces for and against the attainment of the desired socio-economic state. With the use of appropriate technology, steps can be taken to focus attention on increasing the forces for and/or decreasing the forces against the attainment of the desired level of socio-economic development.

Human resource development is viewed as the means for socio-economic improvement in Third World nations because Man possesses untapped resources of vision and creativity as well as moral energies which can be mobilized to bail human-kind out of its predicament. (Botkin et al,1979).

In these nations (and in others), human beings use a small fraction of their potential. It has been estimated that the average person uses only 5 per cent of his or her creative capacity. Thus, it is apparent that all people have creative capacities which can be developed.

We can no longer ignore the truism, especially in formulating solutions to improve the socio-economic level of Third World nations, that in the long run it is better to start with poor initial solutions that improve over time than with good ones that deteriorate over time.

REFERENCES

Arnove, R F (1975) Sociopolitical implications of educational television. Journal of Communication, 25.

Awotua-Efebo, E B (1981) Development strategies and technology for developing nations: The case for human resource development using ETV in Nigeria. Unpublished Ph D dissertation, Wayne State University, Detroit, Michigan.

Awotua-Efebo, E B (1984) Human resource development: A key to breaking the vicious cycle in developing nations. Programmed Learning and Educational Technology, 21, 1, pp46-51.

Botkin, J W, Elmandjra, M and Malitza, M (1979) No limits to learning: Bridging the human gap - A report to the Club of Rome. Pergamon Press, Oxford, England.

Briggs, L C (1960) Tribes of the Sahara. Harvard University Press.

Carnoy, M and Levin, H M (1976) The limits of educational reform. Longman Inc, New York.

Davidson, B (1974) Can Africa survive? Arguments against growth without development. Little, Brown & Company, Boston.

DeGregori, T R (1969) Technology and the economic development of the tropical African frontier. The Press of Case Western Reserve University, Cleveland, Ohio.

Downs, J F (1971) Cultures in crisis. Glencoe Press, Beverly Hills, CA.

Elliott-House, K and Frazier, S (1984) Fleeing the farms: Ortiz family illustrates 'Why rural poor flood into Mexico's capital.' The Wall Street Journal, March 19, p1.

Fafunwa, B A (1969) Educational philosophy and structure for economic development. In Yesufu T M (ed) Manpower problems and economic development in Nigeria. pp 137-138. Oxford University Press, Ibadan.

Fagen, R R (1981) The tranformation of political culture in Cuba. Stanford University Press, Stanford, CA.

Mayo, J K, Hornik, R C and McAnany, E G (1976) Educational reform with television: The El Salvador experience. Stanford University Press, Stanford, CA.

Mody, B (1978) The Indian satelite instructional TV experiment: Its origins, organization, messages, and effects. Paper presented at the International Communication Association, Chicago.

Nishimoto, M (1969) The development of educational broadcasting in Japan. Sophia University, Tokyo, with Charles E Tuttle Company, Vermont.

Pyatt, G and Thorbecke, E (1976) Planning techniques for a better future. International Labour Office, Geneva.

Reddy, A K N (1979) National and regional technology groups and institutions: An assessment. In Bhalla A S (ed) Towards global action for appropriate technology. pp63-137. Pergamon Press, Oxford.

6.5 Facilitating Scientific Thinking in a Third World Non-Formal Setting: An Educational Technology Perspective

A M Stewart and M C A Gunn
Dundee College of Technology

Abstract: The over-dependance on rote learning in Third World countries has been well documented as has the resulting widespread inability to apply concepts and principles to the solving of problems. The literature shows a notable lack of agreement as to what constitutes scientific thinking. The purpose of this paper is to describe a project designed to facilitate scientific thinking in a third world non-formal setting which necessitated an analysis of the characteristics of scientific thinking in relation to Piagetian theories, inductive and deductive reasoning, and hierarchies of learning objectives from an educational technology perspective, and the development of proposals which could be implemented by non-scientific personnel involved in the leadership of children's social/recreational clubs.

INTRODUCTION

Around the world, science and technology are valued because of the resulting benefits of independence, power and prestige which they bring to a society. Science and technology appear to be mutually supportive: science engenders technological progress while technology makes possible many of the major advances of science (Baez,1967). UNESCO(1964) argues that a developing country must strive to build up its own scientific and technological potential. Leaders in most of the developing countries recognize that they must move into the era of applied science and technology if the standards of living of their ever increasing populations are to be improved. It is worth noting that science and technology are emphasized in many development plans and in bilateral and international aid programmes.

President Mubarak of Egypt has made it clear that it is his aim 'to increase production and productivity ... create more jobs for our working force, and ... to absorb the latest technology available', and Hyde(1978) has pointed out that in every plan for every aspect of living in Egypt, the word 'scientific' has an assured place, signifying the enormous importance attached to this comparatively new approach to the problems of the state. The National Centre for Educational Research (NCER) has recognized that Egypt 'lives in an age of science, intellectuality, creativity and inventiveness, an age of rapid development in which supremacy is for thought, intellect and science, one that demands a human capable of permanenetly moving forward in big strides, an age in which human resources are among the most important and serious elements of economic development' (NCER,1980).

Clearly there is recognition that importing science and technology does not make a country advanced: it is scientific thinking and the application of science and technology to the country's problems that are important. The Egyptian educational system purports to provide students, not only with enough scientific background to be able to pursue scientific studies at a higher level, but having the capacity to 'think scientifically' in any situation that confronts them. But is this really the case?

THE TYRANNY OF THE EXAMINATION SYSTEM

Cookey(1976), Dube(1976), Dore(1976), Sam(1975) and Hyde(1978) have all been very critical of the influence of examinations in the educational systems in the developing world. For some time it has been observed that the education provided in many developing countries is not geared towards enhancing the knowledge, skills and values which would help students live more productive lives in society; rather it is geared to preparing students to move from one rung of the educational ladder to the next. The ultimate aim is to pass the examination which allows entrance to university. This quest for university education and the worship of university degrees and diplomas distorts the educational system, and the examinations associated with such progression do little to encourage 'thinking' let alone 'scientific thinking'.

The examination system does not encourage questions of 'how' or 'why' with the requirement being only for the recall of factual information. Accordingly, the teaching strategies frequently result in rote learning, and the learner is seldom required to be involved in the application of knowledge to problem situations. In Egypt, the Ministry of Education recognizes the problem and has stated that education should be 'causing the spirit of innovation and creativity, for the acquisition of basic learning skills, and for the continued pursuit of learning to replace the style of rote learning and memorization which centres attention only on factual details of information' (NCER,1980).

It was in this setting that the following project was prepared.

A PROPOSAL FOR A PROJECT IN 'SCIENTIFIC THINKING'

As part of the United Nations' International Year of the Child in 1979, the Egyptian government considered the important role that education in science and technology plays in their national development. In the conviction that exposure to educational aids at an early age creates an interest for scientific and technical education as well as increasing the prospects for absorbing technological know-how and transfer at a later stage, they sought the support of the United Nations Development Program (UNDP) for a project which would be implemented through the State Information Service of the Ministry of Information in Egypt, and would have the following objectives:

* to determine what technological educational aids would be useful in stimulating mechanical curiosity and a scientific way of thinking in children 6- to 12-years-old;
* to provide prototypes of technological educational aids to selected children's clubs in the Governorates in order to obtain the reactions of these institutions as to their suitability for technical training purposes; and
* to produce prototypes of technological educational aids on the basis of the requirements of utilisers of such educational aids.

In May 1983, Dundee College of Technology was approached for help with the project. It was considered that the title 'educational aids project' had been unfortunate since the emphasis was on the means through which the product was to be achieved rather than on the end product itself – the bringing about of particular styles of thinking. It was agreed that an alternative approach with the major purpose of being the facilitating of scientific thinking in Egyptian children through the utilization of teacher-mediated resource-based learning materials in the non-formal setting of children's clubs be adopted.

As it was the considered judgement of the writers that it would not be possible to bring about scientific thinking in children if their leaders/teachers did not have any idea as to what scientific thinking was, it was decided that the leaders should attend an eight-week full-time course of study with the following aims:

* to facilitate the acquiring of scientific thinking in leaders of the children's clubs so that they, in turn, might facilitate scientific thinking in the children of the clubs, and
* to develop an ability to design and produce and utilize media-based learning materials.

It was also agreed that a learning package would be developed at Dundee for use in the children's clubs in Egypt designed to facilitate scientific thinking.

IDENTIFYING THE NATURE OF 'SCIENTIFIC THINKING'

Although many references to 'scientific thinking' are to be found in the literature, one of the few aspects on which the sources agree is its importance in this age of science. Some references to it have been very vague in their interpretation and little attempt has been made to define or describe the concept. Other references infer that scientific thinking is closely related to, or even synonymous with, such terms as 'problem soving', 'critical thinking', 'scientific process', scientific attitudes', 'scientific method', or combinations of these terms. Some light has been shed on various components of scientific thinking; measures have been created to test for it; but there has been only partial agreement concerning these components as the synonymous terms indicate.

Maskill and Wallis(1982) say that there is an assumption made in research that 'scientists think "better" than other people do and that there is some singular, superior modus operandi which scientists use and which separates scientists from other people.' The present writer would argue that not only is there something singular in their modus operandi but also in their cognitive processes which give rise to that modus operandi, and the attitudinal drive which influence both the cognitive process and the modus operandi.

It is interesting to note that Noll(1935) suggested that 'the persons working in the field of science teaching seem for the most part never to have got the point of thinking scientifically about scientific thinking'. The danger, as Munby(1982) points out is that if the meaning of the terms 'thinking critically' or 'thinking scientifically' is not clear, these phrases will become vacuous slogans beyond translation, teaching methods, and curriculum materials.

The contribution of scientific attitude

The need for a scientific attitude as an objective of education was expressed by Dewey(1934). According to Heiss(1958), the development of a scientific attitude and the development of, and ability to use, scientific methods are two of the goals of science instruction. Also, the common elements of a scientific attitude are curiosity, freedom from bias, critical mindedness, intellectual honesty, belief in cause and effect, and willingness to change belief when new evidence is found.

The contribution of scientific method

Scientific method is basically a systematic way of looking at things and thinking problems through. Although the exact formulation of the steps into which the scientific method can be delineated varies somewhat from writer to writer, the general pattern for soving problems is accepted as:

1. perception of a problem;
2. conduct preliminary observation;
3. generate possible hypothesis or possible solutions to the problem;
4. test validity of hypothesis by observation or experiment;
5. solution of problem.

Developing from this, Burmester(1952) and Burke(1949) have identified what they consider to be the major elements involved in scientific thinking and which can be rationalized as:

1. the ability to sense or recognize a problem;
2. the ability to state or delineate a problem;
3. the ability to recognize and gather facts which are related to the problem;
4. the ability to formulate hypotheses;
5. the ability to plan and carry out tests of the hypothesis;
6. the ability to interpret data;
7. the ability to formulate generalizations based on the data;
8. the ability to apply generalizations to new situations.

This approach is still clearly based in the scientific method. Van Deventer(1958) argues that there is a kind of common denominator which is involved also in everyday living. This common procedure involves data accumulation, tentative solutions, and a simple 'cycle of proof' involving both inductive and deductive thinking.

The contribution of inductive-deductive thinking

Inductive thinking involves reasoning from the particular to the general and is, thus, part of the scientific thinking process as exemplified in the formulation of scientific principles or rules. It is not uncommon, however, for the results of inductive reasoning (someone else's inductive reasoning) to be memorized and regurgitated as recall of information in examinations. In those circumstances, it is difficult to argue for the presence of scientific thinking.

Deductive reasoning, on the other hand, proceeds from the general to the specific. Deductive thinking must involve the application of generalized principles to a specific situation which is almost certainly a problem-solving situation. Its strength lies in the ability to apply concepts and principles when the specific is unknown, and where the problem is then tackled by a reliance on first principles, searching for the best solution to the problem, and applying it.

The authors would argue that it is not uncommon, particularly in developing countries, for a science graduate to be unable to demonstrate deductive reasoning in the application of concepts and principles to the solving of problems.

The contribution of learning hierarchies

It is not necessary here to discuss the various learning hierarchies which have been proposed. It is sufficient to state that a simplified hierarchy could extend from recall of information through comprehension of concepts and principles to application of concepts and principles to problem-solving.

Where rote learning has been encouraged, there is a tendency to stay at the first level and that may include recall of concepts and principles without comprehension. Inductive reasoning would not necessarily be exhibited in such recall. The second level, however, would need inductive reasoning. But, it is only the top level, the application of concepts and principles to problem-solving, which requires deductive reasoning. It is the latter which is so often missing.

An operational definition of scientific thinking

From the approaches outlined above, it seems reasonable to conclude that:

> 'Scientific thinking utilizes inductive and deductive reasoning in the application of concepts and principles to the solving of identified problems.'

Although the comprehension of scientific concepts and principles requires a science base, the present authors are convinced that the scientific way of thinking can be encouraged even where there is no science base. Information can be taken from science, history, or geography, for example, and brought together for the solving of problems. Scientific thinking is not confined to science, but is applicable to all life and can be a way of enriching life.

CONSTRAINTS OF CHILD DEVELOPMENT ON SCIENTIFIC THINKING

As the project undertaken was an attempt to bring about scientific thinking in Egyptian children of ages 6 to 12, it was appropriate to take into consideration the recommendation that 'sound pedagogy should be based upon a knowledge of child development' (Elkind,1962). The conceptual framework of Jean Piaget was considered to be particularly appropriate.

Although Piaget has provided much evidence to suggest that the sequence of stages is fixed - sensory motor/ pre-operational/ concrete operations/ formal operations - and that the thinking at one stage is qualitatively different from that at another, it has been shown that the age at which children reach the varying stages and the rate of progression to the next stage can vary. Ginsburg and Opper(1979), in accordance with Piaget, have pointed out that a child can profit from external information only when his or her cognitive structure is sufficiently prepared to assimilate it. Otherwise, new experiences will have only superficial effects. If the disparity between the type of experience prescribed to the child and the child's current level of cognitive structure is too great, no real learning will take place. The child may learn specific responses, rote memorization of facts, but these responses will have no strength and no generalization can occur.

According to the operational definition of scientific thinking and Piaget's theory of child development, the pre-operational child is incapable of scientific thinking. It might be possible for a young child to learn by rote the definition of a scientific principle but, because he or she could not comprehend it, it would not be possible for him or her to apply it. While it is not possible to reason in a hypothetico-deductive manner until a child reaches the stage of formal operations, young children can understand something of science on a level according to their own cognitive abilities. For the pre-operational child, learning about science could involve encouragement to use his or her observational powers and arouse interest which might lead to the concrete operational level at which science could involve a good deal of physical experience which might lead to formal thought.

OUTLINE OF THE PROJECT

It was in this contextual framework of scientific thinking that the project was undertaken through the offering of a course of study for the leaders, and the development of a resource-based learning package.

Preliminary assessment of the children in the clubs through a series of tests to determine the potential for scientific thinking in the children - conceptual reflectivity/impulsivity, observational and discriminatory skills, inductive reasoning, and problem-solving in a scientific way - indicated that the children seemed to have the potenetial to be scientific thinkers as they seemed to have all the prerequisites that were identified.

The club leaders, having been brough up in the conventional educational process where the examination system dictated their lives, did not show the same potential to be scientific thinkers. Kagan and Kogan(1970) assert that a person's cognitive style develops early in life and remains relatively fixed throughout adulthood. It is therefore possible that it may be easier to bring up a child to think scientifically than to bring about change in the adults.

During the course of study, the leaders studied styles and types of thinking and learning (including scientific thinking), attributes of the media (including graphics, print, overhead projection transparencies, film and video), design and production of media (for the above list), and utilization of media in a learning environment. The whole of the course was within the context of non-formal learning in a developing country. Among the problems encountered with the participants were:

* helping them to see the relevance of scientific thinking;
* encouraging them to change their own style of thinking to accommodate scientific thinking; and
* enabling them to see their role as 'faciltators of learning' in a planned learning environment.

The learning package produced as part of the project is divided into three parts - 'Water for Life', 'Raising the Water', and 'Water-logged Soil' - and was designed to facilitate scientific thinking in the clubs through:

(a) introducing children to scientific method;
(b) enabling children to be more aware of the importance of water;
(c) enabling children to realize the necessity of the controlling the water supply for year-round life-giving sufficiency;
(d) enabling children to identify other advantages of controlling water in Egypt;
(e) ensuring that children appreciate that water for irrigation has to be raised from the canals and how the principles involved in some of the methods used may be found in other everyday actions;
(f) ensuring that children appreciate that all living things require water;
(g) enabling children to realize that the growth of crops can be adversely affected by an excess volume of water in the soil (water-logged soil).

The package consists of three videotapes (each club has a videorecorder), a number of overhead projection transparencies, materials to be used in follow-up activities, and guidance for the leader on how to use the package. The follow-up activities, demonstrations, experiments, and discussions are designed to build on the knowledge provided in the videotape presentation with the intention of bringing the children to a level whereby they can apply the concepts and principles introduced in the tape to problem-solving within their present stage of cognitive development.

It is planned that the package will be implemented in Egypt in the summer of 1984.

ACKNOWLEDGEMENT

The authors wish to acknowledge the support of the United Nations Development Program in Egypt and the government of the Arab Republic of Egypt in carrying out this project.

REFERENCES

Baez, A V (1967) Improving the teaching of science with particular reference to developing countries. Working paper for the Advisory Committee on the Application of Science and Technology to Development. (ERIC: ED033050).

Burke, P J (1949) Testing for critical thinking in Physics. American Journal of Physics, 17 pp527-532.

Burmester, M A (1952) Behaviour involved in the critical aspects of scientific thinking. Science Education, 36, pp259-263.

Cookey, S J (1976) The training and supply of middle-level personnel. Prospects, 6, 2, pp223-230.

Dewey, J (1934) The supreme intellectual obligation. Science Education, 18, pp1-4.

Dore, R (1976) The Diploma Disease - Education, Qualification and Development. Allen & Unwin, London.

Dube, S C (1976) Theories and goals of education: a third world perspective. Prospects, 6, pp349-363.

Elkind, D (1972) Piaget and science education. Science & Children, 10, pp9-12.

Ginsburg, H and Opper, S (1979) Piaget's Theory of Intellectual Development. (2nd ed). Prentice-Hall, Englewood Cliffs.

Heiss, E D (1958) Helping students develop a scientific attitude. Science Teacher, 25, pp371-373.

Hyde, G D M (1978) Education in Modern Egypt: Ideals and Realities. Routledge & Kegan Paul, London.

Kagan, J and Kogan, N (1970) Individual variation in cognitive processes. In Mussan, P H (ed) Carmichael's Manual of Child Psychology 1. Wiley, New York.

Maskill, R and Wallis, K G (1982) Scientific thinking in the classroom. The School Science Review, 63, 224, pp551-554.

Mubarak, President Hosni (undated) In Egypt Your Open Door to Opportunity. Minsitry of Information, State Information Service, Cairo.

Munby, H (1982) What is Scientific Thinking? A discussion paper, Science Council of Canada, Ottawa.

NCER (1980) Developing Innovating Education in Egypt: Policy and Plans. National Centre for Educational Research, Cairo.

Noll, V H (1935) Measuring the scientific attitude. The Journal of Abnormal and Social Psychology, 30, 2, pp145-164.

Sam, L R (1975) The role of educational technology in developing countries. West African Journal of Education, 19, pp307-312.

UNESCO (1964) The Activities of UNESCO in Science and Technology. Unesco Information Manual.

Van Deventer, W C (1958) Simplified approach to the problem of science methodology. School Science and Mathematics, 58, pp97-107.

6.6 Workshop: The Diffusion of Innovations in Training and Education by Simulation Game

R G Dawson and J M Hebein

Human Resources Research Organization, Eppelheim, West Germany

Abstract: The simulation game is designed for educators, trainers, programme developers, and programme administrators who are involved in programmes which are currently or will be undergoing change. The purpose of the game is to provide participants with the knowledge, skills and attitudes needed to implement innovations within their organizations through the application of implementation/change management.

INTRODUCTION

The 'Diffusuion of Innovations in Training and Education' simulation game provides an opportunity for participants to try their hand at being change agents. The goal of the game is to obtain as many adopters as possible for a specific innovation which, in this version of the game, is computer-assisted instruction (CAI) within an adult skills training centre.

Participants work in two-person teams which initially receive only their game board, tokens, and adoption checklist. The team interacts with a game monitor who provides them with information and feedback cards based upon the diffusion strategies that they select. Every strategy employed has a cost in time which is represented by tokens each worth one week, and every strategy has a result which will either enhance or impede progress towards adoption.

Entirely through experiential, discovery learning, participants accomplish the objectives of the game which are to:

1. Identify major variables which determine the rate of adoption of an innovation in a given setting.
2. Classify example personality profiles according to the various 'adopter types'.
3. Predict the likely impact of a variety of diffusion activities.
4. List and describe the psychological phases which typically precede the adoption or rejection of an innovation.
5. Relate a variety of diffusion strategies to different 'adopter types' and different phases of the adoption process.

ELEMENTS AND STRUCTURE OF THE GAME

The major elements of the game are summarized in Table 1.

At the start the game, players must request information about five people in the centre. Information on up to five people is obtained for one token, and players can spend more tokens for additional information if they choose after obtaining information on the first five. There are 24 staff members at the centre whose titles are listed on the game board. In return for the one-week token, the monitor gives the team five information cards which describe the specified people. Since the cards are needed during the game, they are placed in the space provided on the game board. Other information regarding committee structure, social acquaintances, and lunch mates may also be obtained.

Based upon the information they have received, players decide to engage in one of the diffusion strategies. In return for the specified number of tokens (one to six), the game monitor provides a feedback card containing the results of the strategy. This feedback card

Information Types	Diffusion Strategies	Adoption Phases	Adopter Types	Key Individuals
Personal	talk to	awareness	innovator	formal leaders
Social	ask help	interest	early adopter	opinion leaders
Committee	pilot test	appraisal/	early majority	gate keepers
Lunch-mates	site visit	trial	late majority	
	print	adoption	resister	
	presentation			
	demonstration			
	workshops			
	mass-media			
	compulsion			
	confrontation			

Table 1 Major elements of the game

indicates the number of influence points gained by the strategy for specific people. The game monitor has a decision board which guides the selection of the appropriate feedback card from the set of 133 cards.

As the players obtain influence points for the centre staff, the staff members move through the four phases of the adoption porocess. This progression towards adoption of the innovation is indicated by checking off the boxes on the adopter checklist.

The game is designed to demonstrate the factors which have been shown to impede or facilitate the diffusion of innovations. As the participants identify these elements and act on them, they gain adopters. Although the element of chance is built into the game, random actions generally yield poor results.

The game is played in two one-hour rounds, each of which represents 36 weeks. Between the rounds and at the end of the game, the monitors conduct debriefing sessions so that the participants are able to organize and synthesize the change factors which they have identified during the game.

EVALUATION

Following the workshop, participants completed an evaluation form. Mean scores on a seven-point scale (1 = low, 7 = high) were as follows:

enjoyability of workshop	6.5
clarity of objectives	5.72
work of co-ordinators	6.44
level of interest in ideas and activities	6.0
scope/coverage	5.5
benefit of attending workshop	5.67
recommendation to a colleague	6.28

ADDITIONAL INFORMATION

These materials were adapted from a project developed by the University Consortium of Instructional Technology and Development under a US federal grant in 1975.

Additional information about the game and the workshop can be obtained from either Dr Hebein or Dr Dawson by writing to Kleiststrasse 4, 6901 Eppelheim, West Germany.

Section 7:
Media Production and
Assessment

7.1 From Ronald Reagan to Smoking Cessation: The Analysis of Media Impact

J Baggaley
Concordia University, Montreal, Canada

Abstract: The educational media producer requires fast and precise feedback about a programmes' impact. Ideally, this research facility should be available during the production process so that the production's eventual effectiveness may be guaranteed. The effect of production format as well as subject matter need to be pilot-tested on the widest possible target audience, and fluctuations in their responses noted.

The following paper reviews recent development in the techniques and facilities of production research. It illustrates audience research techniques developed by the Children's TV Workshop (Sesame Street) in New York, TV Ontario in Toronto, and by the author in Montreal. These techniques provide the media producer with a second-by-second account of reactions to programming as they vary between individuals.

The new electronic facilities for production research have found immediate application in the advertising industry, where they are used to pilot-test, for example, beer commercials. If audience interest, attention, or other responses are found to lapse even momentarily, they may be regained by an appropriate modification of visuals and/or soundtrack. Similarly, a campaigning politician may receive immediate feedback on audience reactions to his or her TV or platform performance, and adjust it for maximum impact.

So may the teacher and educational producer adjust their performance. In studies sponsored by the Canadian Cancer Society and other agencies, the writer has investigated the impact of health education materials on urban and rural audiences featuring the educated as well as the functionally illiterate members of society. The paper summarizes the finding of these studies and their implications for effective programme design.

THE ANALYSIS OF MEDIA IMPACT

Methods for testing and developing educational media materials were first studied in the 1920s, in the wake of intensive uses of film for World War I training purposes. Lashley and Watson (1921, 1922) reported tests of motion picture effectiveness in U S social hygiene campaigns. One such film, Fit to Win, was field-tested on 4,800 people representing male/female and black/white American audiences, and its educational value was indicated prior to its general release. Research into the commercial impact of radio and film productions accumulated dramatically during the 1930s and 1940s, and attempts to develop principles of effective media production were widely made by educationalists (Doane,1936; Dale,1939; Hoban,1938,1942; Tyler,1942; May,1946; Lumsdaine,1947). By the 1950s, the 'educational technology' movement was firmly established, devoted to classroom applications of the modern media, and drawing on the theories of instruction promoted by, for example, Skinner(1938,1958), Rose and van Horn(1956).

In parallel, during the 1950s, a general interest in communications theory was stimulated by Lasswell(1948), and Shanon and Weaver(1949); and the widespread domestic availability of television triggered intense study of the media's social impact. Four American surveys conducted between 1952 and 1964 provide evidence of the ways in which different sectors of the community use the media as sources of information (Wade & Schramm,1969). In areas of current affairs reporting, the general trend has been one of increasing dependence on television. While in 1952 less than 40 per cent of American adults cited television as a major source of political news, in 1960 and 1964 nearly 60 per cent did so. The general reliance on television for topical information has continued during the 1970s (Aronson,1973; Baggaley and Duck,1976) and will develop further as TV technology is incorporated into modern computerized and satellite-based systems (Baggaley,1979-81).

In the field of public health education, the impact of television and film have been felt to a lesser degree than that of the print media. Wade and Schramm(1969) indicate that newspapers, magazines and other reading matter are more likely to serve as the dominant sources of health information in view of their greater capacity to treat such specialized topics in depth. Women, they report, are more likely to read about health than men, and better educated people more likely do so than lesser educated ones. The early trends in these directions (Swinehart,1968,1976) are shown to apply currently. Thus, Cantor et al(1979) and Miller and Cantor(1980) find newspapers consistently more effective as a source of health information than either television or radio, and information about cancer more readily recalled than information on other health matters (ie, drug abuse and sickle-cell anemia). Basing their conclusions on a telephone survey of 185 people in South Carolina, Cantor et al report that 29 per cent recall cancer announcements having been made in the newspapers, compared with 19 per cent via television, and 6 per cent via radio. Younger age groups, urban and black populations deviate from this pattern in reporting a higher recall for televised announcements than for either newspaper or radio announcements.

Certainly, during the 1970s, large-scale attempts have been made to increase the role of television and film in public health education, and Butler and Paisley(1976) list 30 recent public education programmes concerning cancer alone. These stress a variety of media and communication strategies, and are directed at varied target audiences. The evidence that any of these have had substantial impact, however, is thin. As a review by the Rand Corporation shows (Lau et al,1980), the methods used in evaluating public health campaigns have been either inadequate or inconsistent, and the results inconclusive. Gunaratne(1980) blames the failure of media producers to define or improve the impact of health eduation methods upon the 'the poverty of research about individual, cultural, societal and health behavior, and the nature, motivations and determinants of health learning ..'. The matter of designing educational materials for a particular purpose, or for particular community groups, thus remains distinctly hit-and-miss. One may conclude, as Atkin (1979), that the media can play an important role in communicating health information to the public, but that reliable strategies for this purpose have not as yet been prescribed.

This current position is essentially the same in all other areas of media communication: news and current affairs, educational and community development, and in general training and therapeutic contexts. The public is immensely resistant, or even oblivious, to attempts made by the media to persuade it of new beliefs or a new course of action. Despite a generation of study (Hyman and Sheatsley,1947; Klapper,1960; Griffiths and Knutson,1960; Goldstein,1965; Bogart,1967; McGuire,1969; Bauer,1971; Cartwright,1971; Lazarsfeld and Merton,1971; Katz, Blumler and Gurevitch,1974; Ramond,1976; Schlinger,1976; Adler,1977; Schlegel,1977-78; Atkin,1979) no sure way of overcoming public inertia on, eg, medical self-help matters, has been estalished. Thus, in a televised anti-smoking campaign (O'Keefe,1971), the greatest persuasive effects were on the non-smokers rather than on those for whom the campaign was intended.

Indisputably, social and behavioural research methods have yielded useful findings for the designers of public health materials. But at present they seem to be too generalized, with insufficient reference to the techniques of presentation required in directing materials at specific audience types (Baggaley,1980). Advertising researchers have been able to show that particular advertising strategies appeal differently to different types of audience, and that fashions in this respect constantly change (Ramond,1976; Adler,1977; Atkin,1980; Burnett and Wilkes,1980); but the application of such principles, in health campaigns at least, remains a matter of intuition on the part of the media producer. As Flay et al(1980,1982) indicate, the only way to be sure that public health information is likely to reach and impress its intended audience is to systematically pilot-test it before transmission; yet, as Windsor et al(1980) point out, such systematic evaluations are generally neglected in health education programmes certainly to date in public cancer education - owing to the lack of financial or technical resources.

A major exception to the rule of thumb in instructional media production has been the scientific approach used by producers and researchers of the Children's TV Workshop, New York. In conjunction with TV Ontario, the CTW producer of major TV series such as Sesame Street, Feeling Good, and 3-2-1 Contact - has developed techniques which permit precise insights into the effectiveness of production techniques in particular situations (Cambre, 1981; Nickerson,1981). Essentially, they have overcome the dual problem of:

(a) examining varied audience responses second-by-second as the presentation develops,
(b) feeding this information back into the production process fast enough for the producer to act upon it.

Such moment-by-moment feedback, known as 'formative evaluation', is provided by a program evaluation analysis computer system (PEAC), comprising an APPLE 48K microcomputer and a series of hand-held reponse units, one for each member of the audience. The system's applications in educational, training, and community development have been described by Baggaley and Smith(1981) and Baggaley(1982b).

An example of the manner in which the PEAC technology may be used is given in Figure 1. Nineteen viewers (of voting age, though with no distinct political preference) were asked to view the 1980 TV debate between then-President Carter and Presidential hopeful Reagan. The Figure indicates which of the two debaters, from one moment to the next, is perceived by viewers as 'winning the most votes'. The viewers were directed to respond on the basis as often or as seldom as their opinion altered. They viewed the debate in their own homes during its original live transmission.

Their responses were denoted via either a 'Carter' button or a 'Reagan' button, or a 'Don't Know' button. As the Figure indicates, Carter - the incumbent President - carried the majority of their votes for the first 20 minutes, even when Reagan is speaking Reagan is seen to gain ground from that point onward. (The vertical lines in the Figure represent the debate's successive sections.)

For the media producer, as for the politician, the benefits of this methodology are immense. He or she receives speedy and incisive feedback about the audience impact of his or her subject-matter and techniques, and may adjust his or her delivery accordingly. When such research is conducted during the production process - as 'formative evaluation' (Cambre,1981), the production may be fine-tuned for maximal impact. Any measure of audience response may be collected via the system, from interest value and clarity to complex factual or attitudinal responses prompted by multiple-choice routines. In advertising and political campaigning, such powerful techniques are becoming commonplace. Their application in educational media development, however, is virtually undiscovered. No such research has previously been published in connection with health educational materials.

THREE IMPACT STUDIES

In March 1982, therefore, the Public Education Committee of the Canadian Cancer Society, commissioned an impact study, involving the electronic response measurement technology, of a range of existing CCS films on smoking prevention/cessation. The most recent summaries of this field by Bergler (1982) and at the 20th International Congress of Applied Psychology (Eysenck,1982) had indicated that guidelines for the production of smoking prevention materials remain purely speculative. The advertising industry has access to much relevant, and closely guarded, information on smoking persuasion techniques; but those who would use the media to discourage smoking have little or no specialized information of this type.

The library of films used by the Canadian Cancer Society to encourage smoking prevention/cession was therefore examined. Two films were selected as appropriate for testing on an adult audience, being produced in English, for men as well as women, and within the previous eight years. These are Smoking: The Unconscious Act, was produced for the CCS in 1977, and Let's Call It Quits, was produced for the American Cancer Society (1974). A further film, designed primarily for high school audiences was selected as suitable for screening to adult audiences also: You Don't Smoke, Eh? (Canadian Cancer Society, 1980).

The first impact study (You Don't Smoke, Eh?) has been reported in full by Baggaley(1982a). Sixty-three subjects were tested, varying in age from 15-55 years, in education (adults above Grade II vs below Grade 9), sex and smoking habits. It became apparent during this study that further psychological factors - eg, degree of pessimism regarding cancer, and previous experience of cancer in the family - may exert still more basic effects upon perceptions of anti-smoking films than the above socio-demograophic factors. In the analysis of any one film it is impossible to control for every one of these variables without involving at least one hundred subjects. An audience selection design was therefore adopted, balancing these factors appropriately across the complete series of studies.

The sampling of audience types for each film is summarized as follows:

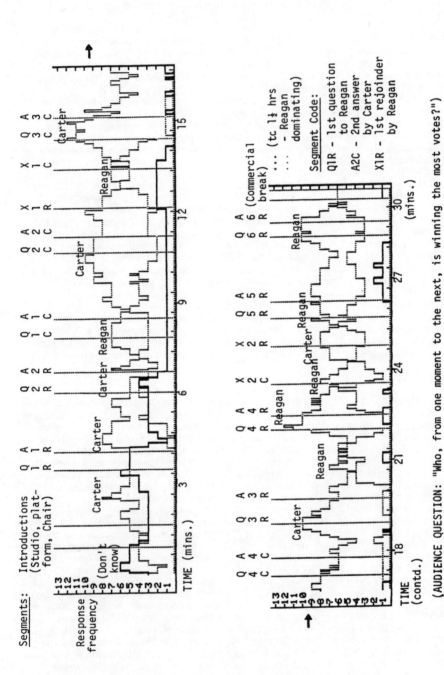

Figure 1   The Carter–Reagan TV debate (November 1980): first half-hour

1. You Don't Smoke, Eh? A preliminary comparison was made between responses of the three basic socio–demographic groups: education, age, and sex. The numbers of viewers in each category do not guarantee the isolation of further factors (eg, relating to prejudice or cancer experience); though the possibility that such factors exert effects transcending the basic demographic factors can be examined. (Film length: 120 mins; total number of subjects = 63.)
2. Let's Call It Quits A similar sample was examined, though the numbers were increased in order to examine a further variable (St John's area vs other areas of Newfoundland). (Film length: 27 mins; N = 46.)
3. Smoking: the Unconscious Act (1) A balanced sample of literate and illiterate viewers was examined in numbers sufficient to permit the analysis of interactions between demographic factors (age, smoking habits, cancer in the family), and psychological variables (eg, levels of optimism/pessimism towards cancer). (Film length,150 mins; N= 93.)

PROCEDURE

The three films were screened to successive Newfoundland audiences in St John's (urban area), Corner Brook and Stephenville (rural areas) between March and September 1982. Each session was conducted by two female research assistants, and lasted between 30 and 50 minutes depending on the length of the film. All groups were told that the work was conducted on behalf of the Canadian Cancer Society; it aimed to show whether the Society's film productions were useful or could be improved.

Each viewer was asked to complete a pre-test of general attitudes to smoking and cancer, and a post-test designed to measure any immediate effects by the film upon these attitudes. Each test lasted between 5 and 10 minutes. All responses were signified by a check-mark in the appropriate box of the questionnaire. Viewers with a reading problem were given non-directive assistance by the researchers.

Following the pre-test, the procedure for using the rogram evaluation analysis computer's manual response units was explained. These units are constructed like conventional hand-held calculators with a four by four matrix of buttons individually coded to represent different responses to a presentation over time. In the present situation, viewers were instructed to use the top row of buttons only, coded from left to right as A) Good, B) Fairly Good, C) Not Very Good, and D) Poor. A digital display at the head of the unit was programmed to indicate the last response made. The subjects were told that they should respond to the film on this scale, whenever anything occurred in the film to change their attitude towards it. Responses could be made as often or as seldom as the individual viewer chose.

After a minute's practice in the art of 'touch-typing' the response unit using the two thumbs and without looking away from the film, the film was presented on a 16mm projector. All films were in colour.

OVERALL IMPACT OF THE THREE FILMS

The responses to the pre- and post-test were analysed, and the distribution or demographic characteristics in the three adult audiences was examined.

The most effective film, according to overall audience opinion, was Let's Call It Quits: 77 of the 96 subjects viewing the film (80 per cent) rated it either very or fairly effective as a tool for 'persuading people to give up ,smoking'. The corresponding ratings for You Don't Smoke, Eh? and Smoking: the Unconscious Act were 67 per cent and 65 per cent respectively.

Analysis also reveals several systematic interactions between attitudes to smoking/cancer and socio–demographic factors. Thus 49 per cent of the functionally illiterate audience indicate that they are currently smokers, compared with only 37 per cent of the literate audience. Simultaneously, 41 per cent of illiterates report an incidence of cancer in their immediate family, as opposed to only 27 per cent of literates. The level of pessimism regarding cancer is also higher in the illiterate group: 61 per cent believe that a person will live for less than two years once cancer is detected, compared with only 39 per cent of the literate group (the majority of the latter group believes life expectancy will exceed two years). These results underscore the urgent need indicated by the earlier telephone survey for cancer education in the functionally illiterate community. The incidences of smoking, cancer in the family, and general pessimism regarding cancer are all substantially higher in this group than among the more educated viewers.

The need for emphasis on cancer prevention in schools is also noted. The incidence of smoking in the sample of 15- to 17-year-old schoolboys is, at 60 per cent the highest in the study. This is compared with a 37 per cent rate among schoolgirls of the same age. Both boys and girls report a high level of pessimism about the cancer prognosis (58 per cent). A possible causal link is suggested in the general population between pessimism about cancer and the incidence of cancer in the family. The subjects with a family background of cancer are 1.55 times more likely to be pessimistic about life expectancy than to be optimistic (57 per cent as compared with 37 per cent). Those claiming no incidence of cancer in the family are only 1.2 times more likely to be pessimists than optimists (53 per cent as compared with 44 per cent). Similar statistics indicate a higher degree of pessimism among smokers than non-smokers.

The socio–demographic factors were next related to the tendency to give a or negative judgment of each film. Ratings of the films (as a 'very' or 'fairly effective' smoking prevention tool) were regarded as a positive reponse; ratings of 'not very effective' and 'very ineffective' were regarded as a negative reponse. The frequencies of positive and negative responses in each demographic category were compared via the chi-square test.

Positive judgments about You Don't Smoke, Eh? (YDSEh) were found to be significantly more common than negative judgments among the schoolgirls, non-smokers, cancer pessimists and those who have not had cancer victims in their family. Smoking: the Unconscious Act (SUncA) is predominantly well received in the educated group (all female), the non–smokers, and - once again - the viewers who have not known cancer in their family. This film is also judged, on balance, positively by cancer optimists. Let's Call It Quits (LCIQ) is significantly well received by all except the schoolboys.

On the above basis, we may conclude that the most successful of the three films is LCIQ. Only the schoolboys fail to show a significant tendency to approve of it as a smoking cessation aid, and this result may be due to an inadequate number of subjects in their group. The tendency for cancer optimists to approve of SUncA, and for pessimists to approve of YDSEh will be related to more detailed evidence of their attitudes later on in this section.

When the composition of the 'positive' and 'negative' audiences for each film are compared, relatively high proportions of cancer pessimists and no–cancer–in–family subjects are found in both categories. The only socio-demographic factor predicting a different level of positive versus negative judgment for all three films is smoking behaviour. Thus, 62 per cent of all positive judgments about YDSEh are made by non-smokers, compared with the 38 per cent who are smokers. Negative judgments of YDSEh are divided equally between smokers and non-smokers. Similar statistics are observed for SUncA and LCIQ. For the film producer, of course, such information is interesting, but it only goes so far. What are the specific elements of a film that cause it to have an overall effect? One may consider this question by reference to the computerized record of audience responses to the films second-by-second.

MOMENTARY IMPACT OF THE THREE FILMS

The computer–based audience measurement technology described earlier allow inspections of a) a programme's moment-by-moment effects, and b) variations between the responses of individual audience members. In the present study, the momentary responses of all film audiences were examined for fluctuations at regular intervals. In the case of the longest film (Let's Call It Quits), the interval was every four seconds; in the other three cases, the interval was every three seconds.

An example of the complete moment-by-moment analysis of audience responses to one of the films (You Don't Smoke, Eh?) has been given by Baggaley (1982a). The present analysis focuses upon the momentary reactions of those viewers whose overall reactions have been shown to contrast significantly in the section above. Thus, overall judgments of each film's effectiveness have been found to vary according to whether or not the viewers currently smoke. Positive judgments (that the films will be effective in persuading others to give up smoking) are primarily associated with non-smoking, and negative judgments with smoking. Each of the films is regarded as effective on balance, although the proportion of smokers giving a positive overall assessment of each is markedly lower than the corresponding proportion of non-smokers.

Three specific subgroups of the audience will therefore be of interest in the moment-by-moment analysis of the films' impact. A prime measure of success in a smoking prevention film is clearly the extent to which it can evoke a positive overall response from smokers ('Smoke/Pos' subgroup of each audience). A measure of its failure is the extent to which it draws a negative overall reaction from smokers ('Smoke/Neg' group). The responses of the remaining viewers ('Non-smoke' group) clearly have limited criterion value, since these are not the films' primary audience; but they may be isolated for reference purposes.

The particular moments in a film which contribute to a successful overall impact may thus be defined as those at which 'Smoke-Pos' viewers react positively, and 'Smoke/Neg' viewers do not. The moments contributing to an unfavourable impact are defined as those at which 'Smoke/Neg' viewers react negatively and 'Smoke/Pos' viewers do not. Occasionally, positive and negative effects of this type may occur at an identical moment. By pinpointing the critical moments of a film in this way, guidelines for effective future production may be indicated, and the techniques yielding little or no educational benefit discounted.

PRODUCTION EFFECTS

From the analysis of You Don't Smoke, Eh? (Baggaley, 1982a), the following production effects became apparent.

1. 'Negative' viewers in general show increasing disapproval of the film at moments when it becomes stern or dramatic in its anti-smoking message. For instance, the effect is noted during a 12-second comment by a cancer specialist as to the regularity with which he must tell lung cancer patients they are incurable. The 'positive' viewing group shows a contrasting tendency at such points - towards approval of the film; but, as already noted, these viewers tend to be the non-smokers in the audience (ie, its 'converted' members).
2. The contrasting effects of this type upon positive and negative viewers are not necessarily restricted to the moments which provoke shock or fear by verbal means. Visually symbolic moments with an obvious anti-smoking intent have similar effects (eg, the two shots of an automatic smoking machine and the smoke and litter it produces). They attempt to debunk the insidious techniques used by cigarette advertisers similarly fails to move the 'negative' viewers, although it has a significantly favourable effect on the 'positive' audience.
3. Shots featuring authority figures (ie, the lung specialist, the pharmacologist, the lady alderman, and the art director) all have deleterious effects on the 'negative' viewers time-based responses. These effects may either be due to the performers' personal image, or to the authoritarian nature of their message, or to both. (The adverse impact of the art director may also be due to the fact that he is smoking as he speaks!)
4. The moments to which 'negative' viewers are apt to respond most positively are those which refer to the benefits of not smoking (eg, the positive effects of smoking cessation on athletic ability and self-esteem). Similar effects are noted at moments when the film acknowledges the problems that the would-be non-smoker faces.
5. The film has a negative effect effect upon the adult illiterate members of its audience from the opening section onwards. It was not in any case intended for those viewers, but for the younger, obviously middle-class audience. The film has a significantly positive overall impact upon schoolgirls, upon those who have not had cancer in the family, non-smokers, and pessimists about the cancer prognosis. The schoolboy sample is less inclined after the film to agree that smoking is an easy habit to break, and less inclined to accept that cancer can be cured.
6. As noted earlier, the film has a significant effect on only one of the ten attitudes measured, reinforcing the belief of the 'positive' (non-smoking) audience that cigarette advertising should be banned.

Analysis of the reactions to Smoking: the Unconscious Act shows very similar effects. The film is divided into two main sections. The first shows the chain-smoking behaviour of a journalist during his typical day; the second shows his attempts to give up smoking and his eventual success. The effects of the smoking sequences are counter-intuitive. Smokers who ultimately regard the film as ineffective respond in a relatively favourable manner during these sequences. Smokers who rate the film positively in the post-test, and non-smokers give increasingly negative reactions to the same moments!

A critical scene occurs in the seventh minute of the film. The main actor, believing that he has left a cigarette burning in his office late at night, runs back into the building to check it. At this moment the 'positive' audience, including some smokers, registers increased approval of the film; however, the smokers who later judge the film negatively react to the scene with disapproval. The sequence apparently raises their defences in the same manner as the overtly anti-smoking moments of You Don't Smoke, Eh?

From this point in the film onwards - ie, throughout the second section containing the more obvious educational messages about smoking cessation the 'Smoke/Neg' group of viewers remains negative in their response. The 'Non-Smoke' and 'Smoke/Pos' group, on the other hand, register increasing approval.

RESPONSE DIFFERENTIATION

Particular moments differentiating the responses of Smoke/Pos and Smoke/Neg viewers are as follows. Whenever the main actor tries particular tricks for aiding smoking cessation (eg, chewing gum/playing with 'executive toys') the Smoke/Pos groups shows approval; however, the Smoke/Neg group does not. During one of these scenes, a colleague is shown smoking in the background and looking at the main character oddly. At this point, smokers in general give an adverse response, possibly because the would-be quitter seems to have become somewhat eccentric. On the other hand, even the Smoke/Neg group expresses approval when a friend is seen helping the actor to persist in his smoking cessation attempt. The positive impact of practical tips for quitting, and of recognition of the quitter's need for social reinforcement, can be clearly identified at these moments.

Unfortunately, its unanticipated negative effects mar SUncA's overall value for the smoking audience in general. It is obviously important that once an actor in a film launches a concerted effort to quit, the chances of his eventual failure should be minimized, and no suggestion should be made that he may emerge from the effort looking eccentric. The specific moments reported above apparently gave negative impressions of this sort.

The impact of Let's Call It Quits has already been shown to be generally favourable. Only 19 per cent of viewers judged it negatively (ie, not very effective or very ineffective as a smoking cessation tool); and this group is primarily identified as being smokers. LCIQ is different from the previous two films in that it takes a light-hearted approach to smoking cessation. It is produced in the style of a television situation comedy, and features well-known sitcom actors. The first section of the film shows the chain-smoking behaviour of a middle-aged man during his typical day; the second shows his unsuccessful attempts to quit smoking, and the third his progress towards eventual success. The scenario is thus similar to that of Smoking: the Unconscious Act.

Momentary effects of the film follow a pattern virtually identical to those of SUncA. Initially, an increasing negative reaction is registered as the main character is seen in one smoking situation after another. Approximately five minutes into the film, the character, his wife and friends agree to a joint effort to quit; at this point general audience approval is shown. During the scenes showing unsuccessful cessation attempts, the Smoke/Neg viewers exhibit a tendency to respond unfavourably, particularly when actors are seen arguing that smoking is too difficult for them to give up. This message is clearly perceived as being defeatist and discouraging.

On the other hand, moments of encouragement - at which, for example, the character's wife helps him to quit - evoke a favourable response, from the majority Smoke/Pos group at least. Prospects of rewards through smoking cessation (eg, weight loss/money savings) evoke high favourable responses from the same viewers. Smoke/Neg viewers are clearly more critical during these scenes, occurring in the final section of the film. Thus they respond negatively to a scene in which the actor falls on his face while jogging, reaches in his pocket and finds a carrot which he eats. As in Smoking: the Unconscious Act, these moments may associate smoking cessation with eccentricity. If necessary at all, they would have been better placed prior to the section of the film featuring the all-out cessation effort.

CONCLUSIONS

The audience responses clearly show smokers' appreciation of practical tips for smoking cessation, and their need for social reinforcement of it. The cessation techniques suggested, however, should not appear quirky; the need for family and friends to give unfailing assistance should be stressed at all times; and cessation itself should be portrayed as increasingly easy and self-fulfilling. These, and the other subtle effects uncovered by the new computer-based research methodology, can now be borne in mind in the production of new smoking prevention materials.

Finally, of course, successful social action against health risks requires a greater degree of intervention than the use of media alone. TV, radio and the press can play a vital role in 'setting the agenda' for a campaign, and the future of the new pilot-testing techniques in this context seems assured. They allow the researcher to provide production staff with practical, meaningful feedback, and they render the producer accountable to both the sponsors and the audience for the educational effectiveness of programming. The new techniques also provide the advertiser or propagandist with precise insights into his or her audience's reactions, which he or she may exploit for less ethical ends. By studying media evaluation techniques and informing the public of their potential, the educationist helps to guard against a '1984 situation' in which the media observe society with ever-increasing finesse. An important role for the educational technologist in society is thus identified.

REFERENCES

Adler, R (1977) Research on the Effects of Television Advertising on Children. Government Printing Office, Washington DC.

Aronson, E (1973) The Social Animal. Freeman, London.

Atkin, C (1979) Research evidence on mass mediated health communication campaigns. Communication Yearbook, 3, pp655-668.

Baggaley, J P and Duck, S W (1976) Dynamics of Television. Gower, Aldershot; and Lexington Books, Mass.

Baggaley, J P (1978) The Impact of TV Production Methods in National Networks Transmissions. Report to Social Science Research Council, UK.

Baggaley, J P (Ed) (1979-81) Experimental Research in Televised Instruction. Vols 2-4, Memorial University of Newfoundland.

Baggaley, J P with Ferguson, M and Brooks, P (1980) Psychology of the TV Image. Gower, Aldershot; and Praeger, New York.

Baggaley, J P (1981) Developing Effective Materials for Cancer Education. Report to Canadian Cancer Society, Toronto.

Baggaley, J P (1982a) Audience Analysis: You Don't Smoke, Eh? Report to Canadian Cancer Society, Toronto.

Baggaley, J P (1982b) Smoking Prevention Materials in Community Education. Report to Canadian Cancer Society, Toronto.

Baggaley, J P (1982c) Electronic analysis of communication, Media in Education and Development. 15, 2, pp70-73.

Baggaley, J P and Smith, K (1982) Formative research in rural education, Media in Education and Development. 15, 3, pp173-176.

Bauer, R (1971) The obstinate audience: the influence process from the point of view of social communication. American Psychologist, 19, pp319-328.

Bergler, R (1982) Advertising and Cigarette Smoking: a Psychological Study. Hogrefe, Toronto.

Bogart, L (1967) Strategy in Advertising. Brace, Harcourt, New York.

Burnett, J & Wilkes, R (1980) Fear appeals to segments only. J Advertising Research, 20, 5, pp21-24.

Butler, M and Paisley, W (1976) The potential of mass communication and interpersonal communication for cancer control. In Cullen, J W, Fox, B N and Isom, R N (eds) Cancer: The Behavioral Dimension, pp205-230. Raven Press, New York.

Cambre, M (1981) Historical overview of formative evaluation of instructional media products. Educ. Comm. Technol. J. 29, pp3-25.

Cantor, A B, Miller, M C, Larisey, E (1979) A study of media effectiveness: for sickle cell anemia education in a rural community. J National Medical Association, 71, 11, pp1055-1057.

Cantor, A B, Miller, M C, Murphy, E and Larisey, L (1979) Comparison of media for dissemination about cancer in rural communities. South Med J, 72, 10, pp1232-1235.

Cartwright, D (1971) Some principles of mass persuasion. In Shramm, W and Roberts, D (eds) Process and Effects of Mass Communication, pp426-447. University of Illinois Press, Urbana.

Dale, E (1939) Critical problems in the production, use, and distribution of school and college films. Proceedings of a conference on the educational production of motion pictures. Ohio State University, Bureau of Educational Research, Columbus.

Doane, D C (1936) What makes a good educational film? Educational Screen, 15, pp203-206, pp239-242, pp271-273, pp305-307.

Eysenck, H J (1982) The Conditioning Theory of Neurosis Revisited. 20th International
    Congress of Applied Psychology, Edinburgh, Scotland
Flay, B (1980) Mass media in health promotion: an analysis using an extended
    information-processing model. Health Educ Q. 7, 2, pp127-147.
Flay, B, Johnson, C A and Hansen, W B (1982) Evaluation of a mass media enhanced smoking
    prevention and cessation campaign. In Baggaley J (ed) Experimental Research in TV
    Instruction. Vol 3, Memorial University of Newfoundland.
Goldstein, H K (1965) Guidelines for drug education through electronic media.
    Drug Educ. 14, pp157-171.
Griffiths, W and Knutson, A L (1960) The role of mass media in public health.
    American Public Health, 50, pp515-523.
Gunaratne, V T (1980) Health for all by the year 2000: the role of health education.
    International Journal of Health Education, 23, pp1-11.
Hoban, C F (1938) Experimental research in instructional films. In Dale, E, Dunn, F W,
    Hoban, C F and Schneider, E (eds) Motion Pictures in Education. Wilson, New York.
Hoban, C G (1942) Focus on Learning: Motion Pictures in the School. American Council on
    Education, Washington DC.
Hyman, H and Sheatsley, P (1947) Some reasons why information campaigns fail.
    Public Opinion Quarterly, 11, pp412-423.
Katz, E, Blumler, J G and Gurevitch, M (1974) In Blumler, J G and Katz, E (eds) The Uses of
    Mass Communications. Sage, London.
Klapper, J (1960) The effects of mass communication. Free Press, Glencoe Ill.
Lashley, K S and Watson, J B (1921) A psychological study of motion pictures in relation to
    venereal disease campaigns. Social Hygiene, 7, pp181-219.
Lashley, K S and Watson, J B (1982) A Psychological Picture of Motion Pictures in relation to
    Venereal Disease Campaigns. Inter-departmental Social Hygiene Board, Washington DC.
Lasswell, M D (1948) The structure and function of communications. In Bryson, L (ed)
    The Communication of Ideas. Harper, New York.
Lau, R, Kane, R, Berrry, S, Ware, J and Roy, D (1980) Channeling health: a review of the
    evaluation of televised health campaigns. Health Educ Quarterly, 7, 1, pp56-89.
Lazarsfeld, P and Merton, R (1971) Mass communication, popular taste, and organized social
    action. In Schramm, W and Roberts, D (eds) Process and Effects of Mass Communication,
    pp554-578. University of Illinois Press, Champaign.
Lumsdaine, A A (ed) (1947) Experimental research and the improvement of teaching film.
    Educational Screen, 26, pp254-255.
May, M A (1946) The psychology of learning from demonstrational films. Journal of Education
    Psychology, 37, pp1-12.
McGuire, W J (1969) The nature and attitudes and attitude change. In Lindzey, G and
    Aronson, E (eds) The Handbook of Social Psychology Vol 3. Addison-Wesley, Reading,
    Mass.
Meyer. M (Ed) (1981) Health Education by Television and Radio. K G Saur, New York.
Miller, M and Cantor, A (1980) A comparison of mass media effectiveness in health
    education. International J Health Educators, 23.
Nickerson, R B (1981) Electronic Analysis of Canadian Television. 4th International
    Conference on TV Instruction, Memorial University of Newfoundland.
O'Keefe, T (1971) The anti-smoking commercials: a study of television's impact on behavior.
    Public Opinion Q. 35, 2, pp242-248.
Ramond, C (1976) Advertising Research: The State of the Art. Association of National
    Advertisers, New York.
Rose, N and van Horn, C (1956) Theory and application of preproduction testing.
    AV Communication Rev, 4, pp21-30.
Schlegel, R (1977-78) The role of persuasive communications in drug dissuasion. J Drug
    Education, 7, pp279-290.
Schlinger, M J (1976) The role of mass communications in promoting public health. Advances
    in Consumer Research, 3, pp302-305.
Shannon, C E and Weaver, W (1949) The Mathematical Theory of Communication. University
    of Illinois, Urbana.
Skinner, B F (1938) The Behavior of Organisms. Appleton-Century, New York.
Skinner, B F (1958) Teaching machines. Science, 128, pp969-977.
Swinehart, J W (1968) Voluntary exposure to health communications. American J Public
    Health, pp1265-1275.

Swinehart, J W (1976) Creative use of mass media to affect health behavior. In Cullen, J W,
    Fox, B N and Isom, R N (eds) Cancer: The Behavioral Dimensions, pp231-242. Raven Press,
    New York.
Tyler, R W (1942) Purposes and procedures of the evaluation staff. In Smith, E R and
    Tyler, R W (eds) Appraising and recording student progress. Harper, New York.
Wade, S and Schramm, W (1969) The mass media as sources of public affairs, science, and
    health knowledge. Public Opinion Q, 33, pp197-209.
Windsor, R (1980) Method and design issues in evaluation of community health programs: a
    case study in breast and cervical cancer. Health Educ Q, 7,2, pp203-218.

7.2 Evaluation of the Use of Structured Materials in the Teaching of Primary Mathematics

M Beishuizen
Leyden University, The Netherlands

Abstract: Early cognitive psychologists like Piaget and Bruner have stressed previous experience with concrete materials and visualizations for the acquisition of cognitive processes. It is here suggested that there is a need to return to more specific approaches to the 'design' issue. There are many differences between conflicting psychological concerns leading to different operationalizations in the use use of concrete materials. For example, Piaget stresses the power of visualization while Galperin stresses the pre-structuring of the mental operations.

   This paper will illustrate the relations between these concepts and the design and use of concrete materials and visualizations. It also summarizes the results of evaluation studies carried out in 1982 and 1983 amongst middle-class and lower-class schools. The results support the view that the Galperin-based approach gives better results than the Piaget-based approach with regards to the quality of problem-solving strategies and the number of mistakes in the response behaviour of the pupils. Current work on computer analysis of the collected data is also reported.

SCHOOL PRACTICE AND PSYCHOLOGICAL THEORY

Since psychologists like Piaget and Bruner stressed previous experience with concrete materials and visualizations for the acquisition of cognitive processes, there is a growing interest for the application of those ideas especially in the field of early and primary mathematics learning (Dienes, 1966). In English school books we have seen fine examples of systematic and <u>integrated</u> use of materials (thanks to the work of Campbell, Price, and Taylor of the British School in the Netherlands). In the Netherlands there is no regular practice and it can only be found in some newer mathematics-methods. However, in our school practice there is also a growing interest, stimulated by a greater emphasis on individualization in education. Many schools now do purchase some sets of Cuisenaire, MAB or Unifix materials. The Abacus is also becoming more popular. These materials are then used in addition to more traditional school books, which do not contain specific directions for their use. Therefore, some local school advisory centres in our country recently started workshops for teachers on this subject, and have a permanent exhibition of arithmetic materials. Of course, there are also some Dutch publications from specialists in the field of mathematics-teaching on this topic of materials. They mainly stem from: practice and theory of the remedial teaching of learning problems. As well as from new insights about the teaching of arithmetic and mathematics as a curriculum in the school.

   Summarizing these introductory remarks as a background for the questions posed in this paper: there is a growing interest and use of arithmetic materials but there is still little theory and almost a complete lack of research data on this subject. The same can be said of the internationally renewed interest in cognitive psychology. Although a lot of energy is spent on research and theorizing on cognitive processes involved in early and primary mathematics learning, until now the role of materials has not been given much attention. Consider Resnick and Ford (1981), who in their recent review on 'The psychology of mathematics for instruction' describe in several pages examples of structured materials (pp 101-127). But their conclusion reads as follows: 'The structure-oriented methods and materials have not been adequately validated by research, and we know little from school practice about the effects of the curriculum reforms upon the quality of children's mathematical learning. The psychological tools for designing the needed research are only now becoming available' (p 126).

In the recent book by Carpenter, Moser and Romberg (1982) which gives an international overview of research and theorizing on 'addition and subtraction' as cognitive processes, materials and visualizations do, of course, play a role in several contributions. But only on the sidelines and not as a main topic. As a matter of fact, Carpenter and Moser (1982) do start their own chapter with a rather confusing remark on this subject: 'A tacit assumption of most school mathematics programs is that addition and subtraction are best introduced through physical or pictorial representations of joining or separating sets of objects ... A growing body of research indicates that this assumption may be false' (p 9). In their data, Carpenter and Moser report that there is a trend for children at the end of the first grade to move to more abstract 'counting on' procedures when no physical objects are available, whereas they do hang on to concrete 'adding on' procedures when physical objects are still available (p 20). But their data also underline the fact that when problems are difficult for children –in the beginning of the first grade and later on when the numbers in the problems become larger - with the aid of materials more correct solutions are reached than without materials (p 16). Compare also the earlier paper of Moser (1980) with more details, from which the effects of materials can better be traced. In my opinion, the opening remark of Carpenter and Moser about the so-called 'false assumption' in the learning of addition and subtraction with physical objects is too general and too negative. It would be better to state that the aid of concrete materials can have positive as well as negative effects. That is one of the main problems, and to me, therefore, an important research question. Moreover, the negative side-effect of 'hanging-on too long' with materials is not a recent conclusion from research, but a common experience in school practice and remedial teaching which has been well known for years! Maybe psychological theory and research could study this phenomenon and could come up with some suggestions to overcome this problem.

SOME INSIGHTS FROM RUSSIAN PSYCHOLOGY

As is possibly known, Russian psychology – and the theory of Galperin in particular - pays a great deal of attention to the development of mental, cognitive concepts and processes from experiences on a more concrete and materialized level. This approach seems to be in line with the psychological concepts of Piaget and Bruner mentioned earlier. A big difference is that the Russian psychology does not agree with the developmental discovery-learning approach of Piaget and Bruner, but emphasizes that learning takes place by the gradual shaping of behaviour by means of directed instruction (somewhat like in the American behaviouristic views on learning). For Galperin, physical objects are not seen as stimulating conditions for dicovery behaviour, but as materialized orienting bases for the learning of correct behaviour-patterns. Another big difference between these rather diverging psychological concepts is that Galperin's theory pays a lot of attention to the gradual transitions in learning behaviour from the first materialized stage to the last mental stage, via the perceptual and verbalization stages in between.

AN EXAMPLE OF DIFFERENT INSTRUCTIONAL DESIGN OF MATERIALS BY FOLLOWING THE PSYCHOLOGICAL CONCEPTS OF PIAGET AND GALPERIN

Because in the Netherlands there is a lot of influence from Russian psychology - not only in theory and research but also in the practice of the design of new school books - I can illustrate these differences in psychological concepts and their consequences for instructional design by a concrete example. In Figure 1 you see two different operationalizations of teaching the mental addition of larger numbers (20-100), taken from Dutch mathematics-methods. Procedure A mainly emphasizes the visualization of numbers by rods and blocks, which can also be done without the use of a hundred-square by just laying down the configurations of materials on the table. This procedure is rather common in school practice, and goes back to the insights of Piaget with emphasis on visualization (Borghouts, 1978). Procedure B uses more the contextual structure of the hundred-square. After a first stage of concrete displaying numbers it quickly moves on to a more abstract stage, where the numbers are represented in the hundred-square by the manipulation of only one block. In the third stage emphasis is then laid on the representation of the addition procedure by jumping with blocks as well as the verbalization of the procedural steps.

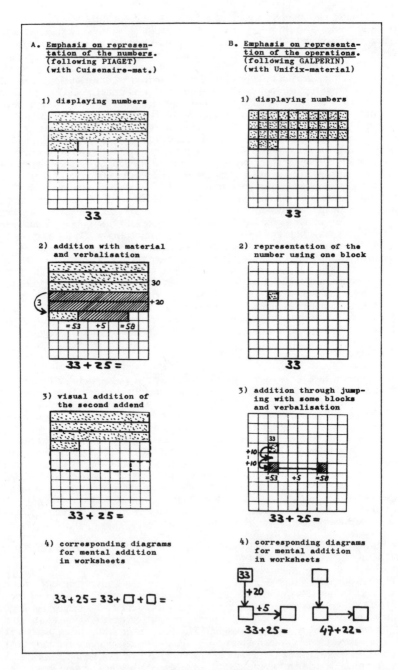

Mathematics teaching in the Netherlands puts more emphasis on
adding and subtracting "mentally" in the area of 0 - 100, and
starts with "written" procedures only beyond the number of 100.

Fig. 1 <u>Instructional design of the addition procedure in 4 stages
following two different underlying psychological concepts</u>

As can be seen in Figure 1 procedure B differs from A in that it gives a more directed pre-structuring of the cognitive addition operation itself. Furthermore, the following diagrams in the work sheets show us a sort-like difference in instructional design between the procedures A and B. In those work sheets the children have to solve the problems if possible without the aid of materials. Procedure B comes from one of our new mathematics-methods, following the ideas of Galperin on gradual and directed transitions from materialized to mental stages in the learning of cognitive concepts and procedures (Buys et al,1980).

THE CONTEXT OF EDUCATIONAL TECHNOLOGY

In this paper I will now concentrate on our evaluation-studies with data about the effects of both these different procedures. But as a last introductory remark, I would like to make a short reference to the field of educational technology. I was once engaged in work and research with programmed instruction (Beishuizen, 1977). In my opinion, since that period educational technology has gone towards broader applications (Kay, 1979), and has more or less lost its theoretical and empirical interest in specific questions of instructional design. Some authors (Salomon, 1980) are trying to make new starts in that old direction. From this point of view materials and visualization for mathematics learning offer, in my opinion, an interesting case for more specific study and research into design questions.

EVALUATION WITH SECOND GRADE CHILDREN (AGE SEVEN TO EIGHT)

Before carrying out our evaluation-studies in 1982 and 1983, an important period was the preliminary orientation into several mathematics methods, arithmetic materials and school practices. In 1980 and 1981, we visited 17 schools and observed lessons, which gave a rather scattered picture of very diverging ways of using arithmetic materials. Rather common was the situation of just providing materials to the children with only a few instructions for their first use. It was rare to find schools with a more systematic and continuing use of materials. Nevertheless, we decided to concentrate on systematic use and long-term effects as a more powerful design for an evaluation study. We therefore chose the second grade - and not the first grade - and schools using systematically the procedures A or B as shown in Figure 1. In the Netherlands the age of children in the second grade of the primary school goes from seven to eight years. In order to be able to generalize we used two comparable schools/classes in each condition, A and B, as well as two schools working without materials as a control condition C. All schools had mainly middle-class children, and were contacted with the assistance of the school advisory centres of the areas Leyden and Gouda in the west of the Netherlands.

Figure 2 gives an outline of both evaluation studies in 1982 and 1983. The children were individually tested at the end of the second grade (May/June) by several postgraduate students of the education sciences department of the Leyden University. Because of the exploratory character of our research-questions and the lack of other comparable data in the literature, we felt the need to gather further evidence on the main conclusions of just one evaluation study. Therefore, we decided in 1983 to carry out a replication study with some methodological improvements. Some of the schools were the same, but in other cases we had to change for reasons such as the appearance of a new teacher or a new method. One methodological reason for a change was that in 1982 our control classes C appeared to be of significantly higher social class level (F 3,38; df 2/141; P .05). In 1983 those levels no longer differed (D 0,21; df 2/124; NS)

TYPES OF PROBLEMS AND SOLUTION PROCEDURES

Figure 3 gives the number problems of the test. They were repeated three times with slightly different numbers. In the first part of the test, problems had to be solved mentally by the children, ie in their heads. In the second part of the test, children were requested to solve the problems with the aid of materials as they were used to before in class. As a matter of fact, the use of materials normally stops half-way during the second grade (February). So at the moment of the test (in May or June) the children had to go back to this materialized level, which caused some problems. Therefore, the second series in the test was preceded by one or two problems -which were not scored - to make them familiar again with this materialized level (ie, refresh their memory).

	Materials:	Use:	N'82:	N'83:
			(Social class: 6-1)	
A	Cuisenaire, Unifix	additional to traditional method, incidental use of 100 square	54 2 classes (3,94)	41 2 classes (3,51)
B	Unifix	integrated in new method, continuous use of 100 square	42 2 classes (3,71)	45 2 classes (3,82)
C	------	no materials, traditional method, incidental use of 100 square	46 2 classes (4,57)	39 3 classes (3,69)
			142 +	125 +

Other conditions:

A	Cuisenaire	systematic use of Cuisenaire, add. to trad. method, incidental use of 100 square	----	20 1 class (3,90)
B	Unifix	additional to new method, continuous use of 100 square	40 2 classes (3,45)	----
B	MAB, Unifix	lower-class schools, int. in new method, continuous use of 100 square	----	45 2 classes (2,11)
C	------	no materials, traditional method, continuous use of 100 square	----	16 1 class (4,00)

total   182 +   206 +

Fig. 2   Conditions in the evaluation studies

1) mentally, by Head
2) with Materials
3) choice by H or with M

1982:	1983:
(direct problems)	(direct problems)
a) 36 + 9	a) 24 + 12
b) 88 + 4	b) 46 + 23
c) 47 + 22	c) 38 + 16
d) 72 - 8	d) 26 - 12
e) 48 - 24	e) 58 - 34
f) 58 - 35	f) 42 - 15
(no indirect problems in series 1, only in ser. 3)	(indirect problems in series 1 and 3)
	g) 42 - . = 34
	h) 15 + .. = 27
	i) 23 + .. = 62
(in series 2: -4 problems to display certain numbers with materials; -4 problems to add or subtract with materials; -4 problems to add or subtract the second number visually, cf fig. 1, procedure A, stage 3)	(in series 2 only 6 problems to add or subtract with materials)
total 26 test problems	total 24 test problems
P-level series 1 (mental)	P-level series 1 (mental)
-direct problems: P .79	-direct problems: P .76
-no indirect problems	-indirect probl.: P .52
split-half reliability of total test: r .56	split-half reliability of total test: r .77

Fig. 3 Arithmetic problems
in 3 test series:

In practice, however, not all children do stop using materials half-way in the second grade. In our classes each child had its own small private set of materials, and several children continued using materials more or less frequently. To evaluate this differentiated use of materials in the last half of the second grade, the third part of the test offered a cho'ce to the children. They might solve those problems mentally or with the aid of materials, just as they wished to do.

As can be seen from the added statistics in Figure 3, the test was not too difficult for the direct problems (P 79 and P 76). In 1983, the problems with one small number were omitted and the problems c) and f) were added, involving passing the number 10. The indirect problems or missing number problems in part 1 of the test, which are more difficult (P 52) as is known from practice and research, were also omitted. The reason those indirect problems were not contained in the first test in the 1983 study was that there is a remarkable difference in this respect between traditional and new mathematics methods. Traditional methods lay more emphasis on a lot of formula exercises as a form of consolidation training. New methods do pay more attention to different types of practice – working with materials, visualizations, solving puzzle-like problems, etc – to enhance concept formation. Also they contain less 'boring' series of formula exercises. We analysed our new method and one of the older ones and Figure 4 gives the number of formula exercises on both sides. As can be seen, the new method contains far fewer formula exercises in direct problems (3044 vs 6285). Also in the new method the difficult indirect problems are much more left till the following third grade, as is also the case with the more difficult direct problems, where the addition or subtractions goes through the 10. Therefore, in 1982 we adapted our test to this basic mastery level, but in 1983 we added those problems because we were more anxious to test the limits and the transfer of the problem-solving capacity of the children.

	old method:		new method:	
	direct problems	indirect problems	direct problems	indirect problems
Small numbers: 0-20	2780	1392	1372	222
Large numbers: 20-100	3505	1360	1672	121
Total exercises:	6285	2752	3044	343

Fig. 4   Number of formula exercises for addition and subtraction in second grade (age 7-8) schoolbooks in the Netherlands.

As a statistical outcome, the variance in the data from 1983 became larger, and presumably also due to some simplification of the second part of the test (Figure 3) the split-half reliability did rise from an unsatisfactory level in 1982 ($r = .56$) to a more satisfactory level in 1983 ($r = .77$).

In Figure 5, we give the solution procedures which we noted by observation and by having the children report their ways of solution at the end of each problem. Counting-on (C) and structuring (S) with 'derived number facts' are well-known categories from the growing research literature (Carpenter and Moser, 1982). The remaining two categories need some explanation because they are less well known. These categories only apply to mental operations with the larger numbers between 20 and 100. In Dutch school practice – and maybe in other countries too – mental arithmetic with larger numbers up to 100 is usual in the second grade. Written arithmetic only starts in the third grade with numbers larger than 100. This is different from the British and the Americam school practice, where written procedures are learned much earlier.

What we called the '10-10' procedure is well-known in the literature as 'decomposition' (Young and O'Shea, 1981) making use of the 'place value' concept (Houlihan and Ginsburg, 1981). Less known in the literature is what we called the 'N-10' procedure, where only the second addend is split into tens and ones, and added-on to the unsplit first addend-number (N) as a sort of 'counting-on' procedure. Most methods – old and new – in the Netherlands teach the last procedure, because N-10 takes lesser steps and prevents carrying-problems, as they direct problems:

C = Counting-on:
$36 + 9 \rightarrow 37,38,39,40,41,42,43,44,45 = \underline{45}$

S = Structuring (or derived Number Facts):
$36 + 9 \rightarrow 36 + 4 = \underline{40} + 5 = \underline{45}$

10-10 = taking Tens together, also the Ones, then combine:
$47 + 22 \rightarrow 40 + 20 = \underline{60}, 7 + 2 = \underline{9}, 60 + 9 = \underline{69}$

10-10-N = taking Tens together, then add the first One, then handle the second One:
$58 - 34 \rightarrow 50 - 30 = \underline{20}, 20 + 8 = 28, 28 - 4 = \underline{24}$

N-10 = not splitting up the first Number but only the second number:
$58 - 34 \rightarrow 58 - 30 = \underline{28} - 4 = \underline{24}$

indirect problems:

C : $15 + .. = 27 \rightarrow 16,17,18,19,20$, etc. $26,27 \rightarrow$ added $\underline{12}$

S : $15 + .. = 27 \rightarrow 15 + \underline{5} = 20 + \underline{7} = 27 \rightarrow$ added $5 + 7 = \underline{12}$

10-10 : $23 + .. = 62 \rightarrow 20 + \underline{40} = 60, 3 - 2 = \underline{1}$,
added $40 - 1 = \underline{39}$

often direction faults: $3 - 2 = \underline{1}$, added $40 + 1 = \underline{41}$
or $3 + 2 = \underline{5}$, added $40 + 5 = \overline{\underline{45}}$

N-10 : $23 + .. = 62 \rightarrow 23 + 40 = \underline{63} - 1 = 62$,
added $40 - 1 = \underline{39}$

also direction faults: added $40 + 1 = \underline{41}$

Fig. 5 <u>Solution procedures of arithmetic-problems.</u>

rise from the 10-10 procedure in subtractions going through the 10 (eg, 42-15 using 40-10=30 and 2-5=?). But, from school practice and remedial teaching in our country, it is a well known fact that children spontaneously incline to the 10-10 procedure! As children also reported in our test situations they see the 10-10 procedures as a sort of easy 'problem-solving strategy', splitting up the 'big' problems with larger numbers in two 'minor' problems: first addition or subtraction with the tens and afterwards separately with the ones (mostly in this sequence). As we saw earlier in Figure 1, both procedures A and B, which use materials in a different way, are aiming at the same objective of teaching the so-called 'N-10' procedure.

As we will see next in this paper the evaluation-results concentrate mainly on the differences and success-rates of these 10-10 and N-10 procedures.

SOME RESULTS AND SOME CONCLUSIONS

In Figure 6 we present some quantitative and in Figure 7 some qualitative results. All groups were split in two levels of arithmetic competency, taking the arithmetic test scores as a criterion. We start with an explanation of the qualitative results, namely the diverging shaping of solution procedures in the three conditions A, B and C. As can be seen from the overall success rates of the solution procedures in Figure 7, the 10-10 procedure appeared to

effects: T = 2 **Testscores** of 1st and 2nd Series: • and ∘
           C = 3 Conditions A, B and C: ═══ = 2 classes as a group
           L = 2 Levels of arithmetic- ──── = + half Ss ⎫ of a class
                     competency: ---- = - half Ss ⎭

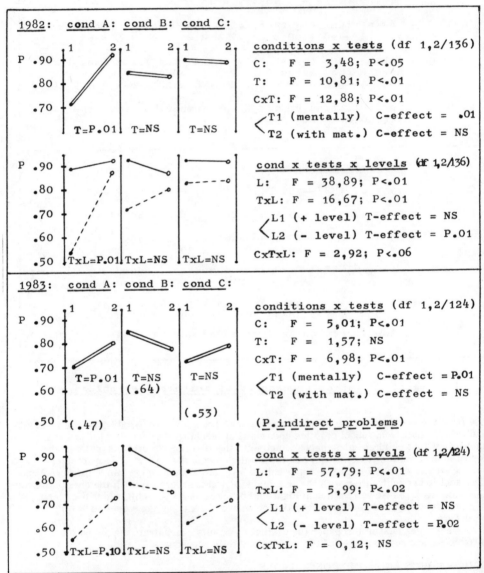

Fig. 6   <u>ANOVA of the arithmetic testscores on the 1st (mentally)</u>
         <u>and 2nd (with materials) series: direct problems</u>.

(% = proportional frequency of all solutions per condition)

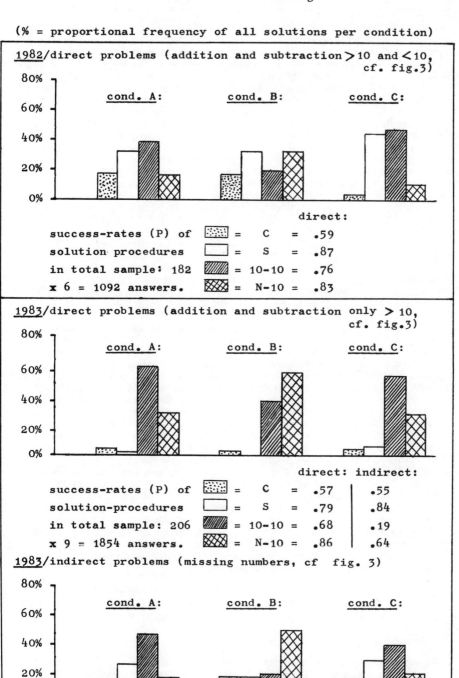

Fig. 7 Frequencies of mental solution procedures in the first test series: direct and indirect problems.

be less successful than the N-10 procedure. Because of the adding of more difficult problems in the test, this trend becomes more clear in 1983, where especially with the indirect problems the application of the 10-10 procedure leads to failures in almost all cases.

For instance in the problem of 23 + .. =62 the 10-10 procedure mostly leads to the solution 20+40=60 and 3+2=5; 45 as the wrong answer means that the direction of the operation is faulty. With the N-10 procedure jumping from 23 - 63 = 40, some direction faults are also made by adding the difference between 63 and 62 = 1 to 40 = 41, but mostly this difference is rightly subtracted from 40 resulting in the right answer of 40-1=39.

Faults due to incorrect direction of the operation are also an important cause for wrong answers with the 10-10 procedure in the direct problems. Our explanation here must be kept short, but as can be seen from the examples in Figure 5, the 10-10 procedure may cause more direction problems than the N-10 procedure. Especially in the case of subtraction we saw a lot of children using the 10-10 procedure, moving to the variant we called 10-10-N: 58-34 - 50-30=20+8=28-4=24. After deducting the tens, the ones of the first number are added, whereafter the ones of the second are deducted. So the 10-10 procedure causes many more direction problems and the taking of decisions than the N-10 procedure, where counting-on or counting-down in one direction always gives the right solution of direct problems (58-34 - 58-30=28-4=24).

Of course, more could be said of both procedures, such as the interpretation of the 10-10 procedure as a more 'invented' and heuristic' procedure, and the interpretation of the N-10 procedure as a more 'learned' and 'algorithmic' procedure. But for the moment we will not go deeper in our analysis. We will return now to our main conditions A, B and C and their effects on the solution procedures of the children taught. We will summarize the results of our evaluation studies in three conclusions, referring to the Figures 6 and 7.

1. In the control condition C we see the 10-10 procedure dominate in the solution procedures. So the instruction in those older mathematics methods, aiming at learning the N-10 procedure is far from effective in a qualitative way. Most children keep following the 10-10 procedure that they spontaneously prefer.
2. In the condition A with materials mainly used as representation of the numbers, the 10-10 procedure also remains the dominating one, and is hardly shaped in the direction of the N-10 procedure. Our impression from test observations is that this use of materials in the very concrete form with ten rods and one block (see Figure 1) is more reinforcing the spontaneous 10-10 solution behaviour instead of shaping it.
3. Only in condition B we see a remarkable qualitative influence on the solution behaviour of the children in the direction of the N-10 procedure. Also remarkable are the rather good quantitative results in comparison with the other conditions (see Figure 6).This is especially the case with the difficult indirect problems, while the children in this condition with a new mathematics method have had much fewer exercises in this respect than children in the other conditions with older mathematics methods (see Figure 4). These results underline in our opinion the power of the N-10 procedure as a more adequate way of operating mentally with large numbers than the 10-10 procedure. Also these results confirm the differential effectiveness of the procedures A and B in their design and use of materials, as shown in Figure 1. Besides the practical relevance there is also theoretical relevance in these evaluation-results, and we will return to that in the discussion.

As a more general conclusion the outcomes of our second replication-study in 1983 strongly confirm the trends we found in our first exploratory-study in 1982. This consistency in the data makes generalization from our findings more satisfactory.

DISCUSSION

Following our evaluation results and relating them to some concepts from the literature, it may be that the psychological effects of the arithmetic materials we studied can be described on two (didactical) functional levels. Considering audiovisual media like film or TV, Salomon (1979) identifies a primary 'supplantation' function of lower cognitive level and a secondary "activation" function of higher cognitive level. Speaking of visual schemes or mappings as an aid to the learning of arithmetic procedures, Resnick (1982) supposes a first 'prohibition' function and a second 'enrichment' function. Both pairs of concepts refer to the possible modelling functions of visualizations for cognitive processes. In the first functions called 'supplantation' or 'prohibition' the emphasis is on following or imitating the model as an explicit step-by-step guide for new or difficult cognitive procedures. On this level there is a strong leaning on the model as a simulator without much internalization of the processes involved. In the second functions called 'activation' or 'enrichment' there is a change to interpretation and internalization of the model by the learner. His cognitive behaviour is 'activated' or 'enriched' in a new direction. As Salomon (1979) states the design of visualizations or models in the first function needs to be more elaborated in a concrete and isomorph way, like some animation techniques in instructional films. But for the second function visualizations or models need to change to a more condensed and abstract-structured form to activate more the cognitive processing by the learner himself.

In our opinion, the two procedures A and B of design and of use of materials and visualizations, as they appear in Dutch mathematics teaching (see Figure 1), can be compared with the concepts of Salomon and Resnick as shown in Table 1.

arithmetic materials	Salomon:	Resnick:
procedure A	supplantation	prohibition
procedure B	activation	enrichment

Table 1 Relationships between procedures and concepts

The different results of the procedures – with B having more shaping influence on the mental, cognitive processes of the learners than A – can be seen as giving more evidence and sharpen the rather speculative ideas of Salomon and Resnick. These may also correspond to the background psychological concepts of Piaget with emphasis on visualization or the first 'supplantation' function, and of Galperin with emphasis on pre-structuring and directed guiding of internalization or the second 'activation' function.

One further finding in our data we can add, which still needs more analysis, but which is relevant because it has to do with the well-known problem of children 'hanging on' too strongly to the support of concrete materials. As can be seen in Figure 6 the results in the test did improve with the second series of problems where mental arithmetic was supported by the requested use of materials. But as the ANOVA analysis confirms, this effect mainly occurred with the children of lower arithmetic competence. As can be seen in Figure 6, this effect most strongly appeared in condition A. We can call this effect the supplantation function of the materials. But there is another side to this effect. The strong rise of the results due to supplantation in part 2 of the test springs from a lower level of mental arithmetic results in part 1 of the test, especially with the lower competence children who had been taught by procedure A. So the interpretation of these findings can also be turned the other way round, namely that especially in condition A the use of materials mainly should be interpreted as a supplantation function, that had too little internalizing effect on the shaping of cognitive processes, especially with the lower competence learners taught by procedure A (see Figure 6). They did hang on much more to the support of materials than the children – also those of lower competence! – who followed procedure B (see Figure 6). There are also other data – such as the choices made in part 3 of the test – which support this 'hanging-on' explanation in relation to the hypothesized supplantation function of materials, but they need more analysis to be presented.

In conclusion, I should like to refer to my remarks above that one of the reasons for going into this research subject of arithmetic materials, was a felt need for more conceptualization on specific design issues in educational technology. I hope that more research with other materials and visualizations will contribute to this subject. I think it is a relevant subject, not only for better describing in psychological terms the many existing materials etc in school practice, but also for better – I mean more didactical-functional – designing of learning materials etc, which applies also to the use of the computer screen as a powerful learning aid in the future.

REFERENCES

Beishuizen, M (1977) Geprogrameerde instructie of tekst + vragen (Programmed instruction or
    text + adjunct questions? Dissertation Free University, Amsterdam), Wolters-Noordhoff,
    Groningen.
Borghouts-Van Erp, J W M (1978) Rekenproblemen: Opsporen en oplossen (Arithmetic
    learning-problems: how to detect and to solve), reeks orthovisies, deel 6, Groningen.
Buys, N, Teunissen, F and Bergen, T van (1980) Handleiding operatoir-rekenen-leerjaar 2
    (Teacher's manual arithmetic-method "Operatoir Rekenen" - second grade).
    Zwijsen, Tilburg.
Carpenter, Th P and Moser, J M (1982) The development of addition and subtraction
    problem-solving skills. In Carpenter, Th P, Moser, J M and Romberg, Th A (eds) Addition
    and subtraction: a cognitive perspective. Lawrence Erlbaum Associates, Hillsdale NJ.
Houlihan, D M and Ginsburg, H P (1981) The addition methods of first and second grade
    children. Journal of Research in Mathematical Education, pp95-106.
Kay, H (1980) Keynote address: Educational technology 20 years on - Sheffield
    revisited. In Page, G T and Whitlock, Q (eds) Aspects of Educational Technology XIII.
    Kogan Page, London.
Moser, J M (1980) A longitudinal study of the effect of number size and presence of
    manipulative materials on children's processes in solving addition and
    subtraction verbal problems. AERA paper. Wisconsin R and D Center.
Resnick, L B and Ford W W (1981) The psychology of mathematics for instruction.
    Lawrence Erlbaum Associates, Hillside NJ.
Resnick, L B (1982) Syntax and semantics in learning to subtract. In: Carpenter, Th P,
    Moser, J M and Romberg, Th A (eds) Addition and subtraction: a cognitive perspective.
    Lawrence Erlbaum Associates, Hillside NJ.
Salomon, G (1979) Media and symbol systems as related to cognition and learning.
    Journal of Educational Psychology, 71, pp131-148.
Salomon, G (1980) The use of visual media in the service of enriching mental thought
    processes. Instructional Science, 9, pp327-339.
Young, R M and O'Shea, T (1981) Errors in children's subtraction. Cognitive Science,
    pp153-177.

7.3 Designing and Manufacturing an Educational Technology Product

I J Winfield and E A Winfield

Abstract: This article chronicles the design, development and marketing of a self-instructional 'package' consisting of skin reponse biofeedback instrument, explanatory booklet, diary and integrated audiotape. As well as examining the rationale for particular design and marketing decisions, the article also highlights the role of chance in product success.

BACKGROUND

Commercially available educational technology products have their own peculiar design history. Whereas, for obvious commercial reasons, the design and marketing of a consumer durable may be shrouded in secrecy an educational technologist venturing into the risky field of design and marketing may feel a strong compulsion to follow the guiding philosophy of educational technology: viz to document and to make public. This is simply because it is argued that the rapid spread of ideas and practices in educational technology can be sped up by adopting the time-honoured conventions of education such as objective recording and publishing results. For the particular product described in this paper, basic 'desk' research had first been carried out over an 18-month period into the psycho-physiological response known as galvanic skin response. This is the activity of the human sweat glands when aroused – part of the sympathetic nervous system popularly known as 'the fight for flight reflex'.

This period of research was followed up by a research visit to the United States to gather data on current developments in the use of biofeedback technology and associated therapeutic practice. Because of cultural differences biofeedback equipment has much more extensive non-specialist prophylactic use in the USA (particularly the West Coast) than in the UK or Europe. A review of the available literature on biofeedback (Winfield, 1983) revealed legions of well validated and controlled experiments upon its therapeutic efficacy, particularly for control and management of stress-related psychosomatic disorders.

However, the review and visit revealed serious shortcomings. While product development undertaken by entrepreneurs often seems superficially 'demand led' or fuelled by a simple desire to fill a gap in a particular market, other deeper more psychological forces are nonetheless present (Winfield, 1984). In the case of the author's product the original motivation can be traced to ideological reasons related to the emergent politics of biofeedback. Biofeedback technology, once hailed as giving 'power to the person'; once hailed as a 'liberatory' low-impact technology had, in practice, become thoroughly medicalized and professionalized. The liberatory technology had, in the words of Illich (1974, 1976) become appropriated by professionals. Biofeedback consultants deliberately rendered esoteric the training processes involved in biofeedback use and a restricted-entry. 'Society' governed legitimation and accreditation in the use of biofeedback.

CASEWORK EXPERIENCE

The first stage in product development consisted of gathering practical casework experience in the use of biofeedback for simple anxiety and stress management. A registered partnership firm called 'Biofeedback Instruction' was formed for legal and contractual purposes. Clients willing to explore the therapeutic use of biofeedback for learning anxiety management were obtained by placing advertisements in local newspapers.

Clients using the equipment eventually formed themselves into a self help network to trade ideas and experiences. The 'Biofeedback Users Group' as it subsequently came to be known held regular monthly meetings – dates and venues were broadcast using the local events listing publication.

At this early stage of casework experience, existing equipment available on the market both UK and world-wide was extensively used. Repeated use of these products revealed certain inadequacies:

* Instruments on the European market were mostly designed for scientific laboratory use. Controls were difficult for the lay person to understand and manipulate.
* All instruments had an off-putting, slightly daunting appearance not suited for domestic use.
* No explanatory text accompanied the instruments.
* There were no guides. What text there was appeared to have been written by engineers or technical experts: it was dense, wordy and heavily jargonized.
* Electrodes were particularly alienating to the lay person.

During case experience and user group meetings clients would frequently request home use of instruments in order to follow extended stress management programmes. Prototype development then took place on an instrument specifically designed for self teaching by the client in their own self chosen environment. Developments at this stage were:

1. A legal hire contract was drawn up between 'Biofeedback Instruction' and the client allowing home use of instruments bounded by contract law.
2. The portable skin biofeedback instrument was made; designed to be robust and with virtually error–proof controls. Control functions were reduced to a simple rotating knob allowing users to establish their own baseline skin responses.
3. Simple procedure strings for stress management exercises in conjunction with the instrument were written, user validated and printed. A general non-technical introduction to skin biofeedback was written along with a 'question and answer' sequence based upon common misconceptions and queries. The explanatory text constituted an integrated workbook whose design was based upon previous research by the author (Winfield, 1979).

Thorough case notes of client progress (or lack of it) and instrument/procedure string performance were kept which subsequently formed the basis for a number of design modifications. Eventually a short self-instruction booklet was derived along with a purpose-built instrument. Observations of user behaviour revealed further insights:

1. Clients preferred to use the instruments in a wide variety of settings – some vastly dissimilar to the architypal Biofeedback relaxation setting of a quiet semi–darkened room.
2. Clients wanted to experiment with their own self–generated procedure strings, modifying the instructional sequence to suit their own idiosyncratic emotional and learning needs.
3. Clients frequently requested a means of self-monitoring their progress on stress management programmes.
4. Some clients requested an integrated audiotape containing verbal instructions on how to use the instrument during relaxation exercise. These clients obviously were unable to switch easily from instrument manipulation to reading and back again.
5. Clients requested modifications to the control–display ratio.
6. Clients found, by accident, less than serious therapeutic uses for the instrument after completing their training programmes. Social use of the instrument in group settings generated party games utilizing the instrument's ability to act as an arousal detector.

All the above demands were incorporated into the final product and accompanying booklet. A diary was developed based on the work of Meichenbaum on self-monitoring techniques (Meichenbaum,1977).

SKINTEC FINAL DEVELOPMENT AND PRODUCT LAUNCH

Before finalizing product design, all attributes that the product could possibly have were reviewed. This is a useful aid to final product design often drawing designer's attention to overlooked features of design. The technique (Crawford,1954) notes that each time an improvement is made in a product or system it is done by changing or varying an attribute. Original invention occurs by improving or varying the attributes (or parts, qualities or characteristics) of an artefact, or by transferring attributes from one situation to another (see Figure 1).

Put it to other uses?	Are there new ways to use the product as it is?
	Can it be modified to do other things?
Adapt?	Is another product similar?
	Does the product suggest other ideas?
	Can ideas be copied/ adapted?
Modify?	A new 'slant' to the product?
	Change meaning, shape, colour, form or other attributes?
Magnify?	Can anything be added?
	Multiply or exaggerate?
Minimize?	Subtract something from the product?
	Make smaller?
	Streamline, split up or understate?
Substitute?	What else instead of existing features?
	Other ingredient/ material/ process/ approach?
Rearrange?	Interchange components?
	Other pattern/ layout/ sequence?
	Transpose cause and effect?
	Change schedule/ pace?
Reverse?	Transpose positive and negative?
	Turn backwards/ upside down/ reverse roles?
Combine?	Consider an amalgam/ assortment or alloy?
	Combine units/ purposes/ appeals and ideas?

Figure 1 Attribute list (after Osborn,1963)

In closely similar vein, ideas checklists can be used to stimulate the production of new ideas (see Figure 2).

A useful practical summary of both these techniques can be found in Osborne (1963), Davis and Houtman (1968) and Bailey (1982).

DISPLAY TECHNOLOGY SECTION

The display interface between instrument and user was a crucial design feature. Here again useful decision-making aids are available, one such flow chart being published in Bailey(1982). Characteristics of product users (generally a low level of technological sophistication) dictated that a simple needle display be used on a swing galvanometer. This was selected over more contemporary displays such as digital reading, LED or LCD. This was a calculated business gamble for it was found from case experience and test marketing that such users easily understood the left/right swing of a galvanometer needle to correlate with subjective mood and bodily states. Direction of motion of display was made in accordance with population motion stereotypes (Loveless, 1969). A commercially available swing galvanometer was overprinted with a vinyl mask using two status words 'relaxed' and 'tense'. Even though strong links have been empirically established between colours and alarm or status words (Warren, 1974), production costs of multicolour vinyl printing prevented this. Target selling price thus became a strong design criteria.

PREPARATION OF A BUSINESS PLAN

The opportunity arose at this point (April,1983) to submit the business idea to the Academic Enterprise Competition sponsored by the British Technology Group. This competition was set up to encourage academics to bring innovations on to the market. Substantial prize money was promised for viable market propositions. Entry to the competition required the drawing up of a formal business plan under the following headings:

    Manufacturing process
    Marketing plan
    Financial forecasting
    Financial funding

Change colour?	New size?	Change shape?	New material?	Add or subtract?	Rearrange things?	New design?
Blue	Longer	Round	Plastic	Strengthen	Switch	Oriental
Green	Shorter	Square	Glass	Make faster	Change	Swedish
Yellow	Wider	Triangle	Fibreglass	Exaggerate	pattern	French
Orange	Fatter	Oval	Formica	Duplicate	Combine	Eskimo
Red	Thinner	Rectangle	Paper	Remove	Another	Russian
Purple	Thicker	5-sided	Wood	Divide	order	American
White	Higher	6-sided	Aluminium	Lighten	Split up	Indian
Black	Lower	8-sided	Nylon	Abbreviate	Reverse	Egyptian
Olive	Larger	10-sided	Cloth	Add new	Upside	Spanish
Grey	Smaller	Lopsided	Cardboard	smell	down	Old West
Brown	Jumbo	Sharp	Steel	New sound	Inside	Roaring
Tan	Miniature	corners	Leather	New lights	out	twenties
Silver	Other size	Round	Copper	New flavour	Combine	Past
Gold		corners	Rubber	Subtract the	purposes	century
Plaid		Egg-shaped	Other	thing that		Next
Striped		Doughnut-	material	does not do		century
Speckled		shaped	Combine	anything		Middle ages
Other		U-shaped	materials			Other
colours		Other shapes				styles

Figure 2 Idea checklist (adapted from Davis and Houtman,1968)

The discipline involved in detailing costings, price fixing, and test marketing strategy was particularly valuable. Instructive too, was the experience gained in raising capital for the venture. The current peculiarities of raising capital for startup manufacturing businesses utilizing UK banking practices is reviewed in Williams et al (1983).

PRODUCT LAUNCH AND TEST MARKETING

A limited company, Self Instruction Limited, was incorporated in February,1982. Mail order was considered to be the best strategy for exploratory test marketing. Many surveys of the mail order business, viz product selection, promotional methods, idiosyncracies of this mode of marketing (Eicoff,1982; Caples,1974; Ogilvy,1983; Roman and Maas,1976; Stone,1979) seemed to indicate that this particular product was well suited to mail order:

* The potential purchaser would not know intuitively where to purchase it in the high street retail outlets.
* There might be slight embarrassment in asking for it in high street shops.
* The product could be construed as 'culturally enriching' with people wanting to tell their friends/neighbours about it.

The package of final instrument design, 24-page biofeedback guide, 16-page diary and audiotape was assembled, packaging produced, information leaflets printed and Post Office Freepost license obtained. Four separate ways were identified of promoting it:

1. Function Based
To promote the product this way involves advertising copy with headlines such as 'Complete Home Biofeedback System'. The 'function' approach presupposed the market understood the concept of biofeedback and its associated therapeutic/prophylactic uses.
2. System Based
It could be promoted by emphasis upon the classic stress symptoms biofeedback is claimed to alleviate. Copy would include stress, tension mangement, relaxation training. Care had to be taken to meet the requirements of the Code of Advertising Practice.
3. Product Name Based
The product, name 'Skintec' could aid its promotion. Headlines in advetising copy would feature this.
4. Fun Uses
Promotion could emphasize its peripheral, fun or social uses. A portable home biofeedback system could be used for party games with the instrument functioning as an arousal meter or 'lie detector'.

The literature on advertising abounds with legions of practical 'how to' texts. Some of the more useful for educational technology products were Roman and Maas (1976), Ogilvy (1983), and Gunning (1971). Mail order outlets for the advertising copy were three broad classes of magazines/journals:

1. Health/Fitness Journals: This included the buoyant publishing sector of alternative health publications. All publications carry flourishing mail order sections. Examples are 'Here's Health', 'Health and Fitness', 'Health Now', 'Journal of Alternative Medicine'.
2. Mass Circulation Sunday Papers.
3. Humorous/Satirical/Listings Weeklies: 'Private Eye', 'Time Out', etc.

Mail order marketing planning is not unlike the preparation involved in conducting a classic 'laboratory' experiment – and the two vocabularies overlap. An environment is delineated – this is the particular market segment to be manipulated. Advertisements are then systematically varied within this segment and the responses (via coded replies) are then analysed. Split half advertising (ie, running differently worded advertising copy consecutively in the same magazine/paper) allows responses to be recorded in an unvarying population.

Innovation ideas for marketing can be generated by considering the possible interaction of markets and promotion method. This is displayed in Figure 3.

Interactions		Market outlet		
		Health/ fitness	Sunday papers	Satirical
Promotion strategy	1. function based 2. symptom based 3. product name based 4. fun uses			

Figure 3 Possible market/ methods interaction

In product launching the universally applicable maxim appears to be 'any exposure is better than none'. Network television spotted the advertisement for the product's peripheral, fun uses. Immediately its value as a parlour game was seen as having television newsworthiness. The product was then demonstrated on television as a modern technologically based family game and seen working by an estimated 3.75 million viewers.

The instrument's ultimate popular usage was therefore radically different from its original design conception.

REFERENCES

Bailey, R W (1982) Human Performance Engineering: A Guide for Systems Designers. Prentice-Hall, New Jersey.

Caples, J (1974) Tested Advertising Methods. Prentice-Hall, New Jersey.
Crawford, R D (1954) The techniques of Creative Thinking. Hawthorn, New York.
Davis, G A and Houtman, S E (1968) Thinking Creatively: A Guide to Training Imagination. Wisconsin Research and Development Centres for Cognitive Learning, Wisconsin University.
Eicoff, A (1982) On Your Money Back. Crown Publishers, New York.
Gunning, R (ed) (1971) The Technique of Clear Writing. McGraw-Hill, New York.
Illich, I D (1974) Disabling Professions. Marion Boyars, London.
Illich, I D (1976) Limits to Medicine. Marion Boyars, London.
Loveless, N E (1969) Direction of motion stereotypes. In Holding, D H (ed) Experimental Psychology in Industry. Penguin, Harmondsworth.
Meichenbaum, D H (1977) Cognitive Behaviour Modification. Plenum, New York.
Ogilvy, D (1983) Ogilvy on Advertising. Pan, London.
Osborne, A F (1963) Applied Imagination. Scribner, New York.
Roman, K and Maas, J (1976) How to Advertise. St Martins Press, London.
Stone, B (1979) Successful Direct Marketing Methods. Crown Books, Chicago.
Warren, A (1974) Norms of restricted colour association. Bulletin of the Psychonomic Society, 4, pp37-38.
Williams, K, Williams, J and Thomas, D (1983) Why are the British so Bad at Manufacturing? Routledge and Kegan Paul, London.
Winfield, I J (1979) Learning to Teach Practical Skills. Kogan Page, London.
Winfield, I J (1983) Biofeedback and counselling: a review. Bulletin of the Psychonomic Society, 4, pp37-38.
Winfield, I J (1984) People in Business. Heinemann, London.

7.4 Workshop: Involving Students in Producing Instructional Materials

H I Ellington, E Addinall and S C Jones
Robert Gordon's Institute of Technology, Aberdeen
K J Ogilvie and W S Telfer
Paisley College of Technology, Paisley

SUMMARY

The workshop dealt with work carried out at Robert Gordon's Institute of Technology (RGIT), Aberdeen and Paisley College of Technology in which undergraduate students were involved in the design and preparation of instructional materials for use by fellow undergraduates. The purpose of the workshop was to allow the students to describe the work they had done and then hold an in-depth discussion on the potential role of students in developing such materials.

After a brief introduction by Dr Ellington, Stephen Jones described his work on the design and production of supportive materials for a second year atomic and nuclear physics course at RGIT. Stephen is a fourth-year honours physics student and this work has been written up as his honours project. He produced six packages of textual materials designed to help fellow students to cope with some of the mathematical and conceptual problems identified by the students who take this course. Dr Ellington was the project supervisor and both he and Dr Addinall have considerable experience in teaching this course.

Mr Telfer then described his work in the Learning Unit in the School of Physics at Paisley and introduced Karen Ogilvie, a final-year chemistry student. Much of the teaching carried out by Mr Telfer is supported by tape-slide programmes and Karen had found the medium difficult to come to grips with. When a series of photographs from CERN became available, she therefore took the initiative and decided to prepare three programmes which she hoped would be of use to her and to her colleagues.

Thus, although the reasons for the student involvement were quite different, here we found two students who were both sufficiently motivated to embark on ambitious programmes of work in educational technology. Their main aim was to provide supportive instructional materials for fellow students, however, in addition to this, they both admitted that they had also managed to learn a great deal about their own subject in the process.

The delegates who attended this workshop were naturally much more interested in the educational processes rather than the detailed subject content of the packages produced, and this was reflected in the discussion that followed these brief introductions. The first question, perhaps an obvious one, was 'Why students?' The two students were keen to point out that they, as students, were well aware of the difficulties as seen by their colleagues and that they were more likely to get 'honest' responses to questions about the course and its difficulties than were the lecturers(!) In addition, they both admirably demonstrated their enthusiasm for the work. When asked how the projects had helped their own situation, they both agreed that their study patterns had changed significantly, and they felt that they now had a much deeper understanding of the subject material.

A range of questions followed on the choice of medium for the presentation of the packages and the feedback that had been received. Naturally enough, the student were also asked how much help they had received from their 'supervisors' and the answer, supported by the people concerned, was 'as little as possible'.

Finally, the students were asked what they would do differently if they had to do it all again. From their replies, it was obvious that they felt they had learned enough to realize that they could do a better job, and, in Stephen's case, might even try a different medium. Karen felt that her programmes were too long and would redesign the three into perhaps five if given the opportunity.

Throughout the dicussion, the three lecturers associated with the students' work kept a very low profile; the delegates were interested in the students' views and not theirs. This became quite clear when, after the end of the formal workshop session, we found that a special extra session had been organized the next evening so that several of the delegates could look over the materials produced and continue their discussions with the two students. The lecturers involved beat a strategic retreat at this news but I can report that the students acquitted themselves very well and the discussion was extensive. Delegates looked at the packages and their reactions were, on the whole, complimentary. Much advice was offered and gratefully received, and it appears that several delegates were going home to try something similar in their own institutions and training establishments.

On the basis of this workshop, it appears that students can play an important role in developing instructional materials for use in a supportive role in undergraduate courses. Both students agreed, however, that they did not think that they would ever replace the lecturer (sighs of relief all round).

Section 8:
Technology Developments

8.1 A Mobile Teaching Unit for Isolated Rural Communities

R Sutcliffe and F Hooper

Abstract: This is an account of the Further Education Unit Research Project No. 110 (CYCLOPS Project). The objective was to identify learning needs in scattered rural communities and devise a system to meet them. The project was aimed at post 16-year-olds and, in particular, to the adult unemployed.

CRITIQUE OF THE 'MOBILE TEACHING UNIT' AS ORIGINALLY CONCEIVED IN THE RESEARCH BRIEF

The research project as originally conceived depends on the credibility of a vehicle as a means of making the resources of the college available to learners in isolated rural communities. There is an assumption here that needs examination, for whatever the vehicle, it is basically a delivery system reaching out over space to those expressing a learning need. In this way the resources of the college are made accessible to those unable to make <u>direct</u> use of them. Thus the vehicle is a kind of distance learning system where the teaching expertise and other resources are carried to the learner.

Any delivery system creates possibilities and also imposes restrictions. What are the particular ones associated with using a vehicle to meet the learning needs of those in remote and thinly populated areas?

<u>Possibilities</u>

Using a vehicle as a 'mobile teaching unit' it is possible to create:

1. a mobile classroom, a mobile workshop, and/or a mobile resource centre. The vehicle provides a space that can be carefully planned to contain the necessary equipment and teaching staff to meet specific learning needs;
2. the traditional face-to-face interaction between teacher and learners/learners and learner that we, the researchers, see a vital element of any learning situation;
3. an individual counselling service which can be either a separate service or one integrated with the teaching situation as is done for example for foundation students of the Open University.

<u>Limitations</u>

The limitations of a vehicle as a delivery system are best revealed by considering the constraints that bear on it.

(1) <u>A vehicle is expensive</u>

A high proportion of educational monies will be devoted to buying, or hiring, a vehicle, maintaining it, paying non-teaching staff, and under-using teaching staff by simply having to carry them from place to place. The bus in the Dorset Community Bus Project is hired at the cost of 40p per mile.

From the above it can be seen that a substantial amount of money will be spent on maintaining the vehicle as an operational delivery system irrespective of how that system is used.

(2) A vehicle has to be large

A vehicle has to be large to accommodate equipmennt, personnel and students using it as a mobile classroom' etc. The Dorset Community Bus Project is a 36-seater adapted to take bookshelves, toy library, book exchanges etc, and in addition provide a learning area with table and chairs. The bus had to be large to be meaningful. A smaller vehicle for example, a minibus, still has to face the questions of what is to be installed and why. What can a minibus achieve that a lecturer in a car cannot?

Certain physical factors compound the problem of accessibility. The very size of the vehicle will prevent it reaching some of the smaller communities. The roads are too narrow, too steep, too twisting for large vehicles. Additional irritations and delays are caused by the difficulty of passing oncoming traffic. The Dorset Community Bus Project encountered all these problems. The weather, which is worst in winter, is a further limiting factor. Winter is also the time when most people in rural areas have the time to avail themselves of new learning opportunities. The problem of accessibility is exacerbated as those places reached with difficulty are likely to become inaccessible as a result of ice, snow, flood and fog. In most winters one or all of these factors could seriously disrupt scheduled visits. Thus the problem of meetimg timetables, seen as imperative by the organizers of the Dorset Community Bus Project, are made worse.

(3) The vehicle is likely to exclude certain section of the target population

The vehicle would normally be operational during term times and in the daytime, and not in college holidays, evenings or weekends. Thus the population that can be reached through using it is that normally in the village, during the day in term time: mothers and pre-school children, the unemployed, the old and the sick. These groups are important to our research project, but not exclusive to it. The working population and, of lesser importance, the school population will be excluded. Thus the effective population that can be reached by a vehicle is reduced in these already low density areas of population. It may be possible to extend the times of operation for a vehicle, but this would involve planning difficulties as different types of people are affected – drivers, maintenance staff, teachers etc.

(4) The operational constraints imposed by a vehicle present the most serious limitations on this form of delivery system

The problem with a vehicle of any kind is that it can only visit one place at a time. The more places it visits the fewer calls it can make to one particular place. The further it travels to a place the fewer places it can visit.

Theoretically, the vehicle can go anywhere, any time, but practially once it has been decided that the vehicle will visit a particular place, it cannot visit others. This operational constraint limits where it can go and how often. Practically, the project will be limited to places within, say, 20 miles radius of the college with a limited number of visits to a relatively small number of places. The only way round this is for staff to be away from home and college for part or all of a week. Inevitably the vehicle will tend to concentrate on the larger centres of population and not relate directly to the small communities that are the focus of this research project.

The practical expression of the general problems identified in sections 1 to 4 above, is demonstrated by the Dorset Community Bus Project.

(a) The bus had crash gears and required an experienced driver. The Manpower Services Commission funded him.
(b) The bus carried three or four tutors, some of which were voluntary under the Adult Literacy Scheme.
(c) The bus had to follow a strict timetable to win and maintain public credibility in the project. A CAB van, it was noted, lost credibility through not following a regular time-table. People never knew when it would appear and, therefore, tended to ignore it.
(d) The bus had to visit each place once a week or at least once a fortnight. Any longer periods between visits did not maintain continuity.

(e) The particular features of an adult literacy, numeracy and basic skills programme, allowed the bus to make flying visits of less than the normal period of one hour. These visits had to be made as scheduled, even if no one came to the bus. This was one of the constraints generated by the need to win public credibility

(f) The bus visited <u>seven</u> places in two days. From the points enumerated, it follows that it must visit the same seven places as long as it was felt that effective contact was being made. The number could not be increased, only locations changed.

(5) The purpose of the vehicle

Behind the general statement that the vehicle is a 'mobile teaching unit', lie a host of details that affect the ends it can serve. Comparison with the Dorset Community Bus Project highlights these issues.

(i) The Dorset Community Bus Project set out to uncover and meet the basic skills, literacy and numeracy needs in rural areas. The organizer and research worker, Mrs Jane Jones, based her approach on the fact that these basic skills etc, can be taught through any medium. She set out to equip the bus so that it would attract as many people as possible. The bus had:

(a) A children's library. This reflected who was in the village when the bus called – mums and toddlers, and associated organizations, for example, playgroups.

(b) A toy library.

(c) A paperback book exchange scheme.

(d) Department of Health and Social Security leaflets on benefits, health care etc.

(e) Details of jobs available in the area, furnished by the Jobcentre.

Mrs Jones recognized that this 'honeypot' approach was necessary to overcome the 'threshold problem'. Even then, people in the initial stages had to be approached, accosted – her word, and asked to visit the bus. The 'honeypot' approach was based on the recognition that anything in English can be used to teach English. The same point extends to basic skills and numeracy, eg, interest in a job demands the ability to contact the prospective employer by telephone and/or letter etc. Even so, Mrs Jones found herself having to persuade her sponsors, ALBSU, that a group of keep fit ladies was an acceptable part of her scheme. She won through by pointing out how health and diet concerns can be vehicles for dealing with literacy etc, and that through the women the rest of the family could be reached

The question is: How would the college vehicle be equipped and why? The Dorset Community Bus Project has shown how, in the field of adult literacy, numeracy and basic skills, a bus can be successful. But, should the college vehicle be based on this model? The college is primarily concerned with specific courses that require basic skills etc, but are specialized beyond them. What would go into a college vehicle? A bit of office equipment? A lathe? Computers? What would be the rationale behind any selection? There is an important limitation here in so far as one learning need may exclude another, eg, the college vehicle could be fitted to meet the demand for motor vehicle maintenance and repairs, but the finite nature of the vehicle means it cannot now meet the demand for office skills and business management. The fundamental point is that deciding what goes into the vehicle also determines what cannot be installed.

It appears to us that this research project is concerned with learning needs above the level of basic skills etc, and that the major resources of the college relate to more specialized forms of education that assumes comepetency in basic skills etc.

(ii) The 'honeypot' approach meant, in the Dorset Community Bus Project, that the bus became a kind of market place. It was possible for people to meet but it was not possible to set up a 1:1 teaching situation because of the background noise. Under the Adult Literacy Scheme this initial contact did lead to such 1:1 teaching situations being established outside the bus. However, group work was possible, and successful, when the group was homogenous and dominated the bus situation.

The particular organizations of basic skills etc, using voluntary tutors, allowed effective follow-up to meet agreed need, and the bus provided a forum for small group work. The college is not associated with such a network of voluntary tutors. The expertise and resources of the college are more specialized and more centralized.

(iii) The Dorset Community Bus Project did, however, point to more specialized learning needs, and also indicated why they are not being met:

(a) They identified a whole area of learning need, which we have also identified –the expressed need for cost cutting skills that can initially be used as a vehicle for literacy and numeracy teaching etc but go beyond that. A good example is the need for elementary courses in motorbike and motor vehicle maintenance and repairs. Unless the Adult Literacy Scheme were fortunate in the pairing of voluntary tutor and student, the more specialized need could not be met. Another example is of one of the first men to use the Dorset bus. He needed basic skills, etc, but above this wanted elementary bookkeeping and office management skills and advice as he was just setting up in business. It was not the objective of the ALBSU bus to meet these revealed needs, but they are the kind of needs that could be satisfied through effective contact with the resources of the college

(b) In almost every village, the Dorset Community Bus Project identified small groups of adult learners who wanted to participate in existing adult education programmes, or could identify a particular course they wished to pursue. The numbers were too small to meet the current class size requirements. Thus some four, five or six could be found, but not the required 12. The small numbers of subscribers for a particular activity appears to us to be a fundamental and intractable problem in small rural communities while the present class size constraint applied. Either the classes have to be heavily subsidized, or cannot run, in spite of the enthusiastic support of some three or four people. Thus, in these communities sporadic attempts are continually made to establish viable courses. A vehicle cannot overcome this problem

So far, we have considered a delivery system that only allows linear and sequential operation. It is possible to create a learning system at A, B or C etc, at different times, but not simultaneously.

Is it possible to design a delivery system that allows simultaneous connections between learners with the same learning needs in different locations simultaneously, and at the same time maintain a high degree of interaction between tutor and students and students and students? Can we meet the class size criterion through this means?

If learners at A are 5, learners at B are 4, and learners at C are 3, and all express the same learning need, we have a 'class', if they can all be taught simultaneously.

IF NOT THE VEHICLE, WHAT?

Our notes on curriculum development indicate our conviction that the ends and means of curricula cannot be separated, but form an integrated whole.

'a curriculum is a thing in balance that cannot be developed first for content then for teaching method then for visual aids then for some other particular feature'.

This is our reason for considering the delivery systems available to us in the early stages of the research project.

A vehicle can best be understood as a distance teaching/learning system that carries resources, including teaching staff, to small groups of learners and operates within their local community. Our analysis of the vehicle as a delivery system reveals severe limitations. It is a cumbersome and expensive method of making the resources of the college available to small groups of learners in distant communities. Its sequential and linear method of operation means that it cannot operate unless heavily subsidized. The vehicle does not point to any solution that can overcome the constraint of class size, the most important single obstacle to any attempt by the college to respond to expressed learning needs in its rural hinterland. We feel it is imperative to seek out a new concept of mobility. A new means of moving information and expertise from the college to the small rural communities it serves.

If the travelling unit is not effective, what existing networks are available to carry information and expertise?

The postal system is the most extensive national network and reaches into every home. It does allow interpersonal communication through letters, tapes etc, but the process is a slow one and depends heavily on the written word. The immediate feedback that characterizes the traditional face-to-face learning/teaching situation is absent. In our view, this is a severe limitation of the system. So, the postal network is viewed by us as a useful, but ancillary system.

The second most extensive system is the telephone network:

'The adult learner, who is often a distant learner, requires non-traditional delivery systems. To reach adults at their home communities, higher education, which is primarily campus-based, must implement new modes of instruction. However, the development of outreach programmes is often limited by budgetary constraints. Instructing students near their homes or places of business is usually not justified economically if an instructor must travel great distances to serve a few participants at each classroom site. What alternative, then, is most economically feasible, makes best use of teaching resources, and effectively meets the educational needs of distant adult learners?'

In response to this question, many educators are turning to the telephone:

'The telephone merits a second look. At first glance it appears to be a limited medium with little potential in education. The telephone has, thus, often been ignored in favour of its more glamorous sisters - television, radio, and computerized instruction. But a second look reveals its particular advantages: the telephone is interactive, flexible, low-cost, widely available, and supported by a well-developed infrastructure. It can also offer a visual communications channel: using telewriters, graphic input devices, or slow-scan televideo systems, a telephone network lends itself to a variety of instructional formats. In short, the telephone is uniquely suited to many educational roles, one of the foremost being the delivery of programmes to adult learners'.

Our preliminary research also shows that new learning needs are being expressed, not only about what is wanted, but also where it is wanted. We share the same awareness as that expressed below:

'Higher education has traditionally focused on full-time, on-campus youth who enrolled in formal degree programmes. However, the new post-secondary student, the adult, has a different view of education and wants learning opportunities to be available in his or her home community. These part-time learners are people of all ages and lifestyles, and they have diverse learning needs. Rather than defining education as a terminal degree programme to prepare one for future goals, the adult learner sees education as a self-directed activity that continues throughout life. Education, conceptualised as lifelong learning, is a vehicle for continual vocational development and leisure pursuits.

Aside from such personal goals, continuing education is increasingly viewed as a necessity in many fields, eg, medicine and engineering. Practitioners are not only strongly encouraged but often required to enrol in continuing education programmes as a practical means of maintaining professional skills amidst rapid changes in technical information. This tendency for professional associations and licensing boards to encourage continuing education will most likely accelerate, forcing educators to revise their curricula and teaching methods.'

It cannot be too strongly emphasized that:

'There is almost universal agreement that two-way communication is a desirable and necessary element of distance education (Holmberg,1981). A telephone network is interactive, allowing students and instructor to exchange information, ask questions and receive immediate feedback. The process of interaction between faculty and students and among the students themselves is perhaps the most important of the educational processes. While television and radio may be appropriate for some ...'

Furthermore:

'The telephone also offers instructional flexibility. Course materials can be modified easily at a reasonable cost. The latest telewriting equipment or slow-scan televideo

274

system can display a variety of graphic or pictorial information to supplement audio
instruction.'

This is where CYCLOPS comes in.

CYCLOPS is an audio/graphic system that requires two telephone lines to each centre and
a telephone bridge which allows all the centres to be connected together. Thus each study
centre has five pieces of equipment – a CYCLOPS box, which controls the system, a
television set to display the pictures; a light pen to create and modify drawings; a modem,
which transmits the picture information down the telephone line, and a loudspeaking
telephone, which links the students and tutor together by voice allowing them to speak over
the system. A student in any centre can then talk or write to all the participants in the
tutorial.

The CYCLOPS system has been researched by the Open University for over two years, in
the East Midlands. The reports and evaluations are encouraging to the point that we feel if
offers a better prospect for meeting learning needs in isolated rural communities than a
vehicle.

We do not envisage this new system will stand in isolation, but we anticipate it will allow
the essential immediate feedback of the face-to-face situation at a relatively low cost when
learners do not have direct access to the resources of the college. A typical course may well
follow the scenario below:

(1) Contact individual learner, expressed need, in particular, localities.
(2) Day or weekend school to introduce learners on the same courses to each other and
    familiarize them with the full delivery system – CYCLOPS.
(3) A period of time when the CYCLOPS system is the main vehicle for interaction.
(4) Intermediate and/or concluding day or weekend courses.

Thus courses would integrate traditional face-to-face teaching/learning situations with the
CYCLOPS system.

Although we have selected CYCLOPS primarily for the degree of interaction it allows
between learners and tutors and learners and learner, it must not be forgotten that CYCLOPS
fulfils other functions that are invaluable to the independed learners:

(a) It can be developed as an information source. Thus it is possible to develop an
    information bank related to the experise and resources of the college. This bank would
    include a local/regional skills register and allow peer matching as well as contain the
    more traditional forms of information. It is possible to link up with national information
    networks, for example, Prestel. Furthermore, connections with other local sources of
    information could be established, for example, the Devon Library Service is actively
    developing the idea of an information network.
(b) It can act as a conventional self-contained teaching machine. Thus programmes can be
    designed for students to complete alone, the only interaction being with the machine.
(c) It can be made accessible to other networks operating in rural areas. For example, at
    an obvious level CAB, may wish to design an information programme for individual
    inquirers to operate. This may help CAB to operate more effectively and meet the
    needs they have identified. It is interesting to note that ALBSU is already working
    with tape cassette programmes as a support system for the 1:1 teaching/learning
    situation.

More ambitiously we are attracted by the idea of a village office. This idea is being
developed by Dartington. A CYCLOPS unit could form an integral part of such an office and
thus extend the concept to include information and learning resources.

The choice of a system created a number of problems and delays. Firstly, we had to re-
submit our research brief as the FEU felt the change in system was a basic change in the
brief. Our re-submission was accepted. We then had to assemble our Darome loudspeaker
telephones, which have only this year (1984) received final authorization from British
Telecom, Darome at the same time were establishing a British office. CYCLOPS equipment
was ordered and received, except for a bit pad. This vital piece of equipment appeared
universally unobtainable. But at last we were able to secure one on loan from the Open
University. The two telephone lines were installed at our three locations and British Telecom
proved both reliable and efficient. Then we had a piece of luck that turned a promising
programme into a possibly revolutionary one. Plymouth Polytechnic had just received a

research contract to develop a telephone bridge in the South West. PACNET, as the system is now called is concerned to develop all aspects of teleconferencing and wish to maximize the use of the 'bridge'. We had our system; we have worked closely with PACNET. Our equipment and system have been tested although we felt some times that the remark attributed to President Pompidou was valid:

'There are three ways to ruination. Gambling is the quickest. Women the most pleasurable. But technology the most certain.'

At last our system was established as shown in Figure 1.

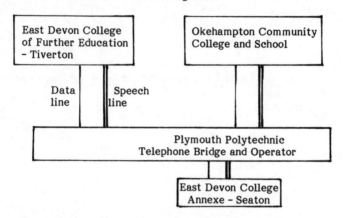

Figure 1. Communication Links

Our first classes based on original responses to our analysis of expressed learning needs and following one-day courses at Okehampton were in 'Shore-based Navigation' and 'Writing and Directing a Village Play'.

The initial response shows the system works for us as well as the Open University. The most memorable remark after the first 'class' from one of the mature students was that it worked better than they felt it would or believed it could.

It was quickly recognized that the CYCLOPS system offered more possibilities than those explored in the original research brief. In addition to extending the kind of work done so far, future development will include:

(1) Siting CYCLOPS with employers. A major development for vocational education is, and will continue to be, the provision of learning opportunities at a distance from colleges. East Devon College is active in Open Tech and Pickup ventures. The siting of CYCLOPS on employers' premises will be beneficial educationally, economically and in terms of accessibility. The interactive nature of the system will greatly reinforce the impact of open learning packages.

(2) Exploring the potential of CYCLOPS as a teaching system in comprehensive schools and community colleges so that:

   (i)   BTEC inputs can be provided for selected students. This will remove the need for students to travel in the case of Okehampton some 60 miles in one day for an equivalent input.

   (ii) Minority subjects can be maintained in the school curriculum, eg, Latin and Greek.

   (iii) The range of subjects offered by the school can include those which small numbers of students have expressed a desire for, eg, Sociology and Psychology A levels.

   (iv) CYCLOPS can be developed as an information point accessing Prestel and other national and local databanks. Already the college tourism course is planning to use Prestel from September and Okehampton sixth forms are already working on local databanks.

(3) The siting of CYCLOPS in a village primary school so that the facilities it offers can be made available for:
   (i)   Specialist inputs into the village primary school. Could this be one way of preventing primary school closures?
   (ii)   A full range of adult education subjects.
   (iii) Information from both national and local databases.
   (iv)   Making the expertise within the village available to other locations on the network.

Theoretically, the whole expertise within the colleges and villages in Devon could be made available to anyone on the network. There is much more research to be done. Effective costings have to be carried out. But CYCLOPS does offer a new teaching/learning system that is highly interactive.

REFERENCE

Holmberg, B (1981) Status and Trends of Distance Education. Kogan Page, London.

8.2 Workshop: Teleconferencing as a Technique in a Graduate Level Distance Mode Educational Technology Course

A C Millar
Victoria College, Australia

Teleconferencing is currently being used by the Department of Educational Technology at the Toorak Campus of Victoria College, Australia, in the distance (or external) mode of the graduate diploma of educational technology course for teachers. The technique (referred to as 'tele-tutorials') has been used in the following ways:

1. Follow-up tutorial to stimulus material such as audio and videotapes, study notes and slide sets.
2. Problem-solving and progress reports on production projects.
3. Playing a simulation game.

A number of educational advantages have resulted from the use of tele-tutorials, including:

(a) Increasing the number of socializing opportunities during the course, thus lessening the isolation factor which is widely recognized as a problem with most distance learning.
(b) Provision of a study framework and regular contact schedule, thus again helping to reduce a traditional problem experienced by distance students.
(c) The creation of frequent opportunities for students to clarify issues and to question the lecturer on content and assessment details.
(d) Provision of experience in exploring non-traditional communication techniques, an advantage that is of particular relevance to a graduate level educational technology course.

Disadvantages experienced include the additional administrative load, lack of visual cues in the communication process and slightly higher costs. However, these disadvantages have not proved to be of great significance.

The workshop was designed mainly for people who have had little, if any, experience in this technique and included:

* Outline information on procedures for conducting tele-tutorials.
* Summary information on costs and equipment.
* The opportunity to experience a simulated tele-tutorial by playing a simulation game in a language laboratory.

ACKNOWLEGEMENT

The help of Professor Tilford and the staff of the University of Bradford language laboratory is gratefully acknowledged.

8.3 Workshop: Teleconferencing for Education and Training

C Humphries, J Watts and R Winders
Council for Educational Technology, London

Teleconferencing was used in Plymouth UK as part of a distance learning project in 1981-82. The potential of teleconferencing as an educational delivery system was then apparent. In order to pursue this initiative, a major new proposal was developed by the Learning Resources Centre at Plymouth Polytechnic, the Council for Educational Technology and British Telecom. An 18-line bridge became available from 1984-86 with funding from the UK government's Manpower Services Commission. The objective is to identify, promote, and evaluate a wide range of applications of teleconferencing in the education and training of the post 16 years old age group. This will include students on distance learning courses, students on work placements, input from experts at a distance, and the full range of conference, committee and professional services. The project will be continuously evaluated by a separately appointed team.

During the presentation, a live demonstration of teleconferencing linking Bradford, London, and Plymouth was given. The presentation team ably dealt with a number of questions, and a lively discussion followed.

8.4 Workshop: Networking your Information Processing System: Simulation of Electronic Mail and Photocomposition

T Hearnshaw
University of Bradford

Office automation has gathered momentum in the UK over the last five years. Competition between manufacturers and suppliers has become intense: technological development has been rapid. Universities have been slow to accommodate to this movement and, whilst large companies have responded positively in order to reduce office costs, the same motivation was not part of general university thinking. As a result, there has been a proliferation of individual ad hoc solutions, each attempting to make the office system more efficient.

At the University of Bradford, we have dealt with the problem systematically. Agreement has been reached on a standard word-processing system for both academic and administrative areas –allowing a co-ordinated approach to training, flexibility of operation, and genuine compatibility between systems. At present, we have 24 screens in full use. To supplement the system an optical character reader (OCR) provides a centralized service. This allows typewritten text, created both inside and outside the university, to be copied to disk and edited on the word-processor workstations. The word-processor and the OCR will eventually be networked to a graphics/typesetting terminal, allowing text to be designed around suitable graphics, typestyles selected from a large menu and printed out on a high quality laser printer. The quality of this output will provide camera ready copy for printing. This network will also enable files to be passed between the word-processing system and the main frame computer and, hence, to other microcomputers.

The demonstration of word-processing stations and network showed clearly the stage at which the system had reached so far.

8.5 Workshop: Inexpensive Computer Graphics for Technical Education

G Pettit
Academic Software, Otley, West Yorkshire

The author currently holds a contract from the Microelectronics Education Programme to write educational software for craft/ design/ technology in secondary education. The packages under development include Boat Hull Design, Ergonomic Anthropometrics, Perspective and Styling, and Visualization and 3D.

Since secondary schools cannot always afford high-precision technical peripherals for their microcomputers (usually the BBC / Acorn micro), methods of input of spatial data using low-cost technology have been developed and were shown in action. These included:

* a joystick with twin 'fire' buttons and with twin thumbwheels for rectilinear input
* a matching digitizer for input from technical plans or working drawings (utilizing wire-wound circular potentiometers mounted at the joints of a double arm).

Software techniques have also been developed (such as gridding to any required accuracy) to compensate for the technical shortcomings of inexpensive input devices.

The BBC micro itself is a low-cost computer for technical education. Software was demonstrated which achieves more complex 3D modelling than would normally be possible in the limited (32k) memory of the unexpanded BBC micro (in particular, the use of overlay coding which enables longer programs to be written without penalizing data storage). The latter is achieved by mounting the BASIC coding (including overlays) on a 'sideways ROM' which makes the computer independent of the cost of disk installation while overlays are called faster than from a disk.

The technical problems of obtaining 'hard copy' output are still acute but, nevertheless, output on a standard dot-matrix plotter for perspectives and other 'impressionistic' output was demonstrated and the techniques for doing this were discussed.

Section 9:
Educational and Training Technology

9.1 The Organization and Administration of an Educational and Training Network

B S Alloway
University of Bradford

Abstract: The complexity of the range of specialism and organizations within the field of educational and training technology presents a considerable problem of understanding, both of function and form. Following some 12 years as a network of programmed learning centres, the members of that organization decided to reform the network function as a group of practitioners in educational and training technology at their annual general meeting in 1982. Having now accomplished two years of work as a network of practitioners, it is perhaps time to take stock and to present our findings to the educational and training technology movement. In this period of time, membership has trebled. Experience has been gained in the networking of information among (i) members, (ii) other ETT organizations, and (iii) education and training organizations in a wide variety of specialist sectors.

  The organization and administration of activities for the membership of the Network of Practitioners in Educational and Training Technology (NPETT) has grown with the increase in the number of members and the holding of quarterly meeting throughout the region. These have been supplemented with special meetings held annually in Scotland and Wales, and with a programme of 'New Directions One-Day Conferences'. Such activities, together with the publication of the Bulletin of Practice four times per year, indicate that NPETT may be able to help a number of people in the ETT movement and some possibilities are discussed.

HOW WE BEGAN - A BRIEF HISTORY

During the late 1960s, the then Association for Programmed Learning (APL) debated the need to form an active wing of programmed learning centres throughout the British Isles. The APL during this period changed its name to the Association for Programmed Learning and Educational Technology (APLET). In conjunction with the Department of Education and Science and a number of other interested bodies, a meeting were held in 1969 and over 20 potential 'PL centres' were identified. These were canvassed and it was agreed that a network would be useful. By 1970, the informal meetings had taken on a formality and the Network of Programmed Learning Centres (NPLC) was created.

  From the beginning, the value of the Network was its sharing of experience, expertise and creative output - valued factors which continue through into today's organization. Regular business meetings of NPLC and a number of one-day conferences were held. Several papers were published. However, in parallel with the changes in the nature and function of APLET, the Network needed to reflect the ways in which members were operating professionally in the late 1970s. APLET agreed to update its image and became the present Association for Educational and Training Technology (AETT). Concurrently, the Network was holding several meetings with titles reflecting many of the new functions carried out by members, for instance curriculum development, training design, audiovisual technology, open learning, research and development. The current NPETT chairman proposed the present title and this has proved its appropriateness when measured by the success of the past two years since we re-formed as the NPETT at our 1982 annual general meeting held at the Royal Naval School of Educational and Training Technology, Portsmouth.

CREATING A NEW ORGANIZATION

Changing the established pattern of organization and administration, created over a decade, required an approach with some sensitivity due to two main considerations:

(a) Many of the existing members of NPLC were at a critical stage in their careers due to a shift in emphasis away from programmed learning. This came from a widening concept of educational technology. Members were becoming responsible for training design, closed-circuit television, curriculum development, open-learning organization, microcomputing etc. At the same time, severe economic cutbacks reduced funding and made the provision of ETT services rather difficult. Hence, any changes made to the Network needed to reflect the new position and provide professional support for members threatened with such diverse changes.

(b) The need to reflect the way in which (in a number of cases) activity had moved away from 'centres' to 'individuals', the latter now carrying a professional responsibility to introduce, develop, and apply a wide range of educational technology within their own educational or training organization.

The initial approach to membership therefore took the following considerations into account within the new constitution which incorporated the following:

'NPETT is a group of organizations and individuals essentially involved in the "practice" of educational and training technology. Such involvement can take many different forms within a range of educational and training backgrounds. The Network seeks to work closely with other organizations who have either:
(a) a similar broad interest in educational and training technology; or
(b) who are prepared to co-operate in educational and training specific joint ventures; these have included meetings, conferences and publications arranged at mutually convenient times during the year.
A number of different categories of membership are available within the British Isles and an overseas provision is made through the corresponding sector.'

CATEGORIES OF MEMBERSHIP

There are three categories of membership available within the NPETT at present, although the standing committee is prepared to consider additional types of membership as new specialisms and demands arise. These are:

Full member: Normally available to units and centres engaged in educational and training work who, on joining the Network, are asked to nominate delegates to represent them. For some of the functions, more than one delegate may attend provided that they are named at the time of delegate registration.
Emeritus member: Will normally have previously represented one or more organization as the nominated delegate, have retired or resigned from a member organization, and have been accepted by a majority present at a meeting of the standing committee or a full meeting of the Network. Individuals who have made an outstanding contribution to educational and training technology over a substantial period of time may also be given emeritus membership following the submission of a description of their previous work and responsibilities.
Corresponding member: This category is designed for members who are concerned to keep up to date with developments in the Network but who are not able to attend many of the quarterly meetings.

Subscriptions for each category of membership are agreed at the annual general meeting each year, normally at a London venue.

EMERGENCE OF THE NEW ORGANIZATION

In the past two years, a pattern of new organization has gradually taken place which, hopefully, reflects the needs and requirements of the above membership. With our background in programmed learning, this can be identified as both an overt and a covert response, as follows:

<u>Overt activities</u>

Quarterly meetings: Central to the idea of a network of practitioners is the need for sharing ideas and conducting business related to educational and training technology. In consequence, quarterly meetings are held throughout the country with both business and professional sub-meetings. For example, the following is a typical business agenda which normally takes half of the day:

Business meeting agenda for the afternoon of 18/11/83
1. Apologies for absence.
2. Minutes of the quarterly meeting, Teeside Polytechnic 15/7/83.
3. Matters arising/ETIC'84 Bradford advance information.
4. Bulletin of practice 3/4/83, issue and discussion.
5. Industrial training - revision of ITB listings and addresses.
6. NPETT microcomputer users survey - progress report.
7. A O B / date and venue of annual general meeting (December).

The professional meeting (in the other half of the day) is designed to give (a) the host organization an opportunity to describe and publicize their current work, and (b) other members a chance to report and demonstrate the latest stages of their own current projects. Linked to the quarterly meetings are the two annual meetings in Scotland and Wales. There, members with particular projects related to their regions identify their special needs. These meetings have proved valuable for other regions of the country as comparisons often allow a new slant on members work. They also lead to co-operative ventures across traditional organizational boundaries.

Standing committee meetings: A small standing committee (of eight elected members) meets each quarter to draft suggestions for future business (for instance, constitutional clauses) and to plan details of special meetings etc. In the process of conducting business meetings, the standing committee is frequently charged with the establishment of working parties, creating links with other bodies, and carrying out investigations. The results are reported at the next quarterly meeting.

Day conferences: The network has established a pattern of one-day conferences which pursue themes of interest to members, to AETT members, and to others with an interest in a specific activity. Our themes in the past two years have been:

* New directions in education and training;
* New directions in the design and production of ETT packages;
* New directions in evaluation and assessment.

Press reports have appeared after each event such as this from Ranmore Hall, Sheffield in February 1983:

'Despite hazardous snow conditions, 30 educational and training technologists attended the second one-day conference on "New Directions", organized by the Network of Practitioners in Educational and Training Technology on Friday 11th February 1983. Delegates this year came from as far afield as Preston, Portsmouth, Mid-Wales, Catterick and Southend-on-Sea to Ranmore Hall, Sheffield, home of the Corporate Services Division of the Manpower Services Commission.
The chairman of NPETT, Norman Allen and the Head of Staff Training, MSC, John Corbett, welcomed delegates to the conference and venue.
Speakers included Denis Timms, Manager of the Midlands Computer-Assisted Learning Project (MIDCAL), Ian Townsend, advisor, National Health Services Learning Resources Unit (NHSLRU), Norman Sykes, advisor, Sheffield City Education Authority at Holly Centre, Major Malcolm Woodhouse, Royal Army Education Corps (RAEC), Ann Howe, Computers in Training as a Resource Project (CITAR), and Professor Edgar Stones who gave a concluding session.
Emphasis was placed upon practice and resources in specific education and training settings. Much current work was demonstrated and vigorously discussed during a full day programme.'

Covert Advantages

In identifying the covert advantages of the professional network, the following seem to be of importance to members (as expressed in correspondance). Consequently the network needs to reflect these factors:

1. Co-operation and consultancy between normally isolated specialists.
2. Publicizing NPETT activity in members' organizations to encourage their recognition as professionals.
3. Approaching all links with other organizations by jointly contacting our member there and by writing to the principal, thus aiding members' kudos.

Additionally, much verbal encouragement has been given to our members when the image of ETT in practice has been seen in reports and press releases after our various activities.

BULLETIN OF PRACTICE

The coming together of individuals from education and training technology practice, the holding of national and regional meetings (as described above), and the exchange of correspondence indicated the need for an NPETT publication early after the re-formation. In consequence, the secretary has gradually established a quarterly publication entitled the 'Bulletin of Practice'. It is composed of all the business and professional reports, a review of ETT commercial developments and a vehicle for members to publicise their own work and ideas. A typical issues' contents are as follows:

Reference code BOP 1/4/83
1. General news.
2. New members.
3. Minutes of quarterly meeting, So. Thames Col., 10/12/82.
4. Professional meeting, So. Thames Col., 10/12/82.
5. Publications and related developments.
6. Equipment and Materials Reviews.
7. Ranmore Hall Conference, 11/2/83.
8. Overseas practice news.
9. UK practice news.
10. Action now! (members enclosures A,B and C).

THE FUTURE OF NPETT

The past two years have seen a most encouraging level of increasing activity, with a rise in membership to over 70 in all categories. We have established and maintained links with other organizations, and many new possibilities for wider activity appear on the horizon. It is even possible that we will be able to help, with out ETT, in the socio-economic recovery of the UK!

9.2 Some Considerations in Selecting Courses for Self-Pacing

D J Freeman
Canadian Armed Forces (Navy), Ontario

Abstract: The recent trend to self-pace all the courses in a school appears to be undergoing second thoughts and in many cases there is a move back to the lock-step method. This raises the obvious question – are some courses better suited for self-pacing than others?

   This paper shows the procedure developed by the Canadian Armed Forces for allocating any training course into one of six categories. The higher the category, the greater the ease of self-pacing. Further, the paper covers some of the considerations necessary in completing a cost-benefit analysis of those courses which fall into the higher categories.

HISTORY

With the introduction of every new device – media or method – teachers, trainees and educators tend to see in the device a cure-all for various problems. Thus it was for TV, the overhead projector, programmed learning, films, and – for all I know – the chalkboard. And history is repeating itself with the computer, interactive video, and all other systems used by self-paced or individualized courses. Implementing a self-paced course, only to discover later that the course is not viable in that format, is costly and time-consuming.

   Having very little in the way of money or spare manpower, the training development officers in the Canadian Forces (CF) asked themselves if there was some method whereby a course with certain characteristics would be a 'natural' for self-pacing. A serach of the literature yielded negative results so we found ourselves in the situation well known to all developers – starting from scratch.

   Before proceeding further, it is necessary to define my terms.

DEFINITIONS

Lock-step

Most CF courses are conducted in what is termed a 'lock-step' manner. For example, students are grouped together to form a course which starts and stops on predetermined dates, regardless of the ability of the trainees. The rate of instruction is set by the instructor and the rate of learning is often ignored. The ratio of instructor to trainees from about one to eight to as high as one to 100, and teaching methods are generally limited to the lecture method with some demonstrations. There is a limited amount of feedback, and testing is done at infrequent intervals, often at the end of a course.

Self-pacing

In self-pacing, the course starts whenever the first trainee arrives (assuming the school is able to accommodate him or her) and continues until all the trainees have finished. The rate of learning is set by the trainee and the ratio of instructors to trainees rarely exceeds one to eight except where the use of computers is concerned. Teaching methods and media include the use of programmed texts, adjunct programmes, video and/or audiotapes, films, audiotapes plus 35mm slides, computers etc. Feedback is constant and testing is carried out several times every day. Trainees are assigned to instructors for specific sections, or the entire course, dependent on course length or complexity. The instructor's role becomes one of tutor. Because there is a constant flow of trainees, all in different stages of training, the average in-house population is generally lower than for lock-step courses, and administration controls are necessarily different.

<u>Groups and Teams</u>

(a) In self-pacing, students can be grouped where required and, just as quickly, the groups can be broken up when not required. In such cases, groups are collections of trainees with similar backgrounds who must form together to complete a specific action which could not be performed by one trainee. All trainees are equal and do identical tasks. For example, in the training of stretcher bearers, a group of two is required -one for each end of the stretcher. The two trainees are interchangeable and it does not matter which two trainees on the course are grouped together as long as each have completed the prerequisite training.

(b) Teams are generally collections of trainees with different skills and backgrounds who must work together - performing different tasks - in order for the team to function. Examples are a tank crew, bomber crew, or a submarine attack team on a ship. Such team training is not suitable for self-pacing.

<u>Individualized Instruction</u>

A specific requirement of self-pacing is known as 'individualized instruction'. In this case, specific instruction is assigned to trainees dependent on their background and experience. Generally, a map is prepared listing the subjects to be studied and the order in which to study them. As in self-pacing, the trainees learn at their own rate. Thus, it is possible that at any given time in a school, no two students would be following the same course of studies. The end result, however, is the same as for other methods of self-pacing - all trainees attain the same end results at their own speed. In this paper, for definition purposes, all individualized instruction is self-paced but the reverse is not necessarily true.

INSTRUCTORS

In self-pacing, the role of the instructor changes dramatically. At the discretion of the school, he or she is responsible for a set number of students over a particular section of the course. Because of various backgrounds, experiences and abilities, different instructors may be responsible for different parts of the course and for a different number of trainees. Instructors monitor the trainees frequently - as often as once per hour. Where a trainee is not succeeding, the instructor will tutor him on a one-to-one basis to overcome the difficulty.

It must be emphasized that self-pacing a course does not mean that fewer instructors are required. In smaller courses, especially, it may be necessary to increase the number of instructors or else institute some of the techniques in individualized instruction described above.

COURSE SELECTION

While self-pacing is applicable to a great many training situations, it is not necessarily the best method in every case, nor is it universally applicable. In certain training situations, it can be far better to retain the lock-step approach. A method has been devised for selecting those courses best suited for self-pacing. As indicated earlier, this method applies to the self-pacing of entire courses and not selected segments of a course.

CATEGORIES

Before discussing the factors relating to the selection of a course for self-pacing, let us consider the categories into which a course can be placed. These categories afford an assessment of a course's potential for self-pacing. There are six categories in descending order of priority as follows:

1. Should be self-paced now (meets all requirements).
2. Should be self-paced now (meets most requirements).

3. Should be self-paced when possible.
4. Could be self-paced sometime.
5. Major changes are predicted – reconsider course at a later date.
6. Should never be self-paced.

FACTORS

The category into which a course falls is determined by one or more factors.

Aims

Certain courses have unwritten aims. One such type of course is basic or recruit training in which one of the highly stressed but often unstated objectives is to foster a feeling for, and an acceptance of, members working as part of a team. While there is also a great emphasis on the acquisition of knowledge, the exposure to effects of 'team spirit' far outweigh any advantages that would be gained by self-pacing the course. The observation of the recruit while in the team plus the experience gained by the recruit while working, suffering and winning with his or her team, is so important that nothing should interfere. Consequently all recruit courses are assigned to category 6.

Role Model

In some training environments, it is necessary for a trainee to see, hear, and be exposed to, the effects of a 'role model'. Leadership training is such an example: instructional technique is another. It is one thing to acquire all the knowledge and theory of leadership but quite another thing to watch a successful leader in action. Such a varied, on-going demonstration cannot be self-paced. Therefore, where the requirement can be identified, courses requiring 'life or role models' should be relegated to category 6.

Teams and Groups

As discussed earlier, groups can be trained in a self-paced mode but teams generally cannot. There are, however, many definitions of team. In this paper, for clarification, team training has been divided into two types:

(a) Collective training. The purpose of collective training is to produce a functioning team from trainees who have similar but distinct skills, background or experience. The team members are not, basically, interchangeable one with another (for example, aircraft flight crew). Self-pacing is not possible for collective training.
(b) Group training. The purpose of group training is to give students experience either in working together as a team or in working in the different positions in a team, not necessarily for the purpose of learning a skill but to expose the trainee to the functions of the different positions. All trainees in this type of training have similar identical skills and/or experiences (for example, firefighting teams, drill platoons). Self-pacing is possible for this type of training.

Note: In many training situations, various sized collections of trainees are often formed for the convenience of control or administration, or for instructional purposes. Such groups are often referred to as classes, serials, syndicates etc. For the purpose of this paper, none of these groups should be considered teams in the sense described above.

Changes

From time to time, courses and schools undergo revision or change. Because self-pacing tends to be more expensive to set up, any courses being considered for self-pacing for which changes are predicted, should be placed in category 5 until the changes have been implemented.

Staff, Facilities and Equipment

Any self-paced course has a requirement for dedicated staff, facilities and equipment. In most schools, any give classroom or laboratory is used for a variety of purposes and courses.

Likewise, instructors may teach more than one course. In lock-step courses, this is not only necessary but often desirable as there are often gaps between courses. In self-pacing, generally, the course is continually in-house. Hence instructors and equipment are always in demand, and the classroom and other facilities are in constant use. These items cannot be shared.

It should be noted here that, although certain facilities and equipment are in constant use, the actual quantities required are often less than in a lock-step course. For example, in your lock-step course there may be 20 students per course which is conducted ten times per year, requiring 20 pieces of equipment on which the trainees learn and practice and a room 20ft by 40ft in which to hold this equipment. In self-pacing, you may only have an average of eight students in-house and thus the requirements for equipment should drop from 20 to 12, allowing for occasional overload as well as any future expansion. In addition, you could probably use a smaller room.

ALGORITHM

An algorithm in the form of a flow chart has been developed for classifying a course in accordance with the factors outlined above.

For the quantity of students per year and for the length of the course in training days, the numbers are arbitrary and can altered to suit the situation. Generally, the fewer the students, the less cost-effective is the self-pacing. Similarly, the longer the course, the more difficult and costly it becomes to self-pace.

Once a course is classified, however, it is necessary to complete some form of cost-benefit analysis to determine whether or not it is cost-effective to self-pace the course.

CONCLUSION

Self-paced instruction is not a cure for all training ills and the decision to self-pace a course must not be taken lightly. As can be seen from the preceeding discussion and regardless of the media or method employed, self-pacing does provide certain advantages and selected savings but only when appropriately used. If we can consider lock-step instruction to be a piston engine, then self-pacing is a jet engine. Both have their place in society but the jet engine requires finer tolerances and works effectively only in selected areas. In other areas, the piston engine is superior.

9.3 The Problems of Training Intended Teachers in Educational Technology: An Analysis of a First Attempt

P Glover

Rhodes University, Grahamstown, South Africa

Abstract: The paper covers four reasons for providing such a course, Cape Education policy, the acceptance of 'media centres', the necessity for teachers to be able to operate educational technology equipment effectively, and the importance of demystifying the 'machine'. The four main problems were found to be the provision of adequate 'hands-on' experience for large groups, limited staff resources, ensuring that all teachers had access to whatever equipment was available in the schools themselves, and the education of school administrators as well as teachers about the new media possibilities. Implicit in these problems is a classic 'vicious circle'.

INTRODUCTION

This discussion is related to simple 'tools technology' - mainly for assisting teachers in classroom and lecture situations. However, it is also relevant to pupils being instructed through the medium of the more sophisticated technological devices which have been demonstrated at this conference.

The problems of training intending teachers in educational technology fall into several categories which are related to:

* the established academic order or ethos
* the demands made on the lecturing staff
* the perceptual baggage which students bring into the course.

Before one mounts any course, one should properly engage in a needs analysis of one's clientele. Obviously one must also examine very carefully one's reasons for considering the course. The reasons for our course are:

1. It is the policy of most of the various departments of education in South Africa to supply schools with reprographic equipment, audiovisual aids, and the means to manufacture material for such audiovisual aids.
2. The concept of 'media (or resource) centres' has been accepted as official policy and schools are being encouraged to develop these.
3. It is our belief that an ability to operate such equipment can enhance the quality of instruction given. Furthermore, it is our belief and experience that, as the pupils become more sophisticated, their demands on teachers become more exacting. Therefore correct and efficient use of various teaching aids (as opposed to over-use) is part of the teacher's armoury and part of the intending teacher's survival kit.
(It is the general belief in the education department at Rhodes University that the one year course of postgraduate teacher training is a survival kit or a launching pad for what one hopes is a successful entry into teaching. The <u>savoir faire</u> which is built up subsequently depends on:

* this grounding in essential practical and theoretical background
* enough practical know-how to help the new teacher overcome the trauma of initial entry

* the new teacher remaining in the profession long enough to put down roots and begin professional growth.

Too many young teachers leave because they are ill-equipped for the job and also because they are given an unrealistic set of expectations about teaching.
4. Finally, we see an important motive for our tools technology course in the 'demystification of the machine'. With almost all the primary trainees and up to 70 per cent of secondary trainees being female, we find it necessary to introduce the gadgets in a systematic and non-threatening way. The fact that fear of machinery applies largely to the women students is not to suggest that it applies solely to females nor that it applies to all females. But we consider that the causes of psychological and sociological stereotyping require some purposeful counter-measures. Another possible reason for the fear that some people have for gadgetry is that, as the pupil becomes a student and then a graduate education student, there is often no allowance made for the student's relation to the machine or gadget. While at school (and even at university), the student is on the receiving end of the technology. At the teacher training level, the student must modify this relation from that of receiver to one of controller. I feel that this switch must be managed gently, especially for some.

These are the reasons for mounting the course, although I have said little so far about needs analysis. However, the need was felt to exist and this perception is shared by a comforting majority of the students. As more equipment of this type is provided at schools, the more the question is asked by the teaching profession, 'Why don't your students know how to operate so-and-so?' Therefore, the old ad hoc basis on which machine operation was taught is clearly woefully inadequate.

FOUR MAIN PROBLEMS

Problem One

How to enable large numbers of students to get 'hands-on' experience of various reprographic apparatus, audiovisual aids and machinery for manufacturing audiovisual aids subject to:

* only seven to 10 weeks available before their first teaching practice session
* the requirement of an adequate level of proficiency in all students
* the finding that a group larger than four to five students, learning the basic operation of a piece of apparatus, cannot be taught in less than about one hour which is the time allotted per standard session.

This leads on to:

Problem Two

Large classes and small groups mean a heavy teaching input by staff and a great duplication (multiplication) of lessons implying that:

* those staff who are willing and able to help must work many extra hours during this period of intensive training, but
* because of global departmental requirements, there cannot be experts allocated to single activities like this which have an intensive but short input.

The two problems outlined above suggest the following:

Question 1: Given the limitations imposed on the course, is the present solution to our perceived needs the most effective one? (Implicit in this, of course, are the assumptions that our needs analysis and, more importantly, the fundamental rationale for the course are accurate and valid.) This question leads to another:

Question 2: Are first-time teachers who enter the profession without these skills less likely to develop them than those who have been taught the skills at teacher training level? In partial answer to this latter question, we encounter a third problem.

Problem Three

Getting 'hands-on' experience at schools can be more difficult because the equipment is sometimes part of somebody's 'empire', or where the equipment is available for use, a new teacher might have difficulty in finding a tutor because the attitude of schools often is that these skills should have been learned by the teacher in training. (The availability of 'resources persons' at schools is still not sufficiently widespread for this problem to be taken seriously at the moment.) These points lead to:

Question 3: Is it possible to appreciate fully the power and the limitations of any medium unless these are actually handled and then used in the proper context, ie in the classroom? (It is only with use, and some unhurried critical evaluation of the medium in use, that one can get a 'feel' for when a particular medium is appropriate, and which medium is the most appropriate.) This leads now to:

Problem Four

Schools, practising teachers, and lecturers need to be educated so that the new media will be explored and used with confidence and ingenuity. In more detail:

1. The new media need to be demystified and hence 'democratized' so that they do not become cornerstones of individual empires and certain teachers' power and esteem (in the same way that an esoteric school subject – and the unique knowledge incorporated in that subject – can become one teacher's property).
2. It is easy to take the popularity of the new technology for granted. But many in positions of importance are suspicious of technology which is beyond their own expertise (possibly due to psychological feelings of inadequacy). It may be a conspiracy theory, but it is nevertheless possible that such people could block the spread of new technologies in education (by their denigration of the technology or their example of non-use) in order to protect their own world-views.
3. New technologies may be tainted by the bad press (following the excessive claims of some acolytes), prejudices and uninformed opinions which grew up around the advent and development of programmed learning and teaching machines.

Implicit in the problems and questions raised above is a 'vicious circle' or even, perhaps, 'downward spiral'. Pupils, ignorant of the type of control needed by a teacher over educational technology, become student teachers fearful of coming to terms with the technology and, in turn, become teachers unwilling to use the technology even where it could be a powerful aid. (Obviously, one excludes here the few teachers who negotiate innovations independently and with relative ease.) This all leads to:

Question 4: How and where do we enter the spiral in order to develop a balanced and confident perspective on educational technology? This question, although developed from a consideration of problems surrounding a tools-technology course, has relevance for all educational technology which involves machinery of any sort.

DISCUSSION

The following points and suggestions were made in response to the questions posed above:

1. The battle to gain active acceptance of educational hardware is a political battle within departments and/or the establishment.
2. One should involve students in their own learning, ie let them produce packages illustrating the use of hardware and allow peer assessment of these packages.
3. Identify teachers in the schools who will ensure, during teaching practice, that student teachers use the hardware.
4. (a) Ensure that university staff use the hardware;
   (b) Encourage the students to become 'hyper-aware' of poor and ineffective use (and non-use) of educational media so that they put pressure on teaching staff to improve their presentations;
   (c) Get students to employ their new-found expertise to help staff build up their own resource banks.

5. The timing of educational technology courses is crucial: students must be able to use knowledge gained as soon as possible after these courses.

6. Teacher-training departments should try to put pressure on schools to free hardware for general use where 'empire-builders' are hogging equipment to enhance their personal esteem.

7. The best (and the worst?) student work should be put on display for the learning benefit of succeeding intakes. Possibly the same should apply to staff productions?

8. Local teachers should be encouraged to bring and demonstrate their work and general use of media.

9. Microteaching sessions could be used in which careful note is taken of the students' use of media.

9.4 Educational Technology in Transit

N D C Harris and R M Strachan
University of Bath

Abstract: This paper is a lighthearted (even frivolous) look at the development of educational technology from programmed learning to microcomputers. It will develop from a van (possibly transit) to consider the following aspects: learners, teachers, media, analysis and design techniques. These will be viewed from a visitor's point of view (the visitor possibly being from outer space). It is illustrated by cartoons and elaborated by fables, stories and/or truth. (Any resemblance to known or unknown persons in the fiction or cartoons is unintentional.)

In recent years there has been no lack of articles and papers suggesting that educational technology has not lived up to its early promise and confident expectations. No doubt some of these expectations were over-optimistic, and, for example, the establishment of a discrete body of theory and practice has proved difficult, if not impossible. It is clear that educational technology has entered an important period of transition and, while it is possible to say what it is moving away from, it is much more difficult to predict what it should move toward. Like all good learning situations the outcome of this transition is likely to be intended.

One way of describing this transition is to see it as the process in which a very considerable body of highly complex and diverse practice is searching for a new and more satisfying theoretical base. The positivist 'certainties' of behavioural psychology have proved inadequate in explanations of the intricate and involved personal and social motivations of human intentionality, purpose and meaning. Yet it is precisely these factors which must be grasped in order to be able to understand classroom interactions. This can be done, some critics argue, if educational technologists acquire a greater familiarity with social psychology and interpretive sociology. Others suggest that this kind of understanding is unnecessary since independent learning systems will be the order of the day. Some critics predict that educational technology is heading towards a well-deserved terminal state. The report of such an impending demise is probably an exaggeration. A critical appraisal of the state of the art need not be unduly pessimistic, and certainly does not need to be conducted as a memorial tribute.

One way of illustrating some of the present problems and future trends is to look at the technology of education from the perspective of an imaginary outsider. Consider the fragmented impressions which might be received by the hypothetical inhabitants of our nearest neighbours in space. Naturally they would want to examine how things are done here and, with profound apologies to Arthur C Clarke (1972), 'A Report on Planet Three -the State of its Technology of Education' might contain some of the following comments ...

The following documentary fragments have just been deciphered for the Intergalactic Archaeological Commission from a long-vanished 'Report on Planet Three' carried out by our Martian neighbours. These fragments concern the state of the technology of education on Earth in a distant time period:

The recent close approach of the Third Planet has once again revived speculation about the possibility of intelligent life upon our nearest neighbour in space. Recent improvements in sensoring equipment have enabled scientists to penetrate the amazing variety of electronic emissions which were once thought to be Earth's sole form of

Figure 1   'Report on planet three': Educational Technology in transit...

educational transmission. We now know that the strange and enigmatic episodes of
Earthling behaviour centering on 'Ambridge' and 'Crossroads' are, in fact, imaginery, and
bear no resemblance to normal life on Earth. Indeed it may shock and disturb members
of the Martian Academy of Arts to realize that such episodes were apparently meant to
be entertaining...
...ideas of human behaviour and motivation based, surprisingly, on the limited
performance of laboratory animals are being abandoned as the main theoretical basis for
theories of learning, but there seems to be growing technological determinism.
Certainly there is no lack of methods, systems, techniques and sophisticated computer
hardware and software for use in classrooms, yet some practitioners still seem concerned
with stubborn questions of educational 'Quality' and 'Worth'. It is difficult for us to
understand precisely what is meant by these terms as those who use them freely have
difficulty in defining them ...
We have been able to identify the real centres of Earth learning where ideas and
materials for education are being developed. These places are large clusters of buildings
called Univerities and Polytechnics to which many Earthlings go for long periods during
which they appear sometimes to learn, sometimes to teach, but often to argue and
transmit huge volumes of paper to each other. Exactly what this latter activity
represents is still a mystery...
There seem to be several popular models of learners and learning' ...

*   The Jug Syndrome
*   The Receiver Syndrome
*   The Sniffer Syndrome
*   Independent Learning
*   Active-Passive

... Younger Earthlings seem to go to smaller clusters of buildings called 'Schools'. It is
not clear what happens here. There seems to be some kind of major change going on,
with paper and argument being replaced by some sort of button pushing equipment.
Some of the older Earthlings in these places seem unconcerned about the processes going
on inside the cranial activities of the younger ones ...

Figure 2 The Jug Syndrome

Figure 3 The Receiver syndrome

Figure 4 The Sniffer syndrome

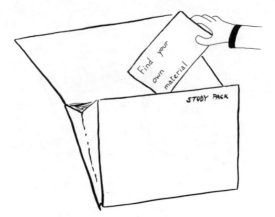

Figure 5   Independent Learning

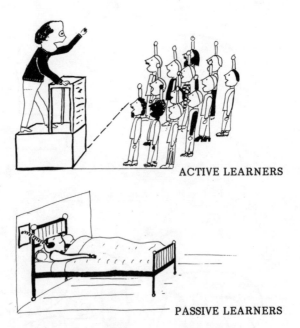

ACTIVE LEARNERS

PASSIVE LEARNERS

Figure 6   Active and passive learning

... A similar kind of equipment, though in larger form, appears to exist in Earth's universities and polytechnics. It is possible that this crude and elementary equipment represents the first steps towards achieving true Artificial Intelligence ...

Figure 7   'School' for younger earthlings

Figure 8   They may not be able to read and write by the time they leave here but they certainly know how to press a button

With acknowledgements and apologies to Martin Honeysett

Figure 9   The new issue system in the university library

One puzzling feature of all these establishments is a peculiar form of soft white rock, often concealed in storage places or ledges. It is used to produce hieroglyphics on vertical dark coloured surfaces. As far as we can determine, the purpose of these hieroglyphics is to enable Earthlings, young and old, to copy the identical hieroglyphics onto a horizontal surface – this time using a dark marking fluid on a light surface! Many of the older Earthlings seem addicted to the use of this strange method and material ...

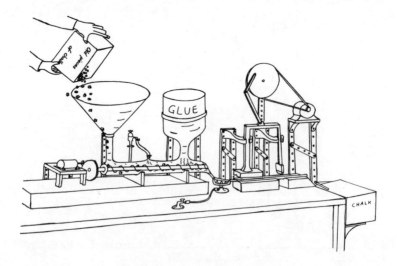

Figure 10 Economy of chalk use

... Many of these centres of Earth learning seem to have two types of people working there. One type is in daily contact with learners and is clearly of low status. The other is incomprehensible to us, but they occupy positions of high status and power in these places. Their title is 'Administrators' ...
... We have been very puzzled by the occasional reference in documents to Educational Technologists. We have found education and technologist, but the two words together seem to suggest some systematic art of education. These beings seem to live in a highly

organized yet bizarre world of their own from which they derive great personal satisfaction ...

... These educational technologists seem to be very fond of 'networks', some sort of idea which we have only found in some of the earthling leisure pursuits ...

Figure 11 Network analysis

... Clearly these 'networks' must be considered as a type of inter-cranial activity akin to high thought processes, and definitely reserved only for superior beings ...

... Lately it seems that these same earthling educational technologists are nearly always closely associated with the button and picture gaming equipment even when not actively working in centres of learning ...

... In their homes they use the same equipment – apparently to send endless electronic messages to each other ...

Figure 12 Hacker at home

... The picture sort of game seems to come in two varieties, one in colour, the other in black and white. Occasionally the picture seems to move into a sort of mosaic pattern (we have found an Earthling writer named McLuhan who talked about this phenomenon)...

Figure 13 Television has ... mosaic format

... Another aspect of learning has been identified which seems to have little connection with the centres mentioned earlier. Some learners it would appear, have abandoned these centres and either receive the hieroglyphics via a messenger system or by using the push button and picture games. This type of learning is called Distance Learning (sometimes Open Learning – a term we have not been able to understand as there do not appear to be any examples of "closed learning") ...

Figure 14 Distant study system

These 'fragments', although designed hopefully to amuse, raise a number of issues.

First, most learning takes place in direct social interaction, in peer groups, families, clubs, schools and so on. Such learning situations form a complex web of meanings to which all participants contribute from their own stock of experience, understanding and skills. There seems to be an opposing tendency which would reduce personal and group contact and individualize learning wherever this was technically feasible.

There is also an over-dependence within educational technology on jargon, on sophisticated software and hardware and on analyses. To many teachers faced with classroom problems this view of the technology in education seems mechanistic and distant from their more real experience.

This gap between theory and practice, between those who implement curricula forms and packages, and those who initiate the forms and who appear to theorize on and criticize practice is a fundamental barrier.

It is interesting to consider why evaluative strategies have moved toward people centred techniques (groups, interviews, open ended) rather than mechanistic objective statistical techniques. Over simplifying there are two obvious strands: those being evaluated have a more participative and a more controlling role; and the evaluative strategies have put some of the power back with the chalk face of face to face tutor.

The second issue follows from the first, the gap between the theoreticians and the practitioners. It is with the advent of microcomputers that the gap has at times become very large. There has been a large amount of time and effort put into developing hardware and software based on quick marketing. Unfortunately, this technology in education has taken little account of the educational value of the materials to learners or to teachers. The practitioners have become stranded again as they were when books, magic lanterns, files, television were introduced. Not only is the technology in education seen as a threat to roles, but more particularly to jobs. When will we learn strategies of diffusion, dissemination, innovation and change? When will we consider the actors in the play and realize that the lighting and the set are only part of the production?

The third issue follows again, with the jargon and hardware associated with complex systems alienating the user. Slide projectors, overhead projectors and taperecorders are now reliable, well-used technology in education. The costs are realistic, the use is controlled in the learning <u>milieu</u>. Television has moved in that direction, but microcomputers and information retrieval systems still either require an intermediary (too much trouble) or provide the learner with the chance of being more knowledgeable than the teacher (threatening). Probably the most exciting impact of information systems is the potential for learning together: learners and teacher - a nearer approach to the social interaction which is so often missing in some individualized learning.

Figure 15 <u>Satisfaction of lecturer</u>

The better examples of individualized learning are built around that social interaction - the aspect of learning to learn. The actors are able to produce unintended outcomes, the process is as important or more important than the overspecified or heavily disguised intended outcomes.

The view of educational technologists held by some is 'a mish mash of empire builders attempting to use a systematic process based on behavioural psychology, with ignorance about real life, but well versed in jargon, overkill, and learning as individuals in horse boxes'.

Educational technology should be based on technology not technique, ie, 'systematic treatment on the art of educating' rather than the 'mechanical or formal part of an art'.

Perhaps a new theoretical base is needed, taking into account the process, the social psychology, and the interpretative sociology - where account is taken of meanings given by individual actors to events and phenomena whether intended or not by the designer.

Innovation of individualized learning systems merely removes problems of social context to less accessible areas. Is such an electronically-assisted system always appropriate? Are such schemes attractive because they remove teacher interference and awkward questions of social/educational worth and value?

There is a need to lose the present identity as Experts, Empire Builders, Disciples of New Education Disciplines. Perhaps there is no separate breed of Ed. Tech. since all teachers are or should be more aware of being educational technologists. .

REFERENCE

Clarke, A C (1972) Report on Planet Three and Other Speculations. Corgi Books, London.

9.5 Current Trends in Research and Development of Educational Technology in Japan

M Inoue, F Shinohara, S Yokoyama, M Nambu, K Mitsuhashi and N Kurai
Tokyo Gakugei University, Japan

Abstract: This paper will discuss the current trends on research and development of educational technology in Japan, limited to five aspects:
1. General information on the education system in Japan.
2. Educational technology with respect to the utilization of educational media.
3. Educational technology with respect to the improvement of teaching-learning systems.
4. Educational technology with respect to the improvement of school environment.
5. Educational technology with respect to new information technologies.
In each respect mentioned above, the problems and perspectives stressed in the improvement of the teacher training are discussed.

INTRODUCTION

General Information on Educational System in Japan

The structural organization of the present system of public education in Japan consists of kindergartens for pre-school education, elementary schools for primary education, lower and upper secondary schools for secondary education, and universities, graduate schools, junior colleges, technical colleges, special training schools and miscellaneous schools for higher education. Besides these, there are special education schools through pre-school and secondary education.

General and special education through the elementary and lower secondary school level is compulsory; thereafter, and in other types of schools, it is voluntary. In principle, success in an entrance examination is one of the prerequisites to enter any school beyond the compulsory school level.

Teacher Certificates in Japan

Teachers at kindergartens, elementary and secondary schools in Japan have a relevant teaching certificate as provided for by the Educational Personnel Certification Law and other statutes concerned.

Certification requirements vary with school level. Teacher certificates for kindergartens and elementary schools are available for all subjects, while those for lower and upper secondary schools are available for specified subject areas.

Teacher certificates are divided into regular certificates and temporary ones. Persons who hold regular certificates are qualified for a full teaching post. These types of certificate are subdivided into first and second class certificates. The basic qualifications for second class certificates for kindergarten, elementary and lower secondary teachers are to have studied for two years in a university (or the equivalent) and achieved 62 credits. The basic qualifications for first class certificates for elementary and lower secondary teachers and second class certificates for upper secondary teachers are to hold a bachelor's degree, while first certificates for upper secondary teachers are granted to those who hold a master's degree or who have studied for one year and have acquired 30 credits beyond the bachelors' degree.

The students in teacher training courses are required, in addition to the above basic qualifications, to acquire the prescribed number of credits in two subject groups in courses approved by the Ministry of Education, Science and Culture; general education subjects, teaching and specialized subjects.

For certificates for teaching in lower and upper secondary schools, the prescribed number of credits in teaching subjects varies with the subject area. The number of credits required for obtaining teacher certificates in social studies, science, homemaking, industrial arts and vocational education subjects is more than that required in other subject areas.

Teachers seeking higher class certificates must earn additional credits and must have served for the prescribed number of years with good records as school teachers. The required credits may be acquired through in-service training (eg, correspondence and other off-campus courses approved by the Ministry of Education, Science and Culture), or by attending regular university courses.

Teacher certificates are granted by prefectural boards of education. Regular certificates are valid in all prefectures and for life, while temporary certificates are honoured for three years only, and valid only in the prefecture issuing them.

In the very near future, the curriculum for teacher training courses will be changed because of the needs in the new technological society as well as the needs to promote better teacher training programmes being developed in the universities.

In-service Training of Teachers in Japan

The Ministry of Education, Science and Culture, prefectural boards of education, prefectural educational centres, and some institutes or centres of national universities provide opportunities for systematic in-service training for public school teachers, principals and supervisors. Some of the larger municipalities and educational study groups also hold workshops and study meetings for in-service training.

The Ministry yearly holds 'central workshops' for intensive in-service training of principals, vice-principals and experienced teachers (eg, curriculum co-ordinators, heads of teachers' groups teaching the same grade or the same subject in a school), who are selected and sent by every prefectural board of education. Tsukuba Annex of the National Education Centre is specially facilitated and equipped for the workshops, which are usually composed of lectures of high quality and seminars related to school administration, curriculum theory, instructional method, etc.

Prefectural boards of education also make programmes for in-service training and carry them out. The prefectural education centre, which has lodging facilities, educational equipment and apparatus, and professional staff, takes an important role in in-service training. Recently, the Ministry and prefectural boards of education have been concerned in providing in-service training with newly recruited teachers and younger teachers with some five years' teaching experience as well as with those in charge of managerial affairs.

Universities and education study groups which are voluntarily organized by school teachers also hold workshops and study meetings. The Ministry of Education, Science and Culture gives grants to prefectural boards of education and educational study groups for in-service training.

In Japan, the predominant aim of in-service training is in improving teachers' professional abilities and participation in an in-service training programme is not normally rewarded with salary increase. Like the pre-service teacher training being changed, the system and the way of thought of in-service teacher training should be changed to meet the needs of the information society and those of the idea of life-long society.

CURRENT TRENDS IN AUDIOVISUAL EDUCATION IN JAPAN

Audiovisual Equipment in School and Social Education

With the exception of videodisk-computer systems, which are still under development, audiovisual aids and equipment are well diffused in school education in Japan. The Ministry of Education, Science and Culture has developed a set of National Standards for Educational Materials and Equipment and is continuing systematically to provide assistance in securing audiovisual equipment. Costs are shared, half by the Ministry of Education, Science and Culture and half by local government.

Diffusion of Audiovisual Equipment in the Schools

There has been a steady increase in the amount of audiovisual equipment available in the schools in recent years. The increasing use of videotape recorders has been most striking. Generally speaking, schools are better equipped than social education facilities. The exception to this is 16mm projectors, with which the social education facilities are better equipped.

1. Audiovisual equipment in the schools
In Japan, 98 per cent of all schools have television; actually 100 per cent of the elementary schools are so equipped. Statistics on the number of sets per school for those schools with television show that the elementary schools are again highest with an average of 16 per school. Lower secondary schools have an average of seven, upper secondary schools an average of six and kindergartens an average of four sets each. Nearly all of the schools, 98 per cent, also have audiotape recorders, with the ownership rate increasing as one goes up the educational ladder. This is also true for the number of audiotape recorders owned by those schools which have them. With the exception of kindergartens, where only 53 per cent have them, nearly all schools in Japan are also so equipped with overhead projectors. Elementary and lower secondary schools have an average of ten projectors each while the upper secondary schools have an average of six. Looking at film projectors of various types, slide projectors have a diffusion rate of 96 per cent, followed by 8mm projectors at 72 per cent and 16mm projectors at 56 per cent.
   Overall, the rate of ownership for videotape recorders is 64 per cent. Just as for audiotape recorders, this rate is higher for the higher school levels, being 97 per cent at the upper secondary school level. The average number of recorders per school is also higher at the higher school levels. Upper secondary schools have an average of three videotape recorders each. The availability of television cameras seems to parallel the availability of videotape recorders. While the overall ownership rate is 44 per cent, the rate for upper secondary schools is 78 per cent.

2. Audiovisual equipment in social education
The rate of ownership of 16mm projectors is higher for social education facilities than it is for schools (schools – 56 per cent; social education – 63 per cent). The rate is especially high for children's nature study centres – 83 per cent, and for public halls – 80 per cent. In comparison to an overall school ownership rate of 98 per cent, the rate for television receivers in social education facilities is only 65 per cent. Even so, the rate for women's education centres is 83 per cent and for public halls it is 81 per cent and is above 70 per cent for youth houses and children's nature study centres. The rate of ownership of audiotape recorders for all social education facility ownership is 70 per cent, the highest of any single item of audiovisual equipment. Comparing this figure with a prior survey shows that ownership of audiotape recorders has also evidenced the greatest growth rates (for example, for public halls an increase from 50 per cent to 75 per cent and for museums from 41 per cent to 60 per cent). Social education facility ownership of videotape recorders is also lower than it is in the schools. The overall average is only 35 per cent, but is slowly on the rise. Today, 48 per cent of the public halls and 41 per cent of the women's education centres are so equipped. Colour television camera ownership is also slowly increasing, the overall rate of ownership (including black and white cameras) is now 19 per cent.

Rates of Ownership by School Levels

1. Kindergartens
Starting from the top, the highest rates of use are for television receivers (colour) –93 per cent; slide projectors – 84 per cent; closed–circuit audio broadcasting systems –79 per cent, and audiotape recorders (cassette with radio) 73 per cent. Combining various models into single categories increases the ownership rate for television receivers (black and white plus colour) to 96 per cent, for audiotape recorders (open reel plus cassette) to 93 per cent, and for radio receivers (including those built–in to audiotape recorders or record players) to 91 per cent.

2. Elementary schools
Again starting from the top, the highest rates of ownership in the elementary schools are for overhead projectors – 99 per cent; closed–circuit audio broadcasting systems – 98 per cent;

television receivers – 98 per cent, and slide projects – 97 per cent. The rate for black and white and colour television receivers combined and that for all models of audiotape recorders combined are the same as for overhead projectors, all three being 99 per cent.

3. Lower secondary schools
Starting from the top, the highest rates of ownership in the lower secondary schools are for overhead projectors – 99 per cent; slide projectors – 98 per cent; closed–circuit audio broadcasting sytems –98 per cent and television receivers (colour) –94 per cent. Grouping various models into single categories increases the rate for audiotape recorders (open reel plus cassette) to 99 per cent and for radio receivers (including those built-in to audiotape recorders and players) to 98 per cent.

4. Upper secondary schools
Starting from the top here also, the highest rates of ownership in the upper secondary schools are for overhead projectors – 99 per cent; slide projectors – 99 per cent; closed–circuit audio broadcasting systems – 97 per cent and 16mm projectors – 97 per cent. Grouping various models into single categories increases the rate for audiotape recorders (open reel plus cassette) to 99 per cent and for television receivers (black and white plus colour) to 97 per cent.

STANDARD CURRICULUM FOR TRAINING IN AUDIOVISUAL EDUCATION

In 1973, the Social Education Bureau, Ministry of Education, Science and Culture, published a Standard Curriculum for Training in Audiovisual Education in order to promote training in the method of use and general operation of audiovisual aids, as well as to promote their use in increasing educational effectiveness. It was hoped that this would be used for reference when making recommendations for improving and perfecting audiovisual training seminars for educators. The standards are divided into three levels (elementary, intermediate and advanced) with minimum hours of instruction stated for each. Subjects and audiovisual equipment covered by the standards include the following:

* Slides and filmstrips
* Overhead projectors
* Motion pictures
* Tape recorders
* Language laboratories
· Sheet recorders
* Response analyser systems
* Use of broadcasting (social education)
* Use of broadcasting (school education).

These standards are unique in that they tie training in actual operation of audiovisual equipment and study of the theoretical bases of instruction into a single unit. They have been used since 1973 in the preparation of numerous training seminars throughout Japan. At the same time, it must be admitted that courses in audiovisual education and educational technology in the universities tend to be strongly centred around theory and knowledge for its own sake.
   These standards have been in effect for ten years. However, during this time, (1) from a pedagogical point of view, there have arisen demands for greater unification of theory and practice based upon the fact that there is not enough practice, drill or clinical research, and (2) from a technical point of view, there has been a growing outcry urging reconsideration of the content of the curriculum as outlined in the standards.
   In 1982, the Ministry of Education, Science and Culture organized a consulting committee for making guidelines for the utilization of advanced technologies. In March 1984, it published, first of all, the guidelines for promoting utilization of microcomputers in school and social education.
   Based upon a careful reflection of the above, one possible hypothesis for determining a framework for the content for this training might be as follows:

Slides/movies	8mm, 16mm
Microcomputers	Production and utilization
	Processing educational data, to
	include response analyser systems
Individual learning devices	(ie, teaching machines) to include sheet recorders
Communications, means, techniques	Telephones, telecommunications, videodisk, etc
Integrated instructional systems	language laboratories, individual learning systems (CAI, CMI), closed-circuit audio systems, CCTV
Broadcasting	(to include distance education) regional UHF, educational broadcasting, school broadcasting, CATV, wired television
Libraries	(to include resource centres) audiovisual libraries, instructional centres, other types of centres, libraries, museums

Also, one means for improving instructional methods in social education would be to develop on-line systems using computers and telecommunication lines to connect audiovisual centres and other facilities with libraries. Concrete measures will undoubtedly be undertaken in the near future in order to enrich, expand and develop organizations for research and training at these various centres as well as for prefecture-wide broadcasting.

CURRENT STATE OF THE EDUCATIONAL USES OF MICROCOMPUTERS IN JAPAN

The uses of the computer in education have developed since the sixties, yet it is the advent of the microcomputer in recent years that opens up a wider scope for their uses in the instructional systems and hence triggers off a drastic increase of research in this area.

Three roles of the Microcomputer in Education

At the present time, the microcomputer has three distinct roles to play in education in Japan.

1. learning about the microcomputer
Regarding the first role, the microcomputer is used as an object to be studied. This type of learning is usually referred to as education for computer literacy and for information services. It includes two main areas:

   (a) Learning about how computers operate and developing the knowledge and skills of programming, and
   (b) Learning about its social implications, usually known as computer awareness.

2. using microcomputers to process research data
The second role is related to using microcomputers as a tool for processing data on educational research. This includes statistical analysis of educational data from the viewpoint of research and utilization of microcomputer software on information processing.

3. using microcomputers to assist the learning/instructional process
The third role is perhaps the most fast growing role for microcomputers in education. Their uses in this area can be divided into three categories:

   (a) Microcomputer assisted audiovisual education
   This refers to using microcomputers for audiovisual presentation in an instructional system. There are four posible areas for such usage:

   * visual and graphic presentation of teaching materials
   * visual presentation of simulation
   * audiovisual presentation of teaching materials
   * development and control of educational equipment and devices.

(b)   CAI

The microcomputer is used to administer instruction according to the program written by the courseware authors. Students interact with the computer program/courseware via terminals, the courseware which programs the computer determines the mode of interaction. Such mode of interaction may be divided into several non-exclusive categories: tutorial, drill and practice, simulation, instructional gaming, demonstration, information and instructional management. The effectiveness of such a system on promoting learning depends on the quality of the courseware being used.

(c)   CMI

The microcomputer is involved in the management of an instructional system. Their uses in this area may be identified as follows:

* to design, store and retrieve instructional materials
* to sort and retrieve educational information
* for evaluating and improving classroom instruction
* for assisting educational administration
* for assisting evaluation and assessment.

Uses of Microcomputers in Schools and Facilities for Social Education

In 1983, the Ministry of Education, Science and Culture conducted a survey on the computing facilities in local schools. According to this survey, as of 1 January 1983, the percentages of schools installed with microcomputers might be said to be very low. Only 0.1 per cent of the elementary schools and 1.8 per cent of the lower secondary schools have microcomputers. However, the percentage is much higher in upper secondary schools - 45.6 per cent. The same survey also includes the data from the various facilities catering for social education such as in public halls, libraries, museums. The percentage of these facilities having microcomputers range from 0.05 to 3.5 per cent.

Regarding the uses of microcomputers in schools with computing facilities, it was found that 70 per cent of the elementary schools use microcomputers in CAI, but 70 per cent of the lower secondary schools and 63 per cent of the upper secondary schools use them in CMI. Among some of these schools, microcomputers are also being used in computer literacy classes or club activities. Seventy-eight per cent of the microcomputers in facilities for social education are being used in CMI.

The above data seem to give the impression that microcomputers are not popular in Japan. This is true to some extent in the school setting, but it is certainly a true reflection of the extent to which research on the educational usage of microcomputers is being carried out in Japan. Over the past few years there has been an increasing interest in research on microcomputers and their educational usages.

The number of research papers in this area, especially in CAI, has increased significantly in the past three years. Also, many microcomputer (based upon CAI) systems have been developed recently by commercial firms or university research groups. These systems are less costly than the minicomputer based system. Typical examples are:

* a stand-alone type simple system called Yalkee by Yuasa Electric System Co
* Seiko Map CAI device by Hattori and Bunri Companies
* Takuben CAI device by Japan CAI system
* Off-line 10 key-typed system in Tokyo, Metropolitan Mukoogaoka, Koyamadai and Choofu-minami high schools
* T.H.E. system in Waseda University
* 'Learn up' system by Japan Univac
* Milestone CAI system in Tsukuba University.

Some of the systems listed above have been installed in some selected schools and are currently being used for teaching subjects such as science and mathematics. Besides the above-mentioned, other systems have been developed:

* Takezono Higashi Elementary School installed with a 44 terminals CAI system in 1978
* Kohuku Senior High School with a 52 terminals system installed in 1983
* Shinjoh Junior High School installed with a 45 terminals system in 1983.

Courseware Development

The development of courseware in the form of writing computer programs has been carried out not only by commercial firms' researchers, but also by individual teachers on their own initiative and by research groups in many universities. Most of the programs are written in drill and practice or simulation modes for subjects such as mathematics, physics, languages and engineering. Though there are various kinds of programmes. When it comes to the quality of the programme, it might be said there are so few, that it should be considered the quality of those (in terms of the efficiency) as well as motivation of the students.

A MAJOR WAVE OF CHANGE IN FUTURE EDUCATION

New Era to be in Light or in Darkness

The prospect for the new era is mixed with light and darkness, optimism and pessimism.

On the one hand, the US economy for the present is on the rise and the Japanese economy has bottomed out. There are signs that the European economy is getting out of sluggishness. However, on the other hand, the American economy has not improved its basic health as it is still faced with a huge government deficit and high interest rates. Consequently, the dollar is priced higher in relation to the yen in foreign exchange rates and the world economy is far from achieving balanced development. Thus, world politics are beoming unstable, pregnant with a confrontation among advanced countries. In such a situation, how can one predict what the future holds?

One of the authors himself predicts that the dozen or so years remaining in this century will be a period conspicuous for its two faces - light and darkness, represented by creativity and instability. The basis of his prediction is his judgement that one era ended with the adoption of foreign exchange fluctuations and the oil crisis in 1973.

This did not simply mean an end to the period of high post-war economic growth that lasted a quarter of a century on a global scale. Judging from various indications in technology, and domestic and international society, it meant an end to the 'twentieth century system' that started in the 1870s. In other words, we are actually in the first phase of the 'twenty-first century'. And past examples indicate a strong possibility that the initial phase of a new era will create new technologies, but at the same time bring about domestic and international instability as society finds it hard to cope with new technologies.

Major Change

Evidence that a major change is about to occur is recognized in various fields. A wave of change is surging upon us, namely, a shift from the twentieth century technology symbolized by energy consumption and huge machines to the twenty-first century technology represented by information and computers.

Durable consumer goods such as automobiles, television sets, electric washing machines and air conditioners are symbols of the twentieth century. However, demands for such durable consumer goods is reaching saturation point in the advanced nations, including Japan. A brake is being put on the trends towards making enterprises into giant corporations and huge government spending on welfare based on Keynesian economics.

A new era has already started in the technical field in the form of computers, robotics, automation of offices and factories, and an advanced information and communications system. From a global point of view, Japan is particularly enthusiastic about new technologies. There are more than a few people who consider the call for an 'information society' simply a dream, but broadly speaking history is moving in that direction. If the Japanese people are hesitant, it is inevitable that someone else will promote the move towards an information society. In this respect, the 1980s or the 1990s will be a very active era in technical creation.

However, education cannot easily catch up with great strides in technology. The period of post-war, high economic growth was actually a period of technical application rather than technical creation. Yet we all know society was forced to undergo great changes. It is expected that a change in the more fundamental education system will be needed when new technology is created.

How will education, benefiting by new information tehnology, come about? There are a flood of expectations. A change in organization and systems will be inevitable when the way of the flow of information is changed. The existing popular industries will decline relatively as the stucture of industry naturally changes. Yet, above all, the nature of our work will undergo changes. A great deal of manual labor will be handled by computerized machines.

New Legislation

There will be a change in the idea of the right to assets regarding information and software. There will probably be changes in the idea of the right to privacy or the role of education. A society capable of coping successfully with these changes - particularly a society that will not keep workers replaced by the computer in unemployment - is most likely to take the lead in the next century.

NEW SERVICES AND FACILITIES IN EDUCATION APPEAR IN THE NEAR FUTURE

CATV

The year of 1984 will see the opening of an era of new media on a full scale.

In 1983, CATV fever hit Japan, and CATV companies were set up in many parts of the country. These companies in 1984 will start preparations to go into operation by applying for licence from the Ministry of Posts and Telecommunications and by laying cables. 'International Cable Network' in Machida, Tokyo, which is the first urban CATV enterprise, has started the construction of facilities to open a station in 1985, having gained the approval of the Ministry of Posts and Telecommunications in November 1983.

Experts on new media say that 'it must be doubted whether CATV will pay as an enterprise in Japan'. Nevertheless, a flurry of moves connected with CATV are likely to be made.

CAPTAIN

The CAPTAIN (Character and Pattern Telephone Access Information Network) system, which is representative of the wire-system new media, will start operation in the metropolitan area in November 1984. Under this system, people can select at will, the information accumulated at the CAPTAIN centre in Ginza, Tokyo, by telephone for screening in their own homes. They can also do home shopping and make reservations of plane tickets by connections with computers of department stores and aviation companies. This system will also be started in Osaka by April 1985, and in other parts of the country later. The telephone charge will be fixed at the uniform rate of 30 yen for three minutes.

Satellite Broadcasting

Satellite broadcasting, too, will be started in May 1984, following the launching of a broadcasting satellite, 'BS-2' (two channels) in February. The two channels of the Japan Broadcasting Corporation (NHK) will be sent from this satellite. The public can then see over the television distinct pictures even on a remote mountain like Hokkaido and an isolated island like Ogasawara-jima, if they purchase a parabola antenna and receiver (priced at about 200,000 yen) and set up the antenna in the garden or on the roof.

Character Multiplex Broadcasting

Character multiplex broadcasting, which NHK started in October 1983, follows the pattern system and has only eight programmes. It was started only for those people in Tokyo and Osaka who have difficulty in hearing. The hybrid system, which NHK and commercial broadcasting companies are testing, will make it possible to broadcast more than 50 programmes through one channel. Broadcasting by this system will be started in the spring of 1985. It is said that 'the new system is likely to develop rapidly, because it can broadcast a large volume of information'.

Character multiplex broadcasting uill make it possible for the public to obtain as much information as they like, free of charge, by just installing an adapter. It will develop into an important information service for local districts, because it can send a large volume of detailed information concerning shopping and events.

High Definition TV, PCM, Still Picture and Facsimile Broadcasting

In addition, high definition TV which shows pictures as distinct as colour photos, PCM (Pulse Code Modulation) broadcasting which can transmit high sound quality, still picture broadcasting which can send several tens of still pictures through one channel, and facsimile broadcasting which may be termed the 'electronic newspaper' because it sends video information to homes by electric waves (with the use of facsimile printers) are waiting for their turn, with the solution of almost all technologicl problems in sight.

POSTSCRIPT

It has even been said that 'new media have left the cradle and entered an era of incessant strife'.

9.6 Curriculum Development and Educational Technology: A Case Study

A C Millar
Victoria College, Australia

Abstract: The purpose of the paper is to examine the role and programme of an educational technology department in a post-secondary college on the Toorak campus, with particular reference to a policy shift over the last four years. The department operates within a faculty of teacher education on a multi-campus post-secondary institution in the south-eastern metropolitan area of Melbourne. Since its inception in the early 1970s, the department has operated on the basis that its twin roles - the teaching and the practice of educational technology - are not only compatible but mutually supportive. At the beginning of the 1980s the view developed in the department that the existing range of production experience was limited and, in order to provide more benefit to the teaching programme, the educational technology practice or service role needed to be broadened and deepened in scope.

This paper examines several changes that were made to extend the range of experience. The perceived advantages and disadvantages of the shifts are examined and an attempt is made to evaluate the changes. It is assumed that the importance of this apparently introspective exercise will be evident to those experienced in the teaching of educational technology at tertiary level. Those not so involved may not realize that the normal and understandable expectation of educational technology students is that teaching staff should 'practise what they preach.' The paper is designed to share the experience of a department at a time when administrative changes - particularly the amalgamation of colleges - are making more difficult the undertaking of teaching and production roles within the college by the same department and staff. Apart from the need to be consistent with the principles inherent in their own teaching, many educational technology staff believe that in an area as fluid and dynamic as educational technology one of the most effective methods of keeping abreast of current developments is to be involved in the production of learning materials.

DEFINITIONS

The Australian Society of Educational Technology defined educational technology in its first Yearbook (Hutton,1976) as 'The design, application, evaluation and development of systems methods and materials to improve the process of human learning.' The Toorak approach is compatible with the above and could be described as being closer to the curriculum development than the audiovisual extreme of the educational technology continuum.

The staff at Toorak can also identify with the recent Rowntree (1982) description of educational technology as 'Essentially, ...a rational problem-solving approach to education, a way of thinking sceptically and systematically about learning and teaching.'

HISTORICAL FACTORS

To better understand this case study, four key stages in the development of the department should be listed:

1. In 1968, a closed-circuit TV system was initiated in a new building complex - Toorak Teachers College. The purpose of the the TV unit was to provide services such as videotaped demonstration lessons from training schools, lectures and interviews with visiting subject and other specialists, and videotaped special purpose lectures. In

addition the unit provided the teaching and equipment resources for introducing TV to students as a valuable and versatile classroom support medium.

2. In 1973, following an invitation from the education department of Victoria, the staff of the TV unit mounted a one-year full-time diploma course for qualified and experienced teachers interested in training as school educational technology specialists. This event was significant because it not only required the recruitment of further teaching staff who were skilled in the educational application of graphic design, photography, film, audio and reprography, but it also indicated the recognition of the wider range of educational media available to complement TV in the classroom. The course was the first of an increasing number of in-service courses to be offered by the college and represented a significant diversification away from the single-purpose role of the training of primary school teachers. Such diversification was becoming common at that time in Australia, UK and many other countries.

3. Also in 1973, occurred the granting by the education department of Victoria of academic and administrative autonomy to its 12 teachers colleges. Toorak State College, as it was known, became an autonomous tertiary academic institution with a consequent broadening of its independence and the enhancement of its status.

4. However, the institution had an effective life of less than a decade. In December 1982, Toorak State College with two other former teachers colleges was amalgamated with the Prahan College of Advanced Education to become Victoria College with a total enrolment of approximately 5,000 effective full-time students.

PROFESSIONAL GROWTH STRATEGIES

During the 1970s, the belief of the staff of the department in the appropriateness of the twin role philosophy, ie the teaching and practice of educational technology, was confirmed. However, while the college retained its mainly primary teachers college identity, a factor existed which served to limit the scope of the practice role. Nearly all the lecturing staff were trained and experienced teachers and, as in many comparable institutions, they saw the role of the department of educational technology as principally that of providing specialist assistance in the use of audiovisual media rather than the broader task of educational development. Consequently, with the exception of TV, the range of professional skills that the staff believed they could offer was not fully tapped and the non-TV tasks were confined to the production of slides and prints, overhead projector materials and some audiotapes. Although a number of departments, centres and units of educational development were established in universities and colleges in the 1970s, most administrators and teaching staff of the former teachers colleges seemed to see little need for such units.

EXTERNALIZING THE COURSE FOR THE GRADUATE DIPLOMA OF EDUCATIONAL TECHNOLOGY

In 1981, 24 external students were enrolled in the Graduate Diploma course - about 16 per cent of the total course enrolment. By 1984, 90 per cent of the course students are external and/or mixed mode students. In addition to traditional correspondence techniques such as the mailing of printed notes and audiotapes, the following are also used:

* videotapes
* slide and slide-tape sets
* tele-conference tutorials
* vacation schools
* supervised practical tasks in regional centres and at Toorak campus.

The videotapes used to date are simply video recordings of the lectures given to on-campus students by the unit co-ordinator and guest lecturers. These tapes are mailed to external students and are followed up by individual tele-conference tutorials. Despite the simplistic approach, research undertaken in the US and at the Royal Melbourne Institute of Technology seems to indicate its appropriateness. Also, our experience tends to support that belief.

After three years' experience in offering this course externally as well as on the campus, a balance sheet of perceived advantages and disadvantages may be attempted.

Disadvantages

The work load on individual staff has been higher, certainly in the materials development phase. Theoretically, staff were to be allowed preparation time but the unfortunate co-incidence of this phase with the college amalgamation with consequent staff trimming meant that little allowance was possible. Now that the first full cycle of the external mode has been run, the problem is less and an off-campus unit load for a member of staff has been accepted by all parties as approximately equivalent to an on-campus unit load.

Another disadvantage of the distance mode is that administration load for the college, department and individual lecturer appears to be slightly heavier (eg, one additional lecturer is now required for the administration of external students). This load factor is relevant to the amount of advance planning required for preparing learning materials, setting up and managing tele-tutorials and organizing vacation schools. However, it may be argued that the distance mode has compensating factors such as less timetabled commitments.

Another slight disadvantage is the loss of some potential students from the Melbourne metropolitan area on the grounds of preference for a course involving evening study only rather than the external or mixed mode. According to the course co-ordinator, there may be some people in this category but it is not regarded seriously by the department since the mixed mode allows students to undertake certain courses in the evening (via another course), the graduate diploma course is available for part and full-time students through daytime on-campus classes, and also because the externalizing of the course has significantly increased the pool of potential students.

There is some inconvenience and added load caused by the vacation schools. Although the external mode tends to lighten the workload during the term, the need for three vacation schools during the year not only lengthens the period of involvement with students but also reduces the opportunity for staff to take blocks of more than one week of recreation leave. This has been partially offset by the use of a mid-year end-of-semester break of two weeks and by other techniques such as rostering staff to be free for all or part of at least one vacation school during the year.

The question of the economics of the external mode is extremely complex. There are some who argue that the external mode is more expensive than the on-campus mode while others argue the reverse. The matter is complicated by the qualitative as well as the quantitative issues involved. This is particularly true of educational technology since the design and production of external materials is a useful exercise in relation to the course content. For this and other reasons, it may be that there is a degree of irreversibility about the externalizing of a course of this kind. One may conjecture what would happen if a hypothetical administrator issued an instruction that a course must drop its external mode. This would then raise a series of questions which do not appear to have been fully answered - eg, how does one define external mode? What are its criterial attributes? Such questions are not directly concerned with the economics of external mode study but do underline the complexity and probably the irrelevance of the economics issue.

Advantages

The most obvious advantage is the experience obtained by preparing the external mode. Not only does it provide an avenue for staff to obtain first-hand experience in course, instructional and message design but also an opportunity for discussion of methodological issues with students. It also gives staff some form of answer to the quite reasonable student question in courses of this kind, viz 'Why don't you practise what you preach?' Then there is the opportunity to explore new technologies. For example, the department has established a regional centre in Canberra at the Bruce College of Technical and Further Education using a loud-speaker telephone link, and a two-way voice link with the ageing NASA communications satllite ATS1. The latter will not only provide experience in satellite communications but also will bring closer the introduction of what are currently being called the 'audio-graphic' technologies, viz facsimile services, the 'electronic blackboard' and slow-scan TV. For technical reasons, these technologies will probably use the telephone system as the carrier rather than the satellite but they will be supplementing the satellite two-way voice link between Toorak and Bruce. The move in this direction is consistent with the apparent convergence of distance education, the use of telecommunications in education and educational technology.

Other advantages of the externalizing process include the opening up of a wider pool of potential students for the course and the offering of greater educational flexibility to students and staff. Examples of the latter include freeing students from regularly travelling long distances to on-campus classes, ability to cope better with late enrolments (on-campus vacation schools excepted) and making staff changeovers and substitutions easier. For example, in 1981, when the department introduced a new course, it was faced with having to conduct two courses, the majority of classes in each which were to have been held in the evening, hence posing a difficult staff constraint. The distance mode effectively solved this problem.

The development of the off-campus mode for the graduate diploma course has proved an interesting exercise and professional challenge. It will be interesting to see whether, in the next ten years, the distinction between on-campus and off-campus study modes is as clear as it is today. If the experience of the department can be taken as a guide, there is reason to believe that the dividing line will not be clear since most of the units on the course are now utilizing on-campus at least some of the materials and techniques originally developed for the off-campus mode.

OUTSIDE CURRICULUM MATERIAL DEVELOPMENT PROJECTS

The other strategy adopted by the staff of the department to broaden their experience base was the undertaking of material development projects for clients outside the college. While this is not a unique practice, it should be stressed that the motivation was primarily professional rather than financial. Indeed, any comparable college or university which has income as its primary goal for this type of activity may be open to the criticism that such production is questionable on the ground of the sales tax and other advantages that such institutions enjoy. In every case to date, this department can argue that the task concerned required the expertise of the academic staff involved and that the professional benefits to the teaching programme of the department have been paramount.

Outside projects undertaken fall into three broad categories. The first is in the area of TV and tasks of this kind were first undertaken in the late 1970s. In all cases, the initiative came from an outside organization such as water safety (life-saving) and teacher groups. The brief was only accepted if staff load permitted and if the finished product was acceptable to the department as capable of being used as a resource on a regular basis in its teaching programme. The second category differed from the above not only because of the different format (usually slide-tape) but because the in-college-use criterion was not applied. Five slide-tape productions were undertaken during 1981-1983 for a municipal library (an introduction to the library catalogue) and a semi-government industrial training authority. These projects were accepted firstly to obtain experience in the costing and financial management of outside projects and secondly to give staff experience in the industrial training area in order to assist in mounting an Associate Diploma of Media Production course in 1981. Both objectives were largely achieved and, in each case, the client appeared to be satisfied with the end product.

The third and most recent category is that of curriculum materials development. Sufficient experience and expertise had been gained in production from the above two categories to provide a base for a submission for an ambitious Australian government curriculum materials project in late 1982. The Department of Immigration and Ethnic Affairs (DIEA) invited nine individuals and groups from Australia (including the Department of Educational Technology at Toorak) to submit proposals for the 'production of a kit which can be used by teachers and students to facilitate the study of population isssues in an interesting and creative manner.' The brief also stipulated that the kit should be 'directed mainly to students in the middle years of high school, but capable of being augmented for use in the senior years. It should consist of a multi-media package ... (and) should be based on a multi-disciplinary approach.' A project team was formed at Victoria College comprising staff of the Department of Educational Technology (Toorak campus), the Department of Curriculum and Teaching (Rusden campus) and the Multi-cultural Education Centre (Toorak campus). A proposal was submitted to the DIEA and, in May 1983, the Victoria College team was commissioned to produce the kit with a budget of just over $90,000 for a two-year period. Currently, the project team is under the joint leadership of the heads of the two departments involved. The progress can be summarized as follows:

1. A needs survey has been completed in order to gauge the attitude of teachers and curriculum and subject specialists towards the 10 topics proposed by the DIEA and to determine the formats most desired for the materials.
   These topics are:

   * introductory material,
   * population size and growth,
   * age/sex structure,
   * spatial distribution,
   * implications of demographic change,
   * interactions between demographic, social and economic variables,
   * world population,
   * population policy – Australia and other countries,
   * immigration policy as population policy,
   * ethnic composition.

   The format preferences expressed in the survey are shown in Table 1.

Format for the materials	Average ranking
Videotapes	1.4
Print-based student activity materials	1.5
Slide-tape programmes	1.6
Print-based information sources	1.7
Computer-based simulation activities	1.7
Computer-assisted instructional materials	1.7
ABC radio/TV broadcast programs	1.7
Slide sets	1.8
Sets of overhead projector materials	1.8
Filmstrip/tape programmes	1.9
Sets of pictures, study prints etc (pupil use)	1.9
Computer games	2.0
Simulation games	2.0
Sets of pictures, study prints (class display)	2.7
Audiotapes	2.7

Table 1 Format Preferences (highest first) from the Survey

2. Inter-state contacts have been appointed to ensure a national flavour for the project.
3. A five-day writing workshop has been conducted in which 30 teachers and specialists worked on draft topic and unit outlines.
4. A content structure has been achieved which includes nearly all the DIEA's topics but re-structures them into three broad areas:

   Part A; People count (the Australian census and its results.)
   Part B; Implications (environmental, economic, social and political.)
   Part C; Past, present and future (Australian population policy and the global context.)

   Unit outlines have been developed for the units within these areas.
5. Unit writers have been commissioned to start work on the writing of some of the units.
6. A paper has been prepared on proposed evaluation strategies.
7. A considerable amount of material has already been gathered to form the basis of the annotated collection which will be an important component in the final kit.

As with the externalizing strategy, there are both advantages and disadvantages to the involvement in outside production work. For example, one problem is the initial work-load on staff. This difficulty is being reduced as the project team is augmented by the recruitment of outside staff. Initially some staff within the department felt threatened by the existence of the project. Again, this problem has disappeared as the professional benefits to the department become evident and as staff realize that they are under no obligation to participate if they do not wish.

The major advantage lies with the educational technology and curriculum-development teaching work of the department. Two major issues have produced lively debate within the project team. First is the question of whether media opportunities should dictate the shape of the project or whether the content structure should be determined first followed by exploring the media possibilities (the latter view has prevailed). The second issue has been the related problem of how to optimize the potentially conflicting tendencies of the need for a logical content structure and the need to cater for the requirements and interests of students and teachers (ie discovery learning versus a structured approach). This debate is still unresolved but it seems that the solution may be influenced by the outcome of another dilemma – how to package and present the project to cater simultaneously for the DIEA's desire that the kit user should work logically through the whole programme while catering for the reality that many teachers will be interested, not in the whole kit, but in specific parts (eg, geographic, economic, social and political issues).

CONCLUSION

There is little doubt that the two broad strategies outlined above have constituted significant in-service development opportunities for the department as a whole. Mistakes have occurred and problems have been encountered but it has provided the challenge of educational technology at work and benefited all those concerned.

REFERENCES

Hutton, D W (1976) President's report. Australian Society of Educational Technology Yearbook.
Rowntree, D (1982) Educational Technology in Curriculum Development. (2nd ed). Harper and Row.

9.7 Closing Session

J K Sinclair
Chairman, AETT, 1981-84, Stirling

I want, for a few minutes, to do a little more than propose a vote of thanks to the usual list of people. I am grateful to the organizers of the conference for providing time in a crowded schedule for us to think not just about educational and training technology in general but also about our association which exists to promote educational and training technology. Therefore, I shall address myself briefly to a consideration of two characteristics of the association and then to some thoughts about how these characteristics affect the present state of the association and the foreseeable future.

First, it is important to repeat that ours is an independent association. We receive no subsidies and grants. We are not tied to any government policy, and we have no link with any commercial undertaking other than the amicable, mutually profitable contract with our publisher, Kogan Page Ltd.

Second, our association is made up of individuals - and individualists. To check this statement, just look through our current membership list and, if you are of such a vintage, recall to mind the other 'characters' who have been such a colorful part of the APL/APLET/AETT scene over the years.

What have these facts meant to the association?

There has always been a strong tradition of openness about the association. If you wanted to find out more about a development or an innovation, there was no need to wait for the next issue of PLET or until the next ETIC. You telephoned or wrote, and usually you could rely on getting a prompt and authoritative answer.

Within the association, views are strongly held and expressed. It must be said that the annual general meetings are normally placid affairs, perhaps because they are held at times which are unattractive to the man-in-the-street member. It takes an effort to be at the AGM at 10.30am on the Monday morning of conference week ready to raise an objection or voice an opinion. It is therefore not surprising that I claim to hold the record for chairing an entire AGM, from apologies for absence to date and place of next meeting, in something between 20 and 25 minutes.

This is not so with council meetings. I sometimes speculate whether the dominant factor is the personality of the people who offer themselves for election, and particularly those who are elected, or the personality of those elected to the chair of the Council, or the topics appearing on the agenda as drafted by the finance and general purposes committee, or the hidden agenda which suspicious minds find written between the lines, or the time and place of meetings, or the general ambience, particularly after lunch when a glance at the clock shows that the afternoon train has been missed anyway and things could do with a bit of stirring up. Whatever the reason, I can assure you that council meetings are never dull. I know that all my predecessors in the chair of the council and my successors will all agree that chairing council meetings is an experience to be savoured and enjoyed, and the privilege passed on to a successor with a strong feeling of relief.

AETT membership does seem to induce a spirit of camaraderie and friendship. Here I speak personally and seriously. Educational technologists lead lonely lives professionally. They often work in an environment where no one else speaks the same language. Others may use the same words but in a different sense. It may be that 'ed tech' to them equals visual aids and the educational technologist should be able to mend the broken-down TV set, replace projector lamps and blown fuses and (to be a real success), supply videotapes, audiocassettes, colour film and other desirable commodities at the drop of a hat. In such circumstances, it is stimulating to meet with others who know that educational technology has connotations, who share an interest in the applications of the principles of programmed learning and the systems approach to learning and traing situations. I very much regret to say that these people are, in my subjective estimation, becoming thin on the ground, not to mention long in the tooth. We may be in danger, once again, of becoming dazzled by the hardware.

I can say with complete sincerity that membership of the association, and particularly membership of council and latterly the holding of high office, has been of great importance to me. I have learned a lot from conferences and publications but I rate much more highly the contact with other practitioners, the comradeship, and the genuine friendship. I owe a great debt to APL/APLET/AETT.

What of the future? It would be easy to be complacent. Who would have thought a few years ago that we could present accounts to the AGM showing £14,000 in the bank? It is true that we we have a membership list which has held up well and is beginning to grow again. But we must face the fact that we are an ageing population. Just think of the number of pensioners - of the early retirement variety as opposed to old age pensioners we have among us and it should give us pause for thought. This year it has been good to see some new young faces at conference. Let us hope that we see them and others next year and the next. What we need is a lot more young enthusiasts, like we were 10, 15, 20 years ago.

We must be bold and adventurous. I know that it is easy for me to say this, speaking from the privileged standpoint of the early retired. It is also, I suggest, relevant to remember that successful innovation brings kudos to the innovator while unsuccesful innovation results in a tarnished reputation. We have to be careful of the reputation of those we ask to do things on our behalf. If there is praise, it belongs to them. We must take any blame.

Bernard Alloway and Gordon Mills have been both meticulous in their planning and industrious. The result has been a memorable conference. The papers have been mostly of high quality, usually well presented, with media support which still leaves room for improvement although I think that the standard is on an upward trend. Workshops have been real workshops involving participation and have been well attended even when held at unsociable hours when other activities beckoned. The social side has been superb - the City Hall, the Industrial Museum, and the Imax film presentation at the National Museum of Photography, Film and Television. The conference dinner and the speeches defy comment. A lesser point is the innovative approach to lunches which is, in my opinion, most successful.

Our sincere thanks then are due to all who contributed to putting the standing of ETIC back where it belongs. We thank the grades of local staff involved, from the deputy lord mayor and his lady and the vice-chancellor of the university to the technicians, the stewards, the bus drivers, the waitresses and the barmaids. To all of these and to many others who have worked hard on our behalf, the Association is very grateful.

Finally, our thanks are due to the delegates who have made the whole thing possible. We hope to see you next year in London. Perhaps we can take away an adaptation of Dr Sharma's slogan from India where they say, 'Each one, teach one'. We say, 'Each one, bring one'.

****

A J Trott then spoke in his capacity as chairman of publications committee and general editor. He mentioned that PLET was changing its emphasis although remaining as an academic research-oriented journal. He reminded the delegates that AETT engaged in publishing occasional papers, and that they were encouraged to suggest topics or submit manuscripts to him for consideration. One delegate suggested that a news sheet (similar to EdTech News) might go with PLET to libraries and other non-AETT members who subscribed.

Miss Margaret Proctor then introduced the organizers of the next three ETICs:

1985 Nick Rushby, Imperial College, London. This will be a three-day conference starting on Monday, 1 April. The emphasis will be on information technology which would play a significant part in the operation of the conference.

1986 Fred Percival, Napier College of Commerce and Technology, Edinburgh. The last of the Scottish cities to be visited by AETT. By then, there should be much to report on developments in open learning, including Open Tech.

1987 Robin Budgett (vice president), Southampton University. Accommodation booked but no firm plans yet.

John K Sinclair here mentioned the working party set up to run a series of experimental one-day events. The first had already taken place and others would be publicized shortly. A question from one delegate about plans to hold conferences jointly with other organizations was answered by pointing out that this had been suggested for York, the originally intended venue for ETIC84 but the other body had not been in favour of the idea. At the workshop held earlier that morning on joint membership of education and training organizations, members had agreed that AETT should continue to try to co-operate with any like-minded bodies.

Henry Ellington, chairman of the information & services committee explained that this was a new body combining two previous committees. They intended to overview information and publicity issued about the Association, regularly review the range of services offered to members, to foster links with groups, either geographically based or with special interests. The appointment of an information officer was seen as a high priority.

On this note, the conference concluded.

Keyword Index

audiotapes 145,209,260,287,307,315
authoring languages 12,35,171

behavioural objectives 183
brainstorming 164
British Telecom Gold 26

Ceefax 31
colour graphics 130,131
computer-aided learning 75,118,130
computer-assisted learning 33,38–
  41,93,98,138,172–175,230
computer-based training 11,118,169–
  171,175,181,185–187
computer games 15,41,42,116
computer programs 21,47,51,57,99,
  100,136,311
computers 13–20,34,37,40,77,104,
  120,130,173,174,187,237,271,287,311
course objectives 152,155,202
creativity 223,224
curriculum development 26–28,30,104,
  109,155,272,284,314,319

databases 13,19,49,66,85,96,97,106,
  115,117,119,276
distance education 200,269,273,309,
  316

electronic notebook 42,46–48,52,53
Engineering Industry Training Board
  (EITB) 75,80
evaluation 108,109,170,174,202,205,
  231,249,285
experiential learning 156,163,230

feedback 57,59,145,207,230,235,237,
  243,259,273,287
film studies 237
formative assessment 36,155

group instruction 121,168,230

human resources 143,215–223

illustrations 132,191–195,198
individualized instruction 288
industrial training 9,10,75,143,158,
  159
information systems 303
information technology 10,13,28,30,
  31,35,102,115,116,145,150,311,321
in-service education 82,83,163,306
instructional materials 82,247,265,318
instructional strategies 81,92,201
intelligence 57,186
interactive video 12,73

Japan 81,121,305

learning strategies 45,57,194
learning theories 39,40,53,59
lecture method 72,287
libraries 102,105,116,174,270,271,
  309,317
lifelong learning 38
LOGO 17,19,43,55,56,60,62–66,94,
  135–137

management training 163,185
Manpower Services Commission (MSC)
  9,11,143,159,150,159,169,270
mathemagenic behaviour 43
media research 235
memory 30,44,120,171,249
microcomputers 9,10,12,31,33,36,38,
  49,60,62,77,85,86,92,94,96,103–106,
  115,120,121,126,170,177,180,295,
  303,309,310
Microelectronics Education
  Programme (MEP) 9,25–28,30–34,
  104,106,108,119,280
mobile teaching unit 269

networks 92,144,172,177,272,273,279,
  283–286,301,312
New Training Initiative (NTI) 143,149,
  156
nursing education 172–176